# The Southern Argus

Obituaries,
Death Notices,
and
Implied Deaths
June 1869 through June 1874

*Compiled by:*

Michael Kelsey, Nancy Graff Floyd, and Ginny Guinn Parsons

HERITAGE BOOKS
2008

# HERITAGE BOOKS
*AN IMPRINT OF HERITAGE BOOKS, INC.*

### Books, CDs, and more—Worldwide

For our listing of thousands of titles see our website
at
www.HeritageBooks.com

Published 2008 by
HERITAGE BOOKS, INC.
Publishing Division
100 Railroad Ave. #104
Westminster, Maryland 21157

Copyright © 1996 Michael Kelsey, Nancy Graff Floyd, and
Ginny Guinn Parsons

Other books by the authors:

*Miscellaneous Alabama Newspaper Abstracts*
*Miscellaneous Alabama Newspaper Abstracts, Volume 2*
*Marriage and Death Notices from the South Western Baptist Newspaper*
*Miscellaneous Texas Newspaper Abstracts - Deaths, Volume 1*
*Miscellaneous Texas Newspaper Abstracts- Deaths, Volume 2*
*Texas Masonic Deaths with Selected Biographical Sketches*

All rights reserved. No part of this book may be reproduced or transmitted in any form or by any means, electronic or mechanical, including photocopying, recording or by any information storage and retrieval system without written permission from the author, except for the inclusion of brief quotations in a review.

International Standard Book Numbers
Paperbound: 978-0-7884-0513-6
Clothbound: 978-0-7884-7606-8

# THE SOUTHERN ARGUS - DEATHS - JUNE 1869 THROUGH JUNE 1874

## INTRODUCTION

The *Southern Argus* was a product of the turbulent reconstruction era. During this period many newspapers failed to survive the hardships brought about by the Civil War and the financial retractions of the early 1870's. The scarcity of southern newspapers for this interval reflects the importance of the genealogical data abstracted from the *Southern Argus*.

One of the largest and most ably edited weekly newspapers published in the South, the *Argus* was published at Selma, Alabama, by Colonel Robert McKee. McKee edited and published the *Argus* from 1869 to 1878, at which time he moved to Montgomery to serve as private secretary to Governor Cobb and later as secretary to Governor O'Neal.

The *Argus* provided more news and a greater variety of news than any other paper. A large portion of its space was devoted to the interest of planters and the laboring class. Local, city, county, state and international news items were published by McKee as well as Masonic, Grange and Church news. McKee was so prolific in coverage of the Alabama press that it was said "if a person kills a rattlesnake in Alabama it seems to find its way into the *Southern Argus*." Readers in Texas were asked to promptly send news of marriages, deaths, sickness or accidents among them. Consequently, by publishing a weekly summary of Texas news, marriages and deaths, the *Argus* contained more Texas items of interest than any other newspaper outside of Texas.

The *Argus* circulated extensively throughout Alabama and its columns were filled with items that revealed the story of people's lives. From these columns the authors abstracted deaths, implied deaths, accidents, illnesses, and murders, which occurred from June 1869 through June 1874. Included is a name index of about 10,000 entries for more than 3,850 surnames.

In the case that a news item was not abstracted verbatim, such as the complete hymn or praise in an obituary, a "..." was used to denote that information was not included. Some issues were very difficult to read, and even though great effort was made by the authors to abstract correctly, every conceivable spelling of a surname should be examined. Often hard to differentiate were u/n, e/o/a/s and i/l.

Master negatives of the *Southern Argus* are located at the Alabama State Archives, Montgomery, Alabama, and a microfilm copy has been deposited by Michael Kelsey at the Temple Public Library, Temple, Texas 76501.

Michael Kelsey<br>
Nancy Graff Floyd<br>
Ginny Guinn Parsons

## THE SOUTHERN ARGUS - DEATHS - JUNE 1869 THROUGH JUNE 1874

### TABLE OF CONTENTS

NEWSPAPER ABSTRACTS . . . . . . . . . . . . . . . . . . . . . . . . . . . . . . . 1

NAME INDEX . . . . . . . . . . . . . . . . . . . . . . . . . . . . . . . . . . . . 360

## THE SOUTHERN ARGUS - DEATHS - JUNE 1869 THROUGH JUNE 1874

NEWSPAPER ABSTRACTS

Issue 6-16-1869

Michael Whelan, an old citizen of Selma, committed suicide last Friday by jumping into the river from the wharfboat.

Last Saturday, in this city, a young man named Maxman was accidentally shot and seriously hurt by a comrade named Shancer. The casualty occurred at the residence of Mr. Eliasberg.

A negro is in jail at Jefferson, Texas, charged with having violated the person of a white lady, a Mrs. Glenn, whose throat he afterwards cut.

R.D. Herndon, convicted of the murder of Miss Lumsden, in Orange County, was taken to Richmond, on the 3rd inst., to be confined for eighteen years in the penitentiary...

John Murphy, convicted of the murder of Lewis Lunsford, was sentenced to be hung, at Maryville, Tennessee, on the 16th of July next.

R.C. Boyd shot and killed H.J. Ainsworth a few days ago at Waxhaxie, Texas, while the latter was lying asleep in his storeroom. An old feud.

Mr. Strickland, in returning home from a short bridal tour, was met at Cowle's Station on the Montgomery and West Point Railroad, a few days ago, by a man between whom and himself an old feud existed, and in the altercation which ensued Strickland was killed.

A little daughter of John Barron of Louisville, Kentucky, was accidentally burned to death on the 6th.

A few days since, John Briggs was shot and killed in Columbus, Kentucky, by Willis Bridgman.

H.J. Barnes, a noted horse-thief, was hung in Shelby County, Tennessee, a few days since.

William Smith was shot through the head and killed last week, at Joyce's Mills, Marshall County, Tennessee, by a man named Gambel.

An old man named Madison was run over by a train of cars and killed near Bowling Green, Kentucky, on the 6th.

# THE SOUTHERN ARGUS - DEATHS - JUNE 1869 THROUGH JUNE 1874

John Murray, a respectable citizen of Portsmouth, Virginia, was shot and killed on the 6th, by Alex Perry, who was accused of seducing his (Murray's) daughter.

Bob Lee, a desperado of the notorious Bickenstaff gang, was killed on the 24th ult. near Lee's residence at Pilot Grove, Texas...

Last Wednesday near Crab Orchard, Kentucky, John Pollard was cut with a hatchet and seriously wounded by a man named Cain.

Tom Hall and Phil. Cunningham, both colored, had an altercation on Desoto Street, Memphis, on the 10th about two women, during which Hall shot Cunningham, killing him...

Perry Nagle, a butcher, formerly of Memphis, was killed in a row house at Helena, Arkansas, on the 10th...

Issue 6-23-1869

Died near Havana in Greene County on the 10th inst., Joseph H. Davis, in the seventy-third year of his age.

Joshua Morse, Attorney General of the State of Alabama, indicted by the Grand Jury of Choctaw County at its last term for the murder of Newell E. Thomas, was before Chancellor Dillard at Demopolis on the 3rd of June by a writ of habeas corpus and admitted to bail in the sum of $1,000.

Parshall, who killed conductor Oates some months ago at Courtland, Alabama, has been bailed in the sum of $15,000.

Mr. John Bramlette was thrown from a mule in a field near Okolona, Mississippi, Saturday week. His leg was entangled in a trace chain, and the mule started at a rapid speed, dragging him a distance of half a mile, tearing out his tongue and two ribs. He died the next day.

Last Saturday, T.M. Lung, a foundryman, was shot and seriously wounded, in Louisville, by a man named Charles Cole. There was a woman in the case.

Ten days ago near Lexington, Virginia, a young lady named Susan Keb was outraged and murdered by a negro named Jesse Edwards, who has been arrested and instead of being hung is in jail.

A man named Dunbar was killed on the 17th near Richmond, Kentucky, by George Tipton, his brother-in-law. Family affair.

## THE SOUTHERN ARGUS - DEATHS - JUNE 1869 THROUGH JUNE 1874

The negro who murdered Adkin Lewis in Georgia a few days since has been arrested.

Strillitz and Selfrank, pantaloon makers, got into a difficulty Tuesday week in Memphis during which the latter was stabbed and killed by the former.

A few days ago Miss Gruber, a young lady of about twenty-two years of age, daughter of Jacob Gruber, Jr., hung herself in the garret of her uncle, Solomon Gruber, near Charlestown, Virginia.

Adkin D. Lewis, residing near Waynesboro, Georgia, was five times stabbed and instantly killed by a negro on the 16th inst. Mr. L. had justly corrected a child of the murderer a few days previous. A little son of the victim was the only person present at the killing.

A number of masked men captured a notorious thief by the name of Howard at Harlem, Missouri, a few days since, tying a rope with a stone attached around his neck, cast him headforemost into the river and drowned him.

On Tuesday afternoon of last week, Mrs. Eliza Ogborn, aged forty years, wife of Mr. Wm. F. Ogborn, who resides near Philadelphia, Georgia, died of suffocation from excessive corpulence. She weighed four hundred and thirty pounds two years ago, but those who knew her intimately say she must have weighed six hundred at the time of her death, as she had not been able to move about much for the last year or two.

Mr. Richard Terrell was seriously stabbed in the arm and back in Meridian, Mississippi, the other day, during an altercation with a youth of thirteen or fourteen years of age named James Head...

A private letter from Jackson, Tennessee, informs the Memphis Appeal that Capt. John Bradford, the noted guerrilla, whose arrest was chronicled a few days ago, while on his way to Henderson County Jail on Saturday last was taken from the hands of the Sheriff and killed...

In Bonesville, Columbia County, Georgia, a few mornings since, a quarrel occurred between a Mr. Walker and wife during which Walker left the house, but, returning shortly afterwards, found his wife lying on the floor in a pool of blood, dead. She had cut her throat from ear to ear with a razor.

Issue 6-30-1869

Thomas Hynes, a released penitentiary bird, stabbed Michael Cochran in Buffalo, New York, on the 21st, fatally. He was arrested.

## THE SOUTHERN ARGUS - DEATHS - JUNE 1869 THROUGH JUNE 1874

Last Wednesday the 23rd inst., Col. Co??us W. Lee died at his residence near Union????.

John Patterson, who stole two horses and killed a man named White near Kingston, Tennessee, in 1866, has been arrested and is in jail at Nashville.

Wm. Winters, an employee on the Memphis and Louisville Railroad, was shot and afterwards beaten to death with the butt end of a pistol by an Irishman named Madden at Mason's Depot on the 20th. Madden escaped.

The first execution in South Carolina under the reconstructed state government took place the other day at Arlington Court House when a negro named Cyrus Cox was hanged for the murder of Robert Suggert, white, in January last...

Sam. Hetterstein, better known along the line of the Memphis and Ohio Railroad as "Sam Tank", recently committed suicide at Okolona, Mississippi, by cutting his throat. Whisky the cause.

Charles H. McDonald, aged sixteen, employed in the Republican office at Frederick, Maryland, committed suicide a few days ago by taking laudanum.

Mr. Wm. Britten shot and instantly killed one of his neighbors named Lapsey, near Greensboro, Georgia, a few days ago. Cause whisky.

Mr. Dulaney shot, some time since, by the negro Lewis Hall near Benton, is dead. The negro is in jail.

Mrs. Catherine B. Paterson, charged with the murder of her husband in Savannah, Georgia, some time since, has been acquitted.

J.A. Galvin and R. Moody, the latter colored, were sentenced yesterday by the Supreme Court of Tennessee at Brownsville to be hung on the 20th of August for the murder of Officer Fenton and Capt. Perry of the Memphis police force about a year ago.

John Cooper, a lawyer, shot through the head and killed a fellow of bad character named Wes. Persell, above West Liberty, Kentucky, on Friday week...

On last Tuesday morning, a Mr. Harrison of Warren County, Tennessee, shot and killed a man named Groves, son of the former Sheriff of the county...

## THE SOUTHERN ARGUS - DEATHS - JUNE 1869 THROUGH JUNE 1874

A young man named Miller was found dead in North River, Tuscaloosa County, a few days since. He had been missing from his home about two weeks.

We learn from the *Greenville Advocate* that on Thursday of last week, Joshua Terrell, living near Rutledge, Crenshaw County, was struck on the head with the heave of an axe by a negro man, breaking his skull. Mr. T., at last accounts, was not dead but considered mortally wounded.

Mrs. Ella Nichols, wife of Dr. Nichols of Nashville and daughter of Mr. J.J. Fackler of Huntsville, was accidentally shot at Nashville Tuesday morning of last week.

A Mrs. Phillips of Greenville attempted to commit suicide a few days since and did inflict a serious wound on the neck.

Issue 7-7-1869

Rev. T.W. Dorman of the Methodist Church died in Mobile on Friday last.

Judge B.L. Whelan, Judge of this Judicial District, died on Monday night in Greensboro.

The other day, John Profit, residing near Cambridge, Saline County, Missouri, was thrown from his mule and so seriously injured that he died four hours afterwards.....about twenty-five years of age, and removed to Saline from Chariton County a few months since.

In Todd County, Kentucky, the other day, R.W. Morrow was convicted of manslaughter in killing W.C. Cheatham and sentenced to the penitentiary for eight years.

A few days ago, L.I. Benton, a prominent lawyer of Robertson County, Tennessee, was killed by J.S. Simpson and his son.

Robert Arnold, negro, will be hung at Washington, Wilkes County, Georgia, on the 30th inst. for the murder of Mr. Thaxon in March last.

A married lady, a Mrs. Garvis, committed suicide on Tuesday night the 8th in San Antonio, Texas, by hanging herself...

Near Crockett, Texas, last week, Mr. Satterwhite snapped a pistol at Mr. Calhoun in a jest. The pistol was loaded and Mr. Calhoun was mortally wounded.

## THE SOUTHERN ARGUS - DEATHS - JUNE 1869 THROUGH JUNE 1874

Saturday night of week before last, a young man named Nolan was killed near West Point, Mississippi, by the accidental discharge of a gun in the hands of D.C. Humphrey as they were returning from a hunting and fishing trip.

Mrs. Nichol of Nashville, formerly Miss Fackler of Huntsville, died the other day from the effects of an accidental shot from a pistol.

Bennett Lee, aged seventy, dropped dead while plowing in his field in Gwinnett County, Georgia, on Saturday of week before last, supposed from heart disease.

Mr. Jackson Templin, an aged citizen of Washington County, Tennessee, living some miles southeast of Jonesboro, committed suicide on the 1?th the inst. by shooting himself through the head.

### Issue 7-14-1869

Col. Daniel Rosser, formerly Sheriff of Wilcox County, died in Grenada, Mississippi, on the 9th inst. at a very advanced age.

A couple of radicals had a shooting match at a radical meeting at Decatur the other day. One Robert L. Garner, scalawag Deputy Sheriff, was shot and badly perhaps mortally wounded.

Major Gunter of Dale County was shot and killed, a few days ago, by some person unknown.

John Deming, an old citizen of Greenville, died yesterday was a week ago.

Dr. Bedell of Henry County died a few days ago from a gunshot wound inflicted upon him some time ago by a man named Culpepper.

The *Greensboro Beacon* publishes an obituary of Henry Fenderson, a negro man famous for his fidelity and good sense, who died recently in Hale County.

### Issue 7-21-1869

George T. Stewart, an old citizen of Montgomery, died in that city very suddenly last week.

George Conway, an old citizen, died near Mobile on Friday night last.

# THE SOUTHERN ARGUS - DEATHS - JUNE 1869 THROUGH JUNE 1874

Died at Charlestown, West Virginia, on the 8th inst., Ellen Lee, widow of the late Rev. N.P. Knapp, formerly Rector of Christ Church, Mobile.

Samuel C. Bonner, aged seventy-three years, died in Pickens County on the 26th of June.

Died in Eutaw, July 2nd, Alexander Jarvis.
Died in Montgomery, July 5th, John M. Williams.

James M. Zimmerman of Elmore County died on the 11th, aged fifty-five years.

John Samuel Peake, formerly a citizen of Lowndes County, Alabama, died in Summerville, South Carolina, on the 14th inst., aged eighty-three years.

Robert Gillespie committed suicide in Louisville on the 15th inst.

Mrs. Mary Walker Pleasants, wife of Samuel Pleasants and daughter of John Robinson, died in Huntsville, July 14th.

Issue 7-28-1869

Mrs. Louisa Kaelin, living near the ???? of Alabama Street, committed suicide yesterday morning by taking arsenic.

Died on the 15th inst. near Tuscaloosa, Frances, infant daughter of Captain and Mrs. W.F. Karsner.

Joseph Dupuy is in jail for killing Lem. Hanna at Whitesburg.

Mrs. Lucy Irby Falconer of Montgomery died on the 13th inst., in the seventy-first year of her age.

On the night of the 21st inst., a man named Rayburn was run over by the cars at Greenville and instantly killed.

R.H. Adams was thrown from a buggy and pretty badly hurt in Montgomery, on the 23rd.

Died July 17th, 1869, at the residence of Mrs. Simonton near Calhoun, Mrs. _____ Wiley, aged about fifty years.

The youngest daughter of Rev. H. Stringfellow, Jr. of Montgomery died in Alexandria, Virginia, on the 21st inst.

# THE SOUTHERN ARGUS - DEATHS - JUNE 1869 THROUGH JUNE 1874

Maj. Thomas C. Price of Sumter County died in Mobile last week.

John E. Brown of Sumter County was stricken with paralysis last week.

Little Norman Lyon, son of George G. Lyon, Esq. of Demopolis, was thrown from his horse on the evening of the 23rd and fatally injured.

Issue 8-4-1869

We regret to learn that Mrs. Inda Ware, wife of Henry H. Ware, formerly of this city, died at Crab Orchard Springs, Kentucky, July 28th.

Died at his residence in Jefferson County, July 9th, 1869, after a short illness, Dr. D. Davis.... He was the father of our fellow townsman, Col. John W. Davis.

On the 28th ult., Benj. Snodgrass, Jr. was shot and seriously wounded at Scottsboro, Jackson County, by G.W.V. Stovall.

Bill Campbell, negro, was killed Saturday night was a week ago in Madison County.

Col. John T. Abernathy died very suddenly at his home near Leighton, Alabama, the other day.

Died at Gadsden, July 22nd, Mrs. Joda M. Echols, wife of Samuel B. Echols and daughter of the late B.F. Pope.
Died near Opelousas, Louisiana, June 20th, 1869, Willie P. Oden, formerly of this county.
Died in Tuscaloosa County, July 22nd, William J. Baggett, aged nineteen years.

Mrs. Elizabeth Wynne died in Warren County, Georgia, on the 18th, at the age of ninety-six years. She was one of the oldest residents of the state.

The youngest son of Mr. and Mrs. R.H. Stickney of Greensboro died in Knoxville, July 20th.

A Mr. Callahan was shot and killed a short time since by a Mr. Scarborough at New Prospect, Hale County.

Haughey was shot by Callin and is dead.

# THE SOUTHERN ARGUS - DEATHS - JUNE 1869 THROUGH JUNE 1874

B.F. Hooper, an influential and leading citizen of Floyd County, Georgia, died near Rome last Wednesday, aged fifty-eight years.

Capt. John C. Lawton, in attempting to swim cross Wateeseea Bayou, Arkansas, on last Sunday, was accidentally drowned.

A man by the name of Patterson was killed by John C. Cason on last Wednesday at Beauregard, Mississippi.

Died in Montgomery County, August 1st, 1869, John Bonham, aged eighty-four years, and Josiah Palmer, aged eighty-two years.
Died July 23rd, 1869, Joseph Silver at his residence at Montgomery Hill, Baldwin County, Alabama, aged fifty-one years.

Will S. McMinn, formerly of Montgomery, died in Topeka, Kansas, last week.

Died in Galveston, Texas, on the 20th ult., Mrs. Ann N. Jones, formerly of Alabama.
Died near Greenville, July 25th, 1869, Mrs. Ann L. Lewis, aged thirty-eight years.

Joseph Westbrook, alias Joseph Lipscomb, negro, is in jail at Demopolis, charged with the murder of Sophy Bell, negro.

Died in Sumter County, July 28th, Rosa Knox, infant daughter of John M. and Mary McDaniel.
Died in Sumter County, July 20th, Preston N. McMillan, aged eighteen years.

Issue 8-11-1869

Died, Columbia, Henry County, July 19th, Edward Wheelock, son of Dr. N.D. and Louisia O. Spottswood of that place, aged three years.

Ben Snodgrass, shot at Scottsboro by Stovall, is dead.

Died at Manack's, Lowndes County, Sunday night, August 1st, Mrs. Meliora A. Graves, the wife of Hon. P.T. Graves.
Died in Huntsville, July 28th, Mrs. Elizabeth Thompson, in the twenty-eighth year of her age.

Thomas Haughey, radical ex-member of Congress was shot and mortally wounded at Courtland the Monday before the election by Dr. A.B. Collins, radical also.

## THE SOUTHERN ARGUS - DEATHS - JUNE 1869 THROUGH JUNE 1874

Dr. J.Q. Johnson of Columbiana was thrown for his buggy last week, and seriously injured.

Died in Lowndes County, August 2nd, J.D. McDonald, age thirty-six years.

Mrs. Pickett of Girard, Alabama sent to the drug store for a dose of Sub-nitrate of Bismuth. The druggist sent her by mistake Corrosive Sublimate. She took it and was dead in an hour.

Died Saturday evening last at his residence four miles west of Selma, Thomas Booth, in the forty-first year of his age.

Issue 8-18-1869

Died on Saturday evening last at his residence four miles west of Selma, Thomas Booth, in the forty-first year of his age. For nearly twenty years, except during the four years of the late war, Mr. Booth had been in active business in this city....At the time of his death he was a member of the firm of Hudson, Kennedy & Co....He was one of the first to respond to the call of Alabama for men to maintain her independence...

John Wesley (negro) was killed last Saturday was a week at Chlorina, Lowndes County, by George H. Staggers.

Col. Montgomery Relf, a leading citizen of Lowndes, died at Letohatchee, August 8th, aged forty-four years.

Died at Silver Run, Alabama, August 2nd, Miss Lucy J. Connally, aged thirty-nine years.
Died in Talladega, August 3rd, Jennie, daughter of Dr. J.H. and Mrs. Elizabeth Logan.
Died in Huntsville, August 11th, Jacob Herts, aged twenty-four years.

Issue 8-25-1869

Died August 14th at Fort Deposit, Ben H. Elsberry of Lowndes County.
Died in Oxford, August 12th, Miss Sallie Goode.

B. Rush Jones, Jr. died in Montgomery, August 18th.

Mr. G.W. Skinner of Washington County accidently killed his sister-in-law, Miss Margaret Hill, a few days since while putting fresh caps on his pistol. Deceased was a niece of the late Gen. A.P. Hill of Virginia.

## THE SOUTHERN ARGUS - DEATHS - JUNE 1869 THROUGH JUNE 1874

Amos McMullen, a notoriously infamous negro was shot in Greenville the other night.

Died at Sulphur Springs, St. Clair County, Katie, only daughter of Jas. P. and Julia A. Powers.

James Berrier, an old citizen of Talladega, died suddenly on the 16th inst.

Ellis Hill killed Thomas McKelvey at Moulton a few days ago by cutting his throat.

Oliver Perkins, negro, stabbed Jeff Bates, white, at Shelby Iron Works last Saturday week and in resisting arrest was himself shot. The wounds were neither of them fatal.

A Mrs. Wallace, living near Fayetteville, Talladega County, was knocked in the head by an unknown party while milking her cows one day last week. She is in a critical condition.

Died at Greenville, August 8th, N.A. Rose.
Died the other day in Madison County, Col. James Nich. Fletcher, an old citizen of that county.

Mrs. Jane Moody, wife of Judge Moody of Tuscaloosa, died in Lynchburg, Virginia, August 9th.

On the morning of the 13th inst. several disguised and unknown men attacked the house of one Dr. Choutteau in Livingston, for the purpose it is supposed of inflicting summary punishment upon Choutteau for incendiary conflict. In the attack, one of the party was killed by a fellow named Coblentza, who was in Choutteau's house, and Coblentz himself was afterwards mortally wounded. The attacking party were tracked by the Sheriff and posse several miles before traces were lost...

Collins, the member of the State Board of Education, who murdered Haughey, is in jail in Tuscumbia.

Issue 9-1-1869

Jeff McCalley, negro member of the Legislature from Madison is dead.

Ed Cook, negro, stabbed severely in Haynesville the other day, Ben. Gilchrist, negro.

# THE SOUTHERN ARGUS - DEATHS - JUNE 1869 THROUGH JUNE 1874

Died in Autaugaville, August 12th of meningitis, Pattie, youngest daughter of Dr. Thos. A. and Dora A. Davis.
Died in Tuscaloosa, August 22nd, 1869, J.M. Mickleboro of Marion, in the thirty-eighth year of his age.

Jefferson Burgin living near Elyton was accidently shot and killed the other day by his friend George Barton.

Died in Madison County, August 14th, Mrs. Elizabeth Johnston, aged eighty-four years.
Died in Courtland, August 17th, Mrs. Elizabeth Rebman.
Died in Huntsville, August 23rd, Mrs. Elizabeth Schaffer.
Died August 24th in Decatur, Col. Henry Fennel, aged sixty-two.

Maj. James T. Dent of Tuscaloosa died last week, aged about eighty years.

Nich. Davis and Preston Drake had a fight in Huntsville a few days ago. Drake knocked Davis down and Davis cut Drake with a knife.

Died August 21st near Butler, Joseph P. Abney.

Daniel Jackson living near Eastaboga and A.R. Barclay living in the vicinity of Talladega, old and influential citizens, died last week.

Died in Jackson County, August 21st, I. T. Jones.

August 23rd, a little son of D.R. Phelps of Eufaula was killed by lightning.

## Issue 9-8-1869

Abel Hill, an old citizen of Selma, died last Saturday.

A Mrs. Foster, living East Selma, was shot by her husband Monday night and mortally wounded. The shooting is said to have been unintentional.

Died in Talladega, August 28th, Mrs. Elizabeth McAfee.
Died near Union Springs last week, Mattie, the little daughter of Mr. John Laslie, who was badly burned some weeks ago; the wife of Dr. Fonville from tuberculosis; and the son of Col. Rhodes from congestion.

E.A. Gunter of Lowndes County died near Gordonsville on the 1st inst.

Died near Jefferson, Marengo County, August 26th, Anna Grant ? daughter of G. W. and M.J. Sandusky.

# THE SOUTHERN ARGUS - DEATHS - JUNE 1869 THROUGH JUNE 1874

Died in Hale County, August 31st, John C. Kennaird, aged thirty-three years.
Died in Greensboro, August 29th, Levin A., infant son of James A. and F.I. Sledge.
Died in Monroe County, Alabama, August 13th, Wm. Moore, aged seventy-three years.
Died in Pickens County, Alabama, August 15th, Walton Black, son of John A. and Mary C. Black.

The remains of the late Rev. Mr. McKee, drowned some months ago in Pea River, have been recovered.

Maj. James T. Dent, who died in Tuscaloosa on the 24th ult., was at the battle of Lundy's Lane during the War of 1812.

Died in Marion, August 28th, John H., son of John H. and M.E. Poole, aged four years.

Thos. E. Winston, a valued citizen of Tuscumbia, died August 24th.

Died in Huntsville, September 2nd, Mrs. Hannah Mann, aged sixty-three years.
Died in Limestone County, August 22nd, Thos. B. Collier, aged sixty-seven years.

Bob Timmons, negro, is in jail in Huntsville for stabbing Wm. Simpson.
   Mr. Simpson, living near Whitesburg, was stabbed by a negro man in his employ on the 31st ult., from the effects of which it is learned he will die.

Green Fearn, negro, was killed in Marshall County, August 28th, by some of the Evans band...

On the 27th of August, Stephen McCally, a negro man on the "Underwood place," a negro man near "Hogue's grocery," two negroes at the "Junction," and one negro at Hamburg, all in Perry County, were killed by lightning.

Died in Eufaula, August 30th, Mrs. Martha J. Cato, aged thirty-eight years.

The negro who stabbed Bryant Richardson of Sumter County about a year ago, now admits that he was pr--pted to do so by Chotteau, who, unfortunately, was not killed in the attack made on his house three weeks ago.

## THE SOUTHERN ARGUS - DEATHS - JUNE 1869 THROUGH JUNE 1874

Issue 9-15-1869

Col. J. B. Bibb of Montgomery died in that city yesterday morning.

Died at Montgomery, Tuesday, Daisy, infant daughter of Mr. and Mrs. E.T. Ledyard.

Died in Eufaula, September 1st, Alice Gertrude, infant daughter of John J. and Ella Virginia Carter.

Died in Tuskaloosa, September 10th, Maj. B. F. Hardwick.

Rachael Williams and Susan Williams, white, and Sol Murphy and Louis Ashford, black, are in jail in Butler County, charged with the murder of Jack Jones, negro.

Mr. William Ott was way-laid and killed Friday night was a week ago near Garland on the M. & M. R.R. by unknown parties. His horse was also shot and killed.

Died in Mobile on Friday morning, 3rd inst., Martin McVoy, aged fifty-four years.

Died at St. Paul, Minnesota, on the 27th of August, Miss Maggie Redus, daughter of Mr. J. R. Gates of Mobile.

George Champion, a democratic negro, was murdered at Rocky Mount, August 28th, by a band of negro Ku Kluxes.

Died in Marion, after a short illness, W.B. Lawson, in the sixty-fourth year of his age.

Mrs. A.E. Stamps, wife of Perry Stamps of Talladega, died on the 7th inst.

Mr. McGrath, white, and Phil. Nash, colored, were seriously injured on the 6th, by the fall of the scaffolding on which they were at work plastering the Presbyterian Church at Demopolis.

Died in Montgomery, September 5th, Mrs. H. Bassel, aged twenty-two years.

Died in Macon County, August 20th, Charles T., infant son of Charles T. and Ellen A. Goodwyn.

Died in Sumter County, September 1st, Mrs. Lucy P., consort of Dr. W. G. Little.

Died September 5th in Hale County, Mrs. Bettie, wife of Mr. J.E. DuBois and daughter of T.H. Davis of Mobile.

Died in Greene County, August 27th, William Josephus, infant son of Rev. C.M. Hutton.

# THE SOUTHERN ARGUS - DEATHS - JUNE 1869 THROUGH JUNE 1874

Jerry Cabaniss, negro preacher, preached himself crazy and died at Stevenson soon after.

Friday afternoon, Henry Herron, a bookkeeper in the banking house of Farley, Smith & Co., Montgomery, was shot and, it is supposed, mortally wounded by his brother-in-law, Robert H. Knox.

Died August 30th, 1869 at Lowndesboro, Mrs. Harrison (nee Walker), wife of Mr. Irvin Harrison.
Died September 1st, 1869 at his residence near Gordonsville, Lowndes County, Mr. Erasmus A. Gunter, an old and respected citizen.
Died near Pickensville a few days since, Zach Pulliam, an old citizen of Pickens County.
Died in Walker County, August 29th, Mrs. J.T. Shearer, wife of John T. Shearer.
Died in Morgan County, September 3, Capt. W. H. Williams.
Died in Lexington, Virginia, on the 31st of August, after a protracted illness of nine months, Mrs. Mary Grace Pratt, wife of Rev. John W. Pratt, formerly of Tuskaloosa.
Died in Etowah County, September 8th, Mrs. Mary Ringo, aged seventy-eight years.

Issue 9-22-1869

Sidney Womack, Clerk of the Greene Circuit Court, is dead.

Died at Wetumpka, September 2nd, Inez, only daughter of W.H. and Laura Alexander.

Wilson B. Farris, acting Postmaster at Huntsville, died in that city on the 1?th inst., aged forty-three years.

Died in Marengo County on the 9th inst., Mrs. Lucie G. Nixon, wife of W.G. Nixon, in the thirty-fourth year of her age.
Died in Brownsville, Alabama, the other day, Mrs. Susan Martin, aged seventy-one years.
Died in Cherokee County, September 5th, Mrs. Adkinson.
Died in Tuskaloosa County, September 16th, Mrs. Frances McMath.
Died in Wilcox County, September 9th, Thomas J. Williams, aged fifty-four years.
Died at Pleasant Ridge, Alabama, August 21st, Mrs. Martha Leonora McMullen, wife of the late Rev. J.P. McMullen.
Died in Demopolis, September 15th, William Drake, infant son of Capt. A.P. French.

## THE SOUTHERN ARGUS - DEATHS - JUNE 1869 THROUGH JUNE 1874

Died in Pickens County, September 11th, James Hammonds, an old and much respected citizen.

Mrs. Rebecca Harris died in Haynesville on the 10th inst.

Mrs. Henry L. Smith died in Lowndesboro on the 13th inst.

Allen Cooper, fifty years a citizen of Huntsville, died last week.

On the 8th, John Carpenter was shot and killed in Clinton, Greene County, by W.T. Eatman.

H.M. Glass, employed at the steam saw mill near Elyton, was thrown against the saw the other day and his leg was so badly mangled that amputation became necessary. At last accounts his recovery was doubtful.

Simon Allen, negro, is under arrest in Montgomery for killing Jerry Cox, negro.

Mr. Wm. Mattchett shot and killed a negro man named Jack Bibb at Farmersville Mill in Lowndes County the other day.

Issue 9-29-1869

Died in Pickens County, September 15th, Lewis W. Ball.
Died at Haynesville, September 18th, Dr. Burrell Boykin Rudulph, aged fifty-seven years.
Died September 10th in Lowndes County, Mrs. Crum, wife of Jacob Crum.
Died September 17th in Lowndes County, Jacob Crum.
Died August 31st in Benton, Mississippi, Adora Young, aged twenty years.
Died in Decatur, September 1?th, Miss Jane Cantwell, daughter of Dr. J.Y. Cantwell of that city.
Died near Munford, September 18th, Mrs. Lelitia Walker, wife of Rev. A.J. Walker.
Died at Bashi, Clark County, August 1st, Oliver Starke Huske, aged eighteen years.
Died in Shelby County, August 24th, Mrs. Mary Ann Cross, wife of A.J. Cross, Jr.
Died at Patona, September 6th, Mrs. Anna Greene, formerly of Columbiana, aged twenty-two years.
Died in Talladega County, September 17th, Hauce Hendrick, aged seventy-five years.
Died in Limestone County, September 23rd, little Benny Irvin.
Died in Limestone County, September 20th, Mrs. Martha Easter.

# THE SOUTHERN ARGUS - DEATHS - JUNE 1869 THROUGH JUNE 1874

James Leake of Montgomery County was killed near Mt. Meigs last Sunday was a week ago by his horse running away and throwing him out of the buggy.

Isaac W. Landers of Limestone County was accidently shot and killed a few days ago while out hunting.

Died in Meridian, Mississippi, September 14th, Mrs. Eunice Early, formerly Miss Eunice Willingham of Greensboro.

A negro man named Hartwell shot and killed another negro named Jim Mastin near Huntsville on the 17th inst.

Benjamin Hill on the track of the Decatur and Nashville Road near Athens, was struck a few days ago by the cow-catcher of a passing train and fatally injured.

The Mr. Glass so badly injured last week near Elyton by being thrown against a circular saw in motion is getting well.

A diffculty occured on Sunday morning was a week ago on the plantation of Capt. John W. Turner, some nine miles below Rome, Georgia, between Lewis Bray and Isaac Tutt, freedmen, about some hogs, which resulted in the former shooting and killing the latter. Bray is now in jail.

Issue 10-6-1869

We learn from the *Gadsden Times* that on the day of the Allen Springs barbaque, Calvin Tinker, living near Fort Payne, was run over by a train and had both legs so badly crushed that he died two days thereafter.

The *Gadsden Times* says that Dr. Jack met with a serious accident as he was returning on a hand car from a call to attend Calvin Tinker, hurt at Allen Springs barbaque. The hand car struck a rail and was thrown off the track, whereby the doctors knee joint was dislocated.

Died in Limestone County, September 20th, Mrs. Martha Jane, wife of F. Easter and daughter of Thomas W. Pettus.
Died in Greenville, September 17th, Lula Rhidoria Burkett, aged one year and five months.
Died in Franklin County, September 18th, W.H. Hart, in the twenty-second year of his age.
Died at Dr. B.W. Whitfield's near Demopolis, September 18th, John Enzor Bouchelle.

## THE SOUTHERN ARGUS - DEATHS - JUNE 1869 THROUGH JUNE 1874

Died near Harpersville, Shelby County, September 22nd, Samuel Wallace, aged eighty-six years.
Died in Lowndes County, September 24th, Mrs. Amanda M. Singleton, wife of J.C. Singleton, aged twenty-eight years.
Died in Lowndes County, September 22nd/28th, Jonathan Mealing, aged eighty-six years.
Died in Mobile on the 1st inst., Parker C., youngest son of the late Rev. J.J. and Mrs. Ellen B. Nicholson.
Died in Montgomery County, October 1st, James Ray.
Died in Montgomery, September 20/29th, Charlie, son of Prof. G.F. and Mrs. Josie McDonald.
Died near Mt. Meigs, Montgomery County, October 3rd, Col. J.C.B. Mitchell.

A man named Garrett was killed one day last week at Dunn's store in Tuskaloosa County by another named Upton.

Died last week in Butler County, Mrs. Julia Ann Peagler, aged about one hundred two years. She had been for sixty years a member of the Baptist Church. She was the mother of eight children and lived to see twenty-three grand-children and eighteen great grand-children.

Mr. W.R. Mason ? late Register in Chancery in Macon County, died in Tuskegee on the 27th.

September 28th, Dr. Burnett of Georgetown, Macon County, accidentally shot and killed a negro girl.

Issue 10-13-1869

A Mr. Hendricks, working near the Hopgood place in Franklin County, was run over, October 2nd, by a freight train on the Memphis and Charleston Railroad, and killed.

Died in Lowndesboro, October 3rd, Julius H. Kendrick, aged thirty-five, a gentleman of fine culture and high position in society.
Died a few days ago in Marshall County, Capt. Thomas Harris, late a gallant officer in the "4th Alabama."
Died in Hale County, September 20th, John DuBois, child of J.B. and Lucy McMillan.
Died near Mt. Willing, September 22nd, Jas. Murphy, aged twenty-one years.
Died at Florence, September 29th, Jos. M. Roberts, a member of the firm of Perryman, Roberts & Co. of Mobile.
Died in Livingston, September 28th, Margaret Ann, wife of David H. Trott.

## THE SOUTHERN ARGUS - DEATHS - JUNE 1869 THROUGH JUNE 1874

Last Thursday night, a negro named William Bell was killed by another negro named Harris. The homicide occurred on the plantation of Dr. H.W. Reese in Marengo County.

A second amputation of the leg of Mr. Glass, mangled by a circular saw near Elyton some time ago, has been rendered necessary. He still lives.

On the 28th ult., a negro named Sanders was murdered near Snow Hill by unknown parties.

Issue 10-20-1869

Ex-Chancellor N.W. Cocke died in Greenville, October 10th.

Mr. Irvin, who lives seven miles southeast of Athens was shot one day last week, while at work in his own field, and seriously wounded by a drunken man named Stone, who had no provocation.

Capt. A.M. Godfrey, proprietor of the Battle House, Mobile, committed suicide on the 14th.

Rev. T.F. Mangum, previously reported dead, preached to his congregation in Demopolis last Sunday was a week.

In Bullock County last week, a negro named Carey Gilmore committed a terrible outrage upon the person of a Mrs. Brown and was forthwith captured and hung.

Monday morning was a week ago, Miss Lizzie Shaver, daughter of Rev. F.L.B. Shaver of Lowndes County was thrown from her horse and killed.

Died in Florida, October 12th, Edmund Alonzo, only child of Dr. E.R. and Mrs. M.M. Prince, formerly of Greene County.
Died in Newnan, Georgia, October 10th, Dr. W.T. Whelan, formerly of Greensboro.

James Carpenter, a highly respectable citizen of Greene County, was shot on the night of the 8th inst. while seated by his own fire and instantly killed.

Died in this city, Tuesday morning, October 19th, Eliza Mary, daughter of Capt. George W. and Angleique C. Colby, aged four years, seven months and twenty-four days.

## THE SOUTHERN ARGUS - DEATHS - JUNE 1869 THROUGH JUNE 1874

On Friday morning last, a lad named Attaway, endeavoring to pass from one train of cars to another, fell between them and was run over and instantly killed.

Mr. Simon Hugo of Mobile died at the Ackerman House Monday night.

Died near Clinton, Greene County, September 27th of "yellow fever," Miss Mollie Baker.
Died in Greene County, September 17th of "yellow fever," James Nusom Pippen/Pipper, aged eight years.
Died in Greene County, September 13th of "yellow fever," Miss Laura Dunlap.
Died in Greene County, August 26th of "yellow fever," Francis Marion Doss, aged twenty-nine years...
Died in Greene County, October 10th, Mrs. Jane Jones, aged forty-two years.
Died in Huntsville, October 13th, Gen. Daniel Morgan Bradford, in the seventy-sixth year of his age.
Died near Meridianville, Madison County, September 24th, Samuel A. Thompson, aged twenty-three years.
Died in Montgomery County, October 10th, Mrs. Precilla E. Farley.
Died in Newbern, October 12th, David Walker, aged twenty-one years.
Died in Talladega, October 6th, Mrs. Susan H.H. Miller, wife of George Miller.

Mr. I.C. Browder, an old citizen of Barbour County, died at his residence in Eufaula on the 12th inst.

Mrs. Louisa Dickinson died at Montgomery on the 15th.

Issue 10-27-1869

Died October 18th, 1869, at the residence of Col. G.C. Phillips near Selma, Katie, daughter of J.C. and Mary Kinkle. Huntsville papers will please copy.
Died October 17th in Newbern, Mrs. Mary Jane, wife of Maj. S.G. Spann.

William Anderson of Bullock County died last week.

William H. Waugh, an old citizen of Union Springs, died on the 17th.

Died in Troy, October 9th, Thomas G.L. Cook.

A.A. Griffin of Troy died a few days since.

Died in Huntsville, October 22nd, Geo. W. Neal.
Died in Columbiana, October 13th, Mary Fannie, infant daughter of Willis and Mary Ann Roberts.

## THE SOUTHERN ARGUS - DEATHS - JUNE 1869 THROUGH JUNE 1874

Died in Greene County, October 8th, Miss Laura Stone, in the twentieth year of her age.
Died in Greene County, October 6th, Augusta Belle, daughter of William H. and Mary M. Pippen.
Died in Sumter County, October 18th, Mattie Alma, daughter of W.A. and M.A. Selliman, aged four years.
Died in Tuscumbia, October 11th, Mrs. Elizabeth C. Green.
Died in Tuscumbia, October 18th, Mrs. Sarah M. Oliver, aged seventy-eight years, six months and sixteen days.
Died in Jacksonville, October 6th, Mrs. Mary Blackwell, aged eighty-one years.
Died in Henry County, October 14th, Mrs. Susan M. Pearre, wife of E.E. Pearre, aged forty-two years.
Died in Fort Valley, Georgia, October 15th, Mrs. Mary A. Dyer, formerly of Montgomery.
Died in Perry County, October 1?th, J???? Edward, son of Major J.H. and Mrs. Josephine Wiley.

In Madison County on the 14th, A.H. Smith, a young man about twenty-nine years old, committed suicide by cutting his throat.

Issue 11-3-1869

Died in Greene County, October 25th, Capt. R.T. Nott, aged about seventy years.
Died in Greensboro, October 25th of malarial kakama, Miss Mary E. Shannon, aged about twenty years.
Died in Greensboro, North Carolina, October 23rd, Samuel Nutting of Greensboro, Alabama, aged sixty-five years.
Died near Radfordsville, September 19th, Mrs. Nancy Francis Austin, in the twenty-fourth year of her age.
Died in Madison County, October 24th, James A., infant son of Levi W. and Mrs. Mollie D. Esslinger.
Died in Columbiana, October 15th, Hattie Wagner, second twin daughter of Willis and Mary Ann Roberts, aged two months.

Mrs. Camille D. Girrard died in Montgomery, November 1st.

Died October 18th near Mt. Willing, Burrell Jones.
Died in St. Clair County, October 23rd, Maggie Brown, daughter of Mrs. Sue Dillon, aged ten years.
Died in Gadsden, October 18th, Eva Theresa, infant daughter of R.B. and M. Kyle.

## THE SOUTHERN ARGUS - DEATHS - JUNE 1869 THROUGH JUNE 1874

Died October 11th near Benton, David A. Steele ?, aged about sixty-eight years.

Died in Greene County, October 11th, Mrs. Elizabeth Dunlap, aged seventy-two years.

Nat Ragan was killed the other day at Echols' Mill in Cherokee County by a log rolling over him.

A few weeks ago near Cedar Bluff, Samuel Reed was shot and killed by Thomas Angle...

$800 reward is offered for the arrest of E.D. Martin, charged with killing John W. Norman in Franklin County.

On the 18th of October, James Littlejohn of Calhoun County was thrown from his wagon and fatally injured.

Dr. Joseph E. Moore of Jefferson, Marengo County, died in Mississippi, October 19th.

Issue 11-10-1869

S. Boldan, an old merchant of this city, died on Sunday last, unexpectedly to his many friends. Mr. Boldan was a Hungarian and under the heroic Kossuth, participated in the last struggle for the independence of his country...

An old man named Mumford in Talladega County went to sleep on the railroad track a few days ago and was killed by a passing train.

Col. John S. Smith, late Adjutant of the 20th Alabama (Confederate) Regiment, was shot and killed in Marion last week by Capt. William A. Forrest.

When Joseph Pizzala of Montgomery found he must die, he sent for Father Manuccy of the Catholic Church to administer the Sacrament. Father M. refused to do this until the dying man had renounced Free Masonry.

Wm. Wood, for many years a citizen of Greenville, died suddenly last week, at Kingston, Georgia.

On the 20th of October, George Early, an old white man living six miles from Tuskaloosa, was found hanging to the limb of a tree, dead. He had been beaten before he was murdered. Negroes are accused of the murder.

# THE SOUTHERN ARGUS - DEATHS - JUNE 1869 THROUGH JUNE 1874

Trenton Foster, son of Charles M. Foster of Tuskaloosa, was thrown from a buggy last Friday upon the heels of a frightened horse and kicked to death.

At Fairfield in Pickens County a few days ago in an affray between Ed. and John Billings on one side and Thomas and William Price on the other, one of the Price's was dangerously and the other seriously wounded.

Frank T. Hall, formerly of Talladega, died in Montgomery, Monday.

G.W.N. Stovall has been indicted by the Grand Jury of Jackson County for manslaughter in killing Ben. Snodgrass last August.

Robert Johnson and his son, Hope Johnson, have been indicted by the Grand Jury of Jackson County for the murder of John Card.

Alfred Norton of Mobile committed suicide in that city on the 4th inst. by shooting himself through the breast with a pistol.

Died at Lower Peach Tree, October 16th, Mrs. Ella McLeod, wife of John McLeod.
Died October 30th near Belmont, Leonidas Rushing, aged forty-two years.
Died in Coosa County, October 25th, Allen J. Taylor, aged twenty-seven years.
Died October 30th, four miles from Hayneville, Mrs. Callie, wife of George W. McQueen.
Died November 2nd near Gilmer's Station, Miss Mary Chappel, daughter of Hon. J.J. Chappel.

Joseph Pizzala died in Montgomery, November 2nd.

Died October 30th near Mt. Willing, Miss Carrie Lee, daughter of Rev. David Lee.
Died in Madison County, November 3rd, James M. Wilson, aged fifty-two years.
Died in Huntsville, October 31st, Mrs. Viora C., wife of A.J. Bolton.

Issue  11-17-1869

Dr. A. Howard, aged seventy-two years, died in Montgomery, November 11th.

Col. N.B. Markle of Troy was thrown from his buggy a few days since and seriously hurt.

# THE SOUTHERN ARGUS - DEATHS - JUNE 1869 THROUGH JUNE 1874

Sheriff P.J. Doyle and J. Polk Wright of Madison County had an altercation in Huntsville the other day, resulting in a rough and tumble fight during which the latter was shot and killed by a son of the former.

At Rome, a village near Loachapoka, on Monday of last week, a fellow named Brewer attempted to assassinate Col. M.J. Bulger by shooting him with a shot gun. The wound inflicted is a very serious one. Brewer has fled.

George E. Monette of Livingston, a lad of sixteen years of age, was accidentally shot and killed last Wednesday by Robert T. Harriss, a companion of about the same age.

E.J. Cook, formerly of Lowndes County, now of Arizona Territory, recently lost his wife by death.

Milton Kirkpatrick, living near Calhoun, was thrown from his horse, a few days ago and seriously injured.

Died near Bragg's Store, November 1st, Mrs. Mary Lester, aged sixty years.
Died in Bullock County, November 4th, John P. Blackmon.
Died in Perry County, November 2nd, Mrs. M.A. Belcher in the forty-seventh year of her age.

## Issue 11-24-1869

Peter M. Cobb, an old citizen of Bibb County, died a few days since.

James A. Owen, an old citizen of Choctaw County, was stricken down with paralysis last week.

Miss Jennie Boyd was found dead in her bed at Eufaula the other morning from the effects, it is supposed, of an over-dose of chloroform.

Gus Walters, negro, was found a short time ago, dead in the Bigbee River. When last heard of alive, he was hog hunting.

Jesse Cox, living near Childersburg, was killed on the 16th by a negro.

The widow of Newell E. Thomas (who was murdered by the Attorney General of Alabama), late Editor of the *Choctaw Herald,* is teaching school in Butler.

Died at Randolph a few days since, Jos. M. Tucker, aged about forty years.
Died in Limestone County, November 5th, Mrs. R.A. Parham in the fifty-fourth year of her age.

# THE SOUTHERN ARGUS - DEATHS - JUNE 1869 THROUGH JUNE 1874

A.E. Sinclair, an old citizen, died at Notasulga last week.

Died in Choctaw County, November 17th, Mrs. Rosina Roach, wife of J.D. Roach.

Issue 12-1-1869

Died at her father's residence near White Bluff, Dallas County, Alabama, October 11, 1869, Mrs. Sarah F. Hall, wife of R.C. Hall, and daughter of E.C. and N.N. Tarry. She was born March 2, 1838 in Mecklenburg County, Virginia...

McIvor Knox, the second son of Maj. W.S. Knox, a young man of high character and rare promises, died in this city last Saturday, in the twenty-first year of his age.

Hiram Hill, one of the earliest settlers of this county to which he removed in 1818 and in which he lived until two years ago, died in Carroll County, Mississippi, November 2nd, in the ninety-first year of his age.

John Christian of Tuscumbia was kicked by a horse, just over the left eye, and dangerously hurt a few days ago.

Daniel C. Sellers, a prominent citizen, died at his residence near Camden, November 15th.

A Mr. Goodwin was killed by a man named Thompson at Tallassee last week.

Gen. Wm. Kerr, formerly of this city, died two weeks ago on his plantation in Greene County.

Capt. Pleas. Todd, well known as an old steamboat captain on the Tennessee River and recently a respectable citizen of Guntersville, died at his residence on the 18th inst.

Mrs. Polly Shelley, wife of the late Capt. Jacob D. Shelley, formerly of Talladega, died in Austin, Texas, on the 14th inst.

Capt. Jas. A. Fowler, an old and estimable citizen of Talladega, died in that place on the 15th inst.

Died on the 18th of November on the steamer *Jennie Rogers*, T.J. Sorsby of the Havana neighborhood.

## THE SOUTHERN ARGUS - DEATHS - JUNE 1869 THROUGH JUNE 1874

Peter M. Cobb, an old citizen of Bibb County, died a few days since.

Major A.M. McIver of Wilcox County died last week.

A man named Smith, who had been living in Cherokee County but a little while, died November 17th from the effects of drinking whiskey out of a kerosene oil can.

Hon. F.M. Hardwick, one of the leading citizens of Cherokee County, died November 19th, aged sixty-three years.

Meyer Cramer, who died in Eutaw, November 8th, aged one hundred two years, fought under Napoleon till the final fall and banishment of that great chieftain.

Collins Tarry, a young son of Gen. J.P. Tarry of Marion, was accidentally killed at that place Saturday was a week ago, by being run over by a heavily loaded wagon.

Died in Claiborne, Alabama, November, 6th Peter J. Galliard, aged thirty-two years.
Died at Randolph a few days since, Joseph J. Tucker, aged about forty years.

A.E. Sinclair, an old citizen, died at Notasulga, last week.

Died in Greene County, November 11th of typhoid pneumonia, Carr Merriweather, aged sixty-two years.
Died in Eutaw, November 17th, Mrs. Frances C. High.
Died in Mobile, November 27th, Thomas Lesesne.

Died in Tuskegee, November 19th, Mrs. Bettie, wife of Gen. G.W. Gunn.
Died in Limestone County, November 19th, Joseph Price Vasser.
Died at Jefferson, Marengo County, Susan Westbrook, relict of the late Rev. John Ivy Westbrook.
Died November 18th near Candy's Landing, Mrs. Fariss, wife of Mr. Lafayette Fariss, aged about twenty-five years.

Issue 12-8-1869

Died at Cahaba on the morning of the 5th inst., Miss Mary J. Ulmer, relict of the late Dr. E.G. Ulmer.

## THE SOUTHERN ARGUS - DEATHS - JUNE 1869 THROUGH JUNE 1874

In attempting on last Monday night to arrest Peter Rhodes (negro), charged with attempting to kill, last summer, John Tarrant (negro), Sheriff Craig was compelled to shoot and kill Rhodes, who was armed and resisted arrest. The killing occurred on the place of Frank Childers.

George Holly, negro, confined in the jail at Opelika for the murder of a Mr. Watson about a month ago, was taken out of jail and killed on the 1st.

In Cherokee County last week, Joseph E. O'Neal got his head caught in the machinery of a cotton press, and was seriously, perhaps fatally hurt.

Six negro men are in the Calhoun Jail for wounding Frank Embrey, negro, and murdering Frank's wife, the cause of the attack being a belief that Frank, possessed of unnatural powers, could fill them with aches and lizards, etc. or make a mark to cross which was death, &c.

Last Sunday was a week ago on Dr. Hussey's plantation in Limestone County, Bill Hussey (negro) was shot and instantly killed by John Hamilton (negro).

Mrs. Amanda B. Rice, wife of ex-Judge S.F. Rice, is dead.

Died in Jackson County, November 20th, William Woosley.
Died in Huntsville, November 30th, Francis J. Levert, aged seventy-eight years.

Last Friday was a week at the residence of W.W. Ferguson in East Perry, Gabriel Moon was shot and seriously wounded by Ferguson.

Clarissa, a former slave of the late Col. F.M. Hardwick, is in the Cherokee Jail on a charge of infanticide.

Died of heart disease in Shelby County, November 25th, Mrs. Mary Hazard, wife of John B. Hazard.
Died near Camden, November 26th, William C. Sterns.
Died in Wilcox County, November 27th, E.A. Pharr.
Died in Camden, November 25th, Toliver Forsyth, aged seventy-nine years.
Died in Cherokee County, November 28th, R.W., son of Rev. O.D. McNeely, aged sixteen years.

Col. J.B. Kennedy died in Montgomery on the 26th ult.

# THE SOUTHERN ARGUS - DEATHS - JUNE 1869 THROUGH JUNE 1874

## Issue 12-16-1869

Mr. James George, formerly a citizen of Alabama, and for some years past a citizen of Texas, died in the latter state on the 13th November last. He was seventy-four years of age.

Died at Forkland, November 5th, 1869, Mrs. Mary Amelia, wife of W.K. Taylor and daughter of Jos. H. and Cormelia A. Bragg.

At Stevenson last week, Tony Lawrence was badly cut by James G. Caperton.

Henry C. Shelly has been dangerously ill at his father's house in Talladega. He is convalescent.

Henry Monier, an old citizen of Talladega, died in that city on the 4th inst. of apoplexy.

A.M. Hinds, a brother of mail-contractor for the State of Alabama Hinds, was buried at Decatur on the 1st inst.

On the 5th inst. near Decatur, Henry Gregory (negro) was shot and mortally wounded by John Young (negro). Young was pardoned out of the Georgia penitentiary not long since.

Miss Mary Corbett of Montgomery was among the killed by the accident some weeks ago on the Pacific Railroad.

Died in Tuskaloosa, December 7th, J.S. Caldwell.
Died in Tuskaloosa on the 7th inst., Jno. Pickford, a native of England but a resident of Tuskaloosa for two years.

Among the confederate dead recently reinterred in Battle Grove Cemetery, Cynthiana, Kentucky, was Thos. Rowland of Jacksonville, Alabama.

## Issue 12-23-1869

Died in Dallas County last Sunday evening, little Maggie, daughter of the late Robert and Mrs. Serena McIlwain, aged about three years.

Maj. Nat. Sledge, an old citizen of Opelika, died on the 16th inst.

## THE SOUTHERN ARGUS - DEATHS - JUNE 1869 THROUGH JUNE 1874

The *Jacksonville Republican* of Saturday last says: We learn that on Saturday last, about dark, D.B. Moore was killed at Cross Plains, by J.L. Thompson, who beat him to death with a club.

Harry Humphrey, negro, of Limestone County was murdered by some one unknown last week.

Mr. Thos. A. Patterson who had for several months been under bond for killing W.W. Bryant of Gainesville died of pneumonia on Thursday of last week.

David Porter, negro, got drunk in Demopolis the other day, went to sleep on the railroad track, and waked up a dead corpus.

Jarrot Flournoy (negro) resisted arrest by the Sheriff of Macon County and was killed.

Died in Mooresville on the 16th, Carrie, daughter of W.G. Martin, aged eight years.
Died in Limestone County, December 13th, Mrs. Lyda V., wife of John W. Stewart, aged twenty-six years.
Died in Huntsville, December 12th, Mrs. Elvira G. Lock, aged forty-two years.
Died near Whistler, December 5th, Mrs. Mary S. Reeder, aged seventy-four years.
Died in Eutaw, December 11th, Thompson Chiles, aged sixty years.

Issue 12-30-1869

Died in Sumter County, December 19th, Thos. A. Scales, aged twenty-two years.
Died in Sumter County, December 16th, Thos. Jarman, Jr., aged seventy-two years.
Died in Tuskaloosa, December 25th, Mrs. A.C. Campbell, wife of E.F. Campbell and daughter of Judge Wm. F. Pierce.
Died in Rockwall, Texas, November 9th, Mrs. Fannie Kimbrough, consort of Dr. G.R. Kimbrough of Green County, Alabama.
Died in Greenville, December 21st, Mrs. T.F. Potter.
Died at the residence of Wm. Howell in Marion on the 17th inst., Mrs. Elizabeth Hindes, in the seventieth year of her age.
Died at the residence of her husband in Marion on the morning of the 19th inst., Mrs. Eliza Dunkin, wife of Elias Dunkin.
Died on the 17th inst. in East Perry, Thos. B. Sprott, aged about forty-five years.

## THE SOUTHERN ARGUS - DEATHS - JUNE 1869 THROUGH JUNE 1874

Died in Limestone County, December 17th, Mrs. Margaret Foote, aged about forty years.

Two weeks ago, little May Speak, an interesting daughter of H.C. Speak of Moulton, was run over by a loaded wagon and killed.

We learn from the *Meridian Mercury* that at York the other day, a young man named Trott, while on a drunken spree, killed two negroes and was killed by the companions of the latter.

Mrs. Sarah M. Flemming, relict of the late Col. Wm. Flemming, died at her residence in Huntsville, December 18th, aged about seventy-five years.

Mrs. Keziah Stewart, wife of Rev. Chas. Stewart, formerly of Purkins County, died in Noxiebee County, Mississippi, on the 23rd of September last.

Mrs. Sallie B., wife of Judge C.N. Wilcox of Choctaw County died on the 17th inst.

Samuel Snoddy of Greene County was murdered last Saturday night was a week ago between Union and Eutaw. A negro named Sam Colvin has been arrested as the murderer.

A few days ago, George Shelton of Blount County resisted an attempt to arrest him by the Sheriff and was shot and mortally wounded by one of that officer's deputies.

Drew Milan, a Tallapoosa farmer, was brutally and terribly beaten over the head a few nights ago in the city of Montgomery.

Mrs. Kelley, an old and well known resident of Benton, died in that place two weeks ago.

Issue 1-6-1870

Died at Montgomery last week, J.D. Randolph.
Died in Eufaula, December 25th, Frank Dennis, infant son of Maj. L.F. and Mrs. M.T. Johnson, aged about ten months.
Died in Tuskaloosa, January 1st, Alexander T. Dearing, aged twenty-six years.

W.T. Judkins died last Saturday at his plantation, six miles from Montgomery, aged sixty years.

# THE SOUTHERN ARGUS - DEATHS - JUNE 1869 THROUGH JUNE 1874

At Fort Decatur a few days ago, a section master named Collins was murdered by a negro.

A small child of Mr. Fountain of Greenville was burned to death on the 28th of December.

On the 22nd ult., Martin Roberts of Cherokee County was thrown from a mule and had his ankle so badly broken that amputation was thought necessary.

D.A. Gray and his daughter, Fannie, late of Troy, Alabama, have recently died in Griffin, Georgia.

Issue 1-13-1870

On the 29th ult., Monroe Howell was found dead in his bed at Lebanon, Alabama.

Died near Six Miles, Bibb County, January 1st, Wm. J. Peters, aged about sixty-four years. Mr. Peters was formerly a prominent citizen of Shelby County and once represented that county in the State Legislature. He had lived in Bibb County for ten years past...

In a difficulty at Payneville, Sumter County, two weeks ago between a Mr. Hopper and a Mr. Boyd, brothers-in-law, the latter was shot and mortally wounded.

Died in Monroe County, December 24th, Daniel McCorvey.
Died at Fort Deposit, December 26th, Mrs. Frances C. Blake, wife of Thomas Blake.
Died near Tuscumbia, December 30th, Mark Gilhland.
Died in Tuscumbia, December 27th, Mrs. Susan Hart, aged sixty-nine years.
Died in Nashville, Tennessee, December 31st, John S. Morgan of Tuscumbia, Alabama, aged sixty-two years. Mr. Morgan formerly lived near Selma, and his eldest son, John S. Morgan, now lives at Montevallo.
Died in Mobile, January 7th, Willie, son of J.H. Daughdrill.
Died in New Orleans, December 28th, Benjamin P., eldest son of William Bancroft of Mobile, aged thirty-five years.

Issue 1-20-1870

Milly Morrill, negress died a few days ago, in the Lowndes County Jail, where she had been confined eighteen months for lunacy.

# THE SOUTHERN ARGUS - DEATHS - JUNE 1869 THROUGH JUNE 1874

Sam Colvin, Jr., and Henry Miller (negroes) are in the Greene County Jail for killing Samuel A. Snoddy a few weeks ago.

A little son of A.A. Hamiel of Greenville, playing with a pistol, shot and killed a negro playmate.

Died near Montevallo, December 27th, Capt. John P. Morgan, a member of the Legislature in 1857-8, and Secretary of the Senate in 1863-4. [see below]
Died in Centreville, January 11th, Mrs. E.H. Courson, aged thirty years.
Died in Greensboro, January 13th, Mrs. Annie Whelan, aged about thirty years.
Died in Bullock County, some days ago, Capt. W.J. Lee, formerly a merchant at Union Springs.
Died in Mobile, January 13th, Daniel D. Wyatt, for many years the foreman of the composition room of the *Mobile Register*.
Died in Blount County, January 5th, Hezekiah F. Garner, aged thirty-two years.
Died in Mobile, January 11th, Philip E. Lavallette, in the forty-seventh year of his age.
Died in Louisville, Kentucky, January 12th, Mary Jane Wylie, wife of N.W. Raphael of Mobile.
Died in Colbert County, January 9th, Samuel P. Morgan, aged thirty years. His brother, Hon. J.P. Morgan of Montevallo, died December 27th, and his father, J.S. Morgan, Esq., died December 31st. [see above]
Died in Evergreen, December 22nd, the wife of Col. James A. Stallsworth.
Died in Eufaula, January 9th, Mrs. Mary Herring, aged eighty years.
Died in Huntsville, January 16th, Mrs. Mary Jane White.
Died at Elmington, Clarke County, December 20th, Thomas McCormick, in the sixtieth year of his age.
Died in Benton, January 8th, little Bessie, only daughter of Charles and Emma B. Douglas.

The *Huntsville Independent* learns that the Pillows killed near LaGrange, were nephews, not sons, of Gen. Pillow...

At Jonesboro, in Franklin County, last Thursday was a week ago, a man named Sewell was shot and it is supposed mortally wounded by Walter Sherrod.

Last Thursday was a week, a negro boy in the employ of Daniel Wilson, in Cherokee County, made a murderous assault upon the two daughters of that gentleman, inflicting dangerous injuries upon one of them. He was arrested and subsequently hung.

## THE SOUTHERN ARGUS - DEATHS - JUNE 1869 THROUGH JUNE 1874

On Saturday the 8th inst. in Somerville, James Simmons was shot and killed by a Mr. Patterson.

Christmas Eve, the son of Mr. Clinton of Fayette Court House, was stabbed and killed by a son of Judge Jones of the same place. The parties were mere boys.

It was Hopper not Boyd who was killed in the Payneville, Sumter County affair some weeks ago.

On the 28th ult., J.J. Ramsey of Franklin County was found near Cherokee with his throat cut but still living. He said that the cutting was done by an unknown negro whom he described. He died on the 1st instant.

Issue 1-27-1870

On the 13th in Colbert County, William M. Gibson, a lad of thirteen, accidentally struck a younger brother with an axe and instantly killed him.

E.J. Belser is under bond for $5,000 to answer for killing W.H. Hogan in Montgomery last week.

### DIED IN ALABAMA

Died in Talladega, January 12th, John F.M., infant son of John F. Autery.
Died in Nashville, Tennessee, January 12th, John A. Winbourne of Talladega.
Died in Huntsville, January 15th, John A. Reedy, aged sixty years.
Died in Athens, January 12th, John W. Crenshaw.
Died near Uniontown, December 25th, John L., son of A. and Mattie Harris.
Died in Greensboro, January 13th, William P., only son of James E. and Mrs. Lemula Webb.
Died in Mobile, January 20th, Mrs. H.J. Charles.
Died in Etowah, January 8th, W.G. Jordan, aged seventy years.
Died in Huntsville, January 20th, Jabez N. Leftwich.
Died in Mobile, January 20th, Mrs. Harriet Fowler, consort of the late Capt. John Fowler.
Died in Mobile, January 20th, James, son of Capt. C.J. Campbell, aged five and a half years.
Died at the Roper House, Mobile, January 19th, Willis V. Hare of Gainsville.
Died near Claiborne, January 15th, Mrs. Virginia P. Strode, relict of the late Charles Bayard Strode of California.
Died near Union Springs, January 15th, Louis Smith.
Died in Conecuh County, January 12th, Pat. S. Whelan.

# THE SOUTHERN ARGUS - DEATHS - JUNE 1869 THROUGH JUNE 1874

B.J. Hughes, formerly of Montgomery, was killed a few days ago by the cars at Rappahannock Station, Virginia.

On the evening of the 18th in Montgomery, Wm. Hogan was shot and killed by E.J. Belser.

Two young men named Phillips and another, have confessed to the assassination of the Pillows. An old difficulty. Now let them be hunted down and hung to the first limb.

Issue 2-3-1870

Thos. Hedges was kicked to death by a mule at Mobile, on the 24th ult.

We learn from the *Marion Commonwealth* that the little girl of Gen. Walker, burned some time since, at the King House, is dead from her injuries.

Carbolic acid was given to a child of W.C. Brewer of Tuskegee, last week, in mistake for syrup. The mistake was not fatal.

At a party at William Anderson's in Cherokee County, January 19th, there was a disturbance, in which Joseph H. Stewart, a deaf and dumb man, was accidentally shot and wounded.

Issue 2-10-1870

### DIED IN ALABAMA

Died in Marion, January 20th, Emma, daughter of John and Emily A. Moore.
Died January 14th near Syllacogga, Talladega County, Adelia Hill, infant daughter of Mr. and Mrs. C.C. Douglas.
Died at Russellville, January 10th, Mrs. Lucy, widow of the late Richard S. Jones of Aberdeen, Mississippi.
Died in Sumter County, January 12th, William Culbert, aged forty seven years.
Died in Sumter County, January 8th, Mary Eleanor Lowe, consort of G. B. Lowe, in the forty-first year of her age.
Died in Mobile, January 22nd, Elisa M., daughter of Edwin and Elsie M. Tardy.
Died at Union Springs, January 20th, Joseph Henderson.
Died at Auburn, January 24th, William Hamp Smith.
Died near Greensboro, January 22nd, Alexander P., infant son of R.M. and A. J. Mellown.
Died in Cherokee County, January 20th, Mrs. Epsa Harwell, aged sixty-four years.

## THE SOUTHERN ARGUS - DEATHS - JUNE 1869 THROUGH JUNE 1874

Died in Eutaw, January 21st, W.R.B. Hatter, in the twenty-sixth year of his age, a citizen of great worth, a lawyer of great promises.
Died in Mobile, January 27th, H.B. Turner.
Died in Mobile, January 27th, Mrs. Rebecca Adeline Clausen.
Died in Athens, January 23rd, Mrs. Rebecca E. Cook.
Died in Athens, January 22nd, Jason Samuel Tanner, eldest son of John T. Tanner, aged eighteen years.
Died in Montgomery, January 30th, E.J. Belser.
Died in Montgomery, January 29th, Capt. Thomas H. Smith of Wetumpka.
Died in Camden, January 22nd, John J.R. Jenkins.
Died in Mobile, January 26th, Joel Allbrook, infant son of Ada. L. and the late W.F. Cleveland.
Died in Montgomery, January 31st, Mr. St. Lanier, formerly of the Lanier House, Macon, Georgia, and the "La Farge," New York, and the "Exchange," Montgomery.
Died in Monroe County a few days ago, Hon. R.G. Scott, formerly a Representative in Congress from the Richmond (Virginia) Dist.
Died in Mobile, January 25th, Nathan Meeker, aged fifty-five years.
Died in Marion, January 29th, J.P. Potts of Newbern, aged forty-five years.
Died in Coosa County, December 31st, John Varner, who was Clerk of the Lowndes Circuit Court from 1831 til 1842, aged eighty-six years.
Died in Bullock County, January 28th, John Rutland.
Died in Perry County, January 24th, John Brand, in the eighteenth year of his age.
Died in Claiborne, January 22nd, Stephen R. Seymour, aged fifteen years.
Died in Monroe County, January 3rd, R.L. Vick, infant son of J.D. and E. Vick.
In Jackson County, February 1st, John Chitwood was shot and killed by a Mr. Bullard.
Died near Greensboro, January 30th of typhoid pneumonia, Mr. Allen Stewart of Mississippi, a student of the Southern University.

A negro man on the plantation of B.F. Howard, near Tuskegee, was killed a few days since by the accidental discharge of a pistol which he was carrying in his pocket.

James Bell of Cherokee was killed January 22nd by being thrown against a tree by a mule.

While the remains of the late W. V. Hare of Gainesville were awaiting interment, a dove flew into the room, alighted upon the coffin, and only flew away when an attempt was made to catch it.

# THE SOUTHERN ARGUS - DEATHS - JUNE 1869 THROUGH JUNE 1874

### Issue 2-17-1870

William Curtis for more than a half a century a citizen of Dallas County, died at his residence in Cahaba on the 26th of January, in the eighty-eighth year of his age.

Died in this city on Saturday the 29th of January, Mrs. Mary Kinkle, widow of the late A.J. Kinkle of Huntsville.

In Limestone County, last week, Frank McClure was shot and killed by James Ethridge.

We regret to learn that Dr. S.G. Todd was yesterday called away to visit his mother, who is seriously ill at her residence in Maryland.

Mrs. Jones, an old lady of Calhoun County, wandered away from home several days ago, and has not been found several days afterward.

### Issue 2-24-1870

Died in Mobile, February 6th, William B. Lightfoot, aged fifty-eight years.
Died near Montgomery, February 8th, Mrs. Eveline Croom, aged about sixty years.
Died near Silver Run, Talladega County, February 6th, Mrs. Rachel R. Hendrick.
Died in Lowndes County, February 5th, Mrs. Beasly, wife of Major J. Beasly.
Died in Hale County, February 5th, J.J. Morris, aged twenty-three years.
Died in Clay County, January 2nd, Mrs. Frances Maria McCullough, aged twenty-seven years.
Died in Franklin County, February 1st, Bryce, infant son of James. E. and Josephine Wilson.
Died in Athens, January 28th, Mrs. Mary D. Crenshaw.
Died in Mobile, February 12th, John Perey, only son of Burgess and Mary I. Garner.
Died in Mobile, February 8th, Miss Kate M. Anderson.
Died in Washington County, January 25th, Boling C. Evans.
Died in Mobile, January 31st, Mrs. Margaret Frank.
Died on Steamer *St. Charles*, Saturday night, February 5th, 1870, in the sixty-third year of his age, Robert Bates of Perry County.
Died in Marion, February 13th, Mrs. Fiquet, wife of J.B. Fiquet.
Died in Marion, February 18th, Mack Chapman, son of J.H. Chapman, aged sixteen years.
Died in Conecuh County, February 12th, Judge William A. Ashley, the most prominent man in the county.

## THE SOUTHERN ARGUS - DEATHS - JUNE 1869 THROUGH JUNE 1874

Died in Henry County, February 11th, Mrs. Jabez McRae.
Died in Pickensville County, February 11th, James Stinson, one of the oldest citizens of Pickens County.
Died in Mobile, February 18th, John Sands, son of Robert L. and Mary A. Yuille.
Died in Mobile, February 19th, Charles Smith.

Marcus Rogers was arrested at Montgomery on the 16th, charged with killing a negro girl named Elsey Stark in 1868.

C.D. Southard was shot by a Mr. Ferguson, at Cuba Station, on the 12th and severely wounded.

### Issue 3-3-1870

Died February 13th near Autaugaville, Mary Lewis, daughter of L.M. and Mary Jane Whetstone, aged five years.
Died February 23rd in Mobile, John Lynch.
Died February 8th, in Mobile, Mrs. Minnie Forney Smith, wife of Col. Melanethon Smith of Quitman, Mississippi, and daughter of the late Maj. Daniel M. Forney of Lowndes County, Alabama.

### DIED IN ALABAMA

Died February 23rd in Mobile, infant daughter of John W. and Maggie Jackson.
Died February 22nd in New York, Mrs. Walter S. Pierce, daughter of Mr. and Mrs. Cheney of Montgomery.
Died February 22nd in Demopolis, George Kohlen.
Died February 25th in Newbern, Mrs. Huggins, wife of R.A. Huggins.
Died February 22nd in Greene County, Mrs. J.W. Jolly, wife of Arnold Jolly, in the fifty-third year of her age.
Died February 25th in Mobile, Miss Mary Munnerlyn, aged seventeen years.
Died February 25th in Mobile, Miss Mary Ann Weldon.
Died February 25th in Mobile, Mrs. Octavia Ferrell, wife of Henry Ferrell and only daughter of Mrs. W.C. Sutton.
Died February 22nd at Oxford, Mississippi, Thomas H. Maxwell, son of Thomas Maxwell of Tuscaloosa.
Died February 21st near Scottsboro, Alison Brewer, aged twenty-three years.
Died February 8th in Madison County, George C. King, aged twenty-two years.
Died in Guntersville, February 14th, Mrs. Henry, wife of Patrick Henry.
Died in Atlanta, Georgia, February 12th, Samuel Clay Pelham, son of Dr. Pelham of Calhoun County, and brother of the late Maj. John Pelham.
Died in Scottsboro, February 12th, Mrs. Proby.

## THE SOUTHERN ARGUS - DEATHS - JUNE 1869 THROUGH JUNE 1874

Died in Greene County, February __th, Col. James A. Anderson.
Died in Greene County, February 12th, Hill Carter, aged thirty-five years.
Died in Greene County, February 5th, J.J. Morris, aged twenty-three years.
Died in Mobile, February 19th of lockjaw, Dr. Robert D. England of Perry County.

Col. W.D. Young of Gadsden fell over an embankment on the night of the 22nd ult., and so seriously injured himself that he died the next day.

The late Willis V. Hare of Gainsville had his life insured just nine days before his death.

Robert Pesknell and his wife were fired upon, on the 19th ult., near Riddle's Bridge in Talladega (or Calhoun) County, by some unknown party. He was instantly killed, and his wife injured it is thought fatally.

W.H. Danforth of Madison County and a negro were found during the late cold spell near Whitesburg, the negro frozen to death and Danforth insensible from cold.

An old lady named Patterson, who lived near Cross Roads, in Madison County, fell down the stairway of her house a few days ago, and was instantly killed. She was ninety years old.

Issue 3-10-1870

A boy eight years old, son of Mrs. Sam Pearson, was frozen to death in Madison County, on the 17th ult.

Last Wednesday night was a week ago, James Nix of Sumter County was run over by the cars near York Station and instantly killed.

Died in Bullock County, February 24th, Mrs. S.J. Baskin, aged about twenty-nine.
Died in Bullock County, February 25th, Perry Germany, aged about twenty-one.
Died in Union Springs, February 27th, a child of Mr. Cole of that city.
Died near Uniontown, February 26th of pneumonia, Mrs. Sarah Underwood, in the seventy-first year of her age.
Died at Six Mile, Bibb County, February 24th, Rev. John W. Starr of the Methodist Church South.
Died in Marion, February 28th, Thomas M. Benson of East Perry.
Died at North Port, February 22nd, in the fifty-six year of his age, George A. Parker.

# THE SOUTHERN ARGUS - DEATHS - JUNE 1869 THROUGH JUNE 1874

Died in Etowah County, February 5th, Ruel, son of O. McIlwain of Jefferson County, aged twenty years.
Died in Linden, February 10th, Ida Loyette Drake, infant daughter of C.L. Drake.
Died in Marion, February 22nd, James P., infant son of Capt. J.H. and Pattie T. Speed.
Died in Wharton, Texas, in January, David T. Stevens, formerly of Greensboro, Alabama.
Died near Forkland, Greene County, William F. Kennon, aged thirty-seven years.
Died near Bellevue, February 27th, Willie, infant son of Dr. B.M. and Mrs. F.B. Perryman, aged eighteen months and four days.

The *Centerville Apprentice* of March 4th reports the four following deaths, without other particulars, as occurring the week before: Near Pleasant Hill, Mrs. Fondreu, aged about fifty-five years. In the edge of Perry County, Andrew Woolley, aged about seventy years.

Died in Bibb County, ten miles below Centreville, James Abercrombie, aged about fifty years. Died at Jericho, Perry County, John Phillips, aged about sixty.
Died in New York, February 24th, Mrs. Lydia Ann Massey, formerly of Mobile.
Died in Vicksburg, March 5th, Mrs. Hattie Gibson, wife of Maj. A.C. Gibson, formerly of Mobile.
Died in Huntsville, February 28th, James Neely, an old citizen.

### Issue 3-17-1870

Mr. S.P. Houston, for many years a citizen of Dallas County, died in Bibb County, on the 4th inst., after a lingering illness, aged about fifty-six years.

Died at Burnsville, on the evening of the 15th inst., in the fifty-fifth year of her age, Mrs. Mary McCollum, relict of the late James McCollum, and mother of Mr. William M. McCollum of this city.

On the night of the 10th inst., as Mr. Wilkinson of Camden was leaving his store to go home, he was assaulted, beaten until he was thought dead, and robbed of $475; and then his store was fired...

### Issue 3-24-1870

Died in this city on the evening of the 16th inst. of consumption, in the thirty-fourth year of her age, Joanna, wife of David White. Charleston (South Carolina) papers will please copy.

## THE SOUTHERN ARGUS - DEATHS - JUNE 1869 THROUGH JUNE 1874

A Mr. McDaniel of Calhoun County was killed by a tree falling on him one day last week.

A negro named Henry Oliver was killed on the plantation of J.F. Smith, near Montgomery, on the 16th, by a knife in the hands of another negro.

Two weeks ago last Tuesday, a Mr. West, a cross-tie contractor on the A. & C. R. R., was murdered by parties unknown, at the Cano Creek bridge, on the road from Gadsden to Ashville.

### DIED IN ALABAMA

Died in Woodbridge, N.J., March 4th, Samuel Barron, Esq., formerly of Mobile.
Died in Hayneville, March 15th, Watson Landingham, aged twenty-nine years.
Died near Tuskegee, March 14th, W.M. Ham.
Died in Mobile March 17th, Bloodworth Taylor, aged seventy-three years.
Died in Mobile, March 17th, Eudora Starr, infant daughter of Jeremy and Lavinia Howland.
Died at Helena, Arkansas, March 7th, Col. O.H. Oates, a former citizen of Lauderdale County, Arkansas.
Died in Montgomery County, March 17th, W.M. Manning, aged nearly seventy years.
Died in Huntsville, March 10th of pneumonia, George Loring.
Died in Meridianville, Madison County, March 15th, Mrs. Maria, wife of John W. Pruit.
Died in Limestone County, March 10th of pneumonia, John R. Evans, aged thirty-six years.
Died in Jackson County, March 15th, Daniel Cain.
Died in Montgomery, March 6th, Lovedy Bettie, youngest daughter of Judge David Campbell, in her eleventh year.
Died in Limestone County, February 20th, Emmett Curry, aged seven years.
Died in Camden, March 1st, Hector McNeill.
Died near Maysville, February 27th, Mrs. Eliza Wall.
Died in Montgomery, March 4th, Mrs. F.A. Turner of Lowndesboro.
Died in Tallassee, February 24th, Dr. John Hughes Thomas, aged about seventy-five years.
Died at Cedar Bluff, Cherokee County, February 17th, Annie Low Laney, aged twelve years.
Died in Mississippi, February 22nd, Mrs. Mary Elizabeth Edwards, formerly of Talladega.
Died at Orphan's Home, Tuskegee, March 3rd, Mary Jane Hollyman, aged twelve years, the first death so far at the Home.
Died in Eufaula, March 6th, Lewis Coalman.

# THE SOUTHERN ARGUS - DEATHS - JUNE 1869 THROUGH JUNE 1874

Issue 3-31-1870

Died in Mobile, March 22nd, James Marsh.
Died in Mobile, March 22nd, Henry Shumaker, Sr.
Died in New Brunswick, March 11th, Mrs. Mary L. Caro, formerly of Mobile.
Died in Mobile Bay, on board the British ship "*Dorset*", March 23rd, Capt. George Gruzelier, aged thirty-four years and thirteen days.
Died in Jefferson County, March 14th, R.B. Walker, one of the best citizens of the county, aged eighty-three years.
Died at Calvert, Louisiana, February 28th, O.R. Wilkins, son of the late R.R. Wilkins of Mobile.
Died in Montgomery, March 20th, Mrs. Sarah A. Walker, wife of Judge A.J. Walker.
Died in Tuscumbia, March 22nd, Timothy Cooley.
Died in Kingston, Autauga County, March __th, Henley Brown, a citizen of this state since 1818 and the first Probate Judge of Autauga County, which office he held till 1862.
Died in Molino, Florida, March 21st, T.J. DeYampert of Mobile.
Died in Lowndes County, March 22nd, Miss Louisa Haigier, aged twenty years.
Died in Eufaula, March 21st, George, little son of Mr. and Mrs. J.H. Pruden, from the effects of a gunshot wound from a gun in his own hands.
Died in Talladega, March 23rd, Wm. Rice, brother of Judge S.F. Rice.
Died in Russellville, March 10th, Mrs. Martha Ann Trimble, wife of Dr. Joseph A. Trimble and daughter of Col. R.S. and Lucy Jones.
Died in Carrollton, March 21st, Rev. John William Taylor, principal of the Carrollton Academy, aged thirty-two years.
Died in Greene County on the 18th, M.M. Williford, in the thirty-third year of his age.
Died in Greenville on the __ inst., Mr. Day of New York.
Died in Montgomery on the 23rd inst., Mrs. Mary Ann Holt.
Died in Calhoun County on the 23rd inst., Mrs. Eigleberger.
Died in Tuskaloosa, March __, Miss Susan C. Potter.

George King, a working man on the Florence bridge, fell into the river the other day and was drowned.

William Wheeler, a former citizen of Franklin County, was killed a few days ago, in Illinois, by the falling of a shed upon him.

## THE SOUTHERN ARGUS - DEATHS - JUNE 1869 THROUGH JUNE 1874

Issue 4-7-1870

Last Friday night, the store of John Burson & Sons, at Snow Hill, in the absence of the sons, was entered, and the old man, badly afflicted with rheumatism and otherwise quite decrepid, was murdered and robbed.

Died in Mobile, March 27th, Montgomery F. Roulston.
Died in Cherokee County, March 25th, Mat Pollard, aged thirty years.
Died in Wilcox County, March 22nd, Jeremiah Jones.
Died in Hayneville, March 27th, Mrs. Cox, wife of George S. Cox, Esq.
Died in Mobile, March 29th, James Whiting.
Died in Mississippi, March 27th, Wm. Wright of Madison County, Alabama.
Died in Mobile, March 31st, Mrs. Matilda B. Haupt, aged sixty-three years.
Died in Greene County, March 24th, C.A. Barbour, aged seventeen years.
Died in Jackson, Mississippi, March 20th, Mrs. Louisa H. Wilson, wife of S.G. Wilson, and daughter of the late Dr. W.T. Hendon of Newbern, Alabama.
Died in Perry County, March 26th of consumption, John L., Walthalf/Waltall? aged about fifty years.
Died in Talladega, March 29th, Merritt T. Ely.
Died in Mobile, April 2nd, Miss P.M. Gary.
Died in Mobile, March 30th, William Henry, infant son of Joseph E. and Eliza Cady.
Died near Alexandria, Virginia, March 27th, Maj. W.W. Herbert, a native of Alabama.
Died in Mobile, April 1st, Capt. B.C. O'Connell.
Died in Greenville, March 26th, George Leroy Porter Henry, infant son of George L. and Ina. M. Henry.
Died in Sumter County, February 19th, James Edwin, son of Dr. C.W. and Jennie Silliman, aged four years.
Died in Montgomery, April 3rd, Eldridge E., only son of Mr. and Mrs. E.E. Atkinson.
Died in Montgomery, April 2nd, Alabama, infant daughter of Gen. and Mrs. J.H. Clanton.

The body of John Hines, formerly a policeman in Mobile, was found concealed in some bushes near that city, a few days ago, with such marks of violence upon his person as to induce the coroner's jury to render a verdict that he had been murdered.

At Gainesville, a few days ago, Ellison Meredith was shot and killed by W.W. Rogers.

# THE SOUTHERN ARGUS - DEATHS - JUNE 1869 THROUGH JUNE 1874

Issue 4-14-1870

Died in Talladega, April 2nd, Mrs. M.D. Henderson, wife of A.M. Henderson.
Died in Madison County, April 1st, James H. Bibb.
Died in Mobile, April 4th, James H. Caldwell, Jr.
Died in Montgomery, April 5th, Katie, daughter of Mr. and Mrs. John W. Powell, aged three years.
Died in St. Louis, March 27th, Robert Taylor Bradshaw, son of R. Bradshaw of Gainsville, Alabama.
Died in Wilcox County, March 25th, Mrs. Jennie, wife of Dr. John Purifory, aged thirty years.
Died in Mobile, April 6th, Peter Ferrent, killed by being run over by a railroad locomotive.
Died in Mobile, April 8th, Miss Kittie Beach, in the twenty-fourth year of her age.
Died in New Market, April 4th, Mrs. Alice Whitman.
Died in Gadsden, on the 29th ult., Mary, infant daughter of Capt. W.P. Simpson.
Died in Choctaw County, March 19th, Rev. B.F. Seale.
Died in Tuskegee, April 4th, Erastus Cox. [see below]
Died in Clay County, April 1st, Mrs. Eliza Mitchell, aged sixty years.
Died in Mobile on the 7th inst., John Clausson.
Died in Mobile, April 9th, Ann L.N. Butt.
Died in Mobile, April 9th, Caroline Froman.
Died in Montgomery on the 7th inst., Edward Lewis.
Died in Barbour County, March 31st, D. Sylvester, aged seventy-four years.
Died in Mobile, April 11th, Mrs. Julia McClelland.
Died in Mobile, April 9th, F. Baudion.
Died in Montgomery, April 12th, Mrs. M. Barclay.
Died in Macon County, April 4th, Erastus Cox. [see above]

At Pine Apple, Wilcox County, on the 3rd inst., John Douglas was stabbed and killed by his brother William.

Issue 4-21-1870

Died at Union Springs, March 15th, Wm. Henry, infant son of Dr. J.A. and Mrs. Fannie E. Hays.
Died in Morgan County, April 13th, Frederick Raoul.
Died in Montgomery on the 13th inst., Dr. Clopton, aged eighty-six years.
Died in Monroe County, April 6th, Capt. Jno. Snell, aged seventy-six years.
Died in Tuskaloosa County, April 5th, John S. Beallo, aged eighty-two years.
Died in Mobile, April 12th, Andrew Stewart.

## THE SOUTHERN ARGUS - DEATHS - JUNE 1869 THROUGH JUNE 1874

Died in Perry County, April 1st, Miss Mary Jane Lester, in the sixteenth year of her age.
Died in Marion, April 8th, Mary, infant daughter of Mr. and Mrs. M.A. Wyatt.
Died in Tuskegee, April 9th, Wm. Varner, aged seventy-seven years.
Died in Montgomery, April 12th, a son of Dr. P.H. Owen.
Died in Mobile, April 13th, P.H. Parrott.
Died at Bradford, Coosa County, April 7th, Elizabeth Abigail Dixon, daughter of the late Sam'l H. Dixon.
Died in Tuscumbia, April 6th, Willie Winston, son of R.B. and Sarah M. Lindsay.
Died in Arkansas, March 17th, Emmet Cockrill, formerly of North Alabama.
Died in Frankfort, March 28th, Katie, child of J.G. and Kate Bentley.
Died near Pleasant Ridge, March 27th, Henry G. Jones, aged sixty-nine years.
Died in Mobile, April 14th, Capt. Pete Murray of the steamer *Ocean Wave*.
Died in Madison County, April 5th, Ida Leslie, daughter of Rev. N. Hensley and Mary J. Grubbs.
Died in Mobile, April 11th, William Lawless, aged thirty-eight years.
Died near Centre, on the 12th inst., Ashley Baker, aged sixty years.
Died in Elyton, on the 14th inst., J.L. Jones of Downsville, Mississippi.
Died in Sumter County, April 10th, from the effects of a fall from a horse, Jesse E. Wolf, aged thirteen years.

Last week, a young daughter of John Lowry, Esq. of Jackson County was near her father's saw mill picking up some chips when a saw-log suddenly became disengaged and rolled over her, completely crushing her body.

Some days ago, Peter Sprott (negro) of Perry County was shot and killed by _____ Lewis, (negro)...

Issue 4-28-1870

Died in Gadsden, April 3rd, Anna, daughter of D.T. and M. Ryan.
Died in Montgomery, April 18th, Mrs. Catharine Vaughan.
Died at Whistler on the 19th, B.C. Bennett.
Died in Mobile on the 20th inst., Mrs. Maria Kelly.
Died in Montgomery on the 20th inst., N.M. Horton.
Died near Rome, Georgia, April 11th, George Pulliam, son of Mr. and Mrs. Pulliam of Talladega.
Died in Booneville, Missouri, April 14th, Mrs. Mary B. Cobb, formerly of Athens, in this state.
Died in Troy, April 17th, Elisha Reddick.
Died in Pike County, April 17th, John Summersault.

# THE SOUTHERN ARGUS - DEATHS - JUNE 1869 THROUGH JUNE 1874

Died near Tuscumbia, April 14th, Elizabeth Jane, daughter of G.S. Henderson.

Died near Cooksville, Mississippi, on the 13th inst., Mrs. Charlotte Warren, consort of Dr. R. Neilson, late of Tuskaloosa County, in the thirty-ninth year of her age.

Died at Monroeville on the 19th inst., S.M. Davidson, Editor of the *Monroe Journal*.

Died in Talladega County on the 19th, Mrs. M. Jemison, wife of S.M. Jemison and daughter of J.E. Groce.

Died in Jefferson County on the 16th, Mrs. Margaret Foster, daughter of Isaac Brown.

Died in Hale County on the 18th inst., Col. Eugene Hill, aged thirty-five years.

Died in Gainesville on the __th inst., Mrs. John Moore, a daughter of Judge Reavis.

Died in Bibb County on the 15th inst., Mrs. Isabella Steele, wife of Washington Steele.

Died in Marion, April 14th, Mrs. Jennet Carrel, nee Graham, relict of the late N.B. Carrel.

Died in Lowndes County on the 13th inst., Judge Philip H. Cook, aged forty-eight years.

Died in Wilcox County, April 15th, Miss Eliza Tindale.

Died in Lowndes County, April 7th, Rev. J.A. Fonville, aged sixty-five years.

Died in Tuskegee, March 24th, Mrs. Catherine A. Hanks.

Died in Gadsden a few days ago, Mrs. Rodon/Roden, a daughter of Mr. Tallman, formerly of Greensboro.

Died near Carthage on the 17th of March, George B. Miller.

Mr. Allen Nichols, formerly of Livingston, and father of the late J.W. Nichols, committed suicide in Meridian on Friday last was a week ago by taking strychnine.

## Issue 5-5-1870

Died near Athens on the 21st of April, William W. Mobley, aged thirty-eight years and two months.

Died in this city last Saturday morning of disease of the heart, Susanna Evans, in the thirty-second year of her age.

G.J. Hayes, a child of eight years old, was drowned in Mobile one day last week.

The *Shelby Guide* of the 26th ult., says: "We learn that a negro named Geo. Adams, was killed yesterday evening near Mardis' Ferry by a party of white men named Elias Weaver, Jack Owen, Jr., and Bob Owen...

## THE SOUTHERN ARGUS - DEATHS - JUNE 1869 THROUGH JUNE 1874

On Wednesday last, James V. Culver, a promising young lawyer of Crenshaw County, fell from the platform of a car, near Fort Deposit, and was instantly killed.

Died in Mobile, April __, Rosa Alfred, infant daughter of Robert and Rosa Waddle.
Died in Mobile, April 26th, Edith, aged two and a half years, daughter of Rev. Dr. Fulton.
Died in Mobile, April 25th, Andrew Leslie, son of John and Margaret Goodbrad, in the fifth year of his age.
Died in Perry County, April 24th, Miss Margaret, daughter of the late Green L. Wallace.
Died near Talladega, April 26th, Mrs. Litton, relict of the late Miles O. Litton.
Died in Montgomery on the 26th ult., Marcus Rodgers, son of the late John R. Rodgers.
Died in Union Springs on the 21st ult., George W. Baskin.
Died in Mobile, April 27th, John P. Campbell.
Died in Huntsville, April 27th, John Lee Rogers.
Died in Huntsville, April 24th, George B. McCrary, aged nineteen years.
Died at Fort Deposit, April 22nd, Edward Nutting, aged nineteen years.
Died in Montgomery, April 28th, Mrs. John P. Figh.
Died at Eutaw Landing, April 19th, Thomas C. Smith.
Died in Mobile, April 28th, Charles Walkley, son of James and Annie C. Young.
Died in Mobile, April 29th, Alfred Liebman, aged twenty-one years.
Died in Boonville, Missouri, April 14th, Mrs. Mary B. Cobb, formerly of North Alabama.
Died in Tuscumbia, April 26th, Miss Constantia Dickey.
Died near Courtland, April ___, Mrs. Italyne Pointer, in the twenty-ninth year of her age.
Died near Whitesburg, April 25th, Mrs. Isabella A. Collins, wife of W.D. Collins, in the thirty-six year of her age.
Died in Autauga County, April 26th, B.F. Boon, Treasurer of the County.
Died in Gwinnett County, Georgia, March 25th, E.C. Tipton of Cherokee County.
Died at Tuskegee, a few days ago, Charles A.T. Price of Montgomery.
Died in Mobile, April 29th, Virginia Lee, daughter of Amanda and John Wilhelm.
Died in Pike County, April 21st, Isaac Hale.
Died in Calhoun County, a short time ago, Elijah Hendon, in the eighty-third year of his age.
Died in Troy, April 26th, Mrs. Elizabeth, wife of James C. Cade.
Died in Wills' Valley, a few days ago, Dr. Charles A. Wheeler.
Died in Pollard on the 26th ult., Mrs. Sprout of Burnt Corn.

## THE SOUTHERN ARGUS - DEATHS - JUNE 1869 THROUGH JUNE 1874

Died in Montgomery, April 30th, Mrs. Mary W. Evans.

Dr. George B. Smith of Randolph County was killed by lightning on the 27th, and several others in the room with him narrowly escaped.

### Issue 5-19-1870

Died in this city on Saturday last, Philip G., infant son of V.G. and Ella F. Weaver.
Died at Centenary Female College, May 1, 1870, Miss Mary Phelps Smith, daughter of Dr. S.P. Smith of Prattville, Alabama.

W.J. Gilmore was tried ? in Mobile the other day as accessory to the murder of N.E. Thomas, June 8th, 1868, and acquitted.
    Joshua Morse has been acquitted in a Mobile Court of the charge of murdering Newell E. Thomas.

Charles Clements was cut in two by a circular saw, at Spring Hill, one day last week.

Died in Montgomery, May 2nd, Mrs. E.J. Ball.
Died in Montgomery, May 2nd, Walter, son of Mr. and Mrs. C. D. Jackson.
Died near Hayneville, April 29th, Henry W. Adams.
Died at Evergreen, April 27th, Agnes A. McDonald, in the sixty-first year of her age.
Died in Mobile, May 4th, Alice Lillian, daughter of J.A. and Mary Affron Stuart.
Died at the residence of Mrs. H.C. Taylor in Lavaca County, Texas on the 18th of April 1870, St. George S. Lee, formerly and for many years a citizen of Mobile.
Died in Bullock County, April 29th, John R. Siler, Tax Assessor and Notary Public.
Died in Wilcox, April 20th, Mrs. Sarah E. Haddox.
Died in Talladega, April 30th, Mrs. Mary, wife of Dr. J.C. Knox.
Died near Russellville, April 28th, James Oakman, aged eighty-one years.
Died in Colbert County, April 25th, H.L. Glover, aged sixty-one years.
Died in Madison County, May 5th, S.S. Clark, in the fifty-fourth year of his age.
Died in Calhoun County, April 27th, Letitia Cirruth, in the ninety-second year of her age.
Died in Fayetteville, Tennessee, April 29th, Galenas M. Steele, formerly of Huntsville.
Died at Sandy Ridge, Lowndes County, May 1st, John L. McQueen.
Died in Gaston, Sumter County, April 24th, Lynn Boyd Humphries, aged twenty-eight years.

## THE SOUTHERN ARGUS - DEATHS - JUNE 1869 THROUGH JUNE 1874

Died in Montgomery, May 5th, little Ella, daughter of John and Emma Williams.
Died in Madison County, May __th, Mrs. Nancy McClenahany, aged about seventy-six years.
Died in Montgomery, May 10th, Mrs. Laura E. Cox.
Died in Montgomery, May 10th, a son of Mr. and Mrs. W.H. Garside.
Died in Marion, May 8th, Felix Sidney Amand, infant son of Capt. Charles and Louisa Desiree Corege.
Died near Marion, May 6th, Katie Lewers, infant daughter of Mr. and Mrs. T.A. Craig.
Died near Marion, May 6th, Mrs. McCracken, widow of the late Rev. Mr. McCracken.
Died in Bullock County, May 7th, Mrs. H.W.B. Price.
Died in Montgomery, May 11th, Mrs. Margaret Kirby.
Died in Montgomery, 7th inst., infant son of Mr. and Mrs. John McLaughlin.
Died in Montgomery, 2nd inst., Walter Hall, youngest child of C.D. and Ellen K. Jackson.
Died in Mobile, 9th inst., Bertha, daughter of Martin Werneth.
Died in Newbern, 7th inst., Mrs. Maria W. Telfair.
Died in Tuscumbia, 7th inst., Robert Bruce, only son of Hon. R.B. and Mrs. S.M. Lindsay.
Died at Frankfort, April 28th, Hartwell B. Sargent, aged forty years.
Died in Tuscumbia, 11th inst., Mrs. Sarah E. Pope, aged forty years.
Died in Eutaw, 7th inst., Lowndes Womack.
Died near Clinton, April 25th, in the sixty-fourth year of his age, Alfred Thacher.
Died in Calhoun County on the 5th inst., Jacob J. Aderhold.
Died in Madison County, 12th inst., Gen. Jno. N. Drake.
Died in Courtland, May 8th, C. Ludwig, aged seventy years.
Died in Huntsville, May 11th, William F. Elgin, aged forty-three years.
Died in Greenville, 9th inst., suddenly, William Rowe.
Died in Evergreen, 11th inst., Mrs. Martha Pearson, aged fifty-eight years.
Died in Mobile, 11th inst., Sarah M., daughter of I.C. Dubose.
Died in Macon County, 4th inst., W.H. Stafford.
Died in Autauga County, __th inst., Ephraim S. Morgan.
Died in Escambia County, April 24th, Mrs. Margaret Griffith, aged ninety-two years.

Arnold Lee, Joseph Henry and Henry Wallace have been arrested in Sumter County, charged with murdering Isaiah Hunter, in that County, on the 27th ult.

# THE SOUTHERN ARGUS - DEATHS - JUNE 1869 THROUGH JUNE 1874

Issue 5-26-1870

Died in this city on the 16th inst., Robert C., infant son of John and Mary J. White.

Died at her residence, near Harrell's Cross Roads, on Tuesday evening last, Mrs. Amanda, wife of Dr. G.W. Monroe.

John Merrell Ashurst, formerly a member of the Alabama Legislature from Montgomery County, died some weeks ago in Santa Fe, New Mexico.

Issue 6-2-1870

John Fay, an Irishman, was murdered on or about the 14th near Winston's (formerly Clinton's) plantation, in Pickens County.

Fourteen negroes are in the Greene County Jail charged with burning the house of Shumake & Anderson and murdering young Markham.

Issue 6-9-1870

Died in Eufaula, 15th ult., A.H. Yarrington, aged sixty-four years.
Died in Montgomery on the 17th ult., a child of Mr. and Mrs. E.F. Goode.
Died in Marion the 13th ult., Mary P., second daughter of C.C. and Florence N. Crowe, aged eight years.
Died at Judson Female College on the 15th ult., Miss Estelle Zimmerman, in the seventeenth year of her age.
Died in Dyer County, Tennessee on the 25th of April, 1870 of congestive chills, Mr. James A. Howze, formerly a citizen of Marion, Perry County, in the fifty-ninth year of his age.
Died at Louisville, Kentucky on the 17th ult., Mrs. S.E. Fearn, widow of the late Dr. R. Lee Fearn of Mobile.
Died in New Orleans on the 16th ult., Mary J. Milwee, wife of Samuel M. Williams, aged thirty-four years, a native of Franklin County, Alabama.
Died near Mt. Willing on the 15th ult., Miss Sarah W. Hinson, aged fifty-seven years.
Died in Monroe on the 4th ult., D.T. Fore, aged twenty-eight years.
Died in Mobile on the 18th ult., Mary, wife of James F. Smart.
Died in Mobile, May 21st, Mrs. S.C. Bancroft.
Died in Mobile, May 21st, Willie, son of Michael Casey and wife.
Died in Mobile on the 12th ult., Mary E., daughter of Victor and Eloise Desporte.
Died in Madison County on the 13th ult., Joseph W. Duryee.
Died in Mobile on the 19th ult., Rone LaForce, youngest child of the late Dr. and Mrs. R. Lee Fearn.

## THE SOUTHERN ARGUS - DEATHS - JUNE 1869 THROUGH JUNE 1874

Died at Gadsden on the 20th ult., Col. John H. Wright.
Died at the Insane Hospital on the 7th ult., Payton Parker, an indigent patient from Limestone County.
Died in Montgomery on the 21st ult., E.M. Hastings.
Died in Montgomery of the 23rd ult., Patrick Corniff.
Died in Montgomery on the 22nd ult., Mrs. Phelan, wife of the Hon. John D. Phelan.
Died in Hale County on the 25th ult., Miss Virginia True.
Died at St. Louis, May 15th, Joseph, youngest son of S.M. and M.E. Houston, aged ten months and four days.
Died at St. Louis, Missouri, May 16th, Robert Samuel, son of S.M. and M.E. Houston, aged four years, two months and twenty-four days.
Died in Huntsville on the 25th ult., Benj. Tyson Moore, aged sixty-seven years.
Died in Marion, May 23rd, Julia Alviee, daughter of Mr. and Mrs. Mark A. Wyatt, aged sixteen years.
Died in Marion, May 22nd, Robert S. Saunders, aged thirty-eight years.
Died in Marion, May 23rd, Eva Mattie, infant daughter of Mr. and Mrs. John G. Apsey.
Died in Fayette County two weeks ago, Samuel McCraw.
Died in Fayette County on the 4th ult., Mrs. America J. Davis, daughter of Rev. L.M. Wimberly.
Died in Opelika on the 11th ult., Mrs. Fannie L. Phillips.
Died in Bullock County on the 10th ult., Mrs. Sarah Waugh, aged thirty-five years.
Died in Union Springs, May 21st, Leonard Cunningham.
Died in Wilcox County, May 4th, Willie N., eldest son of W.W. Moore.
Died in Eufaula on the 14th ult., L.M. Thweatt.
Died in Mobile on the 22nd ult., Everett, infant son of Jacob F. and Susan R. Hoffman.
Died in DeSoto, Missouri on the 19th ult., Lydia A., wife of F.H. Stringfellow of Mobile.
Died in Conecuh County on the 19th ult., R.B. Higdon.
Died in Eufaula on the 23rd of congestion, Mrs. Clark, wife of Col. Whitfield Clark.
Died in Tuskegee, May 31st, P.W. Stark.
Died at Jacksonville, May 21st, Dr. R.E.W. McAdams.
Died in Mobile, May 22nd, Charles B. Cummings.
Died in Mobile, 31st ult., Mrs. S.R. Williamson.
Died in Montgomery, 30th ult., J.S. Aikenhead.
Died in Greenville, 27th ult., William Harris.
Died in Etowah County, 30th ult., Terrill Gregory.
Died in Athens, on the 31st ult., Miss Martha M. Scott.
Died in Huntsville, 31st ult., Charles A. Donegan.

## THE SOUTHERN ARGUS - DEATHS - JUNE 1869 THROUGH JUNE 1874

Died in Huntsville, on the ___ inst., Ebenezer M. Cowles.
Died in Huntsville, 27th ult., Mrs. Sarah A. Wilson.
Died in Germantown, Pennsylvania, 23rd ult., Samuel Hazzard, formerly of Huntsville.
Died in Pickens County, 25th ult., Mrs. Regina Lyles.
Died at Judson Institute, Marion, Miss Lizzie, daughter of Jason G. Jones of Montgomery County.
Died in Tuskegee, ___ inst., Bolling W. Stark.
Died in Mobile, June 2nd, Charles S. Christopher.
Died in Mobile, June 2nd, Charles Zepernick.
Died in New Orleans, June 1st, A.J. Bowen of Alustee, Alabama.
Died in Philadelphia, June 3rd, Lewis M. Hamman, formerly of Montgomery.
Died in Mobile, June 4th, John M., infant son of J.M. Thompson.
Died in Mobile, June 4th, Mrs. Mary Weldon.

Henry Oppenheimer, who had died in Cuthbert, Georgia, was buried at Eufaula on the 26th ult.

Jim Harris (negro) fell from a boat and was drowned at Mobile, a few days ago.

J.L. Ryan of Lee County was killed by lightning a few days ago.

Issue 6-16-1870

Thomas Baker, a lad of twelve years of age, was shot and killed, in Henry County, a short time since, by Thomas Newby.

Miss Sallie J. Haralson, daughter of our venerable fellow citizen, Col. W.E. Haralson, died in this city on Sunday last, in the 22nd year of her age.

Masonic tribute upon the death of S.N. McCraw.

Henry Fabush, an employee on the A. &. C. R. R., was run over and killed near Jones' Bluff, a few days ago.

Julius Johnson of Montgomery was killed by lightning yesterday was a week ago.

Col. Wm. Duerson, an old soldier of 1812, died in Louisville on the 7th.

Baz. Richards was shot by unknown persons and fatally wounded, near New Lexington, Tuskaloosa County, May 20th.

## THE SOUTHERN ARGUS - DEATHS - JUNE 1869 THROUGH JUNE 1874

David Clouch of Colbert County committed suicide the other day by drinking ivy tea. He was seventy-two years old.

Issue 6-23-1870

Died in Fayette County a month ago, William Dodson.
Died in Fayette County, 21st ult., Mrs. Jinkins.
Died in Fayette County, 30th ult., John Gaddis.
Died near Centre, June 6th, Mrs. Purcilla Sheatly, aged seventy years.
Died in Mobile on the 8th, Mrs. Sarah H. McGuire.
Died in Conecuh County, 6th inst., Robert Ivey, aged eighty-three years.
Died in Pike County, 30th ult., Col. McLeod.
Died in Greene County, 31st ult., John Hail, aged seventy-five years.
Died in Mobile, 21st ult., J.B. Fuller of Greene County.
Died in Tuskaloosa County, 1st inst., Mary Spiller, aged twenty years.
Died in Tuskaloosa County, 2nd inst., James Spiller, aged twelve years.
Died in Tuskaloosa, 31st ult., William Tippett of East Tennessee, aged nineteen years.
Died in Tuskaloosa, 1st inst., Wallace F., infant son of F.P. and M.K. Turner.
Died in Mobile, 6th inst., Michael Brady.
Died in Mobile, 8th inst., Amanda Stickney, wife of L.P. Hill.
Died in Mobile, 6th inst., E. Armer.
Died in Centre, 12th, R.W. Wood.
Died in Demopolis, on the 7th inst., Caroline, wife of E.T. Rhodes.
Died in Tuskaloosa County on the 10th inst., John Matthews, aged seventy-eight years.
Died in Mobile on the 13th inst., G.W. Walker.
Died in Mobile, 8th inst., Julius A., infant son of J.A. and F.A. Smith.
Died in Greenville, 3rd inst., Mrs. Emma Henderson.
Died in Mobile, 16th inst., Mrs. Harriet H. Caleff.
Died in Mobile, 15th inst., Asa Waters.
Died in Mobile, 14th inst., Joseph Pollard.
Died in Evergreen, June 16th, Mrs. Eliza Jones.
Died in Jackson, Mississippi, 7th inst., George Clint, formerly of Mobile.
Died in Mobile, 16th inst., Simon H., son of M. Foreheimer.
Died in Jacksonville, 14th inst., Robt. Eugene, infant son of Charles and Kate Beyseigel.
Died in Jacksonville, Jun. ___, infant child of J.W. Strain.
Died in Helena, Arkansas, 12th inst., James E. Russell, formerly of Athens.
Died in Tuscumbia, 16th inst., Sydney C. Green, aged seventeen years.
Died in Madison County, 13th inst., Mrs. Rosa B. O'Neal.
Died at Mars, Bibb County, 13th inst., Rev. Robert Oldham.
Died in Morgan County, 9th inst., Albert E. Moore.
Died in Marion, June 18th, Col. C.C. Crowe.

## THE SOUTHERN ARGUS - DEATHS - JUNE 1869 THROUGH JUNE 1874

Died in Taylorville, Tuskaloosa County, June 11th, Ella, infant daughter of T.C. and L.C. Smith.

Tribute of respect from the pupils of the Pleasant Hill Academy on the death of fellow student Edward S. Walker.

Robt. McMinnis, brakeman on the Decatur and Nashville Road, was run over by a train, between Athens and Decatur, and fatally injured a few days ago.

Issue  6-30-1870

Died in this city on Monday the 27th inst., after a long illness, Mrs. M.D. Philpot.
Died near this city Sunday morning, June 26th, Willie Lewis, son of N.W. and F.D. Phillips, aged ten months and eighteen days.

Mrs. Mary Butler, wife of John J. Butler of this city died in Cahaba on Monday last.

We regret to hear of the death on Tuesday of last week at Oxford of Miss Josie Johnson, a sister of our esteemed friend and neighbor, Capt. Euclid Johnson of the firm of E. Johnson & Co. Miss Johnson was a teacher in the Oxford Collegiate Institute...

A man named Stewart was shot, last Thursday, at Mt. Rozell, Limestone County, by Mr. Lynn, a merchant, and fatally wounded.

Thomas Newby, who recently shot and killed a son of Thomas Baker of Henry County, has been captured and lodged in jail.

The *Autauga Citizen* has heard that Benj. May was shot and killed on the night of the 22nd, by a man named Jarett. The killing was done in Autauga.

On the 24th, a little son of Mrs. Gertrude Gray of Montgomery, and a negro boy were drowned in a pond in which they were bathing.

Two weeks ago last Sunday night, J.T. Etheridge, living near Jones' Bluff, a law-abiding and estimable citizen, was shot and badly wounded by one W.E. Holloway, who with a man named Nagle and one named Knight, had gone to Etheridge's for the purpose of whipping a negro woman living there. Mr. Etheridge, a Democrat and a subscriber to the *Argus*, interfered in behalf of his servant, and was shot as above. Knight and Nagle have been arrested. Holloway has fled.

## THE SOUTHERN ARGUS - DEATHS - JUNE 1869 THROUGH JUNE 1874

E.C. Hannon, an old citizen, Secretary of the Life Association of the South, dropped dead upon the streets of Montgomery one day last week.

On Sam. Steele's plantation, near Benton, a few days ago, Brooks Mock, negro, was killed by Randall Edwards, negro.

Issue 7-8-1870

Died in Talladega on the 17th, Miss Minnie Daughdrill, daughter of Mr. and Mrs. J.H. Daughdrill of Mobile.
Died at Spring Hill on the 22nd, Elizabeth Adell, youngest child of J.G. and A.P. Mordecai.
Died in Mobile on the 22nd, Mary, infant daughter of B.H. and E.M. Richardson.
Died in Mobile on the 9th inst., Eliza Amanda, infant daughter of William and Virginia Allen.
Died in Monroe County on the 13th, I.M. Henderson.
Died in Eufaula on the 18th ult., Miss Mary Dobbins.
Died in East Lowndes on the 21st inst., Mrs. Ben. W. Walker.
Died in Knoxville, Texas, Mrs. Mary Ridgill, formerly of Wilcox County.
Died in Mobile on the 21st ult., Sam'l Lindsey Hill of New Orleans.
Died in Tuscumbia on the 21st, Mattie Lou, daughter of S.F. and M.J. Sharp.
Died in Tuscumbia on the 22nd ult., Mrs. Mary Cheatham.
Died in Greenville on the 23rd, an infant son of C.C. Brawner.
Died in Mobile, June 29th, Helen Gordon, oldest daughter of C.M. Bancroft.
Died in Talladega on the 28th ult., Miss Letha, daughter of Mr. and Mrs. S.W. Williams.
Died in St. Clair County on the 28th ult., Mrs. Louisa J. Donohoo.
Died in Mobile, June 27th, Emily Gale, infant daughter of Max and Emma G. Demoney.
Died in Mobile, June 28th, Caroline A.H. Marshall.
Died in Mobile, June 26th, Alexander L., infant child of Chas. H. and Laura V. Pope.
Died in Shelby County, June 3rd, Bunch Ella Harris, daughter of P.T. and Mary G. Harris.
Died in Dooly County, Georgia, Gideon Roberts, formerly of Alabama, aged fifty-four years.
Died in Uniontown, June 25th, Mrs. Mary B. Eldridge, aged sixty-nine years.
Died near Greensboro, June 27th, Mrs. Sarah Idom, aged sixty-seven years.
Died in Holly Springs, Mississippi, June 13th, Judge Henry Stith, formerly of Pickens and after of Hale County, Alabama.
Died in Conecuh County a few days ago, Nathaniel Coker, aged eighty-two years.
Died in Mobile, June 20th, Thos. McGlynn.

# THE SOUTHERN ARGUS - DEATHS - JUNE 1869 THROUGH JUNE 1874

Died in Eufaula on the 28th ult., W.D. Etheridge.
Died near Huntsville, June 25th, Charles McCalley.
Died in Huntsville, June 29th, Robert Hamlet, Jr.
Died in Huntsville, June 25th, George, infant son of L.E. and M.R. Baker.
Died near Prattville, June 25th, Martin Burt, aged sixty-five years.
Died in Greenville, June 15th, infant son of E.M. and M.L. Hughston.
Died at Scottsboro, June 24th, Watkins, son of H.C. and Annie Bradford.
Died in Mobile, June 20th, James Osborne Ryder.
Died in Mobile, June 2?th, Mrs. Eliza Mooney.
Died in Mobile, June 29th, Willie, son of V. and F. Gab.
Died in Calhoun County on the 16th ult., Archie Demarcus, infant son of H.A. and M.E. Evans.
Died in Bibb County on the 24th ult., Sallie, infant daughter of Marshall and Eliza Pratt.

A three year old son of G.W. McQueen of Lowndes County fell into a tub of scalding water the other day and was dangerously injured.

On the night of June the 30th, a young man named Robinson (a white man and democrat) was assassinated on the streets of Asheville.

A few days ago on J.N. Pugh's plantation, in Bullock County, Dave Gardner, negro, was killed by Ed. Miles, negro.

Benj. May was not killed in Autauga County by one Jarett as reported last week by the *Citizen*.

Messrs. Brizziolari and Phelan, citizens of Memphis, fought a duel the other day, in which the former was dangerously wounded.

J.T. Martin of Harrison County, Kentucky, a member of the State Senate, died last week.

Dr. J.R.N. Owen, formerly of Tuskaloosa, recently shot and killed a man named Allen, at Hamilton, Nevada.

Drowned at Bails Landing, Tennessee River, on the 25th ult. Joe Extima, a German.

Died near Liberty Hill, in this County, on the 29th ult., Minor Willis, son of James and Ellen F. Stewart, aged seventeen years, two months and two days.

## THE SOUTHERN ARGUS - DEATHS - JUNE 1869 THROUGH JUNE 1874

We regret to learn that Col. Thomas M. Matthews of this County is dangerously ill at the residence of his son, J.E. Matthews, Esq., in Pensacola.

Issue 7-15-1870

H.B. Twithey, a brother of Capt. S.C. Twithey of Limestone County, Alabama, was shot and killed in Indianola, Texas, a few weeks ago.

John Tutt, was drowned at the railroad bridge on the 3rd inst., by trying to swim across the Bigbee River.

At Suggsville, a short time ago, James B. Mobley was shot and seriously wounded by R.R. Portis.

On the 4th, in Jackson County, Dennis Gamble was accidentally shot and wounded by Thomas Anderson.

Dr. Charles A. Pope, who committed suicide at Paris on the 15th inst., was a native of Huntsville.

On the 4th inst., a negro named Tom was shot and killed in Huntsville by one W.J. Edwards of Tennessee.

W.B. Lloyd of Huntsville was shot and wounded on the 2nd inst., by Jim Edwards of Maysville, Alabama.

Issue 7-22-1870

Our friend George Robbins, Esq. lost an interesting child, Statira, last week.

Mrs. Anna Whaley Pritchard, formerly of this city, where she was greatly admired and loved, died at Huntsville on the 14th.

Died in this city, July 14th, Charles Alexander, infant son of A.J. and Elizabeth Niel.
Died in Murfreesboro, Tennessee on the 25th ult., Mrs. Sarah H. Cherry, formerly of Athens, Alabama.
Died at Uniontown, June 25th, Mrs. Mary E. Aldridge, aged seventy years.
Died in Mobile on the 6th inst., Dennis Lucy.
Died in Mobile on the 6th inst., Hattie, infant child of W.W. and J.E. Boyd.
Died in Mobile on the 7th, Sidney Riley, son of J.S. and E.A. Cain.
Died in Mobile on the 8th, Mrs. Eliza Weldon.
Died in Mobile on the 7th, Mrs. M.J. Chapman.
Died in South Butler, June 26th, Eli Hudson.

# THE SOUTHERN ARGUS - DEATHS - JUNE 1869 THROUGH JUNE 1874

Died at Blue Pond, Cherokee County, June 28th, Lewis Griffin.
Died at Florence, June 27th, Robert James, infant son of Robert and C.W. McFarland.
Died in Bullock County on the 5th, Mrs. John Eady.
Died in Mobile, July 5th, Everett Brooks, infant son of L.F. and M.B. Irwin.
Died in Livingston, June 22nd, Mrs. Julia Wilson.
Died in Greensboro, July 6th, Stephen Nelson Owens, aged ten years.
Died in Mobile, July 7th, David Woodbury.
Died near Talladega, on the __ inst., Mary R., infant daughter of R. and J.J. McKibbon.
Died near Ferryville, St. Clair County, on the 6th inst., A.P. Coleman.
Died near Montgomery on the 11th inst., W.A. Taylor.
Died near Montgomery on the 1?th inst., John Taylor.
Died in Tuskegee on the 12th, Mrs. Ella Steadman of Montgomery.
Died at Sandy Ridge on the 5th inst., Oliver R., infant son of J.A. and A.H. Robertson.
Died near Gilmer's on the 7th inst., Mrs. M. McGee, aged seventy-two years.
Died in Greenville on the __ inst., Albert Gafford.
Died in Kansas some time since, I.W. Harvy, formerly of Greenville.
Died in Huntsville on the 14th, George W. Atwood.
Died in Madison County on the 13th inst., Robert S., infant son of J.V.A. Hinds.
Died in Madison County on the 8th inst., Miss Ada Neely.
Died in Huntsville on the 11th inst., Joseph H. Conner.

At Scottsboro on the 11th inst., Thomas Wallace was killed by George Steely.

Some days ago, the house of Mr. Paty, in Edwardsville, Cleburne County, was burned, and his wife and child perished in the fire.

Mrs. Mary W. Sherrill, the last surviving sister of Father Grant of the *Jacksonville Republican*, died in Columbus, Texas, July 2nd, aged sixty-seven years.

On the 15th inst., Thomas J. Ballard of Pickens County was killed by an accidental discharge of his gun.

In Lawrence County, some days ago, Jas. M. Warren was shot and seriously wounded by John Odam.

Judge A.H. Longstreet, author of "Georgia Scenes", died a few days ago in Oxford, Mississippi, eighty years old.

## THE SOUTHERN ARGUS - DEATHS - JUNE 1869 THROUGH JUNE 1874

Col. R.C. Myers, David W. Myers, and Washington Hardy, who were convicted for the killing of Colonel Millican, in Brazos County, Texas, some time since, and who have been confined in jail for several months, were pardoned by Governor Davis a few days ago.

### Issue 7-29-1870

At Newbern, on the 15th, Emmet B. Jackson committed suicide.

On the Perry place, near Greensboro, a few days ago, Hill, negro, was shot and killed by McCann, also negro. A night or two after, a band of negroes took McCann out and shot him several times, leaving him for dead, which he is not.

A lad about twelve years old, a son of Perry Cook of Pike County, was drowned last week.

Mr. Dennis St. Leger, well known in Eufaula, was drowned at Brunswick, Georgia some time ago.

A little boy, six years old, named Williams, was drowned in the river near Florence, a few days ago.

We regret to learn that Hon. George D. Shortridge died on Tuesday last at his residence at Montevallo.

Major James Penn, the oldest Mason in Tennessee, died in Memphis on the 22nd.

### DIED IN ALABAMA

Near State Line, Mississippi, June 26th, Joseph Daniel, formerly of Perry County.
In California, July 4th, Dr. Lafayette Guild of Tuskaloosa.
In Mobile on the 18th, H.T. Heenan.
In Mobile on the 17th, Gracie Gadder, wife of Joseph Gibbons.
In Mobile on the 15th, Jeannie Marie Francoise Delecamps, aged eighty-nine years.
In Huntsville on the 19th, Gen. W.T.H. Brooks.
In Benton on the 16th, Sandy Brown, formerly of Montgomery.
In Huntsville on the 16th, Ellen, infant daughter of Mr. and Mrs. G.W. Bowman.
In Cherokee County on the 14th, Liberty Freeman.
In Greene County on the 13th, W.H. Lee, aged fifty-six years.
In Greene County on the 10th inst., Charles H. Miller, aged seventy years.

# THE SOUTHERN ARGUS - DEATHS - JUNE 1869 THROUGH JUNE 1874

Near Forkland on the 2nd, Woodson Garrett.

Gen. Le Hardy, Viscount De Beaulieu, a veteran of the old French army, formerly a citizen of Rome, Georgia, died on the 1st inst., at Brussels, Belgium, his birth place, aged ninety years.

Mrs. Gen. Brooks and child were badly injured the other day in Huntsville, by the breaking down of the carriage in which they were returning from the funeral of Gen. Brooks.

Issue 8-5-1870

A negro was shot by E. Martin, near Elyton, on Tuesday last.

Alex Jones of Etowah was killed by Colly Wynne on Tuesday of last week.

Died at Marion, Perry County, on the morning of the 2nd inst., George Henry, the only child of Richard H. and Hattie L. English, age one year, ten days.

Cook, recently shot at Union Springs, by Tarver, who eloped with his sister, was mortally wounded.

Henry Martin, route agent over the Mobile and Montgomery Road, died suddenly in Montgomery on Saturday last.

Lindsay, the seducer of his sister-in-law, was shot and mortally wounded on the 21st ult in the presence of his victim, by her father, at Chester, Virginia.

Last week, Mr. Page of Evergreen was assaulted from behind by one Stallwoth and badly beaten with a cudgel.

Died in Mobile, July 28th, Amie, daughter of Burgess and M. J. Garner.
Died in Montgomery County, July 24th, Dudley Battle.
Died in Mobile, July 30th, Christopher Pryor.
Died in Marysville, California, July 4th, Dr. Lafayette Guild, an old citizen of Alabama.
Died in Mobile, July 29th, Miss Fannie Byrne.
Died in Mobile, July 30th, Alice, infant daughter of Ferdinand and Caroline Hatchmeyer.
Died at Baywood, near Mobile, July 30th, Miss Amelia C. Beers.
Died in Mobile, July 30th, Mrs. Hannah Haas.
Died in Mobile, July 27th, Mrs. Amie Hall.
Died in Etowah County, July 23rd, Mrs. McLeod.
Died in Etowah last week, Mr. Best.

## THE SOUTHERN ARGUS - DEATHS - JUNE 1869 THROUGH JUNE 1874

Died in Gadsden, July 28th, infant daughter of Judge L.E. and Emma Hamlin.
Died in Tuscumbia, July 28th, John A. Pope, aged forty-one years.
Died in Lowndes County, July 23rd, infant child of B.W. Walker.

Issue 8-12-1870

Mrs. Virginia Wilson, widow of the late George W. Wilson of this city, died in Burnsville last Tuesday evening.

On the 15th inst. Thos. J. Ballard of Pickens County, was accidently killed by his own gun.

An Irishman named Weaver, was hung the other day, in Cherokee County, for outraging a little girl aged eleven years.

Died in Newbern, 27th ult., Dr. John T. Barron, formerly a resident of Marion.
Died in Lowndes County, July 20th, little Eugenie, youngest daughter of J.W. and Emma Rast.
Died at Montrose, Eastern Shore of Mobile Bay, July 28th, S. T. Strudwick.
Died in Montgomery on the 3rd inst., Eugene S. Bolling.
Died in Montgomery, August 3rd, Mrs. E.H. Dickerson.
Died in Tuskaloosa, August 1st, Mrs. W.H. Douthit.
Died in Tuskaloosa on the 1st inst., Mrs. W.J. Boyd, aged forty-nine years.
Died in Montevallo, July 27th, Hon. Geo. D. Shortridge.
Died in Whitewater, Pike County, on the 22nd ult. John, eldest child of H.M. and Mary McClure.
Died in Tuskaloosa, July 3rd, S.R. Passmore.
Died at Opelika, July 30th of pneumonia, Wm. Fletcher.
Died at Opelika, August 1st, John Martin, aged one hundred three years.
Died in Union Springs on the 4th inst. after a long illness, Dr. Wm. S. Mabson.
Died near Autaugaville on the 1st inst., Mrs. R. Ann DeBardelaben.
Died in Perry County on the 26th ult., John Lee, aged fifty years.
Died at Newbern on the 12th inst., George F. Huckabee.
Died in Greensboro, August 3rd, Willie, son of W.H. and L. Locke.
Died in Eufaula on the 2nd inst., L. Marburg.
Died in Mobile, August 4th, Geo. G. Sampson.
Died in Jacksonville, last week, Mrs. John A. Findley.
Died in Tuscumbia, 30th ult., Mrs. Susannah Wilson, aged sixty-three years.
Died in Mobile, last Thursday, George G. Sampson.
Died in Greenville, August 1st, Mrs. Dora Webb.

John Morrisette of Uniontown was killed at the late railroad accident in Virginia.

## THE SOUTHERN ARGUS - DEATHS - JUNE 1869 THROUGH JUNE 1874

George Houston, negro Representative from Sumter, was not drowned in the Bigbee as reported.

R.H. and Colby Wynn have been held to answer at the next term of the Etowah Circuit Court, for killing Alex. Jones.

Dr. W.T. Battey of Augusta, Georgia, dropped dead at the dinner table in Wilmington on Monday last.

H.S. Gallagher was drowned in the Ohio River at Paducah last week.

Allen Baker of Franklin County, Kentucky, was killed by his nephew W.B. Newton on Monday of last week.

A young lady named Mary Bell Dewitt has suddenly and mysteriously disappeared from her home in Louisville.

John Hatton of Louisville is now lying dangerously ill from the effects of a spider bite in his arm.

Mock Simmons was killed at Cornwall Iron Works, Georgia on Saturday last by the falling of an ore bank.

The search for the Nathan murderers is pursued with unabated zeal.

Jim Littlepage and Ed. Love, notorious car robbers, were both run over and killed near Meridian a few days ago.

Issue  8-19-1870

John A. Doyle, a printer, for many years employed in one of the offices of this city, died on Wednesday evening last.

On Friday last a man by the name of Loftin was killed by the oar-grinder wheel at Cornwall.

James Norman of Lowndes County has lately lost two children from dysentery.

A young man named Davis of Cherokee was accidentally shot and badly wounded, a few days since.

Young Hamiter of Barbour County lately committed suicide by taking opium and laudnum.

## THE SOUTHERN ARGUS - DEATHS - JUNE 1869 THROUGH JUNE 1874

James Cunningham of Eufaula died recently while on a visit to Cuthbert, Georgia.

Henry Teal fell from a roof in Mobile, a short time since, and was seriously injured.

By the death of the Hon. George D. Shortridge of Shelby County, Alabama has lost one of her greatest intellects and one of her truest noblest sons; and a sketch of his life will not be without interest to our readers.

He was born in Montgomery County, Kentucky, on the 10th day of November, 1814. His father, the late Hon. Eli Shortridge, a distinguished lawyer and politician of that state, being so unfortunate as to lose his estate, sought a new sphere and removed to Tuskaloosa, Alabama, in 1826. Here his son George had the difficulties of poverty and frontier life to contend with in obtaining his education. To raise funds for this purpose, he accepted, at the age of fourteen, a place in the office of the Clerk of the Supreme Court, and subsequently entered the office of Secretary of State at the solicitation of Col. James I. Thornton. He likewise remained for some time in the book store of D. Woodruff. He entered the State University in 1830, where he signalized himself as one of the principal founders of the famous Erosophic Society. In the year 1833, with his friend and future brother-in-law, Burwell Boykin, he read law in the office of his father, and at the same time conducted, as editor, the leading Democratic organ then published at the Capital. He was admitted to practice at the June Term of the Supreme Court in 1834, and the winter following was elected by the Legislature, over several able competitors, Solicitor of the Eighth Judicial Circuit, and removed to the city of Montgomery....

When the storm of 1861 came, he was summoned from his private walks by the voice of the people of Shelby, who had known and trusted him so long; and, in conjunction with the late Judge McClanahan, he represented them in the state convention. He now dedicated all his time and energies to the cause of southern independence, assisting in the organization of companies and regiments, attending and directing public meetings, looking after the wants of the poor and helpless, and taking care of the sick and wounded, and he was only withheld by disease from active service in the army. Eight boys ---one brother, three sons, three nephews whom he had raised to manhood, and his only son-in-law--- gave upon the battle-field the highest evidence of that patriotism with which his teachings had imbued them....

William Parrot dropped dead in Mobile last week.

Watson, murderer of Reese, arrested at Sommerville, was delivered to the Sheriff of Etaw, Monday of last week.

# THE SOUTHERN ARGUS - DEATHS - JUNE 1869 THROUGH JUNE 1874

Died in Mobile, 11th inst., Wm. Sherlock.
Died near Mt. Welling, July 27th, Mrs. Georgia Cunningham.
Died in Cherokee County on the 1st inst. of palpitation of the heart, Jack Boring.
Died in Talladega on the 5th inst., Mrs. Anna M. Jones, in the eighty-first year of her age.
Died at Shelby Iron Works, July 27th, Sumpter A. Horton.
Died at Shelby Iron Works, July 23rd, Union T. Horton.
Died at Shelby Iron Works, Mrs. Frances McDaniel.
Died in Fayette Court House, July 30th, Mrs. Edie Robertson.
Died in Clifton, August 3rd, Wm. B. Watson, infant.
Died near Huntsville on the 7th, Thomas W. Pettus.
Died in Huntsville, 6th inst., Mrs. Cassandra Shoenberger.
Died in Athens on the 3rd, Miss Martha F. Kittrell.
Died in Monroe County, August 2nd, B.B. Kimball.
Died in Choctaw County, July 24th, Capt. A.G. Watters.
Died at Rashia, August 9th, N.O.J. Tisdale of New Orleans
Died in Morgan County on the 7th inst., Miss Jane Morrow.

Frank E. Saywood was caught and crushed between two railroad cars at Hamlin, Missouri the other day.

Died in Union Springs, August 1st, Henry Taylor, infant son of Mr. and Mrs. M.L. Stinson.
Died in Union Springs, July 17th, Emma Isabella, infant daughter of Mr. and Mrs. M.L. Stinson.
Died in Union Springs, 7th inst., Lizzie Rea, infant daughter of W.H. and Lizzie F. Black.
Died in Montgomery County, July 23rd, Wm. Dudley Battle.
Died in Montgomery on the 10th inst., Mr. Lampson, an old resident.
Died in Talladega County on the 5th inst., Wm. Menzo McCargo.
Died at Opelika 1st inst., Mrs. Jane R. Dunbar, aged 6? years.
Died in Eutaw on the 6th inst., Mrs. Eliza W. Williams.
Died in Huntsville on Wednesday of last week, James R. Blunt.
Died near Jacksonville last week of apoplexy, Mrs. Jas. K. Douglas.
Died in Mobile on the 13th inst., Hon. Henry Chamberlain.
Died in Butler County, 8th inst., A.W. Turner.

Issue 8-26-1870

Maj. R.H. Adams, for many years a prominent planter and leading citizen of the vicinity of Faunsdale, a gentleman of enlarged and liberal views, widely known and greatly beloved, died suddenly at his summer residence near Christianburg, Virginia last Sunday.

## THE SOUTHERN ARGUS - DEATHS - JUNE 1869 THROUGH JUNE 1874

Misses Henrietta Moody and Mary Wilson were thrown from a buggy and both badly injured while on their way to preaching in Choctaw County two weeks ago.

Josiah Martin of Conecuh County is held to bail in $500 to answer a charge of assault with intent to kill.

On the 17th instant, near Huntsville, two men were ran over by the cars; one of them (Wood) was killed, and the other (Herman) was so badly injured that he will die.

Lucinda Brown, negress, was murdered in Mobile the other day, by Wilson May, negro.

Died near Oxford, August 13th, Leonidas Gunn.
Died in Montgomery on the 20th inst., Wm. Stacey.
Died in Greenville on the 15th, M.A. Alvin Hazard, infant son of W.C. and Sarah Caldwell.
Died in Mobile, August 19th, Christopher Jacobs.
Died in Huntsville, August 18th, Lafayette Sisk.
Died in Clarke County on the 16th inst., W.B. Riley of the firm of Riley & Vail, Mobile.
Died in Mobile, August 18th, L.D. Gould.
Died in Eutaw on the 16th inst., Mrs. Virginia E. Cockrell.
Died near Eutaw on the 13th inst., Mrs. Bettie Storer.
Died in Eutaw, August 6th, Mrs. Eliza Pendleton Williams.
Died in Huntsville, August 15th, John David Blunt, infant.
Died near Tuscumbia on the 8th inst., John Lewis Hobgood.
Died in Huntsville on the 15th inst., Willie Ables, infant.
Died in Montgomery, August 20th, Mrs. Mattie Robinson.
Died in Union Springs, August 12th, infant child of J.E. Delbridge.
Died in Mobile, August 18th, Mattie May.
Died in Tuskaloosa, August 15th, Mrs. Nancy Keen.
Died in Marion, August 17th, Willis Pleasant.
Died in Perry County, August 16th, Henry Jemison.
Died in Perry County, August 13th, Napoleon B. Curb.
Died a few days ago in Autauga County, Abel K. Harris.
Died recently in Dale County, Willie Edwards, a sprightly boy.
Died in Tuskaloosa, August 18th, W.F. Mallory, brother of the late Secretary of the Confederate Navy.
Died at Pleasant Hill, August 12th of consumption, Miss Selam Webster, daughter of Mrs. Sarah Webster, aged about twenty years.
Died at Collorine, August 14th of consumption, Mrs. Joseph Soles of Farmersville, aged about twenty-five years.

## THE SOUTHERN ARGUS - DEATHS - JUNE 1869 THROUGH JUNE 1874

Died in Mobile, August 22nd, Mrs. Ulmer.
Died in Mobile, August 22nd, the wife of C.A. Bradford.
Died in Mobile, August 22nd, Rev. Father Dominick Gibbons, formerly Priest in Charge of the Catholic congregation in this city.
Died in Jackson, Clarke County, August 21st, Leila Moore Webing, wife of the late H.H. Miller.
Died in Montgomery on the 23rd, Thomas McCarthy.
Died near Talladega on the 16th, Dawson B. Elliott.

Mr. Loftin of Cherokee is not dead as reported, though he is quite ill and not expected to recover.

A son of Dr. Adams, living near Pine Apple, only eight or ten years old, hung himself a few days ago.

W.H. Taylor, who murdered his wife in Chambers County not long since, has escaped from prison.

Adolphus Watson, who escaped from Attalla after murdering young Reese, was arrested in Morgan some days ago.

Joe Williams (negro) was shot on Sunday evening by the watchman at the depot of the M.&E.R.R., Montgomery.

### Issue  9-2-1870

Died at Choctaw Corner, Clarke County, Alabama, July 23rd, 1870, Bettie O. Poole, only daughter of Mr. Charles Poole of that place, aged seventeen years, four months.

A negro named Ball Yarbrough, who was said to be one hundred fifteen years old, died near Athens a few days ago.

Three soldiers, who were arrested on the charge of killing Thos. McCarthy in Montgomery, by throwing him from a balcony, were released for want of proof.

Died in Montgomery, 24th ult., Miss Nettie Ward.
Died at Bell's Landing, August 15th, Jennie Stallworth, infant of J.F. and F.E. Packer.
Died in Larkinsville, August 3rd, Lilly Morring, infant.
Died near Mt. Zion, Madison County, August 8th, T.W. Pettus.
Died near Tuscumbia, August 22nd, little Willie Green.

## THE SOUTHERN ARGUS - DEATHS - JUNE 1869 THROUGH JUNE 1874

Died a short time ago at Florence, Mrs. Martha H. Armstead, aged ninety years.
Died in Marengo County, last week, Richard H. Adams.
Died in Auburn, last Monday week, Calvin Stratton.
Died in Madison County, 24th ult., Mrs. Paul, wife of the miller at the Bell Factory.
Died in Huntsville, August 24th, little Mary Ella Blunt.
Died in Eutaw, August 16th, Ann T. McNutty.
Died in Hale County, August 23rd, Miss Adaline M. Burge.
Died in Montgomery, August 26th, Samuel Holt Pickett.

Issue 9-9-1870

Died at Cahaba, September 5th, Hamilton Coleman, only son of Dr. and Mrs. J.S. Dean.
Died near Bellevue, August 20th, Ora Cena, infant daughter of James I. and M. Craig.

Tribute of respect from Randolph Lodge #258, August 29, 1870, upon the death of Rev. Joseph F. Ray.

Gen. Edwin G. Lee, well known in Alabama, fell dead at Yellow Sulphur Springs, Virginia, a few days ago.

P.W. Whorton was seriously stabbed by two brothers Lewis, in Cherokee County, the other day.

D.N. Williamson had a difficulty with some showmen at Cedar Bluff, recently, and received a serious stab in the back.

Ephriam Webb, a negro of good character, was killed in Eutaw, not long since, by a negro named Jupiter.

Mr. Hollenbach was badly injured by falling through a skylight from the second to the first floor of a store in Huntsville the other day.

John Stoddard was killed last week in Cherokee County, by his brother, who stabbed him.

Died in Opelika, August 25th, Frank, infant son of Capt. Frank Watkins.
Died in Montgomery, August 29th, Roger Fortes.
Died in Auburn, August 29th, Caroline Stratton.
Died in Montgomery, last Wednesday, William Byrd Fountain.
Died in Hale County, August 29th, Mrs. May Frierson.

# THE SOUTHERN ARGUS - DEATHS - JUNE 1869 THROUGH JUNE 1874

Died near Greensboro, 31st ult., Samuel Martin, aged seventeen years.
Died in Green County, last week, William Pettigrew.
Died near Eutaw, during the past week, A.D. Hutton.
Died in Green County, August 23rd, Daniel Sanders.
Died at Pleasant Ridge, Greene County, last month, Johnnie Knox, aged nine years.
Died in Troy, August 31st, Matthew Manning of congestive chill.
Died in Decatur, August 29th of congestion of the brain, Capt. Newton.
Died near Uniontown, last Monday week, Jas. Simms, Jr. of congestive chill.
Died near Uniontown, 25th ult., Maria Mince Adams, aged four years.
Died in Athens, August 25th, Edward Achille Pipin, aged one year.
Died at Notasulga, August 28th, Mrs. E.B. Barber.
Died in Auburn, August 31st, Maggie, infant daughter of L.W. Payne.
Died in Greenville, 1st inst., Florida Powell, aged seven years.
Died in Montgomery, September 2nd, infant child of Oscar and Sarah A. Deoille.
Died in Mobile, 31st ult., Abram Larkin of Sumter County.
Died in Decatur, August 27th, H.E. Willard, aged three years.
Died in Eufaula, September 1st, Mrs. Thomas Brannon.

J.G. Apsey of Marion was last week lying dangerously ill at Nashville, Tennessee.

Died at Pleasant Hill, Dallas County, Alabama, Salena, eldest daughter of the late Thomas and Sarah Webster.

Issue 9-16-1870

Caesar Fleming, negro, indicted in Wilcox County for murdering Spencer, white man, was killed the other day while attempting to escape.

M.P. LeGrand of Montgomery was thrown from his buggy and badly hurt, the other day.

Ed. Nash shot and instantly killed Wm. Miller, at Cowles' Station, last Friday week.

Whorton, severely stabbed by the Lewis brothers in Cherokee County recently, is getting well.

Died in Camden, September 1st, Mrs. Ellen L. Riley.
Died in Hale County, 7th inst., Mrs. Nancy Collins, aged eighty-five years.
Died near Greensboro, September 6th, Mrs. S.S. Mellown.
Died near Elyton, 6th inst., Wm. Killough.

## THE SOUTHERN ARGUS - DEATHS - JUNE 1869 THROUGH JUNE 1874

Died in Demopolis, September 6th, Mrs. Indiana Manning.
Died in Opelika, September 3rd, Emma, infant daughter of T.L. Kennedy.
Died near Gaylesville, 31st ult., infant son of Ebenezer Cunningham.
Died in Eufaula, last Sunday week, Nicholas Christian.
Died in Conecuh County, August 25th, Mrs. Patience A. Brewton.
Died in Moulton, August 31st, Viola Ross McKelvy, aged eight years.
Died near Tuscumbia, 2nd inst., Edmond Ellet.
Died in Huntsville, September 7th, Thos. Kirkland.
Died near Madison Station, 1st inst., Sarah Elizabeth Hughes, infant.
Died in Madison County, 7th inst., Mrs. Emma J. Walker.
Died near Nashville, Tennessee, September 7th, John E. Tucker, formerly of Huntsville.
Died in Limestone County on the 5th inst., America K. Petty.
Died in Tuskaloosa, September 3rd, Thomas Blount Slade.
Died in Nashville, September 4th, Mrs. Mary Lane Johnson, daughter of H.H. Higgins of Athens.
Died in Jacksonville, September 5th, Col. John R. Clark.

An old negro, Randall Miller of Huntsville, fell dead a few days ago.

Elasar Falk of Florence was found dead in his bed on the morning of the 30th ult.

### Issue 9-23-1870

Mrs. Eliza Reese, daughter of Henry J. King, and wife of Dr. A.J. Reese, died at the residence of her husband, at King's Landing, in this County, on the 19th inst.

A little daughter of James Ryals, was choked to death with a bean, at Stone Mountain, last Saturday week.

Ruffin Blair, an inoffensive and worthy lad, was waylaid and shot to death by unknown parties, near Athens, one night last week.

Died in Claiborne, 30th ult., W.R. Agee, Sr., aged sixty-four years.
Died in Camden, September 1st, Mrs. Ella L. Riley.
Died near Talladega, September 12th, Wm. Turner.
Died near Hollow Square, September 14th, Mrs. J.T. Neighbors.
Died in Taylorsville, Tuskaloosa County, Wade Brooks.
Died in Tuskaloosa on the 11th inst., Daniel Clark.
Died at Mt. Sterling, Choctaw County, September 3rd, Earl Gaines.
Died in Huntsville on the 14th inst., William Powers.

# THE SOUTHERN ARGUS - DEATHS - JUNE 1869 THROUGH JUNE 1874

Died in Columbiana on the 12th inst., Mrs. Mary Ann Roberts, wife of Willis Roberts of the *Shelby Guide*.
Died in Mobile, September 17th, Henry Heutsch.
Died in Mobile, September 17th, Henry Wittman.
Died near Robinson's Springs, September 17th, Mrs. Tarrant, aged ninety-four years.
Died in Montgomery, September 17th, Clayton Wilson.
Died in Greenville, September 14th, Lillie, infant child of James and Jane Perdue.
Died in Perry County on the 8th inst., Mrs. Annie E. Wells.
Died in Marion on the 10th inst., Miss Eliza Patrick.
Died in Perry County on the 13th inst., Sidney Reese.

Joe Hanson of Opelika was recently thrown from his horse and killed.

Dimby Petty of Greenville was seriously stabbed by William and Hubb Gandy a few days ago.

Mr. Dent Lamar, who died in Tuskaloosa on Sunday last, was buried from the Baptist Church in this city Wednesday afternoon.

The remains of Mrs. Lucy W., wife of W.M. Ridgway of the vicinity of Macon Station, were brought to this city for interment last Tuesday.

Issue 9-30-1870

Uncle Tom Cowen, an old and respected negro man in Eufaula, was buried on last Wednesday week.

The death of Mrs. Norris, last Monday, soon after her return from Mobile, gave rise to a report that she died of yellow fever.
Died in this city on Monday last, Mrs. Emily H. Norris.

Enoch Boyd, a very bad negro, who had but a short time previous escaped from a mob of his own color, was recently found murdered in Sumter County.

Frank Harrison shot and killed Charles Gilmer, negro, near Hayneville, a few days ago.

M.W. Hawkins was killed by a Deputy Sheriff in Marengo County some days ago.

Died in Pickens County, September 17th, Earnest Foster of Mobile.
Died in Talladega County, September 7th, Ella Lela Wilson, infant.

## THE SOUTHERN ARGUS - DEATHS - JUNE 1869 THROUGH JUNE 1874

Died at Kymulga, September 5th, Asa Caldwell, infant.
Died near Gaylesville, September 13th, Mrs. M.A.L. Henderson.
Died in Montgomery, September 22nd, Absalom Jackson.
Died near Camden, September 17th, Daisy Cumming.
Died in Mobile, September 24th, James Kelly.
Died in Huntsville, September 2nd, infant of E.J. and Martha Trotman.
Died in Jacksonville, September 21st, John Grant Francis, aged six years.
Died in Tuskaloosa, September 20th, John S. Fitch.
Died in North Port, near Tuskaloosa, September 19th, Rosco, son of R. and P.H. Simpson.
Died in Opelika, September 20th, infant daughter of Mr. R.C. Jeter.
Died in Greenville, September 20th, Maggie Metcalf, infant.

Issue 10-7-1870

John Grider, a merchant, was seriously stabbed by W.R. Moore, a planter, near Thomasville, last Thursday week.

Died at Hayneville, September 26th, Mrs. Kate McLean.
Died near Lowndsboro, September 23rd, Miss Sallie Craig.
Died in Montgomery, October 1st, Carrie Schular.
Died in Greensboro, 24th ult., Hattie, infant daughter of E. and M. Nutting.
Died near Greensboro, September 24th, A.D. Idorn, aged twelve years.
Died in Hale County, on the 25th ult., Mrs. L.W. Ridgeway.
Died near Erie, September 27th, J.W. Monette.
Died in Greensboro, September 16th, Madison Lumery.
Died near Eufaula, Sunday week, very suddenly, Mrs. C.A. Mallory.
Died in Huntsville, September 25th, Willie Hardcastle Blair.
Died in Meridianville, 21st ult., J.G. Bentley.
Died in Mobile, September 30th, Mrs. Joseph Cohill.
Died in Mobile, 1st inst., H.R. Kelly.
Died at Bridgeville, Pickens County, September 27th, Miss Sallie Gardner of Mobile.
Died in Tuskaloosa, September 19th, Daniel N. Clark.
Died in Tuskaloosa, 26th ult., Harry Pegues Martin, aged one year.
Died near Tuskaloosa, September 22nd, little Lottie Ogburn, infant.

Jos. Autunez was accidentally drowned at Mobile the other day.

Dr. F.G. Godbee of Burk County, Georgia, was last week stabbed to death by a negro who escaped.

Henry Davis, negro, was killed by the falling of an embankment, on the Grand Trunk Railroad, seven miles from Mobile, on the 29th ult.

# THE SOUTHERN ARGUS - DEATHS - JUNE 1869 THROUGH JUNE 1874

Issue 10-14-1870

Laurence Ackerman, father of the late J.C. Ackerman of Mobile, died in New York on the 2nd inst.

Died near Midway, October 2nd, J.M. Taylor, aged fifty-eight years.
Died in New Orleans, September ??th, D. Irwin Rast, formerly President of the Marion Female Seminary.
Died in Montgomery, October 4th, Mrs. Anne F. Howard.
Died near Letohatchie, October 2nd, Annie Lee Haigier, aged seven years.
Died in Marion, October 2nd, Susan Smoot.
Died near Tomkinsville, Choctaw County, October 3rd, Mrs. Sarah Lyon, aged seventy-seven.
Died in Richmond, Virginia, September 4th, Mary G. Freeland, formerly of Madison County.
Died near Madison Station, October 1st, Sarah Elizabeth, infant daughter of E.J. and S.H. Hughes.
Died near Crockett, Texas, September 2nd, Mrs. G.A. Hester, formerly of Hale County.
Died in Hale County, September 25th, W. Oberry.
Died in Mobile, October 6th, Blanche E. Deas.
Died in Huntsville, October 3rd, James E. Copeland, aged two years.
Died in Mobile, October 7th, Maj. J.D. Carpenter.
Died in Marengo County, September 30th, David W. Magruder.
Died in Mobile, October 8th, Henry Davenport.
Died in Mobile, October 1st, Harrison R. Kelly, infant.
Died in Montgomery, October 8th, Frank Douglas, aged ten years.
Died in Camden, October 4th, Geo. W. Caldwell.
Died in Mobile, October 1st of yellow fever, Waldemar L. Marivitz.
Died in Mobile, October 3rd, Z. Townsen?
Died in Mobile, September 30th of yellow fever, Mrs. Margaret Cahill.
Died near Tuskaloosa, October 2nd, W.T. Sartain.

Andrew Norrell was run over and killed by a train on the S.R. & D.R.R., near Sugar Valley Station, a few days ago.

Kitt McGree was waylaid and dangerously shot by two negroes near Tuskegee several days ago. The following night in the same neighborhood, Tobe Davis, white man, was shot and badly wounded by a negro. The guilty parties yet escaped detection.

In consequence of the death of his only son, Chancellor Felder held no court in Hayneville last Monday week.

## THE SOUTHERN ARGUS - DEATHS - JUNE 1869 THROUGH JUNE 1874

A.H. Marschalk has been forced by bad health to sever his connection with the *Demopolis Exponent*. F.P. Ferris becomes sole editor and proprietor.

Ashfield Harwood of Union Springs was accidently shot and seriously wounded last Sunday week.

Alfred Bryant, negro, was mortally shot in Montgomery last Sunday morning by Wm. A. Gunter, while attempting to rob his premises.

Thos. Key and John Pickett of Salem exchanged shots Friday week, the latter being mortally wounded and the former receiving a slight wound in the hand.

Issue 10-21-1870

Died near Burnsville, Monday evening last, aged over seventy years, Josiah Brown.
Died in this city, October 14th, William Chambliss, infant son of Mr. and Mrs. F.S. McClelland.
Died in Cahaba, October 15th, Leila, daughter of Dr. A.L. and S.A. Arthur.
Died in Prairie Bluff, October 6th, James Robert, only son of John A. and E.W. Erwin.
Died in this city, October 14th, Mrs. Merritt Burns.

Miss -- Shelby died near Valley Creek Church last Saturday.

Dr. Burke formerly and eminent physician in Glenville, died in Mobile last week of yellow fever.

An affray occurred in Uniontown last, in which Thos. J. Norton was dangerously shot by John Horn. Henry Morgan, a bystander was also wounded.

Died at Fayette C. H., October 7th, Mrs. William Walker.
Died in Evergreen, October 2nd, Pinkney James.
Died near Claiborne, September 8th, Laura Stabler.
Died in Lowndesboro, October 8th, Thomas R. Williamson.
Died near Lowndesboro, October 8th, a young man named Cravy.
Died in Mobile, October 12th, M.B. Dane.
Died in Mobile, October 10th, Wm. A. Brown.
Died in Mobile, October 11th, Chas. M. Quigley.
Died in Mobile, October 11th, Blocker Montgomery.
Died in Demopolis, October 13th, Judge E.B. Bailey, aged seventy-seven years.
Died near Columbiana, September 27th, Miss Ellen Trague.

## THE SOUTHERN ARGUS - DEATHS - JUNE 1869 THROUGH JUNE 1874

In Mobile, October 7th, Peter Hicks.

Died in Mobile, October 4th, Mrs. Adele Betrie, aged seventy-nine years.
Died near St. Stephens, October 1st, Hattie Fannie Floyd.
Died near Greensboro, October 8th, Ida McMillan.
Died at Cuba, Sumter County, October 4th, D. V. Patterson.
Died in Troy, September 27th, Mrs. John Post.
Died in Macon County, October 10th, Milton A. Williams.
Died in Mobile, October 12th, Perry Clifton.
Died in Pickens County, September 25th, Capt. M. Cook, aged seventy-six years.
Died in Camden, October 4th?, Geo. W. Caldwell.
Died in Camden, October 9th, Miss Emily Mahew, one of the teachers in Wilcox Female Institute.
Died in Tuskaloosa, October 11th, Irby, infant son of T.B. and C. Slade.
Died in Tuskaloosa, October 13th, Wiley B. Thompson.
Died in Tuskaloosa, October 13th, Mrs. Minora Spinner.
Died in Montgomery, October 17th, Dr. T.J. Goodwin.
Died at Spring Hill, October 15th, Capt. J.G. Mordecai.
Died in Mobile, October 10th, Harry D. Houston.
Died in Mobile, October 7th, Mrs. Margaret Mercer Nevins, wife of Rev. R.D. Nevins, D.D.
Died in Mobile, October 17th, W.P. Hammond.
Died in Mobile, October 10th, Ann Clay Cuthbert.
Died on the Eastern Shore, a few days since, Mr. Short.

The negro burglar, Aleck Mack, shot last week in Montgomery, is dead.

Ashfield Harwood accidently shot in Uniontown, is recovering.

Abram Moss, one of the negroes wounded in the Zion Church tragedy at Tusegee has since died.

Issue 10-28-1870

Died at Burnsville, October 24th, Polk C. Randle, aged about twenty-five years.

The yellow fever in Mobile has carried off Drs. Herndon, Burke, Toxey, and Anderson.

In three weeks, four members of the Cravy family near Lowndesboro have died of measles.

## THE SOUTHERN ARGUS - DEATHS - JUNE 1869 THROUGH JUNE 1874

Charley Williams, negro, is in the Eufaula Jail for shooting Wyatt Ryan, negro, some time ago.

Young Horn, shot by Norton in Uniontown last week has since died.

Issue 11-4-1870

A little son of Mrs. Bett??? Ervin, near Prairie Bluff, was so badly crushed in a cotton gin a few days ago, as to cause the amputation of his leg, from which he died a few hours after.

Died in East Selma, November 2nd, Cleveland Grant.
Died near Selma on Sunday last, John C. Lilly, aged about twenty-five years.
Died at the Troup House in this city on the night of the 27th, A.B. Finlayson of Wilcox County.
Died in Mobile, October 18th, Edward Girard, two years old.
Died on Eastern Shore Mobile Bay, Wm. Phinn Hammand.
Died in Mobile, October 20th, Wm. Henry Ramond, aged five years.
Died in Mobile, October 1st, Myron B. Dane, aged twenty-nine years.
Died in Mobile, 13th inst., Robt. Benjamin Huston.
Died in Mobile, October 21st, Henry Chambers.
Died in Mobile, October 20th, John Welsh.
Died in Mobile, October 6th, John Edwin Banta, aged twenty-two years.
Died in Montgomery, October 22nd, Mrs. Rufus Figh.
Died in Mobile, October 20th, Miss Libby C. Pearce.
Died in Huntsville, October 16th, W.A. McGaha.
Died in Tuscumbia, 16th inst., Georgia Evans.
Died in Tuscumbia, October 19th, Hattie Sloss Roland.
Died in Wetumpka, 7th inst., Rev. J.D. Williams, aged seventy-one years.
Died in Wetumpka, October 15th, John C. Miller, Sheriff of Elmore County.
Died in Tuskaloosa, 20th inst., John M. Hoyt.
Died near Montgomery, 21st inst., Mary Mathews Hughs, infant.
Died in Huntsville, October 28th, Mrs. Felicia Chapman, wife of ex-Governor Reuben Chapman.
Died in Perry County, October 8th, Jesse H. Lide.
Died in Cherokee County, October 23rd, Mrs. Virginia Tripp.
Died in Mobile, October 21st, Miss Minnie Edmondson.
Died in Mobile, October 18th, John Speake, infant.
Died in Camden, October 24th, Fulton Moore of Bourbon County, Kentucky.
Died in Camden, October 27th, Conrad Hoffman.
Died in Montgomery, October 29th, Thomas Bunting.
Died in Montgomery, October 29th, John Lawler.
Died in Montgomery, November 1st, S.C. Austin.
Died in Mobile, October 31st, Col. D. Belthoo?er.

# THE SOUTHERN ARGUS - DEATHS - JUNE 1869 THROUGH JUNE 1874

Died in Mobile, October 27th, Miss Zoe Atkins.
Died in Mobile, October 31st, Mrs. Libbie Tutill White.
Died in Mobile, October 31st, Henry T. Gunthorpe.
Died in Talladega, October 31st, Lillie P. McAfee, infant.
Died in Camden, October 7th, John Paul Wheadon.
Died near Evergreen, October 15th, Joel Adams, aged sixty years.
Died at Monroeville, October 6th, Mary Catherine ?ynes/Guynes/Haynes?.
Died near Benton, October 14th, John Edwards, aged forty-three years.
Died in Mobile, October 19th, Robt. L. Burfoot.
Died in Mobile, October 19th, Robt. Torrence.
Died at Spring Hill, near Mobile, recently, Mrs. Mary Berney Smith.
Died in Mobile, October 18th, Hugh McGonegal.
Died in Mobile, October 13th, David P. Ried.
Died at Pleasant Ridge, Green County, October 7th, Mary T. Steele.
Died in Gadsden on the 21st, Mrs. Oglesbie.
Died in Etowah County, recently, Rev. T.H. Whitby.
Died in Mobile on the 20th, Miss Libbie C. Pearce.
Died in Mobile on the 20th, Dr. Dabney Herndon, an eminent physician.
Died in Huntsville, October 21st, Elizabeth M. Coltart, infant.
Died in Mobile, October 15th, D.W. McGaughy, aged eight years.
Died in Mobile, October 18th, Thomas Hunt McGaughy, aged thirteen years.
Died in Mobile, October 18th, Mrs. Sarah Higgins.
Died in Mobile, October 25th, Michael B. Graham.
Died in Mobile, October 17th, Miss Laura Frank.
Died in Montgomery, October 29th, C. Remhard.
Died near Greenville, October 19th, Mary Jane Horn, four years old.
Died in Greenville, October 21st, F.M. Walker.
Died in Greenville, October 11th, Mrs. Elizabeth Bragg.
Died in Greenville, October 25th, James Ellington.
Died in Mobile, October 28th, Wm. Travis.
Died at Pollard, October 17th, Wm. Welsh.
Died in Eufaula, October 28th, J.J. Servatius.

Issue 11-11-1870

Died in East Selma, November 7th, Mrs. E.C. Stickle.
Died near Burnsville, November 7th, little Mollie, only daughter of E.P. Cothran.
Died in Limestone County, October 14th, Oscar Moyler Perry, infant.
Died in Huntsville, October 29th, Levi Emsell of Bloomville, Ohio.
Died in Mobile, November 4th, Margaret Weldon.
Died in Mobile November 4th, Chas. Lang.
Died in Evergreen, November 30th, S.F. Sharp.
Died in Evergreen, November 1st, Z.T. Christian.

## THE SOUTHERN ARGUS - DEATHS - JUNE 1869 THROUGH JUNE 1874

Died in Evergreen, October 29th, Isaac Smith.
Died near Beuna Vista, October 20th, Mrs. Caroline E. Rikard.
Died near Monroeville, recently Julia T. Nettles, infant.
Died in Huntsvill,e October 31st, Michael Callighan.
Died at Cross Keys, October 19th, Mrs. C. Louise, wife of J.D. Cottingham.
Died in Bullock County, October 29th, Dr. A.B. Brashear.
Died in Pickens County, October 10th, David S. Connerly.
Died October 12th, near Braggs, Edgar Moorer, aged about thirty years.
Died October 18th, near Braggs, Augustus Hobby, aged about nineteen years.
Died near Braggs, October 21st, a child of W.J. Underwood, aged about two years.
Died near Braggs, October 21st, two children of Mrs. J. Hobby, aged respectively two and four years.
Died near Braggs, October 26th, Willie, son of James Hobby, aged about seven years.
Died in Mobil,e November 1st, John Smith.
Died in Charlotte, North Carolina, October 26th, Dr. Jas. Young Bryce, brother of Dr. Peter Bryce of Tuskaloosa.
Died in Tuscumbia, October 26th, Edward Josephus Shackelford.

Monday was a week ago, a little son of W. A. Schoolar of Bibb County fell into a large pile of ginned cotton and smothered to death.

October 27th, W.G. Musten, a white man and democrat, tax collector for Pickens County, was murdered and robbed.

Issue 11-18-1870

Died in Durand's Bend, Friday, November 11th, Mrs. Sarah Bilberry. [See Harrell]
Died at his residence near Benton, Sunday, November 13th, Henry Gunn.

In a drunken frolic near Bellevue, Tuesday night, John Anderson, negro, was shot and killed by James Porter, negro.

Died near Cahaba on the 7th inst., Ann E.M. Walker, relict of the late Geo. Walker and the daughter of the late Uriah G. ??

Obituary. Death has again visited our community and claimed for its victim little Mollie, only daughter of E.P. and E.J. Cothran, aged four years......

Died in Opelika on the 8th, James T. McCoy.
Died in Marion on the 5th, Mrs. Rosanna Womble.

# THE SOUTHERN ARGUS - DEATHS - JUNE 1869 THROUGH JUNE 1874

Died in Monroe County, October 22nd, Eddie Hestle.
Died in Monroe County, October 24th, Mrs. Matilda Thompson.
Died in Greensboro, November 6th, Mrs. Eliza J. Hamilton.
Died in Perry County, November 5th, Mrs. Jane P. Jenkins.
Died in Jackson County, November 9th, Maj. G.W. Graham.
Died near Gainesville, October 19th, Mrs. Euphemia Mobley Chapman.
Died at Columbus, Kentucky, November 3rd, Dr. Benjamin Hunter of Green County.
Died in Sumter County, October 30th, Mary Julia Robertson.
Died in Mobile, November 14th, Wm. F. Parker.
Died in Gadsden, November 12th, infant child of Ed. Cox.
Died in Camden, October 26th, Robert Franklin Armstrong, infant.
Died in New York, November 11th, Mrs. S.E. Waring, wife of Moses Waring of Mobile.
Died in Mobile, November 12th, F. Ludeman.
Died in Mobile, November 11th, Rev. A. Laser.
Died in Colbert County, October 30th, James A. Huston.
Died in Limestone County a few weeks ago, Robert Rainey, a veteran of the War of 1812.
Died in Limestone County, October 31st, Lillie Beuford Tisdale, infant.
Died in Arkansas, October 9th, Dr. A.W. Jones, formerly of Limestone County, Alabama.
Died in Mobile, November 12th, Mrs. E.C. Benge.
Died in Mobile, November 11th, Pauline Norand.
Died in Talladega County, November 4th, Robert Jemison, Sr. aged eighty-two years.

Last week, Polk Green was killed in Talladega County by a man named Jordan.

Brother Stearns of the *Evergreen Observer* is recovering from a serious illness.

Married in Durand's Bend, November ? by Jerry Johnson, Esq., Mr. Harrell to Miss ? B.? Billberry?---the times of Tuesday last,----announcement of the death of Mrs. Harrell ---- the day after her marriage as above.

Issue 11-25-1870

On Dr. James Foster's plantation, in Bullock County, on the 15th, G.W. Hubert was killed by Joe Barker and Geo. Johnson. He was charged with seducing a sister of Barker's.

## THE SOUTHERN ARGUS - DEATHS - JUNE 1869 THROUGH JUNE 1874

On the 16th inst. in Greenville, Dr. T.D. Stallings was killed by Ransom Seale, in a street fight.

At Warrior Stand in Macon County last week, an old man named Boune was killed by one Morrison.

In Russell Circuit Court the other day, Peter Williams was guilty of murder in the second degree and sent to the penitentiary for ten years.

Col. Robert C. Forsyth, brother of Col. John Forsyth of the *Mobile Register*, died suddenly in Mobile on the 14th inst.

Stephenson Cobb of Green County was gored to death on the 11th by a cow which he had undertaken to drive out of his garden.

On the 15th inst., Charles A. Johnson of Greensboro was dragged on the ground, and fatally injured by a horse which he had fastened by a halter to his waist to lead him by.

Mr. A.C. Jackson died in Meridian, Mississippi, on the 10th inst., aged fifty-five years.

Issue 12-2-1870

Died in this vicinity on Friday the 25th inst., Charles Savary.

A.M. Sanford of the vicinity of Plantersville was found murdered on the city wharf last Saturday morning.

Mrs. Adah V. Webster, daughter of James R. Butler, deceased, of Pleasant Hill, Dallas County, after an illness of some weeks from consumption, fell asleep in the arms of her savior.

In Somerville on the 21st ult., Alexander King was killed by William Adkins.

Dr. Skegog, living near Leighton, shot killed his wife a few days ago.

The house of a Mr. Watson, in Marshall County, was burned a couple of weeks ago, and in it two idiot children.

Died in Mobile on the 24th ult., Mrs. Elizabeth J. Steele.
Died in Mobile on the 24th ult., Robinson Miller Ingersoll, infant.
Died in Mobile on the 20th ult., Mrs. Ann Stramler.
Died in Mobile on the 26th ult., Mrs. Jane Boyle.

# THE SOUTHERN ARGUS - DEATHS - JUNE 1869 THROUGH JUNE 1874

Died at Spring Hill, recently, Mrs. Nancy Ballard.
Died in Madison County on the 4th ult., Robert Hunt.
Died in Courtland on the 18th ult., little Mattie Acklen.
Died near Huntsville on the 18th ult., Theodore Acklen.
Died at Red Sulphur Springs on the 15th ult., Judge Fred Tate of Huntsville.
Died in Tuskaloosa on the 18th ult., Miss Mary Stillman.
Died in Camden, October 31st, Mrs. Caroline Matthews Forniss.
Died in Camden on the 24th ult., W.T. Wear, aged twenty-two years.
Died in Autaugaville on the 18th ult., Capt. J.H. Golson.
Died in Vienna, October 20th, Bettie Baxter Cook, infant.
Died in Bullock County on the 1st inst., Mrs. Josephine L. Walker.
Died at Lowndesboro on the 5th ult., Mrs Finnie Blair.
Died at Hayneville on the 19th ult., Miss Eugenia A. Witcher.
Died in Haynesville on the 23rd ult., D.D. Davis.
Died near Letohatchie on the 18th ult., Mr. Alderburg.
Died at McMaths on the 16th, Henry W. Nave of Jefferson County formerly of Marion.
Died in Henry County on the 5th, little Lizzie Smith.
Died in Tuskaloosa on the 19th, Mrs. Smith, aged about forty-seven.
Died at West Point on the 16th, Mrs. James Baker.
Died in Mobile on the 10th, George L. Cadliff.
Died in Mobile on the 1?th inst., Sallie B. Thurber.
Died in Mobile on the 18th, Mattie A. McGovern, infant.
Died in Tuscumbia October 22nd, little Wallace Barner.
Died in Florence on the 12th, Letitia C. Sloss, infant.
Died in Sumter County on the 8th, Mrs. Ellen Parker.
Died in Talladega County on the ?th, Mrs. Eveline Mauldin.

Dr. Howard and R.W. Russell of Lowndesboro each lost a child week before last.

?. C. Efurd, tried in the Barbour Circuit Court for killing Calvin Smoot, has been acquitted.

In Russell County on the 16th ult., Alfred Thompson was shot and killed by William Bray.

About a month ago, Thomas Atkins of Marshall County got one of his hands badly crushed in a cotton gin and died on the 12th ult. from the effects of the injury.

## THE SOUTHERN ARGUS - DEATHS - JUNE 1869 THROUGH JUNE 1874

Issue 12-9-1870

Mr. J.H. Brantly, recently of this vicinity, was assassinated at Macon, Mississippi, last Monday morning.

A dispatch from Macon, Mississippi, says that Mr. J.N. Eskridge of this vicinity had been arrested charged with killing J.H. Brantly, in that city, last Monday.

November 23rd, Greene Cone of Marion was found dead in his buggy in the road near Newberne. His death is attributed to epilepsy.

H.J. Walton, late of ?????, Montgomery County, was called to his door, one night about two weeks ago, and shot to death.

Wm. Thompson, an aged citizen of Lowndes, recently undertook to walk from Fort Deposit to his home seven miles distant, but wandered from the road and perished by the wayside.

Joe Lampkin was killed by Jack Clark, at Even Station, Bullock County, two weeks ago. Both negroes.

A negro cabin on the plantation of G.W. Bates, in Sumter County, was burned on the 23rd ult., and a child two or three years old perished in the flames.

Belden Reed, negro, was shot and killed the other day, in Mobile, by Henry Lindsey, negro.

J.L. Colby of Mobile committed suicide a few days ago.

November 25th, near Hurtville, Russell County, A.J. Harris was called to the gate, and shot five times. His wounds were mortal.

Issue 12-16-1870

Died in this city, last Monday, Mrs. Lewis, the mother of the late Honorable Dixon H. Lewis, Senator in Congress, aged eighty-six years.

At Society Hill, Russell County, on the 4th inst., J.J. Dumas was murdered by O.H. Field.

Capt. George Evans of Colbert County was thrown from his mule a few days ago and seriously injured.

## THE SOUTHERN ARGUS - DEATHS - JUNE 1869 THROUGH JUNE 1874

E.D. Duncan, formerly of Gadsden, was dangerously shot by a negro a short time ago.

Last week, Dr. Pennington of Coosa County was assassinated by one of his nephews.

Albert Bedell, a step-son of B.S. Barker of Livingston, was thrown from a horse last week and severely injured.

In the Butler Circuit Court last week, Sol Murphy and Bill Ashford were convicted of murder and the first was sentenced to death and the other to life imprisonment..

Died in Southington, Connecticut, November 17th, Lewis B. Langdon, formerly of Marion, Alabama.
Died in Marion, November 26th, Mrs. M.E. Thompson.
Died in Marion, November 28th, Wm. King, son of Major and Mrs. W.B. Modawell.

Near Bragg's Store, November 17th, Levy Hobdy.

Died in Perry County, November 28th, Emma Eugenia Stoudenmire, infant.
Died at Lowndesboro, November ?0th, Mrs. Robert W. Russell.
Died in Union Springs, November 27th, John W. Basken.
Died in Union Springs, November 27th, S.J. Humphries.
Died in Oxford, November 26th, Mrs. Amanda F., wife of Samuel Morgan.
Died in Marengo County, November 7th, Mrs. Priscilla Aldridge.
Died near Clinton, Greene County, November 28th, J.M. Spencer.
Died in Clinton, November 23rd, James R. Pettigrew.
Died in Forkland, November 23rd, Miss Anna High.
Died at Union, November 10th, John G. Brown.
Died in Hale County, November 18th, Mrs. Elizabeth Roberts.
Died in Hale County, November 9th, Mrs. F. Wynne.
Died in Mobile, November 20th, little Charlie Winters.
Died in Pike County, November 16th, Mrs. Nancy Ballard.
Died in Pike County, November 17th, Miss Fannie J. Brady.
Died in Jacksonville, Mrs. Andrew Adams.
Died in Huntsville, December 1st, Saml. Clark, Jr.
Died in Huntsville, December 1st, Mrs. Eliza Ann Dyer.
Died in Columbus, Mississippi, a short time since, Jesse W. Bryan, formerly of Pickens County.
Died in Opelika on the 25th ult., Mr. McClure, aged eighty-eight years.
Died in Mobile, November 30th, David L. McClure.

## THE SOUTHERN ARGUS - DEATHS - JUNE 1869 THROUGH JUNE 1874

Died at Nashville, Tennessee, November 22nd, Maj. W.A. Clare, a native of Tuskaloosa.
Died in Jackson a few days ago, Frank Proctor.
Died in Wilcox County, November 26th, A.S. Crum.
Died in Mobile, November 27th, Anne Elizabeth Shields, infant.
Died in Demopolis, November 29th, Edward James Halpin.
Died in Gainesville, November 30th, Mrs. Reavis, wife of Turner Reavis.
Died in Mobile, December 8th, Miss Virginia Coyle.
Died near Greensboro, December 4th, Kezia Eudora Kinnaird, infant.
Died in Yazoo County, Mississippi, on the 17th ult., Captain Clifton Walker, son of Hon. Pope Walker.
Died in Texas, October 30th, H.D. Tipton, formerly of Jackson County, Alabama.
Died in Cherokee County, November 30th, Abel Roberts.
Died in Mobile on the 7th, Mrs. Caroline A. Shelton.
Died in Mobile on the 6th, G.O. Warren, infant.
Died in Mobile on the 5th, Mrs. Sarah Ellen Waring.
Died in Mobile on the 5th, James C. Browne.
Died in Mobile on the 9th, Richard P. Giles.
Died in Starksville, Mississippi, November 28th, Mrs. Mary E. Sellers, daughter of W.M. Crenshaw of Limestone County.
Died near Pickensville, November 23rd, Norman Evans.
Died in Marion, December 13th, after a long and painful illness, Miss Anna Huntingdon, daughter of William H. Huntingdon.
Died in Mobile on the 10th, Pichard Perry Giles.
Died in Mobile on the 10th, Jas. E/F Joiner.

Last Thursday night, in Mobile, George Wall was killed by Frank E. Spencer.

On the 1st inst., Anderson Whitman, negro, was shot and mortally wounded, by Edenboro Graham, negro, in Lowndes County.

On the 3rd inst., near Farmersville, Osborn King, negro, was shot and killed by Charley Bennett, negro.

Issue 12-23-1870

In Madison County, a few days ago, Frank Calhoun, negro, was killed by John Adams.

Died in Madison County, December 10th, Mrs. Amanda M. Davidson.
Died in Huntsville, December 14th, J.J. Hardman.
Died in Huntsville, December 6th, Dannie Martin, aged four years.
Died in Choctaw County, November 9th, Mrs. Susan Lightfoot Fluker Ward.

# THE SOUTHERN ARGUS - DEATHS - JUNE 1869 THROUGH JUNE 1874

Died near Benton, December 8th, J.J. Barlow.
Died in Union Springs, December 13th, Benjamin Baskin.
Died in Dadeville, recently, Colonel J.A. Vaughan.
Died in Limestone County, December 3rd, Mrs. Peete.
Died in Limestone County, December 10th, Jacob Peete.
Died in Calhoun County on the 17th, William Whisenant.
Died in Pickens County, November 15th, William D. Fitzgerald.
Died in Mobile, December 17th, William Warner.
Died in Montgomery, last Tuesday, Henry P. Lee.

Issue 12-30-1870

The *Elyton Sun* is draped in mourning for the late Dr. Earle, a noble and good man.

Chas. T. Mills, late of this city, conductor on the Selma, Rome & Dalton Road, accidentally fell from the cars last Monday, at Pinson's Depot and was killed.

Within a few weeks four of the oldest citizens of Pickens County, Green W. Wilder, J.M. Benson, Calvin Taylor and John A. Holder, have died.

Mitchell M. Davis of Cherokee County was shot down by the roadside and killed on the 18th by some negroes, two of whom, it is reported, have since been captured and hung.

Died in Elyton on the 20th, Dr. S.S. Earle, one of the most eminent men in the County.
Died in Limestone County on the 20th, Dr. Van B. Gilbert.
Died near Livingston on the 10th, Mrs. Sarah L. Lake.
Died in Madison County, November 9th, Josie Lee Bowhannon, aged seven years.
Died in Talladega on the 17th, Jesse Fair, aged seventy-six years.
Died in Montgomery, last week, Mrs. Rebecca Holt.
Died in Hayneville on the 15th, Eugene William Renalde, infant.
Died near Lowndesboro on the 13th, Mrs. Philip M. Balzegar.
Died in Mobile on the 10th, Mrs. Keziah Heilen/Hellen.
Died in Lebanon on the 15th, Dr. J.H. Pursley.
Died in Prattville on the 26th, Danuel Hall.

An old man named Harris, living near Montgomery, was killed, his wife was badly hurt, and a little negro living with them was wounded, last Sunday morning, by parties unknown, whose object is supposed to have been robbery.

## THE SOUTHERN ARGUS - DEATHS - JUNE 1869 THROUGH JUNE 1874

Dr. W.B.R. Melford, a professor in the medical college at Richmond, Virginia died on the 27th.

Mrs. Corcoran of Washington City, daughter of Hon. James B. Beck of Kentucky, married about a month ago, is dead.

Issue 1-6-1871

Died in Greensboro, December 25th, Samuel Cowin.

In Jackson County, two weeks ago, Bud Peaks was killed by a Mr. Guess, who was acquitted by an examining court.

Watt Teer is in jail in Pickens County, charged with the murder of William G. Mustin.

Henry Mack, a negro of desperate character, has been arrested in Montgomery, charged with complicity in the murder of Amos Harris.

Gabe Wright, family, and mother-in-law of Rome, Georgia, were lost on the *Nick Wall*.

Benjamin S. Lippincott, one of the most prominent of the early California pioneers, died a few weeks ago.

W. Rucker, late of Clark County, Kentucky, was murdered, in Baldwin County, Mississippi, December 13th.

A.S. Wood, a member of the Mississippi Legislature, committed suicide a few days ago, in the Jackson lunatic asylum.

Allen Battle, negro, is in the Montgomery Jail, charged with the murder of Alfred Sampson, negro.

Rev. Albert Barnes died in Philadelphia on the 24th of December, aged seventy-two years.

Rev. Simon Tucker, the Hebrew Rabbi in charge of the Reformed Temple in Memphis, died December 31st.

Issue 1-13-1871

On the 3rd inst., a Miss Bush was killed by the falling of a tree, near Greenville.

# THE SOUTHERN ARGUS - DEATHS - JUNE 1869 THROUGH JUNE 1874

A week or two ago in Blountville, Frank Burgess was mortally wounded with a knife in the hands of Lewis Ketchum.

A few days ago, a daughter of E. Cobb of Madison County, aged twelve years, was fatally burned by her clothes catching fire.

Alexander Fryer of Perote, Pike County, was killed on the 2nd inst. by the running away of a pair of horses he was driving. He had been married only two weeks.

A Mr. Massingill, aged sixty-four years, was found frozen to death, on the night of December 23rd, at Hickory Grove, Alabama.

A fellow named Motes, living near Mt. Willing, on the 2nd inst., shot and killed a negro named Perry Reese.

Died in Montgomery County on the 6th inst., David Browder.
Died in Colbert County, December 31st, Mrs. Martha A. Rather.
Died in Tuscumbia, December 29th, Thomas Burton.
Died in Barbour County, a few days ago, Mrs. Phoeby Rachels, aged one hundred sixteen years.
Died in Athens, January 3rd, Hellen Brittle.
Died in Limestone County, January 3rd, Mrs. J.D. Beauchamp.
Died in Limestone County, December 23rd, Mrs. Rebecca Elliott.
Died in Tuskaloosa, January 2nd, Thomas H. Ralph.
Died in Jefferson County, from injuries received in being thrown from a wagon, Daniel Anderson.
Died in Montgomery, January 9th, Mrs. Robert A. Beall.
Died in Evergreen, December 28th, Joseph D. Lundy.
Died in Evergreen, January 2nd, D.R. Thomas.
Died in Marion on the 5th inst., W.M. Anthony, a student at Howard College.
Died in Greenville, December 17th, James S. Adams.
Died near Farmersville, December 24th, F. Blackman of meningitis.
Died near Farmersville, December 24th, Wm. Landford of meningitis.
Died in Huntsville, January 4th, Mrs. Martha A. Gill.
Died in Livingston, January 2nd, Daniel L. Ayers.
Died in Eutaw, December 23rd, Laman Marx.
Died in Eutaw, January 3rd, P. Schoppert.
Died in Cherokee County, December 26th, Mrs. Rosanna Daniel.
Died in Colbert County, January 4th, H. Seeforth.
Died in Pike County, J.B. Clayton of Brier Hill, R.E. Park of Orion, and Dr. J.B. Fannen of Troy.

## THE SOUTHERN ARGUS - DEATHS - JUNE 1869 THROUGH JUNE 1874

Issue 1-20-1871

Near Union, Greene County on the 8th inst., W.E. Jones was shot and dangerously wounded by his nephew W.T. Jones.

Maj. Edwin Hickman, once of Huntsville, for several years Mayor of Memphis, died in San Antonio, Texas, December 19th.

Issue 1-27-1871

Died in Pleasant Hill on the evening of the 16th inst., Mr. S.G. Underwood, in the thirty-second year of his age, leaving a devoted mother and friends to mourn their early loss, and his darling Janie, who wiped away the deep-damp from his brow even to his latest breath, to bear her sad bereavement, and to act as guardian angel to minister to the two little ones left with her.

A young man named Tanner was accidentally shot at Attalla a couple of weeks ago.

In the vicinity of Munford, Christmas morning, a man named Jones was burned so that he died a few days afterwards.

David, son of Dr. D.R. Lindsay of Florence, was severely wounded on the 15th by the accidental discharge of a shotgun.

In a shooting scrape eight miles from Athens, two weeks ago, over a crop settlement, a negro named Henry Gregory [see Allison 2-3-1871] and a white man named Bill Allison shot each other, inflicting mortal wounds.

At Blue Pond, Cherokee County, on the 12th, in a drunken frolic, a young man named Arter was shot and killed by a man named Whit.

On the 11th inst., Mr. Sims, living near Ramsey's Station, lost three children by death from meningitis.

John A. Aiken, aged eighty-two years, died in Floyd County, Georgia, last Friday.

Senate---Resolutions in relation to the death of Hon. W.P. Chilton were adopted.
    House---A message from the Governor was received announcing the death of ex-Chief Justice Chilton.
    Dr. J.H. Thompson of Talladega, is Grand Master of Masons in this state since the death of W.P. Chilton.

## THE SOUTHERN ARGUS - DEATHS - JUNE 1869 THROUGH JUNE 1874

Capt. H.A. Gartrell of Rome died in Atlanta on the 19th inst.

Gen. George D. Johnson has been quite ill in Marion.

At Gadsden, two weeks ago, Drs. Bevans of Lottwich, and Petty, extracted a minnie ball from the hip of John Riley, where it was lodged May 22nd, 1863, in an action on the Jackson Road, near Vicksburg.

William Barrett, aged eighty years, one of the wealthiest men of Richmond, was fatally burned on the 20th.

E.C. Delevan, the great apostle of temperance in America, died in Schenectudy, New York, on the 18th inst.

A clue has at last been obtained and the "Nathan" murderer is certain to be speedily arrested.

Judge Byron Payne of the Supreme Court of Wisconsin, died on the 17th inst.

Issue 2-3-1871

Died near Summerfield last Monday, William M. Russell, aged about sixty-seven years. Mr. Russell, when quite young came to this county with his father in 1816, and settled in what is now East Selma.

Flora, a former slave of Charles Dupree, died in Cherokee County, December 24th, aged about one hundred twenty years.

W.D. Allison of Limestone County, who killed a negro [see Smith 1-27-1871] at Harris' Station, January 16th, has died of the wounds he received at the same time.

Wilkins, a stone mason employed by the Alabama and Chattanooga railroad, was run over near Elyton last week, by a train and fatally injured.

In Bullock County, a short time ago, Stephen Gates, an old man, was dangerously and perhaps mortally stabbed by parties whose names are not given.

One Kennedy, confined in Dale County Jail for murder, escaped a few days ago.

Kelso and McPherson, white men, confined in the Butler Jail, one for murder and the other for rape, made an ineffectual effort to escape a few nights ago.

## THE SOUTHERN ARGUS - DEATHS - JUNE 1869 THROUGH JUNE 1874

Issue 2-10-1871

In Memoria: At a regular communication of Marengo Lodge, #28, F. and A.M., held at Dayton, Alabama, on the 5th day of February, 1871, announcement being made of the death of William P. Chilton, M.W. Grand Master of the Grand Lodge of the State of Alabama...

Died at Tensas, January 19th, Tobe Echols.
Died in Cherokee County, January 11th, Miss Sallie Sharp.
Died in Pickens County, January 10th, Miss Clara Howard.
Died in Meridian, Mississippi, on the 8th, L.Y. Tarrant of Marion.
Died in Troy, January 12th, a child of Mrs. L.B. Soles.
Died at Orion, January 1st, R.E. Park.
Died in Tuscumbia, January 17th, Mrs. Jacintha McKay.
Died in Tuscumbia, January 12th, James Halsey, aged eighty-seven years.
Died at Sandy Ridge, January 12th, E.M. Roper.
Died in Mobile, recently, James Conning, aged sixty years.
Died in Montgomery on the 18th, James Terry Smith.
Died in Montgomery, January 20th, Mary Jane Trimble.
Died in Greene County, December 31st, Mrs. Josephine Phillips.
Died in Greene County, December 18th, Macon Phillips.
Died in Greene County, January 2nd, Mrs. Eliza J. Mahaffey.
Died in Greene County, December 20th, Miss Mary Chiles.
Died at Pleasant Ridge, Greene County, recently, infant of Mr. and Mrs. Abston.
Died in or near Auburn, January 12th, J.T. Scott.
Died in Barbour County, January 19th, Aaron Thomas.
Died in Macon County, December 23rd, Dr. W.R. Cunningham.
Died at Benton, January 20th, W.L. Staggers.
Died near Jefferson, Marengo County, January 4th, Mrs. Francis Rawls.
Died in Camden, January 8th, Col. Milton Jenkins.
Died at Spring Hill, January 22nd, Thomas J. Fettyplace.
Died in Mobile, January 23rd, A.B. Wright.
Died in Mobile, January 28th, Mrs. Caroline Roulston.
Died in Montgomery, January 20th, William P. Chilton.
Died in Mobile, January 20th, Fanny Webb Posey, infant.
Died in Tallahatchie County, Mississippi, January 14th, T.C. Keith of Athens, Alabama.
Died in Wilcox County, recently, Matthew Wright, aged sixty-one years.
Died at Pine Apple, January 21st, Jefferson Carte.
Died in New Market, December 24th, Cara Hambrick, infant.
Died at Fayetteville, Tennessee, January 16th, Mrs. Ann Feeney, formerly of Huntsville.
Died in Tuscumbia, January 1st, Mrs. Eleanor Weatherford.

## THE SOUTHERN ARGUS - DEATHS - JUNE 1869 THROUGH JUNE 1874

Died at Lentzville, January 5th, Benj. F. Hargrove.
Died in Coosa County, January 5th, John Connoway.
Died in Mobile, January 13th, Mrs. Margaret Kelly.
Died in Mobile, January 13th, Charles W. Hooks.

On the 1?th ult., J.C. Rupert of Pollard was thrown from the cow catcher of a train on which he was riding, whereby his leg was broken.

Issue 2-17-1871

Died in Huntsville, January 29th, Woodson Withers White, infant.
Died in DeKalb County, January 18th, Col. Wm. O. Winston.
Died near Bladon Springs, January 26th, Jane Wave Lenoir, infant.
Died in Mobile February 1st, Mrs. Catharine Ayers.
Died in Mobile, February 5th, Malon G. Keys.
Died in Pickens County, January 16th, Maj. John D. Johnson.
Died in Huntsville, February 2nd, Miss Amanda J. Carmichael.
Died in Hale County, January 10th, Capt. J.W. Baker.
Died in Greensboro, February 9th, Mrs. Eliza M. Erwin.
Died at Canton Bend, January 8th, Daniel Smith.
Died at Canton Bend, January 16th, Duncan C. Smith
Died in Perry County, January 25th, Mrs. Elizabeth Barton.
Died in Mobile, February 11th, Augustus Brooks.
Died in Mobile, February 12th, Albert Baker Carver.
Died in Hayneville, February 7th, Lafayette Renaldi, infant.
Died in Limestone County, January 26th, Wesley A. Gray.

John Lee, who lived in Etowah County, was shot one night last week, and afterward taken from his house and hung.

C. Moates of Butler County, was tried before Judge Watson a few days ago for killing a negro in Lowndes County in January last. Verdict self-defense.

The widow of Luke, killed at Cross Plains, has sued Calhoun County, under the Ku Klux law, for $5,000 for the alleged killing of her husband by disguised men.

Issue 2-24-1871

Obituary-- God has come very near to the people of Summerfield within the past few months, and spoken earnestly to his church here. Mrs. Dr. Vaughan has been taken from our midst. Her death occurred on the 27th of January 1871... Mrs. Vaughan was the daughter of the Hon. William J. Alston... His daughters, reared under such circumstances would of course be intelligent

## THE SOUTHERN ARGUS - DEATHS - JUNE 1869 THROUGH JUNE 1874

and attractive; but Mrs. Vaughn was naturally lovely... Orphan children and devoted husband... A.H. Mitchell *New Orleans Christian Advocate*, please copy.

Died in this city on the 20th, John H. P. Heinz, infant son of Mrs. P. Heinz.

The skeleton of a man was found a few days ago near Uniontown in a jungle of sugar corn. It is supposed to be the remains of an Irishman named Tony who suddenly disappeared some time since from that neighborhood.

C.R. Woods and James Herring, two old citizens of Eufaula, have recently died.

On the 2nd inst., a little son of Wright Flowers of Barbour County, was caught by the gin band and so mutilated as to cause his death.

Col. J.R. Stevens of Rome, Georgia, committed suicide on the 11th inst.

Mrs. Deale, formerly Miss Adeline Windham, of Tuskaloosa, died a short time ago in Mississippi.

J.B. Land of Collingsville is dangerously ill.

Lawrence Berry (negro) committed suicide in Mobile the other day.

On the 10th inst., Mr. and Mrs. Hill, married the evening before, were thrown from a buggy, in Athens, and were seriously injured.

Issue 3-3-1871

Died in this city, February 25th, Eugene ?, son of H.M. and S.K. White.

Last Monday, the body of W.W. Williams was found, drowned in Valley Creek, at the S.& M.R.R. bridge. Mr. Williams was a comparative stranger here, employed at the time of his disappearance by the Southern Express Company. He had been missing several days; and it is supposed he committed suicide in a fit of mental aberration.

Died near Forkland, Greene County, January 26th, Mrs. Ann E. Goss.
Died in Huntsville, February 10th, infant son of Mr. and Mrs. J.F. Brown.
Died in Perry County, January 20th, Jabez Curry.
Died in Mobile, February 15th, Mrs. L.G. Eastin.
Died in Eufaula, February 11th, R.C. Woods.
Died in Eufaula, February 9th, James Herring.

# THE SOUTHERN ARGUS - DEATHS - JUNE 1869 THROUGH JUNE 1874

Died in Mobile, February 8th, Dr. R. Miller.
Died in South Carolina, recently, Mrs. Ferrie Henshaw.
Died in Montgomery, February 18th, Mrs. Charles Bohlea.
Died near Union, Greene County, February ??, Thomas Colvin, aged seventy-three years.
Died near Clinton, Greene County, recently, Mrs. Virginia E. Thomas.
Died in Tuskaloosa County, February 14th, W.P. Hickman.
Died near Mt. Hebron, February 16th, Ossie N. Jolly, infant.
Died in Hillsboro, Arkansas, January 9th, Dr. J.O. Thompson, formerly of Wilcox County, Alabama.
Died near Coleraine, February 16th, Mrs. Horace D. Rast.
Died at Whitehall Station, February 14th, Mrs. Sarah E. White.
Died near Fort Deposit, week before last, Thomas E. Gurley.
Died in Montgomery, recently, Col. Jack Thorington.
Died near Centre, February 11th, J.B. Jones, aged eighty years.
Died near Centre, February 20th, Pleasant Whitecotton.
Died in Hale County, February 20th, A.B. Drake.
Died near Prospect, February 17th, F.A. Brown.
Died near Tuscumbia, February 16th, Charley H. Huston.
Died in Florence, February 10th, Andrew Amonett.
Died in Tuscumbia, February 22nd, Mrs. Margaret A. Connine.
Died in Cherokee, February 18th, G.W. Malone.
Died near Elkmont, February 15th, Thomas David Holmes, aged seven years.

Dr. J.W. Knight, an eminent surgeon of Louisville, died on the 19th ult.

Elder Curtis J. Smith, an eminent divine, died at his residence near Frankfort, Kentucky, on the 22nd ult.

Joe Johnson, negro, who killed Henry Walton last December, near Pike Road station, on the M. and E. railroad, has been arrested in Columbus, Georgia and will be brought to Montgomery.

Thompson H. McMahon, a leading banker of Galveston, Texas died on the 27th ult.

Gen. Arnold Elzy, of the late Confederate Army, died in Baltimore on the 22nd ult.

Issue 3-10-1871

Col. Jack Thorington is not dead, as reported some days ago by the *Montgomery Advertiser*.

## THE SOUTHERN ARGUS - DEATHS - JUNE 1869 THROUGH JUNE 1874

NEW LAWS: Acts passed by the General Assembly and approved by the Governor, to March 2nd:
To enable John Y. Kilpatrick, administrator of the estate of R.H. Kilpatrick, late of Monroe County, deceased, to sell, either at public or private sale, the residence and medical office owned by said deceased at the time of his death and make title to the same.
To be entitled an act to remove the administration of the estate of John C. Judkins, Sen., from the County of Macon, into the Probate Court of Montgomery County.
To authorize Mrs. Elizabeth Amanda Mabrey, administratrix of the estate of Joshua R. Mabrey, deceased, to sell certain lands in Dale County.
To authorize Mary E. Levie, widow and relict of James H. Levie, to sell and convey by deed certain lands therein named.
To authorize the executrix of the last will and testament of F.S. Denson, deceased, to sell certain land at private sale.
For the relief of James H. Booth, as administrator of the estate of Benjamin F. Boon.
To make an appropriation to pay the funeral expenses of the late Hon. J.F. Morton, deceased.
For the relief of the widow and heirs of David Owen, deceased.
For the relief of Richard H. Clarke as administrator of the estate of William A. Christian, deceased, in the County of Marengo.
To authorize Theodore L. Guerry and William Harrison, citizens of the State of Georgia, to qualify in Alabama as executors of the will of James Harrison, deceased.
To authorize certain proceedings in relation to the real estate of John T. Smith, deceased, within and near the city of Opelika.

Died in Calhoun County, February 27th, William Alonzo Pruett, infant.
Died in Eutaw, February 27th, Mrs. Elizabeth Gilbert.
Died in Sumter County, February 14th, Florence Monette McKerrall, infant.
Died in Morgan County, February 2nd, Mrs. Virginia A. Johnson.
Died in Monroeville, January ??, Henrietta Archer.
Died in Huntsville, February 2?, C.W. Strong.
Died in Mobile, March 1st, Rev. Bishop James Osgood Andrew.
Died in Troy, February 23rd, Mrs. J.A. Benton.
Died in Pike County, February 26th, Mrs. Eli Ford.
Died in Tuskaloosa County, recently, Willis Willingham.
Near Owen's Cross Roads, Madison County, February 17th, Joseph Chapman was shot severely by A.M. Nabors.

February 28th, Jacob Hauser of Mobile County was murdered in his own store.

# THE SOUTHERN ARGUS - DEATHS - JUNE 1869 THROUGH JUNE 1874

Issue 3-17-1871

Fayette Bates, negro, was drowned in the Chickasabigue, near Linden, Monday night of last week.

Ed. Mills, formerly of Boston, committed suicide in Choctaw County a few days ago.

Died in Wetumpka, last week, Mrs. N.W. Green.
Died in Mobile, for the week ending March 11th: Wilmer Forss, George B. Rain, Elizabeth Pollard, G.W. Miller, Mrs. Matilda Cotehett, George Kapahn (infant), Barney Tobey, William James, Amme Secor Garner.
Died near Clinton, February 1st, Mrs. Virginia E. Thomas.
Died near Eutaw on the 4th inst., Willis H. Patten, infant.
Died in Eufaula on the 6th inst., Mrs. Elizabeth McLean.
Died near Huntsville, March 10th, C.D. Williams.
Died in Mobile, March 9th, Mrs. Julia A. Turner.
Died in Bossieur Parish, Louisiana, February 7th, Garrett L. Sandidge, formerly of Madison County, Alabama.
Died in Talladega, March 12th, James Houston Isbell, infant son of Thomas L. and Mattie J. Isbell.

Issue 3-24-1871

Hall of Phoenix Fire Co. Whereas, it hath pleased Almighty God to remove from our midst our friend and brother, Samuel P. Stoddard, one of the oldest members of this company...

C. B. Williams, an old citizen of Madison County, was buried last week.

Prince Green has been sentenced to the penitentiary from Talladega for seven years for killing Jesse Cox.

Adam Herd, Jr., was drowned, some time ago, in attempting to cross the creek at Schmidt & Harmen's Mill in Talladega County.

Isaac E. Young, an old and respected citizen of Tuscumbia, was seized with apoplexy while talking with some friends last week, and died in ten minutes.

William Stillings of Marion, who was so brutally assaulted about six weeks ago by a negro burglar, died last week Saturday and was buried the next day.

Dr. Steadman, former clerk of Clay County, is lying dangerously ill at his residence near Ashland from the effects of a fall from his horse.

## THE SOUTHERN ARGUS - DEATHS - JUNE 1869 THROUGH JUNE 1874

At Evans' Mills, Escambia County, on the 13th, a man named Lowry was killed by one named Franklin.

At Carter's Mill, Conecuh County, recently, Noah Daw was seriously, perhaps fatally, injured in a fight with N.B. Lassiter.

Dr. Wise, merchant at Thompson's Station, on the Montgomery and Eufaula Railroad, was called to the door, a few nights ago, and shot and wounded by unknown parties.

### DIED IN ALABAMA

Died in Greene County on the 2nd inst., infant daughter of Mrs. S.J. Brown.
Died in Opelika on the 13th inst., C. Echols.
Died at Childersburg on the 12th inst., Rev. E.C. Odum.
Died in Clayton on the 10th inst., Mrs. Elizabeth F. Glenn.
Died at Whitesburg on the 5th inst., Mrs. Elizabeth Jane Rayford.
Died in Jefferson County, February 28th, Stephen Hodge.
Died in Madison County on the 13th inst., Dr. G.S. Nuckolls.
Died in Madison County on the 15th inst., Leroy P. McCrary.
Died in Waco, Texas, recently, Dr. John Houston, formerly of Lauderdale County.
Died in Tuscumbia on the 11th, Isaac E. Young.
Died in Claiborne Parish, Louisiana, recently, Josiah Barron, formerly of Chambers County, Alabama.

At Cross Plains on the 16th at Robinson's circus, a difficulty occurred in which a Mr. Keith was shot through the thigh, John Neighbors cut in the arm, Shields Keith cut on the hand, a horse shot, and several bruises given.

In the vicinity of Opelika on the 12th inst., John Elliott, negro, shot and wounded a white woman named Sallie McSquirt.

Issue 3-31-1871

George Richardson, a student at Florence, was accidentally drowned on the 21st inst.

The body of John McAllister, drowned in the Alabama River a few days ago, was recovered last week, at Dutch Bend, eight miles below where the accident happened, carried ashore there and buried.

In the vicinity of Clayton, recently, D.J. Prather and John Turner had a shooting scrape, in which the former was badly wounded.

## THE SOUTHERN ARGUS - DEATHS - JUNE 1869 THROUGH JUNE 1874

James E. Warren and John Glass had a shooting affair near Mt. Andrew, in which the latter got a ball in his shoulder.

### DIED IN ALABAMA

Died at Enon, Alabama, recently, Jeff Seals of Tennessee.
Died in Texas, February 18th, P. Graves Rogers, formerly of Lowndes County.
Died in Montgomery on the 18th inst., William Frazier.
Died in Coosa County on the 6th inst., Thomas Bazemore.
Died in Arizona Territory, February 18th, John Prentice, formerly of Mobile.
Died in Marion on the 12th inst., Catharine Woodfin, aged eighty years.
Died in Perry County on the 20th inst., Abner E. Benson, aged fifty years.
Died in Butler County on the 17th inst., Mrs. Eliza O'Gwynn.
Died in Greenville, recently, infant child of A.M. Goldsmith.
Died in Greensboro on the 21st inst., B. O'Donnell.
Died in Georgetown, District of Columbia, recently, Ben. F. Ficklin, formerly of Greensboro.
Died in Dadeville on the 20th inst., A.G. Adams.
Died in Chambers County on the 19th inst., Mrs. Elizabeth Susan Blakely.
Died in Montgomery on the 24th, Annie E. Blue.
Died in Clay County a few days ago, Dr. Marshal Stedham.
Died in Limestone County on the 19th, Ezekiel Hughey.
Died in Reswill(Roswell ?), Georgia on the 14th inst., infant daughter of W.A. and Nina J. Hansell, formerly of Huntsville.
Died in Mobile on the 23d, Richard Maxwell.
Died in Mobile on the 14th inst., Geo. H. Western.
Died in Montgomery on the 20th inst., Mrs. Henry Horton.
Died near Arlington on the 26th inst., Frank Burgess, in the sixty-first year of his age.
Died in Montgomery on the 28th inst., Mrs. Elizabeth Lowther, aged eighty-three years.
Died in Tuskaloosa on the 27th inst., Mrs. Matilda Whitfield.

On the 14th, in Pickens County, Thomas W. Joy was shot and killed by W.M. Gresham, who was held in the sum of one thousand dollars to answer at the term of the Circuit Court.

### Issue 4-7-1871

Died in Athens, March 26th, Cornie Clayton Hoffman.
Died near Elkmont, March 16th, Johnnie, son of A.P. and J.A. Davis.
Died in Montgomery, March 21st, Annie E., daughter of Rev. O.R. Blue.
Died in Gadsden, March 27th, Mrs. B.T. Pope.
Died in Tuskaloosa, 2nd ult., Mrs. Matilda Whitfield.

# THE SOUTHERN ARGUS - DEATHS - JUNE 1869 THROUGH JUNE 1874

Died in Mobile, 30th ult., James Watt.
Died at Bladen Springs, 27th ult., W.R. Adams, Secretary of the New Orleans and Texas Railroad.
Died in Bellefonte, recently, M.L. Swan.

## Issue 4-14-1871

Obituary: Mrs. Charles Lewis... She was the youngest daughter of the late Dr. George Phillips, one of the early pioneers of Middle Alabama and, at the time of his death, one among the most respected and valued citizens of Dallas County. She was born in Shelby County, November 1818, and died at her late residence in this city, on the 28th ultimo, in the fifty-third year of her age.

On Monday last, Henry Thompson, a stevedore, committed suicide in Mobile.

Last Saturday at 11 o'clock a.m., Dr. L. Martinez of Whistler was shot and instantly killed while sitting in his own office by one George Hahn of Quitman, Mississippi, aided and abetted by Charles Gage and Dr. Sanders of the same place. There was a woman in the case.

In Mobile County, the other day, W.B. Spencer was accidentally shot and killed by his step-father, W.L. Brown.

Peter Carter, negro, is in jail in Pike County, for killing Lewis Lawson, negro.

Charles Peterson, negro, was killed in Eufaula, April 31st, by a man named Sawyers.

In Limestone County, recently, one Caldwell, charged with horse stealing, while resisting arrest, was shot and seriously wounded by Deputy Sheriff Lowell.

## DIED IN ALABAMA

Died in Benton, March 30th, John Dudley, Sr.
Died near Bragg's Store, March 29th, E. Whittle.
Died in Greenville, April 4th, Mrs. Passion Medley.
Died near Oak Bowery, April 5th, John Allen Jones.
Died in Montgomery, March 31st, L. McKinney.
Died in Talladega, March 30th, Miss Addie Best.
Died in Jefferson County, recently, Arthur Truss.
Died in Montgomery, March 29th, Mrs. Joseph H. Bradford.
Died in Gadsden, March 30th, Mrs. B.T. Pope.
Died in Pickens County, March 25th, Archibald Hood, aged seventy-four years.

## THE SOUTHERN ARGUS - DEATHS - JUNE 1869 THROUGH JUNE 1874

Died in Mobile on the 8th inst., Mamie, daughter of Capt. Frank S. Stone.
Died in Mobile on the 6th inst., Perry B. Cayce.
Died in White Plains, March 31st, Dr. J.P. Evins, aged seventy-seven years.
Died near Georgiana on the 2nd inst., N.O. World.
Died in Butler County, on the 2nd inst., Thomas, son of William Ashford.
Died in Mobile on the 2nd inst., Anna Eliza O'Conner, aged seven years.
Died in Mobile on the 7th inst., Charles H. Bostwick.
Died near Tuskaloosa, March 26th, Miss Julia A. Blount.
Died in Tuskegee a few days ago, Capt. Robert A. Peterson, late of the 61st Regiment, Alabama Volunteers.
Died in Marion on the 11th, Dr. J.F. Knight.
Died near Kilpatrick's Station on the 11th, Mrs. George Stowers.
Died in Chambers County on the 7th, Mrs. W.L. Wilson.
Died at Woodstock, Tuskaloosa County, on the 30th ult., Mrs. Laura J. Ray.

Mrs. Cobb, near Milford, Sanford County, was recently outraged and then murdered by a negro.
The negro, by whom Mrs. Cobb of Sanford County was outraged and murdered, has been hung. A Ku Klux outrage.

### Issue 4-21-1871

W.J. Gilmore, Superintendent of Education for Choctaw County, (one of the assassins, we believe, of Newell E. Thomas) had his house burned the other night, and $6,000 of school money was burned up in it!

Saturday of last week, Mrs. Margaret Higgins of Athens committed suicide by jumping into a well.

The boiler of Harwell's mill, at Ramsey's Station, on the Gainesville Railroad, exploded last Saturday was a week ago, killing Mr. Riley, the engineer, and seven negroes, and wounding several.

Mrs. Thomas Green was thrown from a buggy near Bellville on Saturday of last week and was seriously injured.

### DIED IN ALABAMA
Died in Rutledge on the 3rd, Mrs. Flora Moore.
Died in Rutledge on the 5th, Arabella Bell, aged twelve years.
Died in Rutledge on the 7th, T.W. Thompson.
Died near Demopolis on the 14th, Mrs. Augustus Foscue.
Died in Hale County on the 8th, Mrs. M.A. Thorp.
Died in Texas on the 8th of March, Mrs. Mary A. Edwards, formerly of Greene County.

# THE SOUTHERN ARGUS - DEATHS - JUNE 1869 THROUGH JUNE 1874

Died in Montgomery on the 15th, Katie, infant daughter of Colonel and Mrs. W.S. Reese.
Died in Mississippi on the 24th March, Mrs. Marion Shelby Ross, formerly of Huntsville.
Died in Florence on the 4th, Mrs. Elizabeth Kirkman.
Died in Mobile on the 11th, Mrs. Eliza St. John Murrell.
Died in Mobile on the 13th, I.L. Phillips.
Died in Cherokee County on the 9th, H.W.M. Adrain, aged seventy-four years.
Died at LaFayette on the 7th, Peter Bragaw.
Died in Mobile on the 16th, Mrs. Emma R. Touart.

Joseph H. Burt of Conecuh County was seriously injured last week by being run over with a wagon.

## Issue 4-28-1871

Rachel Williams was tried in the Conecuh Circuit Court, at its late term, for the murder of Jack Jones, and sentenced to the penitentiary for life.

### DIED IN ALABAMA

Died in Mobile, April 18th, Mary Orth, infant child of David and Maria Lotspeich.
Died in Tallapoosa County on the 7th, Dr. Allen Kimball.
Died in Wilcox County on the 13th, Charles M. Dear/Dean.
Died in Livingston on the 10th, Mrs. Susan Spratt Cockrell.
Died in Eutaw on the 6th, Mrs. Jane C. Richardson.
Died in Mobile on the 19th, Christian Kearns.
Died in Marion, recently, A.Z. Blair of Greene County, a student of Howard College.
Died in Tuskegee on the 17th, John A. Graham.
Died in Pike County on the 18th, Stephen D. Smilie.
Died at Kymulgee on the 14th of injuries received in a fall from his horse, M. Culpepper.
Died in Greenville on the 16th, Dr. George D. Herbert, aged seventy-one years.
Died in Greene County on the 28th ult., Mrs. Margaret R. Cross.
Died in Opelika on the 16th, Miss Sallie Mallett.
Died in Demopolis on the 20th, Mrs. E.M. Phillips, wife of Rev. J.W. Phillips.
Died in Madison County on the 20th, Thomas Bibb, aged seventy years.
Died in Mobile on the 21st, George F. Boone.
Died in Mobile on the 22nd, George A. Russell.
Died in Mobile on the 8th, Charles H. Bostwick.
Died in Florence on the 17th, Mrs. Lucretia Boardman.

## THE SOUTHERN ARGUS - DEATHS - JUNE 1869 THROUGH JUNE 1874

D.P. Scarbrough of Eutaw has been acquitted in Hale County on the indictment against him for killing Dennis Callahan at New Prospect last spring.

In Clinton on the 7th, Edward Guyler, was shot and killed by James Harkness.

A man named Andrew Olson was drowned at Mobile on Monday last.

In Jackson County, two weeks ago, James Counts was accidentally killed by Thomas B. Reid.

Issue 5-5-1871

The negro boy, Calvin, who was cut by Walter Oliver on the 14th ult. in Gadsden, died a few days ago.

John McIntosh of Marengo County was struck several blows by the Marshal of Linden, a few days ago, while he was resisting an arrest, from the effects of which he soon died.

W.A. Todd of Talladega, who was in Wetumpka as a witness against a lot of negroes charged with highway robbery, has disappeared under circumstances indicating that he has been foully dealt with.

Obituary: Mrs. Carrie Leonard. She was born in Perry County, Alabama, May 15th, 1849. She joined the Baptist Church at Fellowship, at the age of ten, and lived a devoted christian up to the time of her death, which was the 8th of April, 1871. She leaves a pious husband and one little daughter four years of age, mother, brother, and sisters...She has been lingering for two years with that dread disease consumption...her spirit now is with her infant son who preceded her about twelve months.

Ex-Governor Manly of North Carolina died last Monday.

Hon. James M. Mason of Virginia died on the night of the 28th ult. at Alexander of general debility.

Col E.S. Worthington, a distinguished lawyer of Louisville, Kentucky, died last Monday.

# THE SOUTHERN ARGUS - DEATHS - JUNE 1869 THROUGH JUNE 1874

Issue 5-12-1871

Saturday night of last week, near Tuskaloosa, a difficulty occurred between W.F. Samuel, an excellent young man, and a negro in which the latter was killed, and the former it is thought mortally wounded.

In Escambia County, April 10th, a man named O'Farrell was shot and killed by a party of men composed of Halls, living in the same county.

J.C. Rupert of Conecuh, who had a leg broken some time ago by a fall from a locomotive cow-catcher, has had the wounded limb amputated and his recovery is doubtful.

John R. Tankersley is in jail in Evergreen for killing S.P. Sellers recently.

Monroe County sends Clark Jones (negro) to penitentiary for murder.

The other day, on Trawick's place, in Lowndes County, John Chancellor, negro, was killed by Frank Owens, negro.

Recently, on the place of Penn Marvin in Lowndes, Lawrence Crockett, negro, was cut in four places and killed by John McDaniel, negro. John is in jail.

On Calvin Moorer's place in Lowndes County, Dick Moorer, negro, had his head split open with an axe, a short time ago, by Gabe (negro)

John Pullen fell from a fishing smack in Mobile Bay the other day and was drowned.

In Lawrence County, a few days ago, a man named Garley was shot and killed by Thomas H. Jones.

In Huntsville, the other day, William Murrell for killing A.W. Brown in 1866, was convicted of manslaughter in the first degree.

## DIED IN ALABAMA

Died in Mobile on the 28th ult., William Kearney.
Died in Mobile, last week, William G. Baker.
Died in Mobile, April 29th, Helen Davis Baugh.
Died in Mobile, April 27th, Abraham Butler.
Died at Robinson's Springs, April 28th, Mrs. Mary Alston Allen.
Died in Madison County, April 20th, Joseph Jamison.
Died in Tuskaloosa on the 21st ult., Miss Mary P. Dearing.

## THE SOUTHERN ARGUS - DEATHS - JUNE 1869 THROUGH JUNE 1874

Died in Arkansas, April 22nd, Mrs. Agness P. Morgan, daughter of the late L.B. Neal of Tuskaloosa.
Died in Demopolis, April 28th, Mrs. Josephine Smith.
Died in Russell County, April 30th, Rev. B.M. Ware.
Died in Huntsville, April 30th, Alonzo G. Scott.
Died near Madison, April 25th, Mrs. Mary F. Troutman.
Died in Shelby County, April 28th, Mark Duke.
Died in Shelby County, April 28th, Moses Johnson.
Died at Union Springs, April 20th, Col. W.B. Locke.
Died near Eufaula, April 22nd, James R. Poston.
Died near Monroeville, April 3rd, Miss Parmelia Tucker, aged sixty-six years.
Died at Taylorsville, May 1st, Henry Hays Armstrong, infant.
Died in Oktibbeha County, Mississippi, 26th ult., Mary Mosely Barnwell, daughter of the late A.F. Hopkins of Mobile.

C. S. Smith of Mobile was seriously injured last Saturday by being thrown from a buggy.

Issue 5-19-1871

### DIED IN ALABAMA

Died in Springfield, Greene County, April 29th, Samuel R. Murphy, aged seventy-one years.
Died near Union, Greene County, on the 3rd, Mrs. David R. McGraw.
Died in Eutaw on the 4th, John M. Jones of Little Rock, Arkansas.
Died in Mobile on the 9th, Annie M. Belden.
Died in Columbus, Mississippi, April 21st, Dr. W.G. Westmorland, formerly of Greene County.
Died in Eutaw, April 18th, Mrs. Clemmie White.
Died in Greensboro, on the 5th, James McClelland.
Died in Florence, April 24th, James L. Holland.
Died in Butler on the 7th, John Phillips.
Died near Rockbridge, Alum Springs, Virginia, on the 3rd, Capt. J.L. Reddish of Camden.
Died in Mobile on the 13th, John P. Remy.
Died near Nixburg on the 5th, Joseph Day.
Died in Coosa County on the 7th, David R. Staples.
Died at Elkmont on the 8th, H.J. Cartwright.
Died near Scottsboro on the 6th, Mrs. Joanna Coulson.
Died in Mobile on the 15th, Robert Canby, infant.
Died in Montgomery, recently, Mrs. J.A. Diaz.
Died in Mobile on the 10th, William Reynolds Thompson, infant.
Died in Mobile on the 7th, Rigail LeVert Reale, infant.
Died near Talladega, recently, Mrs. Martha Miller.

# THE SOUTHERN ARGUS - DEATHS - JUNE 1869 THROUGH JUNE 1874

Died at his father's residence near Dixie on the 8th, John W. Fuller, aged three years, six months and twenty-five days.
Died in Barbour County on the 6th, Mrs. Joel Sims.
Died in Barbour County on the 3rd, John Bullock.
Died in Barbour County on the 4th, Mrs. Lee.
Died in Barbour County on the 5th, Mrs. Dorman.
Died in Jacksonville on the 11th, Mrs. G.I. Turnley.
Died in Cuthbert, recently, Mr. Hickey of Eufaula.
Died in Montgomery on the 13th, W.J. Turner.
Died at Shelby Springs on the 2nd, Charles Barnes of Montgomery.

Joseph Marx, a peddler, was drowned two weeks ago in the neighborhood of Barnett's Station, Sumter County, while attempting to cross a swollen stream.

John R. Dobbs of Coosa County, arrested for killing his brother, Joseph Dobbs, was discharged by an examining court.

In the Baptist Church of Wetumpka, Saturday of last week, Harper James was stabbed and killed by a Mr. Bugg, whose sister he was accused of having wronged. [see Issue 5-26-1871]

John Copeland, in the DeKalb Jail on a charge of murdering his wife, was taken out of prison some time ago, and has not since been heard of.

A preliminary trial has resulted in the acquittal of J.C.B. Harkness for the killing of Edward Guyler, at Clinton, some time since.

Tribute of respect: On the death of O.H. Chisolm, a beloved student of Erskine College, Due West, South Carolina...from Forts, Alabama, who departed this life on the morning of the 6th inst...

Died near Colerene, Lowndes County, at the residence of R.J. Dudley, Esq., on the 29th of March, John Dudley, Sr., in the eighty-first year of his age.
 The subject of this notice was born in Princess Ann County, Virginia, May 4th, 1790; emigrated to this state in 1818, and settled in Autauga County, where he was married to Miss Julia Reese in 1820, who still survives him; after remaining there twelve years, he removed to Lowndes County, where he principally resided up to the time of his decease...

## Issue 5-26-1871

Zack Lovel was shot a few days ago in Wills Valley by a Mr. Crone.

# THE SOUTHERN ARGUS - DEATHS - JUNE 1869 THROUGH JUNE 1874

Drury Byars of Pickens committed suicide, Tuesday, the 10th inst.

Ann Francis, negro, was burned to death at Montgomery on the 19th by the explosion of a kerosene lamp.

Samuel Bugg, son of Bugg who killed Mr. James at Robinson's Springs Saturday week last, has been committed to jail as accessory or abettor of the deed. [see Issue 5-19-1871]

A child of Mr. Paul Thomas of Limestone County, two or three years old, was drowned in a swollen branch near her father's residence, a few days ago.

An English miner named Pearson was killed at the Brierfield ore beds, on the 10th, by the caving in of a bank.

### DIED IN ALABAMA
Died in Union Springs on the 1?th, E.L. Brunscomb?.
Died in Wilcox, 15th inst., Jere Fail.
Died in Eutaw, 14th inst., Miss Minnie R. Webb.
Died in Eutaw, 16th inst., Captain John J. Winston.
Died in Hale County, 15th inst., Mrs. Amanda Lawrence.
Died near Burnt Corn, 10th inst., Chatlen Doggett.
Died near Evergreen, 17th inst., W.P. Estep.
Died in Conecuh County, 12th inst., Turner Ivey.
Died in Eufaula, 13th inst., Jack Hardman.
Died in Florence, 15th inst., R. Melville Miller.
Died in Florence, 8th inst., Mrs. Frances Ann Mason.
Died in Troy, 16th inst., William Wilson.
Died near New Market on the 4th inst., Colonel George T. Jones.
Died in Wilcox a few days ago, Mrs. McArthur.
Died in Montgomery County on the 18th inst., W.W. Hannon.
Died in Abbeville on the 10th inst., John J. Ward.
Died in Mobile on the 20th inst., R.B. Sutton.
Died in Mobile on the 22nd inst., A.M. Wood.
Died near Lowndesboro on the 18th inst., Mrs. Sue McCurdy.
Died near Morgan Spring on the 20th inst., Mrs. Sarah Thomas, wife of Wm. Thomas.
Died on the 3rd inst. in Hale County, little Bobbie C., infant son of Dr. R.S. and E.A. Jones, aged two years, six months.

Hon. J.J. Chappell, who was a member of Congress from South Carolina from 1812 to 1815, died at his residence near Montgomery, Wednesday last.

George Parsons of Talladega has the inflammatory rheumatism.

## THE SOUTHERN ARGUS - DEATHS - JUNE 1869 THROUGH JUNE 1874

Issue 6-2-1871

On the 23rd ult., a shooting match occurred near Fayetteville, between T.J. Averett and a Mr. Tood. Mr. Averett was badly wounded.

Cato Jones, negro, has been held by an examing court in Montgomery to answer for the murder of Amos Harris, near that city, last Christmas.

Benjamin La?clle of Lauderdale accidentally shot, some time since, by Bub Ellis, is dead.

### DIED IN ALABAMA

Died in Mobile, 25th ult., Thomas Morris.
Died in Lawrence County, 11th ult., Dr. Robert Mason Clark.
Died in Louisiana, March 17th, Alexander P. McQueen, formerly of Montgomery County.
Died in Tuskaloosa, 19th ult., Earnest, child of J.P. and Bella Dawson.
Died in Tuskaloosa, 19th ult., Mrs. Theresa Loveman.
Died in Eutaw, 4th ult., John M. Jones.
Died in Greene Springs, 19th ult., E.I. Ashe, aged seventy-seven years.
Died in Jefferson County, 14th ult., Mrs. Minerva Emmons.
Died in Texas, 8th ult., Mrs. Temple B. Hinton.
Died in Clayton, 21st ult., George E. Macon.
Died in Clayton, 21st ult., the wife of Rev. J.S. Paullin.
Died in Gadsden, May 24th, Jefferson J. Adams.
Died near Huntsville, May 24th, Louis T. Pollard.
Died in New Orleans, 26th ult., Mrs. Sylla Witherspoon, daughter of General Withers of Mobile.
Died at Clayton, 21st ult., Orange Bennett.
Died in Jacksonville, 26th ult., Fielding Snow.
Died in Pickens County, 14th ult., Stephen Stone, Sr.
Died in Montgomery, 28th ult., Theresa Manley, infant.
Died at Spring Hill, 29th ult., Robert Purvis.

Issue 6-9-1871

A Mr. Pettigrew of the vicinity of Eutaw was killed in that town, Monday of last week, in an altercation and difficulty with a Mr. Boggs and his son of Finch's ferry.

B.T. Boggs and his son, both of Greene County, are in jail at Eutaw for killing W.M. Pettigrew on the 29th ult.

# THE SOUTHERN ARGUS - DEATHS - JUNE 1869 THROUGH JUNE 1874

Last Friday evening on the Montgomery and Wetumpka Road, Frank Cochran had a difficulty with some of his negro hands in which he was shot and killed, as was one of the negroes.

John Winbourne, negro employee at Bingham & Brother's steam mill, near Talladega, was killed by lightning 31st ult.

In a shooting affair at Cowles' Station two weeks ago, a Mr. McCluskey was killed and a Mr. Shelton severely wounded.

### DIED IN ALABAMA

Died in this vicinity ____, last ____, Jesse R. Rountree...[see below]
Died in Mobile, June 3rd, Alfred Batre.
Died in Mobile, June 2nd, Warren Witherspoon Foster, infant.
Died near Trickem, Lowndes County, last week, Lewis Kirkland.
Died in Eufaula, 28th ult., Miss Eugenia Hardman.
Died in Huntsville, 25th ult., Colonel Charles W. Cummings.
Died in Gadsden, 24th ult., J.J. Adams.
Died in Tuskegee, 30th ult., Jack Drakeford.
Died in Mobile, 31st ult., Buck Mitchell.
Died in Mobile, 31st ult., Mrs. Anne Walker.
Died in ____, 29th ult., Mrs. Dickerson, wife of A.Z. Dickerson.
Died near Uniontown, 27th ult., Augustas Ives Pearce.
Died in Choctaw County, 20th ult., Thomas L. Roberts.
Died in Eutaw, 31st ult., Abner Perrin.
Died in Uniontown, 2nd inst., Mrs. P.M. Nunnemacher.

Thomas Lindsay, an elder brother of Governor Lindsay, died in Liverpool, England, a few days ago.

### Issue 6-16-1871

Jesse D. Roundtree departed this life on Monday, June 5th, 1871, at his residence in Dallas County, Alabama, aged seventy years. The subject of this memorism was born in Edgefield District, South Carolina, April 3rd, 1801, and moved to Dallas County, Alabama, in 1820, where he resided until his death. He was the eldest of eight children: his father died while he was yet under the paternal roof...he was happily married to Frances C. Brown daughter of the late Josiah Brown... A devoted wife and their affectionate children, together with many friends, are left to mourn his loss... [see above]

At Talladega on the 7th, Thomas McAdams shot and killed George Klein.

# THE SOUTHERN ARGUS - DEATHS - JUNE 1869 THROUGH JUNE 1874

Wilson, confined for killing Belt Nabors, in Columbiana, was before Judge Pelham last week on a writ of habais corpus, and admitted to bail in $3,000.

In Colbert County, 29th ult., Turner Williams, negro, shot and killed Gabe Malone.

### DIED IN ALABAMA

Died in St. Clair County, a few days ago, Walker Keith.
Died in Jefferson County, May 31st, Thomas Anderson, aged seventy-nine years.
Died in Camden, 26th ult., Capt. J.R. Mason.
Died at Palo Alta, Mississippi, May 2nd, Mrs. Harriet A. Hatfield.
Died in Mobile on the 6th, Miss Josephine Irwin.
Died in Eufaula on the 4th, Mrs. L. Florida Wallace.
Died in Talladega on the 4th, Mrs. Mary L. Nash.
Died in Greenville on the 2nd, Thomas Jackson.
Died in Greenville on the 6th, John Caldwell.
Died in Havana, Cuba, May 15th, John T. Greer, formerly of Athens, Alabama.
Died in Pickens County, May 9th, Mrs. Elizabeth Hicks.
Died in Tuskaloosa County on the 7th inst., Robert Ellyson, aged seventy-three years.
Died at Spring Hill on the 12th, Fanny Augusta Field.

Near Fort Deposit, last Monday, J.J. Heard, was shot and killed by "Dink" Holman.

James Kelsoe, indicted in Butler County for the murder of James C. Otts, has been convicted and sentenced to the penitentiary for life.

Ferdinard Myerseay was drowned at Montgomery, Thursday evening last week.

### Issue 6-23-1871

Monday Plummer, negro, was accidentally drowned in the river at Demopolis two weeks ago today.

We are happy to correct the report of the death of John E. Hatcher, to which we gave credit last week.

Commodore Tatnall died at Savannah on the 12th inst.

# THE SOUTHERN ARGUS - DEATHS - JUNE 1869 THROUGH JUNE 1874

Near Shiloh, Marengo County, last Friday, Edward Bradley was shot and killed by Henry Tucker.

The boiler of the new steam mill of B.W. Smith, near Maplesville, exploded last Saturday, fatally injuring a young man named Frazier.

At Brinlee's Mill, Cherokee County, on the 6th inst., a young man named Mitchell was drowned.

A two year old son of the Rev. R.W. Wilks, living near Gaylesville, was seriously and dangerously kicked by a horse a few days since.

### DIED IN ALABAMA

Died in Monroeville, 31st ult., Hugh McLaughlin, infant.
Died in Wilcox, 24th ult., William S. Hazel.
Died in Wilcox, 4th inst., Mrs. Eliza Fail.
Died in Huntsville, 12th inst., Samuel P., son of R.W. and Mattie Coltart.
Died in Wetumpka, 6th inst., Mrs. Lucy Jane Root.
Died in Centre, 6th inst., George W. Sharp.
Died in Limestone County, 12th inst., Mrs. Sallie White.
Died in Hayneville, 13th inst., Mrs. Mary Louisa Smith.
Died in Florence, 11th inst., Mrs. Sarah P. Crow.
Died in Tuskegee, 12th inst., Mrs. Carrie E. Varner.
Died in East Pascagoula, Mississippi, 14th inst., Frank Thompson, infant son of Howard P. Gray of Mobile.
Died in Mobile, 14th inst., Gordon K. Adams.
Died in Eufaula, 13th inst., Henry Reynolds.
Died in Pike County, 25th ult., Thomas L. Fryer.
Died in Greensboro, 13th inst., Mrs. Sarah A. Harvey.
Died in Opelika, 11th inst., Nat. Collins.
Died in Camden, 31st ult., J.P. Jackson.
Died in Choctaw County, 13th inst., Mrs. A.C. Powe.
Died in Mobile, 15th inst., Foster Hayne Holland.
Died in Huntsville, 15th inst., Hollis Barclay Newman, aged three years.
Died in Little Rock, Arkansas, 8th inst., Mrs. Julia A. English, formerly of Limestone County.
Died in Tuscumbia, 9th inst., Hunter Thornton, aged six years.
Died in Mobile, 4th inst., Miers Fisher.
Died in Choctaw County, recently, Dr. M.G. Pritchett.

A son of the late Colonel Beltzhoover of Mobile was drowned near Natchez, Mississippi, last week.

## THE SOUTHERN ARGUS - DEATHS - JUNE 1869 THROUGH JUNE 1874

Emmet Baxter, formerly of Tuscumbia, was thrown from his horse at Lacouia, Arkansas, a few days ago, and killed.

Issue 6-30-1871

### DIED IN ALABAMA

Died in Athens the 21st, Eliza H. Jones, infant.
Died near Mooreville the 11th, Henry C. Bibb, infant.
Died on board the steamer *Clara* the 19th, Capt. Sam Ables.
Died in Tuscumbia the 20th, Joseph Clarke Eve.
Died in Pickens County the 18th, Mrs. Sarah Basham.
Died near Bridgeville the 14th, Dr. D.G. Gardner.
Died in Florence the 19th, James William White.
Died near Talladega the 6th, Mrs. Elizabeth Anderson.
Died in Talladega the 15th, Taul, infant son of Mr. and Mrs. Taul Bradford.
Died in Talladega the 20th, infant daughter of Rev. Mr. Renfroe.
Died at Athens the 20th, Mrs. J.W. Sloss.
Died at Bay St. Louis the 10th, Mrs. Mary Smith Calhoun, formerly of Huntsville.
Died in Perry County the 11th, Mrs. Eliza A. Perkins.
Died near Eutaw the 27th ult., John James Love, infant.
Died in Huntsville, 22nd inst., Mrs. Isophoena Bassett.
Died at Toulminville the 25th, Isaac Wood.

Near Montgomery, last Monday, Jack Taliaferro, negro, was killed by lightning.

John Borden of Cleburne County, the father of the Principal of Oxford College, was waylaid a few days ago and probably fatally beaten with a club.

John Carothers, negro, was shot and killed on the 20th by Colonel W.A. Johnson.

Issue 7-7-1871

John Rogers, negro, was accidentally drowned here last week.

Died at the residence of B.C. Harrison, in this County, on the 5th inst., Mrs. Fannie H. Harrison.

B.F. Boggs, has been committed to the Greene County Jail without bail, for the murder of W.M. Pettigrew, some time ago.

# THE SOUTHERN ARGUS - DEATHS - JUNE 1869 THROUGH JUNE 1874

Died in Dallas County, July 2nd, 1871, of congestion of the brain, George Fletcher, son of Mr. and Mrs. D.B. Thrash, aged five years and five months. The *Chicago Sunday Times* will please copy.

A little son of J. Kohn, while sliding down a post in front of Arnold's store, Montgomery, last Tuesday, struck a splinter two feet long, which entered his groin, passed upwards through his body piercing his lungs and passed out near his shoulder.

Issue 7-14-1871

A man named McDonald, a railroad hand, was found dead on the side of the road near Blyton two weeks ago.

Judge Dwinelle? of San Francisco has again refused to grant a new trail in the case of Mrs. Laura Fair. There seems to be a little doubt of her execution at the time fixed by law.

In Lowndes on the 4th inst., A.H. Marschalk, Editor of the *Marengo Journal*, was dangerously stabbed in a personal difficulty with Joe Barley. He is getting well.

In Mobile last Saturday, Madison Wilson, son of L.M. Wilson, was shot and killed by Braxton Bragg, Jr.

Thomas Boyle, a newsboy on the Memphis and Charlestown Road, fell from the Western bound train on the evening of June 20th, near Lafayette, Alabama, and was killed.

On the 29th ult. near Lafayette, Alabama, a freight train on the Memphis and Charleston Road was thrown from the track, and William Turner and Sam Blacksbeer, brakemen, were killed.

Among the killed at the railroad accident near Nashville last week was Miss M. Ettie Jones of Huntsville.

Died in Mobile, June 30th, James Montague.
Died in Lauderdale County, June 14th, Mrs. Elizabeth G. Robertson.
Died in Montgomery, June 28th, Beauregard C. Baldwin.
Died in Montgomery, June 28th, Willie Sweeney.
Died near Centre, June 20th, Ezekiel, son of J.W. Wood.
Died in Union Springs, June 23rd, master J.C. Lunsford.
Died in Clayton, June 23rd, Robert Dill.
Died in Florence, June 26th, James William Crow, infant.

## THE SOUTHERN ARGUS - DEATHS - JUNE 1869 THROUGH JUNE 1874

Died in Madison County, June 23rd, Charlie Ann Eslinger, infant.
Died in Huntsville, June 26th, Arthur Hampton Lindman, infant.
Died in Mobile, June 29th, J. Metevier, suicide.
Died in Camden, June 25th, Maggie Lee Reddish.
Died in Coosa County, June 11th, C.M. Cox, Sr.
Died in Tuskaloosa, June 28th, Mrs. Carolyne C. Matthews.
Died in Eufaula, recently, a child of N.M. Wyatt.
Died near Union, Greene County, a few days ago, John Upchurch.
Died at Mt. Willing, June 23rd, Mrs. Maples.
Died in East Lowndes, June 21st, John Stephens.
Died in Newbern, July 3rd, Annie B. Hatch, infant.
Died in Greensboro, July 2nd, Herndon Randolph, infant.
Died in Lauderdale, July 1st, William Rhodes.
Died in Memphis, Tennessee, a few days ago, Jacob K. Swoope of Florence.
Died in Columbia, June 24th, Mrs. Martha Bryan.
Died in Stevenson, recently, W.J. Carter, formerly of Huntsville.
Died near Huntsville, July 4th, W.M. McCloskey, late of Pennsylvania.
Died in Gadsden, July 3rd, R.D. Ross.
Died near Centre, July 2nd, Mrs. Dorcas Pratt.
Died near Centre, June 27th, Clementine Thomas, infant.
Died in Madison County, July 7th, Stephen Haynes.
Died in Athens, July 4th, Mrs. A.J. Crenshaw.
Died in Pickens County, June 28th, Miss Nancy J.H. Hudgins.
Died at Ponchatoula, near New Orleans, July 6th, Dr. S.S. Batchelor, formerly of Montgomery.

Issue 7-21-1871

On the 6th of July the livery stable of Mr. Zorkowski of Silver Run was struck by lightning, which killed a little son of Benjamin R. Henry.

We learn from private sources, that A.H. Marschalk, Editor of the *Marengo Journal*, who was stabbed in a personal difficulty, some time ago, died on Sunday night last.

Alfred Cargle of Fayette County committed suicide by shooting on the 28th of June.

Elias Barlow of Conecuh was dangerously hurt by a kick from a horse two weeks ago.

Sylvester G. Hallins, a lad of seven years old, was accidentally drowned on the 12th at the foot of Charleston Street, Mobile.

## THE SOUTHERN ARGUS - DEATHS - JUNE 1869 THROUGH JUNE 1874

Died in Haynesville, July 9th, Miss Francis Cody.
Died near Benton, July 4th, Sarah Bryant, child.
Died in Sanford County, June 28th, Jesse T. Walden.
Died near Havana, July 10th, Henry Harrison Westcott, child.
Died in Iuka, Mississippi, recently, Dr. Hugh Houston, brother of Hon. G.S. Houston of Athens.
Died in Washington City, July 12th, Dr. Joseph Bell Alexander, formerly of Mobile.
Died near Pride's Station, July 7th, S.M. Thompson, infant.
Died in Lawrence County, recently, Mrs. Eliza Eggleston.
Died in Franklin County, Tennessee, June 26th, Mrs. Mary D. Corzelius, formerly of Wilcox.
Died in Talladega, July 4th, Mrs. Nash.
Died in Conecuh County, July 8th, Curtis Page.
Died in Escambia County, Florida, July 5th, Dr. Milton Amos, formerly of Bellville.
Died in Shelby County, July 11th, Frank Jordan.
Died in Wetumpka, July 1st, Mrs. Loomis.
Died in Fayetteville, July 2nd, Mrs. Mollie Pond.
Died in Gadsden, July 12th, O.P. Hill.
Died in Etowah County, June 29th, Mrs. Julia Ann Reeve.
Died in Cherokee County, July 5th, Mrs. Sarah Coker.
Died at Cedar Bluff, July 3rd, Jere Lawrence.
Died in Mobile, July 10th, Armand Boullement.
Died in Marengo County, July 11th, J.G.P. Coleman.
Died in Eufaula, July 10th, Oscar L. Barefield, infant.
Died in Mobile, July 10th, John A. Brady, journalist.
Died in Mobile County, June 22nd, Mrs. Sarah Greer.
Died near Aberdeen, Mississippi, February 1st inst., Willis E. Logan, formerly of Greene County.

Issue 7-28-1871

At Five Mile Post, Mobile County, last week, Albert Harrison, a butcher, was seriously, probably fatally, cut by Burrell Lyles.

The death of Dr. Pugh Houston of Iuka, Mississippi, was erroneously reported. It was Mrs. Houston who died there.

One of the pillars of the porch of Mr. John Collier's residence, near Opelika, fell one day last week, killing a little son of Dr. James Collier, who was playing about it at the time.

Died at Asheville, North Carolina, July 9th, Aquila Miles of Lowndes.

## THE SOUTHERN ARGUS - DEATHS - JUNE 1869 THROUGH JUNE 1874

Died in Lowndes County, July 16th, Murriel J. Varner, infant.
Died near Springfield, July 18th, Jere Cockrell.
Died in Greene County, July 16th, Mrs. Lucy T. Sheppard.
Died in Jefferson County, July 14th, Mrs. Morinda Lyon.
Died in Mobile, July 18th, C.R. Rice.
Died in Mobile, July 18th, under circumstances indicating suicide, Ellen Walker.
Died in Camden, recently, D.F.C. Brooks.
Died in Montgomery, July 18th, D.P. Bray.
Died in Greenville, July 21st, Isaac G. Hutton.
Died in Lauderdale County, July 17th, Edmund Noel.
Died in Mobile, July 20th, Mrs. Georgia Woodruff.
Died in Marion, July 18th, Tommie, son of S.C. and M.P. LeVert.
Died in Athens, July 14th, W.N. Jones.
Died in Greensboro, July 17th, Miss Fannie A. Dorman.
Died in Hale County, June 29th, Miss Kezia McD. Stringfellow.
Died in Tuskaloosa County, July 2nd, Samuel Hosmer.
Died in North Port, July 16th, Frank Haley.
Died in Tuskaloosa, July 17th, Sion P. Skinner.
Died near Payneville, July 11th, Mrs. Pattie Renfroe.
Died in Guntersville, July 13th, Mrs. Elizabeth A. Barclay.
Died near Midway, July 15th, Eddie Isabella Daniel, infant.
Died near Eufaula, July 18th, Olin Wood.
Died near Morgan Springs, July 15th, David Walter, infant son of M.D.L. and M.C. Moore.
Died in Iuka, Mississippi, recently, Mrs. Houston, formerly of Lauderdale County.
Died in Butler, Choctaw County, July 15th, Rosina Winter Ulmer, infant.
Died in Montgomery, July 24th, H.C. Alford.
Died in Autauga County, a few days ago, Dr. J.D. Moody.
Died in Prattville, July 24th, D.A. Suther.
Died near Liberty Hill, Dallas County, Alabama, on the morning of June 22nd, 1871, Nettie Ella Clarance, eldest daughter of W.R. and S.E. Ramsey, aged five years, two months and twenty-five days...

Mr. McCourt of Elyton, was shot and wounded in the hand a few nights ago, by a concealed person.

### Issue 8-4-1871

John A. Moore, an old and respected citizen of Selma for several years, at one time Marshall of the city, was found by the road side last Saturday near Weaver's wood-yard in a dying condition. It is supposed he was killed by a fall from the mule he was riding or a kick from it.

# THE SOUTHERN ARGUS - DEATHS - JUNE 1869 THROUGH JUNE 1874

Lewis Vaughan, negro, was killed near Demopolis two weeks ago by lightning.

July 22nd, between Centre and Cave Springs, a horse ran away with a buggy containing Winston Wester and Miss Smith, who were both thrown out and injured, Mr. Wester fatally. [see Wester 8-18-1871]

At Haysville, Greene County, some two weeks ago, in a street difficulty, Dr. Ed. Sanders and a man named Anderson were badly cut with knives.

B.F. Boggs, committed to the Greene County Jail for killing William Pettigrew, has been granted bail in the sum of two thousand dollars.

Died in Montgomery, July 30th, Mrs. H. Lewy.
Died in Huntsville, July 21st, Capt. David H. Todd, a brother of Mrs. Lincoln.
Died in Linden, July 23rd, Alice Whitlock, aged three years.
Died in Huntsville, July 16th, George W. Herbert, infant.
Died in Huntsville, July 22nd, George Bei?ne Paiton.
Died in Madison County, July 18th, Mary Louisa Banks, infant.
Died in Jefferson County, July 20th, Colonel John H. Barton of Greensboro.
Died in Clayton, July 25th, Duncan Carmichael.
Died in Henry County, July 22nd, Willie Wingate Cox, infant.
Died in Evergreen, July 22nd, Mrs. Dr. J.A. McCreary.
Died in Conecuh County, July 22nd, John Gilmore.
Died near Loachapoka, July 26th, Jonathan Davis.
Died in Auburn, July 27th, George C. Dillard.
Died near Clayton, July 16th, Mathew Clark.
Died at Hickory Grove, July 15th, Miss Lizzie McQueen.
Died near Benton, July 14th, Mrs. Clarisa Hardy.
Died near Benton, July 21st, a child of Leonidas Whatley.
Died in Mobile, recently, John B. Galvin.
Died in Talladega, July 25th, infant child of Thomas Pullam.
Died in Gadsden, July 12th, O.P. Hill.
Died in Gadsden, July 3rd, M.R.D. Ross.
Died near Centre, July 10th, William Goodin.
Died in Cherokee County, July 2nd, Mrs. Dorcas Eliza Pratt, aged seventy three years.
Died near Union Springs, July 21st, Roderick McCall.
Died in Limestone County, July 20th, Ben H. Tucker.
Died in Limestone County, July 26th, Etta, daughter of Dr. J. David Malone.
Died at Cullum Springs, July 19th, Mary E. Tew, infant.
Died in Mobile, July 19th, Frankie Southerland, infant.
Died in Mobile, July 22nd, Mary E. Purdon.
Died in Mobile, July 22nd, Mrs. Mary Dougherty.

# THE SOUTHERN ARGUS - DEATHS - JUNE 1869 THROUGH JUNE 1874

Died in Mobile, July 24th, Mary Seward.
Died in Mobile, July 26th, William A. Wallace.
Died in Mobile, July 29th, Thomas Gleason.
Died in Pike County, July 28th, William Oates, aged seventy-four years.
Died in Florence, July 26th, Mrs. Mary Esther Wood, aged seventy-five years.

Near Jackson's Mill, Crenshaw County, a few days ago, a Mr. Petty was shot and killed by a Mr. Thomlin.

## Issue 8-11-1871

Picket Hammond, proprietor of a saloon on the Bay Road, Mobile, was shot and badly wounded by some negroes, one night last week.

At a barbecue at Wickham's, Limestone County, last Saturday was a week ago, Andrew Strange was killed by Peter Burrus.

In Limestone County, recently, Lafayette Free was shot and killed by J.W. Thompson.

Peter Burrus, who killed Andrew Strange in Limestone County the other day, and was himself wounded, was foully murdered the ensuing night by disguised parties.

Lacy Miller, negro, was accidentally drowned last week in Limestone County.

The wife of Robert Powell of Coosa County, who had been partially deranged for months, was found dead in a marsh near her home two weeks ago.

On Monday evening last in Montgomery County, young Mr. Grigg [see Gregg also] was killed by Fleming Gilmer.

Died in Washington County, July 22nd, James Percy.
Died in Jefferson County, July 12th, William E. Hewitt.
Died in Jefferson County, July 21st, Horton B. Chamblee.
Died in Brazil, May 13th, S.D. Watson, formerly of Talladega.
Died in Troy, July 30th, Rev. J.P. Dickenson.
Died in Pike County, recently, William Law.
Died in Mobile, August 2nd, Henry V. Couch.
Died in Mobile, August 2nd, Miss Amanda H. Walker.
Died in Calera, July 31st, Thomas R. Hunnicut.
Died near Eutaw, July 19th, Johnnie Hall, infant.
Died in Greene County, recently, Green Harris.
Died in Eutaw, July 14th, Eddie Reid, aged two years.

# THE SOUTHERN ARGUS - DEATHS - JUNE 1869 THROUGH JUNE 1874

Died in Canada, July 18th, Mrs. Ann Gilston Marvin, formerly of Hayneville.
Died in Perry County, July 7th, Charlie Thames, aged four years.
Died in Tuskaloosa County, July 28th, Mrs. Hargrove.
Died in Tuskaloosa, July 28th, Sidney Wallace Turner, infant.
Died near Tuscumbia, July 26th, Daniel Gue.
Died, Russell Valley, July 28th, little Annie Doherty.
Died in Lauderdale County, July 25th, Jonathan M. Cunningham.
Died in Lauderdale County, recently, Mrs. Margaret Harraway.
Died in Lauderdale County, July 29th, Mrs. Josephine Banks.
Died near Greensboro, July 30th, Peter Stokes.
Died in Jonesboro, August 5th, Lucy, infant daughter of John and Fanny Nave.
Died in Marion, August 5th, Miss Georgia Sumner, aged twenty-nine years.
Died at Fayette Court House, July 23rd, W.R. Wooten.
Died in Fayette County, July 23rd, J.H. Bryan.
Died in Tuskaloosa, August 6th, George D. Johnson.
Died in Montgomery, August 6th, Col. Jack Thorington.
Died in Atlantic City, New Jersey, July 29th, G.O. Jordan of Montgomery.

August 29th, in Troy, Dick Brown, negro, came to his death of too much kerosene, with which he had attempted to kindle a fire.

Henry V. Couch, formerly of this city, committed suicide by poisoning in Mobile on the 2nd inst.

On the 5th in Reid Horton's store at Spring Hill, Charles Fee was killed by lightning.

Issue 8-18-1871

Old man Fisher of Talladega, shot some time ago by Bowlen, is dead.

The young lady [Miss Smith, see issue 8-4-1871] thrown from a buggy with a Mr. Wester, in Cherokee County, some time ago, has since died from the injuries received. [see 8-4-1871 Smith]

Laura V. Stiff of Centre is dangerously ill.

W.H. Moore of Fayette County accuses his son-in-law E.A. Powell of poisoning his (Powell's) wife to death at their residence in Texas.

Dr. Thomas H. Brasher, formerly of Shelby County, was accidentally killed July 22nd near Bonham, Texas.

# THE SOUTHERN ARGUS - DEATHS - JUNE 1869 THROUGH JUNE 1874

Major A. Benton of Troy, was seriously hurt a few days ago by being struck on the head by a brick falling from the unfinished walls of the new hotel in that city.

A few days ago near Greenville a man named Woodruff fell from a wagon, a bale of cotton falling on him, and was perhaps fatally injured.

Saturday was a week ago M. Sellars of Choctaw County was drowned in the Bigbee.

Last Sunday in Oxford, a Mr. Harris was shot and killed by Samuel Morgan, formerly of this city.

Died in this city, August 6th, Joseph Savory, aged eighty-three eight months four days. Mr. Savory was born in the town of Dunkirk, France, near the coast of Flanders, on the 2nd of December 1787, and grew to manhood among the stormy scenes of the French Revolution.

When scarcely more than a boy he served as drum major in the famous army of Italy and was not year nineteen when he followed Napoleon in the "terrible passage of the Bridge of Lodi," on the 10th of May 1796. On the 5th of November of the same year, he participated in the fearful seventy-two hours battle of Arcole; and shared in the hardships of the veteran army, and its victories at Austerlitz, Jena, and Marengo.

In 1811 Mr. Savory left France and came to America, landing first at Philadelphia, but afterwards came to Alabama to join the colony of French emigrants who had settled in the County of Marengo...

Died in Marion, August 6, Ransom J., son of A.J. and M.M. Pool, aged three years, ten months.

Issue 8-25-1871

## DIED IN ALABAMA

Died in North Port, July 5th, Mrs. Mary F. Savage.
Died in North Port, 7th inst., Littleton Cole.
Died near Havana, July 27th, H.B. Halbrooks.
Died in Havana, 7th inst., W.H. Sheldon.
Died in Greensboro, 9th inst., Annie Lea Atkins, infant.
Died in Greenville, 7th inst., R.L. Gandy.
Died in Escambia County, 5th inst., John R. Downing.
Died in Mobile, 8th inst., J.B. Pidal.
Died in Gadsden, 8th inst., Mrs. Catharine R. Morague, aged eighty years.
Died at Fayette Court House, 4th inst., infant daughter of Dr. Posteur.
Died in Livingston, 8th inst., Julia Elizabeth Garber, aged seven years.

## THE SOUTHERN ARGUS - DEATHS - JUNE 1869 THROUGH JUNE 1874

Died in Columbiana, 9th inst., Samuel Leeper.
Died in Claiborne, July 26th, Sarah A. Brewer, child.
Died in Tuscumbia, 9th inst., infant son of T.C. Vesey.
Died in Dickson, 1st, Mrs. Elizabeth Hudson.
Died in Franklin, Tennessee, 7th inst., S.W. Barr, formerly of Launderdale County.
Died in Centre, 2nd inst., Lela Shropshire, child.
Died in Launderdale County, 7th inst., Willie Daman, child.
Died in Mobile, 9th inst., Cassie Shields.
Died in Mobile, 9th inst., Gustavus Goubil.
Died in Marengo County, 2nd inst., Laura, daughter of Dr. A. J. Wynne.
Died in Marengo County, 5th inst., John Beaman.
Died in Demopolis, 3rd inst., Andrew Young.
Died in Hale County, 6th inst., W.T. Cheney.
Died near Ridgely, 6th inst., Thomas H. Ellis.
Died in Trousdale County, Tennessee, 3rd inst., Mrs. Margaret C. Siddons, formerly of Eutaw.
Died near Clinton, 5th inst., Mrs. Sanders Walker, aged seventy-five years.
Died near Eutaw, July 29th, John Hall, infant.
Died in Greene County, July 29th, L.S. Knowles.
Died in Limestone County, 8th inst., Miss Mary McCormack.
Died in Pickens County, July 23rd, Alma Latham.
Died in Jacksonville, 9th inst., infant child of Frank Pierson.
Died in Longview, Texas, July 25th, Walter M. Wagner, formerly of Lowndes County.
Died in Mobile, 1st inst., John Cabell.
Died in Whistler, July 25th Julia Albertine Marshman, infant.
Died at Grove Hill the 13th, Mrs. Rebecca Woodard.
Died in Etowah County the 11th, John B. Hall.
Died in Tallapoosa County the 15th, J.M. Turner.
Died near Forkland, recently, Mrs. S. Alice Little.
Died at Forkland the 9th, Mrs. Mary Virginia Akin.
Died, Washington County the 3rd, Robert Coleman Stocker.
Died in Washington County, July 23, James Pevey.
Died at Bladon Springs the 15th, H.J. Yates.
Died near Lowndesboro, lately, a daughter of Seymour Powell.
Died in Minnesota the 2nd, Arthur M. Savage, formerly of Lowndes.
Died in Benton the 9th, Mrs. M.A. Garrett.
Died at McMinnville, Tennessee, the 13th, Colonel Howell Peebles of Union Springs.
Died in Greenville, last week, W.H. Thames.
Died in Butler County, July 24th, Ida Alice Smith, child.
Died in Bellville the 10th, Henry Stanley.
Died at Tomlinson's Mills, Conecuh County, recently, Mrs. Arabella Chandler.

## THE SOUTHERN ARGUS - DEATHS - JUNE 1869 THROUGH JUNE 1874

Died in Jackson County, two weeks ago, John Wilson.
Died in Doran's Cove, lately, old Mr. Ferguson.
Died in Mobile the 16th, N. Heidelberger.
Died in Mobile the 17th, W.G. Luter.
Died in Hale County the 4th, Nancy Rebecca McAlister, child.
Died in Cherokee County the 9th, Jerry A. Mann.
Died in Mobile the 17th, Samuel C. Gallier.
Died on Sypsey River, recently, George Washington, aged seventy years.
Died near Rogersville, July 31st, Mrs. Eliza A. Nauce.
Died in Lauderdale County the 7th, Andrew Broadfoot.
Died at Leighton the 7th, Andrew K. Galbraith.
Died in Madison County, July 31th, Luke Pryor Bibb, infant.
Died in Limestone County the 12th, Major David Gilbert.
Died in Jackson County, recently, Captain H.F. Smith.
Died in Tuskaloosa the 13th, E.C. Spragins of Madison County.
Died in Sherman, Texas, the 7th, Mrs. R. P. Baggett of Loachapoka.
Died in Jacksonville the 19th, Annie McGhee, niece of Judge Walker.

Near Cherokee, Colbert County, on the 9th, William Sharp was knocked on the head and killed by a negro.

A lad named Emele Alte/Aite was drowned at Mobile the other day while in bathing.

Sam Morgan was tried before a committing magistrate for killing Harris, at Oxford, and discharged.

In Tallapoosa on the 13th, Selden Jenkins, negro, was shot and killed by another negro.

The Governor offers $400 reward for the arrest of Fleming Gilmer, charged with killing Zack Gregg. [see Grigg also]
    Gilmer, charged with killing Gregg, a short time ago, was arrested near High Log, Bullock County, on the 15th, but subsequently escaped. He was shot at and it is supposed wounded.

Bill Tillery, desperado and horse thief, was killed in Madison County on the 10th by unknown parties.

Near Bragg's a short time ago, a fine mare on which a little son of Esquire Shehan was riding, ran away, run over a cow, threw the lad off and injured him seriously, and fatally hurt herself.

# THE SOUTHERN ARGUS - DEATHS - JUNE 1869 THROUGH JUNE 1874

Died in this county, August 7th, 1871, Florida Hunter, after a painful illness, aged thirteen years, seven months, fifteen days, youngest daughter of Charles and M.A. Hunter.

Mrs. Sarah L. Davidson died at her residence near Uniontown on Sunday the 6th inst. after a protracted illness of several months. She died in peace in the seventy-seventh year of her age...

Mrs. John Brock of Cleburne County was killed by lightening not long ago.

At Park Townsend's, in Madison County, on the night of the 17th, John Markham of Fayetteville, Tennessee, was assassinated by some person unknown.

A Tuskaloosa ladykiller named Carter, after an eighteen months success, turns out to have been all the time a horsethief and murderer named Mooney.

Todd R. Wyatt of Montgomery was found dead in his bed last Friday morning, under circumstances indicating that he committed suicide.

On the evening of the 17th, Clement Richardson, aged twelve years, son of Professor W.C.L. Richardson of Tuskaloosa was drowned in the Warrior River.

## Issue 9-1-1871

In Fayette County, recently, Oliver Wood was shot and seriously wounded by his brother-in-law, William Ham.

A few days ago near Courtland, George Nixon was shot and killed by Sam Melton.

Vivian Darden, third child of W.A. and Cynthia Marschalk, formerly of this city died at Port Gibson, Mississippi, August 22nd, aged twenty three months, eleven days.

J.C. Abercrombie has been appointed Sheriff of Macon County, vice J.J. Padgett, dead.

A convict named Andrews from Selma died in Eufaula on the 22nd.

James and A??nda Dixon have been arrested in Evergreen on a charge of infanticide.

## THE SOUTHERN ARGUS - DEATHS - JUNE 1869 THROUGH JUNE 1874

Hon. T. B. Cooper, the old war horse of Cherokee, has been seriously sick.

On the 12th in Birmingham, Rush Pratt was attacked by two negroes, one of which he killed with his pocket knife.

Mrs. Dr. James A. Kelly, ...B. Skinner, and Mr. Alexander Smith of Coosa have been dangerously ill.

A man named Summerford was killed in Abbeville, Henry County, on the 23rd ult. by a young Mr. Teague.

### DIED IN ALABAMA

Died in Mobile, August 19th, Miss Mary R. McGuire.
Died in Macon County, August 18th, J.R. Padgett.
Died in Russell County, recently, Mrs. Ann Chambers.
Died in Perry County, recently, Z.M. Chandler.
Died near Cedar Bluff, August 9th, Miss Margaret Carrender.
Died in Clarke County, August 4th, Bertha Tait Barnes, infant.
Died in Calhoun County, August 7th, A.O. Kirksey, Jr.
Died in Waco, Texas, August 12th, Colonel James B. Martin, formerly of Talladega.
Died in Camden, August 13th, Miss Mary Gilmore.
Died in Clay County, August 10th, G.W. Wilson.
Died near Midway, August 4th, Willie Thornton, infant.
Died near Pineville, July 20th, Mary Kate Riley, child.
Died in Mobile, August 26th, Felix McCorley.
Died in Mobile, August 21st, Mrs. Mary Frances McKay.
Died in New Orleans, August 20th, John M. Rawlins, formerly of Limestone County.
Died in Huntsville, August 25th, John W. Scruggs.
Died in Greenville, August 22nd, Albert Caldwell, infant.
Died at Blount Springs, recently, infant child of Dr. J.W. Clements of Eutaw.
Died in Greensboro, August 23rd, Elijah Rosser of Georgia.
Died in Greensboro, August 20th, Inez H. Leiser, infant.
Died in Tuskaloosa County, August 23rd, Mrs. T.C. Chandler.
Died at Coleraine, August 18th, Hattie E., daughter of H.G. and E.A. McCord, aged three years and nine months.
Died in Mobile, August 28th, Mrs. Jane O'Hare.
Died in Mobile, August 27th, W.J. Prevost.
Died in Mobile, August 27th, S.S. Bell.
Died in Montevallo, August 26th, A.R. Brown.
Died in Huntsville, August 26th, Mrs. Ruth Cross.

# THE SOUTHERN ARGUS - DEATHS - JUNE 1869 THROUGH JUNE 1874

Died near Autaugaville, Alabama, on the 18th inst., little Lela May, daughter of Robert H. and Maria King, who was born on the 15th of April, 1868, thus being, when she died, three years, three months and three days old.

## Issue 9-8-1871

In Cherokee County, August 27th, two sons of Foster Perdue were killed by lightning.

A son of Mr. Palmer of Madison County fell into a well and was drowned a few days ago.

Amanda Dixon is in the Conecuh Jail, charged with infanticide.

William F. Courson, killed by the Ocean Wave explosion, was a native of Greene County.

A few days ago, Daniel Hawkins was drowned in Choccolocco Creek.

The body of Mr. Fillebrowne, drowned while surveying the Coosa River, has not been recovered.

In DeKalb County, August 24th, Ben Wheeler shot and killed Kinney Kean.

On the 17th ult. near Blount Springs, David Landlingham was cut and mortally wounded by a Mr. Hays.

The widow of Harvey McEachin (negro) of Perry County has sued the county for $5,000 damages under the Ku Klux law, he having been killed by disguised negroes.

Joshua Vickers has been arrested and lodged in the Madison Jail, charged with killing Henry Erwin, negro, last winter near New Market.

An old man named McVay was found dead near the Montgomery and Eufaula Depot, in Montgomery, on the 1st inst.

Andy Miller, an employee of the Mobile and Ohio Railroad, was run over and killed by a passenger train at Columbus, Kentucky, Wednesday night was a week ago.

Rev. D.W. Gwin, pastor of the Montgomery Baptist Church, has been summoned to Alexandria, Virginia by the illness of his mother.

# THE SOUTHERN ARGUS - DEATHS - JUNE 1869 THROUGH JUNE 1874

Obituary: Died in Montevallo, Alabama, August 25/26th, 1871 of apoplexy, Andrew R. Brown. The deceased was born in 1825? He came to Selma in 1863, where he resided until the autumn of 1865, when he removed to Montevallo... He leaves a wife and two children...

Colonel Luther Libby, the owner of the warehouse in Richmond, Virginia, known during the war as the "Libby Prison," died at his residence in New Kent County, Virginia on Monday week last, aged sixty-five years.

On the morning of the 5th, Rhomes? Risen, while only half-awake, walked through a third story window in the hotel at Talladega, in the fall breaking both thigh and fracturing his jaw.

Issue 9-15-1871

Died at his father's residence in Dallas County on the 6th inst., John Hatcher, son of Dr. E.B. Mosely, aged seven years.

Peter E. Harris of Tallapoosa County committed suicide recently by shooting himself.

On the morning of the 10th in Montgomery, W.T. Key was shot and killed by James Flanegan.

Judge John M. Henderson of Evergreen is seriously ill in Florence.

Issue 9-22-1871

Gen. Brown, Governor-elect of Tennessee, has been dangerously ill.

Sterling Price, Jr., formerly adjunct Professor of Languages in the Missouri University, died in the Fulton Asylum on the 31st at the age of forty-one.

Mrs. Joseph Groves is, we regret to learn again, dangerously ill at the residence of her husband in this city.

Mrs. Catherine Conners, sister of Captain Joseph Groves of this city, died in Providence, Rhode Island, on the 24th of August.

John C. Reed, an aged and honored man of Maysville, Kentucky, father-in-law of the editor [Robert McKee] of this paper, died in Dorcherster, Illinois on the 14th inst.

# THE SOUTHERN ARGUS - DEATHS - JUNE 1869 THROUGH JUNE 1874

L.L. Weir of Limestone County was not murdered, as reported, by the men who took him from his house.

Two hundred dollars reward is offered for the arrest of William Cloud charged with killing D.B.W. Jetton of Marshall County.

Two weeks ago, Munroe Peende of Lauderdale County killed with a shot-gun James Futrell, one of his neighbors.

E.D. Nash was tried last week at Tuskegee for killing Mr. Miller at Cowles' Station some time since and acquitted.

J.F. Flanagan has been tried before a Montgomery examining court for killing Mr. Key, and acquitted.

Mathew Dearne, Sheriff of Wilkinson County, Georgia, was gagged and murdered on the night of August 30th.

Wesley Redmon has been sentenced by the Lumpkin (Georgia) Superior Court to twenty years imprisonment for the murder of a colored man.

## DIED IN ALABAMA

Died in Windham Springs, 7th inst., a son of Henry Broadmax of Greene County.
Died in Tuskaloosa County, 2nd inst., Anna Kehoe, child.
Died in Huntsville, 4th inst., Archie Landman, child.
Died in Corinth, Mississippi, 6th inst., James H. Norvil, formerly of Huntsville.
Died in Eufaula, 4th inst., Richard Fulson.
Died in Pickens County, recently, John W. Winbourne.
Died in Pickens County, recently, Benjamin W. Williams.
Died in Pickens County, about two weeks ago, Mr. Parham.
Died in Pickens County, recently, Miss Catharine Graham.
Died in Pickens County, recently, a son of George A. Skidmore.
Died in Pickens County, recently, a son of Jason Williams.
Died in Greene County, 6th inst., Lelia V. Bowers, child.
Died in Troy, 6th inst., Miss Martha Ann Pennick.
Died August 5th, Miss Sarah E., daughter of the late Rev. J.P. Dickinson.
Died in Boonesboro, Arkansas, August 2nd, Col. A.W. McClellan, formerly of Talladega County.
Died in Colbert County, 1st inst., Lasseephin Ligon, child.
Died in Mississippi, August 27th, George S. Holly, an old citizen of Hale County.
Died in Cherokee County, 1st inst., Samuel Beard.
Died in Cherokee County, 4th inst., a daughter of S.L. Russell.

## THE SOUTHERN ARGUS - DEATHS - JUNE 1869 THROUGH JUNE 1874

Died in Marion, August 31st, Miss Rebecca Peeples.
Died at Letohatchie, August 31st, Mrs. Robert T. Shepherd.
Died near Bragg's, August 31st, Fountain Leatherwood, aged thirteen years.
Died in Montgomery, 12th inst., Mrs. N.W. Terry.
Died September 7th, Mrs. Fannie Octavia Stevens of New Orleans, formerly of Mobile.
Died in Barbour County the 10th, Benjamin Shearer.
Died in Louisiana, 26th ult., Young William Graves, formerly of Lowndes County.
Died in Mobile the 7th, Mrs. Daniel Troy.
Died near Opelika the 11th, Hon. James F. Dowdell.
Died in Opelika the 1?th, Mrs. Mary J. Smith.
Died in La Grange, Georgia, the 11th, Mrs. Mary Brady of Opelika.
Died in Troy the 8th, little Portia Daley.
Died in Gadsden the 7th, Mrs. Dr. Bevans.
Died in Bullock County the 9th, Sasha Slaughter, child.
Died in Mobile the 14th, B. Schoenfeld.
Died in Clinton the 9th, Joseph Henderlaing.
Died in Choctaw County, recently, Rev. W. Woodward.
Died near Pensacola, recently, J.M. Henderson of Conecuh County.
Died in Huntsville the 11th, Viola Young Lawler, infant.
Died in Huntsville the 12th, Mrs. Matilda Walker Dox.
Died in Lauderdale County the 10th, Wallace Claiborn.
Died in Cherokee County the 8th, Simson Shields.
Died in Mobile the 15th, Miles M. Carrington.
Died near Clayton the 9th, a little son of M.C. Bell.
Died in Columbiana the 9th, Clemmie Post, child.
Died at Pleasant Grove, Pickens County the ??ult., Robert Cameron.
Died in Pickensville, recently, Calvin Carson.
Died near Pickensville, a few days ago, a young man named Goodman.
Died in Sumter County the 30th ult., Mrs. Margaret Love.
Died near Meridianville the 10th, Robert Walter Pruitt.
Died near Dixie the 1st, a child of Rev. A.A. Greene, aged about six years.
Died at Lower Peach Tree the 7th, Martha Ann Elmira Mayer, child.
Died in Henry County the 31st ult., William Peebles, aged ninety.

David Gillespie killed a discharged convict near Brock's Gap, recently, and was acquitted by Judge Morrow of Jefferson County.

The brother and sister of John Harper, the great Kentucky horseman, owner of Longfellow, were murdered by negroes on the 10th inst.

## THE SOUTHERN ARGUS - DEATHS - JUNE 1869 THROUGH JUNE 1874

Issue 9-29-1871

General James H. Clanton was killed at Knoxville, Tennessee, on the 27th, by Col. D.M. Nelson, in a street fight.

D.E. Hewett of Shelby County was fatally snake bitten on the 19th inst.

C.H. Gay was thrown from his buggy near North Port, recently, and seriously injured.

John Adolphe committed suicide by drowning in Mobile, one day last week.

In the upper part of Clarke County, about two weeks ago, Thomas Nichols, an estimable citizen was shot and killed by Jacob Bradley, negro, who was killed in turn by Frank Payne.

Professor W.Y. Titcomb of Conecuh was seriously hurt by a fall from his horse a short time ago.

The *Evergreen Observer* thus sums up the deaths among the more prominent citizens of Conecuh within the last year: Wm. A. Ashley, the two Higdons, P.S. Whelan, Turner Ivey, Joseph G. Lundy, Daniel R. Thomas, John Gilmore, Henry Stanley, Mrs. J.A. McCreary, Rev. T.W. Postell, Z.T. Christian, W.P. James and James D. Thomas, and then John R. Downing and the lamented Henderson of Escambia...

George Alexander Hamilton, Secretary of the Treasure under Earl Derby, died in Dublin on the 18th inst.

Ex-Governor Stewart of Missouri died on the 21st.

Seaton Grantlan was killed by his father-in-law, Dr. W. W. Carr, in Washington County, Georgia a few days ago.

Governor-elect Brown of Tennessee, who has been dangerously ill, is getting well.

Issue 10-6-1871

Sam Hamer, who killed Si Randall in Madison County in 1870, was arrested last week and is in jail at Huntsville.

Thomas T. Adams of Talladega, indicted for killing George Klein, was tried and acquitted two weeks ago.

## THE SOUTHERN ARGUS - DEATHS - JUNE 1869 THROUGH JUNE 1874

Capt. B.W. Justice, formerly of Tuskaloosa, was accidentally killed in Raleigh, North Carolina the 23rd ult.

Major W.A. McAllister is dangerously ill in Abbeville.

Died in Randolph, 19th ult., in the full triumph of a christian's faith, Tinzy Jones, wife of B.P. Jones.
Died in Allenton, 16th ult., Dr. W.P. Crum.
Died in Mobile, 30th ult., Mrs. Sarah E. Jones.
Died at Choctaw Corner, August 20th, Miss Emma Morrisette.
Died in Dale County the 10th, Mrs. H.H. Blackman.
Died in Camden the 14th, Jacob Levy.
Died in Jacksonville the 15th, Mollie Bolinger, child.
Died in Jacksonville the 19th, Mrs. Smithy Turner.
Died in Huntsville the 17th, Thomas O. Burton.
Died in Vienna the 14th, Katie Connerly.
Died in Mobile the 10th, G.M. Keller, Jr.
Died in Mobile the 23rd, Thomas J. Murdock.
Died in Sunny Side, recently, a daughter of George Ross.
Died at Manack, recently, a child of M.W. Collins.
Died in Mobile the 20th, Mrs. Anna Yuille.
Died in Marion the 15th, Mrs. Catherine M. Callahan.
Died in Arkansas, August 29th, Col. Allan Walls, formerly of Madison County.
Died in Blount County, recently, Major Mace T.P. Brindley.
Died in Blount County, recently, Judge J.C. Gilliespie.
Died in Eufaula the 17th, Professor J.R. Ware.
Died in Tuskaloosa County the 17th, Mrs. Ed. Hagler.
Died in Memphis the 16th, Mrs. Margarite Sunnerer of Florence.
Died in Centre the 16th, Mrs. Mattie Coker.
Died in Cherokee the 18th, infant child of James Coker.
Died in Gadsden the 15th, Miss Mary King.
Died in Hollow Square the 10th, Eddie Chapman, thirteen years old.
Died in Hale County the 10th, Georgie Drummond, child.
Died in Elyton the 9th, George W. Maroney of Greene County.
Died in Greene County the 15th, a child of Dr. J.W. Clements, the third within a month.
Died in Greene County, recently, a child of Dominic Constantine, the third in less than six weeks.
Died near Evergreen the 14th, James D. Thomas, eight years old.
Died in Montgomery the 20th, A.P. Watt.
Died in Marion the 23rd, John T. Livingston.
Died in Perry County, the 24th, Jefferson J. Watts.
Died near South Florence, 25th ult., Mrs. Annie E. Whittemore.
Died in Mobile, 29th ult., David Haig.

# THE SOUTHERN ARGUS - DEATHS - JUNE 1869 THROUGH JUNE 1874

Died near Hollow Square, 27th ult., Fannie Sawyer, aged ten years.
Died in Mobile, 28th ult., F.A. Leslie.
Died in Mobile, 27th ult., Sister Agatha of the Sisters of Charity.
Died in Mobile, 26th ult., Mrs. F.F. Parker.
Died in Mobile, 25th ult., M.T. Perryman.
Died in Springfield, Tennessee, the 24th ult., Rev. E. Strode, formerly of Huntsville.
Died at Berkley's Landing, 15th ult., I.N. Cook, aged fifteen years.
Died at Greenville, 26th ult., William J. Wood.
Died at Union Springs, 26th ult., Dr. James Rumph.
Died at Sandy Ridge, 19th ult., Fannie Lou Brooks, infant.
Died in Hayneville, 25th ult., Mrs. Fannie Mushat.
Died in Montgomery County, recently, William H. Emmerson.
Died in Mobile, 1st inst., Peter Laffre.

A young man named White was mortally cut a few days ago near Gadsden by a young man named Jarvis, who he had attacked.

At York Station, Friday night last, while intoxicated, J.J. Currence murdered his wife and father-in-law.

Rev. W.H. Ellison of Union Springs, who has been quite sick, is convalescing.

A few days ago, a little son of T.H. Dozier of Union Springs was badly hurt by the accidently discharge of a gun.

## Issue 10-13-1871

Elzi Sanders (negro) convicted in Perry Circuit Court of rape, is to be hung November 24th.

David T. Vincent, a native of Maryland, but lately an esteemed citizen of Selma, died in Harpersville, Shelby County, on the 6th inst.

Mrs. W.H. Crusius, formerly of this city, where she had many friends who sincerely mourn her loss, died in Montgomery on the 5th instant.

J.N. Eskridge, formerly of this city, who some time ago escaped from jail in Columbus, Mississippi, where he was confined on the charge of murdering Harry Brantley, also late of this county, has been rearrested in Louisiana.

# THE SOUTHERN ARGUS - DEATHS - JUNE 1869 THROUGH JUNE 1874

While plowing in his field in Cherokee County the 28th ult., Miller Force was shot and killed.
   Frank Weaver has been arrested in Cherokee County, charged with killing Miller Force.

H.W. Dawson, nephew of Capt. J.M. Winston of Sumter County, was murdered at Scooba, Mississippi, on the 3rd inst.

J.F. Dennis, formerly of this city, has had yellow fever in Vicksburg.

We regret to here that Mr. James Lauderdale, agent of the Selma and Montgomery Road in this city, has been seriously sick since Tuesday last.

J.C. Camp of Cherokee County was attacked recently with violent pains in his head, followed by partial paralysis...

## DIED IN ALABAMA

Died near Grove Hill, 21st ult., Rev. L.L. Dewitt.
Died in Mobile, 5th inst., W.T. Townsend.
Died in Eutaw, 29th ult., G.W. Kiser of Kentucky.
Died in Huntsville, 4th inst., Miss Nellie Lee Jolly.
Died in Troy, 26th ult., Miss Anjella Tulles.
Died in Troy, 1st ult., Mrs. Margaret E. Nicholson.
Died in Chunnenuggee, 1st inst., B.J. Brantley.
Died in Tuskegee, 3rd inst., Mrs. Nancy Wade.
Died in Mobile, 4th inst., Miss Rosanna Callahan.
Died in Madison County, 30th ult., Charles Thomas.
Died in Huntsville, 1st inst., Mrs. America Geron.
Died in Huntsville, 2nd inst., "Judge" Willett.
Died in Lowndes County, two weeks ago, a child of J.M. Monerief/Moncrief.
Died at Randolph, September 24th, William Christian, aged about sixty-five years.
Died at Randolph, September 7th, William Houston, aged about nine years.
Died in Mobile, 7th inst., Charles Callenge.
Died near Carrollton, 27th ult., Brice Hodge.
Died in New York, 2nd inst., H.G. Muldon of Mobile.
Died in New Orleans, 5th inst., Milton Boullemet, formerly of Mobile.
Died in Tuscumbia, 29th ult., Mrs. Anna E. German.
Died at the residence of W.A.D. Ramsey in Baker County the 4th inst., J.H. Cocke of Perry.
Died in Mobile, 7th inst., Thomas McConnell.
Died near Mobile, 5th inst., Mrs. Caroline Carrington.
Died at Whistler, 9th inst., Mrs. Elizabeth Clark.
Died near Mt. Meigs, Sunday night last, Franklin C. Pinckston.

## THE SOUTHERN ARGUS - DEATHS - JUNE 1869 THROUGH JUNE 1874

Died in Marion the 3rd inst., Elisha Y. Nelms.

Issue 10-20-1871

Died in Cahawba, October 2nd, Cordelia, only daughter of John and Elizabeth Olds.

Died in this city, Thursday evening last, after a long and painful illness, George C. Swift.

James Gilmer, Esq., an old and honored citizen of this County, is dangerously ill at his residence in Union Beat.

We regret to hear that Mr. J.F. Dennis, formerly a citizen of this place, died one day last week in Vicksburg of yellow fever.

David A. Hobbie who died recently in Troy, was an old newspaper man, having been successively connected with the *Selma Reporter, State Journal, State Rights Democrat, Southern Advertiser* and *Troy Messenger.*

Ruff Stinnett, Jr. was thrown from a horse and killed in Limestone County last week.

A little child of Mrs. Randall of Macon County was drowned in a tub of water a short time ago.

Died in Mobile the 14th, Charles Turner.
Died in Opelika the 11th, Mrs. John O. Singley.
Died at Fort Jackson the 7th, Mrs. Pierce.
Died at Fear Wetumpka the 9th, Mrs. Levins.
Died in Wetumpka the 6th, H.J. Reed.
Died in Wetumpka the 13th, Mrs. J.W. Suttle.
Died in Elmore County, recently, F. Gibson.
Died in Mobile the 13th, Daniel Grimes.
Died in McKinley, July 19th, Addie E. Chapman, aged four years.
Died in McKinley, July 25th, Mrs. Martha E. Chapman.
Died in McKinley, September 18th, Samuel E. Chapman, aged two years.
Died in Mobile the 14th, Francis Huth.
Died in Mobile the 14th, William Rouse.
Died near Autaugaville, a few days ago, W.N. Thompson.
Died in Tuskaloosa the 9th, John E. Chambers.
Died in Montgomery County the 14th, Mrs. M.A. Baldwin.
Died in Mobile the 9th, Peter Collins.
Died in Mobile the 10th, Emanuel Otero.
Died in Mobile County the 10th, Major Boyd D. Simison.

## THE SOUTHERN ARGUS - DEATHS - JUNE 1869 THROUGH JUNE 1874

Died in Mobile the 11th, Thomas H. McGonigal.
Died in Mobile the 11th, Colonel W.C. Griggs.
Died in Mobile the 11th, Mrs. Gabriella Nason/Mason.
Died in Troy the 5th, David A. Hobbie.
Died in Troy, recently, Andrew Franklin Wingate, infant.
Died near Benton, September 28th, little Manie May.
Died in Macon County the 9th, John C. Judkins.
Died in Madison County the 7th, Mrs. Susan Jinkens.
Died in Mobile the 12th, Mrs. E.S. Henstis/Heustis.
Died in the neighborhood of Havana the 6th, Nettie Irene Elliott, infant.
Died in Russell County, recently, Captain R.N. Howard.
Died in Marion the 14th, Berry Rutledge.
Died in Autauga County the 15th, Melton F. Howard.

James M. Spindle of Mt. Hebron fell from the platform of the warehouse at Trussell's ferry, a few days ago, fatally injuring himself.

J.M.N.B. Nix was thrown from his buggy in Talladega, Sunday week ago, by a runaway horse and came near being killed.

The mother of Rev. O/D? W. Gwinn, pastor of the Montgomery Baptist Church, died in Alexander, Virginia, the 10th inst.

Issue 10-27-1871

John T. Wilson, indicted in the Shelby Circuit Court for killing Belt Nabors, has obtained a change of venue to Baker County.

The case of Bowlin charged with killing Fisher, in Talladega County, transferred to Shelby, was continued at the late term of the Shelby Circuit Court.

An old man named Morgan of Eutaw County fell out of his oxcart the other day and broke his neck.

Resolution of respect from Meridian Sun Lodge #88, on the death of John Buster.

In Montgomery, Joe Johnson (negro) has been convicted of the murder of Henry Walton, and sentenced to be hung.

Major James Isbell of Talladega was dangerously ill last week.

## THE SOUTHERN ARGUS - DEATHS - JUNE 1869 THROUGH JUNE 1874

Issue 11-3-1871

Hugh Allicin Lee, lately brutally murdered by a negro mob at Arteria, Mississippi, was born and raised in Carlowville, in this county.

Died in East Selma, Tuesday last, Mr. Joseph Harper...

Old man Creach and his son, in Dale County, died suddenly two weeks ago, and were buried in the same grave.

On the 23rd ult. a shooting match between Colonel W.C. Oates and Alexander McKay occurred in Pike County, in which McKay was wounded.

### DIED IN ALABAMA

Died in Mobile the 16th, Irene Mary Clark, aged two years.
Died in Montgomery the 13th, John Cowley.
Died in Coosa County the 14th, Mrs. Julia B. Garrett.
Died in Montgomery the 21st, Mrs. John P. Dickinson.
Died in Benton the 8th, James H. Gifford.
Died in Autauga the 13th, Charles Hrabouski/Hrabonski.
Died in Claiborne the 13th, A.J. Robertson.
Died in Greensboro the 13th, Miss Maria Odele Dorman.
Died in Hale County the 16th, Mrs. Mary A. Massey.
Died in Tuskaloosa the 16th, Robert Jemison, Jr.
Died at Eutaw the 15th, J.H. Barger.
Died near Camden, September 8th, Mrs. Mary Johnson.
Died in Wilcox County the 7th, Lewis D. Jones.
Died near Centre the 13th, J.P. Camp.
Died near Centre the 9th, Miss Mattie McGhee.
Died in Elyton the 11th, Agnes, daughter of Dr. J.R. Smith.
Died in Colbert County the 11th, Hector Atkinson, aged seventy-five years.
Died near Tuscumbia the 12th, Mrs. Kasper Muller.
Died in Demopolis the 15th, Edward J. McGrath, infant.
Died at Spring Hill the 17th, Mrs. Charolette A. Marston.
Died in Mobile the 18th, Hinson S. Monk.
Died in Choctaw County the 13th, Colonel Thomas McC. Prince.
Died near Fort Deposit the 12th, Mrs. Sampley.
Died in Lowndes County the 12th, Wm. Hornady.
Died in Mobile the 16th, Lizzie Merritt, twin daughter of J.R. and Lelia C. Eagon.
Died in Mobile the 20th, Lavinia Louisa, twin daughter of J.R. and Lelia C. Eagon.
Died in Mobile the 14th, Richard Bledsoe Harris.
Died in Mobile the 21st, George Walter Hewitt.

## THE SOUTHERN ARGUS - DEATHS - JUNE 1869 THROUGH JUNE 1874

Died in Mobile, recently, George Whitney.
Ded in Pickens County the 10th, Miss Ella Ferguson.
Died in Tennessee the 1st, Abraham Eddings, formerly of Madison County.
Died in Conecuh the 14th, Henry Ward.
Died near Tompkinsville the 7th, Samuel Johnson.
Died near Butler the 8th, C.A. Spear.
Died in Eufaula the 16th, Mrs. Sarah Anderson.
Died in Washington County, 16th ult., John Thompson, aged seventy years.
Died in Washington County, 15th ult., A.T. Brown.
Died in Madison County, 25th ult., James W. Burwell, sixty-nine years of age.
Died in Cherokee County, 20th ult., Ebenezer Pitts.
Died in Cherokee County, 15th ult., Mary E. White.
Died near Cedar Bluff, 23rd ult., Dr. S.B. Robinson.
Died in Gainesville, 28th ult., a little son of J.H. Hendricks.
Died in Scooba, Mississippi, 23rd ult., Mrs. E.D. Harwood, formerly of Gainesville.
Died near Rockford, 19th ult., Thomas J. Martin.
Died at Dayton, 21st ult., Mrs. Fannie Wall.
Died at Jefferson, 21st ult., Jordan W. Oakley.
Died in Sumter County, 11th ult., William R. Davis.
Died in Mobile, 28th ult., Mrs. Harriett Slocum.
Died in Mobile, 23rd ult., John W. O'Meara.
Died in Wetumpka, recently, Fletcher Gibson.
Died in Pike County, 21st ult., Simeon D. Wilson.
Died near Greensboro, 4th ult., David Leonidas Smith.
Died in Mississippi, 7th ult., B.A. Carter, formerly of Hale County.
Died in Mobile, 26th ult., Peter Odermatt.
Died in Opelika, 24th ult., Judge A. Lewis of Russell County.
Died in Clarke County, September 26th, Mrs. Catherine Endora Stallworth, daughter of Archibald and Frances Glen, formerly of this county.
Died in Tuskaloosa County, 18th ult., Mrs. Rebecca Haseltine Foster.
Died in Mobile, 2nd ult., Charley Wagner.
Died in Montgomery County, September 28th, John W. Alford.
Died near Letohatchie, September 20th, Henry B. Rolfe.

R.A. Salomon of Eufaula has been very sick.

Humes Carothers of the *Huntsville Reporter* accidently shot himself through the hand a few days ago.

Bird Ohlman of Tuscumbia was thrown from a wagon the other day and had his arm broken.

# THE SOUTHERN ARGUS - DEATHS - JUNE 1869 THROUGH JUNE 1874

Issue 11-10-1871

A little son of A.J. Bransford of this city fell from a tree on Sunday evening and received injuries from which he died in about half an hour.

Kate Gordon, daughter of Rev. Dr. Palmer of New Orleans died the 27th ult.

Died at the residence of Mrs. M.O. Robinson, in Lowndes County, on the night of the 2nd inst., Mrs. R.I. Morgan, sister of Mr. R. Wyatt of this city.

Thomas Anderson, conductor on the Selma, Rome and Dalton Road, was severely injured, at Childersburg, Monday night last, by being caught between two cars.

Died at his residence near this city, Wednesday night, E.W. Barnett, aged forty-nine years.
Died in this city last Saturday night, David Hoffman, from injuries received in a fall from his horse the Monday previous.
Died in Mobile the 16th ult., Mrs. Mary E. Elliott.
Died in Tuskaloosa the 2nd inst., Leighton Cobbs.
Died in Gainesville the 28th ult., Odom Cox.
Died in Pickens County the 24th ult., Mrs. Nancy Wilkerson.
Died in Escambia County the 25th ult., William Matthews.
Died in Conecuh County the 25th ult., David Henderson.
Died in Mobile the 2nd inst., Ruby Livingston, infant.
Died near Lowndesboro the 26th ult., Miss Margaret Polly.
Died in Tuskaloosa County, October 16th, Mrs. Antoinette Farmer.
Died in Troy, recently, little Lowndes Wilson.
Died in New York the 26th ult., W.C. Hallett, formerly of Mobile.
Died in Mobile the 31st ult., Helen Mary Holt, infant.
Died in Huntsville the 4th, William F. Mastin, Mayor of the city.
Died in Claiborne the 4th, Mrs. John C. Arthur.
Died at the residence of C.C. Smith, Perry County, the 27th ult., H.G. Smith.
Died at the residence of her father, C.C. Smith, Perry County, the 5th inst., Mrs. Sarah H. Henley.
Died at the residence of C.C. Smith, Perry County, August 31st, Edmund Henley.
Died in Prattville the 26th ult., Oscar Smith, child.
Ded in Prattville the 27th ult., Thomas P. Smith.
Died in Coosa County the 2nd inst., Thomas J. Welch.
Died in Decatur the 29th ult., Harry Moore.
Died in Mobile the 30th ult., Mrs. Sarah Jane Russell.

## THE SOUTHERN ARGUS - DEATHS - JUNE 1869 THROUGH JUNE 1874

Rev. N.M. Crawford, son of Hon. W.H. Crawford, who was one of the presidential candidates in 1824, died in Whitfield County, Georgia, the 26th ult.

Elbert T. McGehee of Gadsden has been quite sick.

### Issue 11-17-1871

Joseph Sullivan, a member of Mechanic Fire Company, was buried on Thursday of last week by that company.

Henry Carter Edmunds and Dr. J.A. McAlpin of Talladega are dead. The former died at Senatobia, Mississippi, the latter at Philadelphia.

Adam Gresser, a shoemaker, died suddenly in Mobile, Tuesday last.

Major William F. Mastin, Mayor of Huntsville, died on the 4th inst., aged thirty-six years.

By the falling of a shot gun in Centre a few days ago, William Blair and W.M. Meeks were accidentally shot.

Luke Johnson, a condemned murderer, escaped from Nash County, North Carolina Jail.

Died near Hillsboro the 6th, Mrs. Rebecca Mitchell, aged seventy.
Died in Frankfort the 6th, Lemuel Nelson, aged sixty-five years.
Died near Tuskaloosa the 2nd, Leighton Cobbs.
Died near Auburn the 1st, Barton D. Harris of Montgomery.
Died in Columbiana, 24th ult., Susan Rebecca Beggs, infant.
Died in Lowndes County, 2nd, Mrs. Cora Martin of Columbiana.
Died in Mobile the 8th, Lawrence Wachtee.
Died in Memphis, Tennessee, the 9th, Jerome Sheehan of Mobile.
Died in Mobile the 10th, Mrs. E.D. Chilton.
Died in Mobile the 8th, Adelia S. Brown.
Died in Camden the 8th, Johnny Martin, aged eleven years.
Died October 4th, fifteen minutes past four o'clock p.m., at the residence of her mother, Mrs. Mary A.E. Gulley, in Snow Hill, Wilcox County, Alabama, Mrs. Mary E. Jones, consort of Dr. C.C. Jones, aged fifteen years, ten months, and eighteen days...She was married February 1st, 1871...

S.J. Swords of Cherokee County was killed by being run over by the cars at Amersonville, week before last.

# THE SOUTHERN ARGUS - DEATHS - JUNE 1869 THROUGH JUNE 1874

Early Eason is to be hanged at Memphis the 29th of December for the murder of Ed. Lyle.

Among the Ku Klux cases in South Carolina is the pretended murder of Mr. Newman of Chesterfield, whose widow makes affidavit that he was accidentally killed.

Issue 11-24-1871

Mrs. Alice Pettus, the venerable mother of our honored townsman, General E.W. Pettus, died in this city, on Wednesday last.

George Bates, living near Liberty Hill, committed suicide last week.

Died in Anderson County, Texas, October 29th, Mrs. Sarah Rosser, formerly of this county.
Died at the residence of Mrs. S.A. English, near Selma, on the 11th inst., Elisha S. Johnson.

Norman Gilchrist, William Johnson, and J. Frank, all of Hayneville, are quite sick, the former dangerously.

Wednesday of last week, near Jacksonville, a little daughter of Taylor DeArmar was killed by the falling of a small tree.

Mr. Breathwaite was thrown or fell from his horse in the vicinity of Clinton a few days ago, and had his skull so badly fractured that death ensued.

Ed Lipscomb of Alexander accidentally shot his sister the other day. The wound is not dangerous.

Issue 12-1-1871

Died in Gadsden, lately, Mrs. Golightly, wife of William Golighly.
Died in Bullock County, 14th, Colonel J.R. Rann, aged seventy-four.
Died near Newbern, 8th, Mrs. Eliza M. Beatty, aged seventy years.
Died in Greene County, 7th, F.P. Strother.
Died near Florence, 8th, Mrs. Matilda Burtwell.
Died in Tuskaloosa County, 13th, William Willingham.
Died in Greenville, ???, the wife of Terry McCall.
Died in Cross Plains, 13th, James Pierce.
Died near Newbern the 8th ult., Mrs. Eliza M. Beatty.
Died in Colbert County, 22nd ult., Benjamin Wilson.
Died in Montgomery, 27th ult., Dr. T.R. Hill.

## THE SOUTHERN ARGUS - DEATHS - JUNE 1869 THROUGH JUNE 1874

Died in Claiborne, 13th ult., Catherine Martha Ann Miller.
Died in Russell County, 19th ult., Jacob McGehee.
Died in Choctaw Corner, 16th October, Roswell Poole.
Died in Pickens County, recently, James Murphy.
Died near Clinton, 16th ult., George L. Clanton.
Died in Mobile, 23rd ult., Michael Morrow.
Died in Mobile, 22nd ult., Mrs. S.A. McGovern.
Died in Camden, October 31st, James Lawrence.
Died in Mobile, 1?th ult., Walter Brooks Tuggle.
Died in Mobile, 15th ult., Henry Ferrell.
Died in Athens the 12th ult., Mrs. Bettie Cox.
Died in Jackson Springs, Clarke County the 30th ult., D.O. Grady of Mobile.
Died in Meridian, Mississippi, lately, Mrs. Alabama B. Thielyard, daughter of the late Governor Bagby.
Died in Conecuh County, 9th ult., Hardee Deer.
Died in Hayneville the 1?th ult., James Norman Gilchrist.
Died in Radfordsville the 13th ult., Lemmie D. Palmore, child.
Died in West Perry the 19th ult., Miss Ada Jemison.
Died in East Perry the 21st ult., Elias J. Wallace.
Died in Gadsden the 19th ult., Mrs. O.P. Hill.
Died in Sumter County the 11th ult., Samuel M. Arrington.
Died in Madison County the 30th ult., Mrs. Ella Burks.
Died in Limestone County the 19th ult., Sarah A. Roberts, aged sixty-five years.
Died in Eufaula last week, Luke Lott of Ocheesee, Florida.
Died in Macon, Georgia, the 19th ult., from wounds received in the army, John F. Cargile of Eufaula.
Died in Galveston, Texas, a few days ago, Warren Garrott, son of the late Colonel L.W. Garrott of Marion.
Died in Dale County, recently, R.T. Lingo.

Two weeks ago in Colbert County, Armstead Barton, a lad, was caught in the gearing of his father's cotton gin and killed instantly.

In Elyton the 18th, Dr. Gunn was shot and mortally wounded by a man named Thomaston.

Issue 12-8-1871

We regret to learn that Major W.S. Knox is dangerously ill, in Carlowville.

The dwelling of Alvin Anderson of Winston County was burnt a few days ago with all its contents and a child several months old perished in the flames.

## THE SOUTHERN ARGUS - DEATHS - JUNE 1869 THROUGH JUNE 1874

Mrs. Reese D. Gayle, for many years a resident of Cahawba, died in Mobile...

Miss Lilly Weaver, daughter of Leroy Weaver, an accomplished young lady of this city, died in Baltimore last Friday and was buried here on Sunday.

At the late term of the Pickens Circuit Court, Wm. Gresham was tried for killing a man named Ivie, and Watt Tier for killing W.G. Martin, and both were acquitted.

R.T. Burns, formerly of Montgomery County, was found murdered between Pollard and Tensas, two weeks ago last Tuesday.

In resisting an officer charged with his arrest, George King, negro of Eufaula, was recently shot twice and seriously wounded.

The residence of a Mr. Tolson, on Dog River, was blown down on the 25th ult., and Mr. and Mrs. Tolson were badly injured.

Capt. William Forrest was not killed in Texas as reported some time ago. He was arrested in Texas, charged with killing some person there some eighteen years ago, tried for it the 14th-18th of last month, and acquitted.

Sam Anthony, near Elyton, was blowing in a gun to find out whether it was loaded or not, a few days ago, when it was discharged, killing him instantly.

Mrs. Robert of Cherokee County was thrown from her horse and killed some two weeks ago.

A man by the name of Taylor was found dead near Greenville, Tuesday of last week, supposed to have been murdered by a negro named Jim Burnett.

Young Blair, who was shot on election day at Centre, is recovering slowly. Seven shots are yet in his leg.

On the 23rd ult., Elzi Sanders, negro, was hanged in Marion, for rape.

Died in Conecuh County, 15th ult., Willie Parks, aged five years.
Died in Limestone County, 20th ult. Lizzie H. Dawson, infant.
Died in Missouri, lately, Wiley J. Coleman, formerly of Choctaw.
Died in Mobile, 29th ult., Laura Darman Spracklin.
Died in Stevenson, last week, a young man named Griffin.
Died in West Perry, 24th ult. Elisha Ivie.
Died in West Perry, recently, Miss Nannie B. Driver.
Died in Uniontown, 20th ult., little Hattie Kennedy.

# THE SOUTHERN ARGUS - DEATHS - JUNE 1869 THROUGH JUNE 1874

Died in Missouri, lately, Alexander Lyon of Eutaw.
Died in Chester County, South Carolina, 12th ult., James Strait of Clinton, Alabama.
Died in Clark County, 22nd ult., E.S. Pugh.
Died near Fort Deposit, 23rd ult., James Goldsmith.
Died in Union Springs 8th ult., Rev. J.W. Williams.
Died in St. Clair County, 18th ult., Richard Rowan.
Died near Uniontown, 28th ult. Hugh R. Nelson, child.
Died in Calera, December 1, A.P. Turner, Jr. of the firm of Turner & Dare.

## Issue 12-15-1871

A young man named Thompson committed suicide at York Station the 31st ult by drowing himself in a well.

Col. John D. Ashmore, former member of Congress from Abbeville District South Carolina, blew out his brains with a pistol at a hotel in Sardis, 5th inst.

Died in Summerfield the 21st ult., after a long and painful illness borne with christian patience and fortitude, in great peace of mind, Mrs. Massey, wife of Professor John Massey of Centenary Male College.

Died in Carlowville on the 6th inst., Maj. W.S. Knox, an old and honored citizen of Selma, a large hearted, liberal minded, public spirited, business man, a devoted husband and father, a true and worthy mason, and an earnest and consistent christian.

In Pineville, Monroe County, the 29th ult., Jehial Cotten and Enoch Riley, old neighbors and friends, got into a difficulty, which ended in a shooting, in which both parties were killed.

At Rocky Mount, Montgomery County, Mr. Smith, who kept a store there, was murdered by negroes, last week.

In Pike County, a few days ago, William Leonard had his hand caught in the saws of a cotton gin and terribly lacerated.

Holman Pugh, a laborer at the Shelby Iron Works, was accidentally shot and killed the 1st instant by his brother-in-law, a Mr. Bice.

## THE SOUTHERN ARGUS - DEATHS - JUNE 1869 THROUGH JUNE 1874

Maj. [James] Isbell died at his residence in Talladega at half-past seven o'clock, Wednesday evening the 6th instant.
   He was a native on North Carolina. In early life he chose Alabama for his home and settled in Lowndes County. About 1836 he removed to Talladega, where he resided until his death. His age was sixty-five years...

On the 30th ult. a little daughter of a Mr. Buford, blacksmith at the railroad shops in Huntsville, caught fire, and was so badly burned as to cause her death.

Rev. C.B. Parsons, D.D., died in Louisville on the night of the 8th.

J.N. Wilson, near Centre, has been very ill.

Died in Limestone County, 24th ult., Andrew McWilliams.
Died in Conecuh County, 15th ult., Willie Parks, child.
Died in Clarke County, 26th ult., Mrs. Acsah Chapman.
Died in Columbiana, 7th inst., Miss Mary Leeper.
Died in Etowah County, Willis P. Casey.
Died in Birmingham, 30th ult., little Nannie Jackson.
Died in Jefferson County, 1st inst., Colonel James McAdory.
Died at Touminville, 5th inst., Mary Alvarez Prichard.
Died in Texas, October 29th, Colonel T.B. Woodward, formerly of Talladega.
Died in Talladega, 3rd inst., Mrs. Josephine Lewis.
Died near Linden, October 30th., B. Burnett.
Died November 29th, Robert Pinkney, son of E.P. and E.J. Cothran, aged one year and one month...

### Issue 12-22-1871

Near Jefferson, Marengo County, a few days ago, Eilas Westbrook, negro, was dangerously stabbed by another negro.

A Mrs. Murray died in Eufaula last week in very distressing circumstances of want and destitution.

Roland Bryant of Floyd County, Georgia,... was accidently killed a few days ago by a fall from his horse.

### Issue 12-29-1871

At Axem's grocery in Dale County a few days ago, Hillery Woodham was stabbed and killed by a Mr. Windham.

## THE SOUTHERN ARGUS - DEATHS - JUNE 1869 THROUGH JUNE 1874

A.F. Henderson, late joint proprietor and Editor of the *Montgomery Mail*, committed suicide by shooting himself in the head at Tuskegee on the 22nd inst.

W.R. Bugg, tried on a charge of murdering his brother-in-law in Autauga County, last spring, has been convicted of murder in the second degree and sentenced to twenty-five years in the penitentiary.

Died near Middleton, 11th, Lewis S. Meharg.
Died near Florence, 10th, Mrs. Mary Coffee.
Died in Huntsville, 11th, Mrs. Elizabeth W. Fackler.
Died in New York, 11th, Simeon H. Anderson, formerly of Mobile.
Died in Mobile, 16th, Mrs. Fannie A. Williams.
Died in Mobile, 16th, E.J. Bacon.
Died in East Butler, 2nd, Francis Kirkpatrick.
Died in Etowah County, two weeks ago, Jeremiah Taylor.
Died in Perryville, November 17th, Joseph P. Morton, child.
Died in Perryville, 7th, William M. Morton, child.
Died in Mobile, 10th, A.H. Ryland.
Died in Limestone County, 1st inst., Andrew McWilliams.
Died in Limestone County , 3rd inst., Richard Wiggins.
Died in Mobile, 7th inst., Mary McNamarry.
Died in Lowndes County, 31st ult., Mrs. Elizabeth Nall.
Died in Benton, 3rd, infant child of Dr. Mushat.
Died in Tuscumbia, 6th., Major David Deshier.
Died near Courtland, 15th ult., James M. Conners.
Died in Lauderdale County, 26th ult., William Butler.
Died in Madison County, 23rd ult., Dr. W.B. Dunn.
Died in Madison County, 3rd inst., Richard A. Wiggins.
Died in Mt. Pleasant, Iowa, 1st inst., Mrs. Martha Nason, mother of Reuben Nason of Mobile.
Died in Wilcox County, October 31st, Robert D. Strock.
Died at York Station, 6th inst., Dr. J.M. Mayes.
Died in Greene County, 1st inst., Tillery Brown.
Died in Atlanta, 3rd, E.S. Mitchell, formerly of Montgomery.
Died in Montgomery, 14th, Effice Gornlay Hosner, infant.
Died in Montgomery, 13th, William Fuller.
Died in Greensboro, 17th, A. Syd. Nelson.
Died in Stevenson the 15th, Mrs. Cora Morris.
Died in Mobile the 19th, Caroline Augusta Harris, infant.
Died in Eufaula the 16th, T.W. Lane.
Died in Lowndes County the 12th, Mrs. Carter.
Died in Lowndes County, recently, Jimmie Lee Allen, infant.
Died in Tuskegee the 19th, Mrs. Milton Stevens.

# THE SOUTHERN ARGUS - DEATHS - JUNE 1869 THROUGH JUNE 1874

Died in Auburn the 16th, Dr. David A. Reese.
Died in Mobile the 21st, John Anthony Winston, aged fifty-nine years.
Died in Greene County the 15th, Miss Bettie Chiles.
Died in Mobile, recently, Matthew V. Scurry of Lynchburg, Virginia.
Died in New Orleans the 20th, Mrs. Sarah Smith, formerly of Mobile.
Died in Mobile the 23rd, Mrs. Rebecca J. Donovan.
Died in Mobile the 23rd, Louisa Garnett Scott.
Died in Chambers County the 19th, Solomon Seagroves, aged one hundred seven years.
Died in Montgomery the 23rd, Mrs. J.D. Bibb.

At Holley's Landing, a short time ago, a negro made a murderous attack on Captain J.D. Prichett.

Issue 1-5-1872

Died in Mobile, 24th ult., Dr. E.W. Burton.
Died in Mobile, 27th ult., Thomas Douglas.
Died in Mobile the 30th ult., James Stewart.
Died in Ohio the 11th ult., John G. Ernst, formerly of Mobile.
Died in Mobile County the 21st ult., Paul Lyons, aged one hundred and eleven years.
Died in Huntsville the 24th ult., Bendall S. Anyan.
Died in Mobile the 30th ult., Ellen McDonald.
Died in Eufaula, 23rd ult., Mrs. J.H. Prudden.
Died in Eufaula, 23rd ult., E. Veal.
Died in Montgomery, 31st ult., Colonel James A. Rhea.
Died in Jackson County, 22nd ult., Mrs. Ann Gentry.
Died in Stevenson, 22nd ult., James Eshelby.
Died in Huntsville, 27th ult., W.T. Armstrong.
Died at Florence, 25th ult., Rev. W.H. Jordan.
Died in this city Thursday morning, December 28th, Mrs. H.J. DeYampert.

We regret to learn that Colonel William Phillips has for some days been dangerously and is yet very sick.

General R.C. Foster, 3rd, of Nashville, Tennessee, died on the 28th.

At Cedar Bluff, recently, a Mr. Dukes was shot and wounded by E.S. Hardwicke.

Woodyard and Morningstar, two "sports" known in Central Alabama, exchanged shots in Mobile the other day. Woodward was wounded and the other killed.

## THE SOUTHERN ARGUS - DEATHS - JUNE 1869 THROUGH JUNE 1874

Tribute of respect on the death of William S. Knox, Central City Lodge F. & A.M..

James H. Hackett, an iminent actor, died the 27th ult.

Issue 1-12-1872

On the 30th ult., a party of Eufaula fox-hunters came in collision with an old man Nolan and his six sons, in which E.S. Ott received a severe blow on his head, John Wells a cut and two broken ribs, Osborne Wells a fractured skull and a broken cheek bone, and Turner Smith and Dallas Pippin any number of bruises and bumps. The Nolans came off better, only one of them being seriously hurt by a stab. Several of the parties, it is thought, will die of their wounds.

William Graham, a boy between twelve and fifteen years of age, accidentally shot Mr. Paschal High, at Coloma, last week.

It has been ascertained that a young man named Tyler, who left Cherokee County for Texas some two years ago in company with a stranger from that latter state, was murdered on Sand Mountain.

John Davidson, an old and widely known business man of New Orleans, died the 3rd inst.

Samuel Ashley, a lad of fifteen, living near Evergreen, was accidentally shot and killed on the 29th ult.

Saturday evening last, James Fisk of New York was wantonly shot and mortally wounded by Edward Stokes.

J.L. Watson, a brakeman on the Alabama and Chattanooga Railroad, was killed on the 29th ult., at Eutaw, by falling between the cars of a moving train.

Green Bolton, negro, caught stealing cotton, near Camden, was killed the 21st ult., by A.J. Cook.

William Ripley killed James Whitlock at Ladiga, on the 25th ult.
  A few days ago, James Whitlock of Calhoun County died from the effects of a blow on the head received at the hands of William Ripley.

Woodyard, the killer of Morningstar, has been discharged from custody, the shooting having been done in self-defence.

## THE SOUTHERN ARGUS - DEATHS - JUNE 1869 THROUGH JUNE 1874

Philip Swigert, an eminent Kentuckian, died in Frankfort, Kentucky, December 31st.

Issue 1-19-1872

On the night of the 4th inst., Daniel Smith of Black's Bend, Wilcox County, was shot and killed in his own store by a negro fellow.

John Watson of Pike County was assassinated near Mossy Grove on the 16th, being shot with buckshot from the roar side. Jonah Black is charged with the shooting.

At Dudleville on the 8th, Dr. Meadows was severely cut by a Mr. Word.

Lizzie Rash, negro, thirteen years old, near the line of Bullock and Pike Counties, has been committed to jail for the murder of Green Crawford, negro, ten years old.

Died in Mobile, 30th ult., Ellen McDonald.
Died in Bullock County the 28th ult., Dr. John W. Bledsoe.
Died in Blount County, 28th ult., G.W. Weaver.
Died at Florence, 25th ult., Rev. W.H. Jordan.
Died in Colbert County, 23rd ult., Mrs. Parthenia Pearsall.
Died in Huntsville, 1st, Christopher B. Donegan.
Died in Mobile, 4th, John P. McKinnon.
Died in Calhoun County, 21st ult., Elech Aiken.
Died near Cedar Bluff, 24th ult., Colonel James Bishop, aged ninety-two years.
Died in Lowndes, 20th ult., James Thompson.
Died in Union Springs the 2nd, Professor William Threadgill.
Died in Nevada the 12th ult., Perez Coleman, formerly of Montgomery.
Died in Mobile the 7th, Mrs. Lotta Hanlein.
Died in Lee County the 8th, S. Pennington.
Died in Loachapoka the ?th, Miss Mollie Hart.
Died in Hayneville the 6th, Mrs. Virginia Johnson.
Died in Stevenson the 8th, infant son of Mrs. Winter.
Died in Newbern the 31st ult., Dr. W.C. Nichols.
Died at Fayetteville the 8th, James P. Vessels.
Died in Choctaw County the 26th ult., Mrs. George E. Johnson.
Died in Mobile the 9th, Captain Robert Bruce.
Died in Butler the 4th, B.N. Glover, Probate Judge of Choctaw.
Died in Barbour County the 6th, A.A.F. Hill.
Died in Camden the 10th, Dr. William Gully.

## THE SOUTHERN ARGUS - DEATHS - JUNE 1869 THROUGH JUNE 1874

A.H. Roebuck, one of the most prominent citizens of Jefferson County, has been very sick.

### Issue 1-26-1872

A sailor named J.E. Williams was drowned the other day in Mobile Bay.

Died in this city Saturday last, Mrs. William Turner.

Little Anna, infant daughter of Mr. and Mrs. William M. Byrd, Jr. of this city, died on Thursday last.

Died at her residence in this city on Saturday last after a long and painful illness, Mrs. E. A. King.

Mrs. F.W. Andrew, the venerable widow of the late Bishop Andrew, died at the residence of her son, Colonel B.M. Woolsey, in this city, Wednesday last.

Mrs. Caroline J. Chiles of Greene County has lost by death six grown children in as many years.

Two negro women last week attempted the assassination of a Mrs. Miers of Marion, whom they seriously hurt.

Died in Jefferson County the 9th, A.H. Roebuck.
Died in Pollard the 8th, Martin Jones Lyons, infant.
Died in Marion the 16th, Thomas R. Fletcher.
Died in Gadsden the 13th, infant of Mrs. Slaton.
Died in Greene County the 17th, Miss Agnes Child.
Died in Florence the 16th, Francis Moran.
Died in Greene County the 22nd ult., Mrs. Mattie C. Montgomery.
Died in Greene County, recently, Mrs. Ann Hutton.
Died in Glennville the 11th, a little daughter of Rev. J.W. Glenn.
Died in Greensboro the 12th, Major Reuben Seay.
Died in Huntsville the 16th, Minnie W. Hawkins, aged nine years.
Died in Mobile the 19th, J.C. Colsson.
Died in Pickens County the 12th ult., Miss Matilda Berry, aged seventy-three years.
Died in Mobile the 21st, Mrs. Mary Dillon, aged seventy years.

A man named Aberson, in attempting to get on a freight train on the Mobile and Ohio Railroad at Mobile on Sunday last, fell under the cars, which passed over him and severed both legs.

## THE SOUTHERN ARGUS - DEATHS - JUNE 1869 THROUGH JUNE 1874

Rev. John McDaniel, a clergyman of Jonesboro, Tennessee, was accidentally drowned last week while crossing the Nolachucky River.

Mr. Jere Griffith, an old and respectable citizen of Montgomery, dropped dead on the 17th, while walking the street in apparent good health, from disease of the heart.

Issue  2-2-1872

Died in this city on Saturday last, James Burns.
Died at Carlowville the 22nd ult., Captain Jacob S. Allicin, in the seventy-third year of his age..

Mrs. Lizzie L. Wailes Humphreys, sister of Major W.E. Wailes of this city, died in Salisbury, Maryland, the 20th ult.  Mrs. Humphreys was educated at Summerfield...

We regret to hear of the death at or near Meyersville, Texas, on the 15th of January of William G. Hill, recently of this county. Mr. Hill's health had been bad for some time; and only a few months ago he went to Western Texas with what has proved the vain hope of physical improvement...

Died in Mobile, January 25th, Mrs. Georgiana Wildman.
Died in Mobile, January 24th, Samuel Doak Holt, infant.
Died in Huntsville, January 23rd, Charles Hereford.
Died in Lauderdale County, January 13th, Lee Allen Howell, child.
Died in Hayneville, January 23rd, Silvester P. Vermilya(?)
Died at Mt. Willing, January 9th, W.M. Garrett, child.
Died in Eufaula, January 10th, Miss Julia Langston.
Died in Eufaula, January 20th, William Hardman.
Died at Opelika, January 22nd, Mr. Kilgore.
Died in Linden, January 17th, little Mattie Johnson.
Died at Judson Institute, Marion, January 23rd, Miss Lela Seaman of Montgomery.

Issue  2-9-1872

Died at Summerfield the 5th inst., Miss Julia Daniels.

January 11th, James Martin of Dale County was accidentally killed by the falling of a log which he was raising to its place in a house he was building.

The dress of Mrs. John Fulmer of Lowndes County caught fire a few days ago and she barely escaped with a severe scorching.

## THE SOUTHERN ARGUS - DEATHS - JUNE 1869 THROUGH JUNE 1874

W.F. Hurt, Representative from Jackson County, has been very sick.

On the 20th ult. a negro made an assault with an axe on the wife and daughter of Dr. G.W. Files of Gosport, Clarke County, wounding both, the wife fatally it is thought.

George Hogg of Wilcox County was killed a few days since by the fall of a house he was erecting.

At Guntersville, recently, Robert J. Kennedy, Jr. was killed by W. Todd.

Freddie Jones, son of W.A.C. Jones of Livingston, was seriously hurt the other day by an accidental explosion of a powder flask.

Issue 2-16-1872

At Greenville the other day, York Caldwell, negro, was smashed up by the cars.

On the night of 5th, John Willis, a Jackson County lad, fell from a car on the Memphis and Charleston Railroad and was instantly killed.

Maj. Edward Herndon, recently dead, was clerk of the Sumter Circuit Court.

Died in Hale County, January 26th, Frances Isabella Borden, child.
Died near Greensboro, January 27th, infant daughter of L.M. Osburn.
Died in Decatur, January 24th, Mrs. Eliza J. Dykous.
Died in Butler County, January 28th, Dan Shine.
Died in Mobile, January 28th, John Thomas Smith.
Died in Opelika, January 26th, Miss Mary Wilder.
Died in Montgomery, January 26th, J.A. Waller.
Died in Lowndes County, recently, Carlos Barlow.
Died near Scottsville, January 30th, W.D. Skelton.
Died in Jackson County, January 19th, Joab Wilson.
Died in Talladega, 2nd inst., Mrs. C.M. Pritchett.
Died in Monroe County, January 13th, James T. Pritchett, aged one hundred and six years.
Died in Calhoun County, January 31st, Nathan Bowls.
Died in Birmingham, January 18th, Mrs. Sallie Stephenson.
Died in Pickens County, January 24th, Joseph Cunningham, Sr.
Died in Pickensville, January ??, Robert Long.
Died in Memphis, Alabama, January 28th, H.H. Dunn.
Died in Shannon, Mississippi, January 25th, Daniel Gardner, formerly of Pickens County.

## THE SOUTHERN ARGUS - DEATHS - JUNE 1869 THROUGH JUNE 1874

Died in Greenville the 8th, Mrs. Helen M. Wright.
Died in Calhoun County the 31st ult., Maj. M. Bowles.
Died in Evergreen the 3rd, Felice Virginia Mononl(?), infant.
Died at Iuka, Mississippi, a few days ago, Colonel J. Lawrence Moore, formerly of North Alabama.
Died in Limestone County the 3rd, Joel B. Pugh.
Died in Greensboro the 2nd, Miss Julia Cecile Dorman.
Died in Tuskaloosa the 31st ult., Miss Sallie Ann Swoope.
Died in Lebanon, Kentucky, the 9th ult., Thomas J. Foster, formerly of North Alabama.
Died in Livingston the 2nd, Major Edward Herndon.
Died in Mobile the 6th, Levin Gayle.
Died in Mobile the 3rd, Mary E. McAlpine of Greene County.
Died in Marengo County, January 29th, Dixon H. Lewis.
Died in Granby, Connecticut, January 24th, Mrs. Harriett S. Pease, formerly of Eufaula.
Died in Talladega the 2nd, Mrs. C.M. Pritchett.
Died at Shelby Iron Works, January 27th, Alfred Seale.
Died near Monroeville, January 21st, Miss Sarah Broughton.
Died in Monroeville the 2nd, W.E. Lealie/Leslie.
Died in Barbour County, January 26th, J.B. Bishop.
Died in Barbour County, recently, N. Zorn.
Died in Barbour County, January 31st, Arthur Crews.
Died in Mobile the 2nd, W. Jasper.
Died near Letohatchie, a few days ago, Mrs. Morgan.
Died in Mobile the 7th, John William Bolman, child.
Died in Mobile the 7th, Mrs. Clara Sise.
Died in Bullock County the 1st, T.D. Brantley.

Governor Lindsay has offered a $300 reward for the apprehension of Spencer Rice, charged with the murder of Alexander Haskett in Jefferson County.

Died in this city, Tuesday last, Marion A. Givens, late of Illinois.
Died in this city, Saturday last, Luda, daughter of Mr. and Mrs. George Robbins.
Died at Summerfield the 6th inst., Mrs. Theodosia Saunders, relict of Colonel E.W. Saunders, aged sixty-seven years.
Died in Montavallo, Tuesday last, Mrs. John M. Strong, for many years with her venerable husband a resident of this city.
Died in this city, Thursday of last week the 8th inst., Mrs. Mary Ormond, one of the longest residents in Selma, aged eighty-five years.
Died in this city, Saturday last, James W. Moore. Mr. Moore was kicked by a horse some two weeks ago, and died from his injuries.

## THE SOUTHERN ARGUS - DEATHS - JUNE 1869 THROUGH JUNE 1874

Issue 2-23-1872

A team driven by a careless negro in Mobile, on the evening of the 17th, run over and seriously injured James M. White, a lad of thirteen.

Recently, Henry Cooper, U.S. Senator from Tennessee, has lost by death his wife and eldest son.

Thomas Nelson of Baldwin County was accidentally drowned off Point Clear a few days ago.

Recently, Joel B. Pugh of Limestone, while hunting, was stricken with paralysis and soon expired.

William Cameron of Sand Mountain fell from Running Water Bridge, a few days ago, and was killed.

Howard Chapman of Mobile was found on the 12th in an out of the way place and in a dying condition.

Near Shell Mound on the 12th, T.J. Johnson shot and killed Wm. Singleton.

John Wasson is in the Lauderdale Jail for killing Lewis E. Moore in 1862.

Colonel B..C. Grider, an eminent Kentucky lawyer, is dead.

Dr. E.H. Locke of Troy is recovering from a dangerous illness.

Mrs. Mary Mead Hardie, the honored and beloved mother of our distinguished friend and fellow citizen, Major Joseph Hardie, died at her residence, near Talladega, on the 18th inst., aged fifty-nine years and four months. Seven sons and two daughters, reared under her intelligent, pious care, survive her, all grown...

Rev. Robert A. Lapsley, D.D., (father of James W., Robert, and John Lapsley of this city), died in New Albany, Indiana, on the 13th...

Ira H. Bird, Grand Master of Ohio Odd Fellows, is dead.

Miss Ellen Goodwin is, we regret to hear, still suffering greatly from the injuries received in the burning of her dress in the cantata at Edward's Opera House of the 2nd inst....

## THE SOUTHERN ARGUS - DEATHS - JUNE 1869 THROUGH JUNE 1874

In Mobile the other night, E.D. Buckley was almost eaten by some vicious dogs.

The other day, Dr. J.B. Pouncey of Barbour County shot and killed a negro who had attacked him with a pistol.

Granville C. Torbett, an eminent citizen of Nashville, died the 14th.

It is supposed that Charlie Moore, living near Belmont, was drowned in the Bigbee a few days ago.

Issue 3-1-1872

Died in Dallas County the 6th ult., Mrs. Jenie? Purifoy, daughter of our venerable friend, John Mosely.

Captain King of Dauphine Island was drowned off Dog River a few days ago.

Rev. Mr. Scarborough, whose place of residence is unknown to us, died the 19th ult. from injuries received a few days previously in the railroad accident near Clayton.

At Warsaw, Friday last, Captain J.J. Little and Z.T. Reardon were killed in an affray.

The venerable widow of the late Hon. John Bell of Tennessee is living in Nashville in the enjoyment of good health.

Mrs. William Hallowell of Whistler was badly burned by the explosion of a kerosene lamp the other day.

Died in Huntsville the 15th, Miss Lucy Pride Green.
Died in Montgomery the 13th, W.G. Duvall.
Died in Limestone County the 13th, Mrs. Lizzie H. Crenshaw.
Died in Sumter County the 11th, Mrs. Lou Hancock.
Died in Mobile the 14th, Mrs. Lyon.
Died in Mobile the 14th, J.S. Gliddon, Sr.
Died in Mobile the 15th, Mrs. Mary A. Niles.
Died in Coosa County the 4th, John Kosciusko Walker.
Died in New Orleans the 10th, Captain Edward F. Shields of Mobile.
Died in Scottsboro the 3rd, Mrs. Ira T. Cobb.
Died in Scottsboro the 7th, Mrs. William Andrews.
Died near Bridgeport, January 30th, G.N. Potts.
Died near Bridgeport the 8th, Mrs. Sarah Ann Moore.

## THE SOUTHERN ARGUS - DEATHS - JUNE 1869 THROUGH JUNE 1874

Died near Letohatchie the 12th, Robert McDonald.
Died in Tuscumbia the 14th, Rev. B.N. Sawtelle.
Died in Troy the 11th, Charlie Barron, aged five years.
Died in Canton Bend a few days ago, John McArthur.
Died in Montgomery the 17th, Mrs. E.G. Carew.
Died in Elyton the 1st, James Bird Whorton, infant.
Died in Livingston the 12th, Judge George B. Saunders.
Died in Union Springs the 9th ult., Mrs. Catherine Matheson.
Died in New York the 15th ult., James L. Bliss, formerly of Mobile.
Died in New Orleans, 16th ult., Mary Reynolds, formerly of Mobile.
Died in Mobile, 12th ult., Howard E. Chapman.
Died near Evergreen, 17th ult., Mrs. Matilda G. Chapman.
Died near Monroeville, 9th ult., Mrs. Mary Coker.
Died near Letohatchie, 7th ult., Dr. J.G. Turner.
Died in Benton the other day, John Gresham.
Died in Canada, January 19th, Ebenezer Marvin, a citizen of Lowndes County from 1836 to 1853.
Died near Eastaboga a few weeks ago, Mr. Carr.
Died near Greenwood, 8th ult., Mrs. Anna Slaughter.
Died in Wetumpka, 7th ult., Willie Mann.
Died near Athens, 15th ult., Mrs. Martha Tucker.
Died in Huntsville, 17th ult., Eva, infant child of A. and M.J. Bailey.
Died in Livingston, 22nd ult., M.C. Houston, an old and honored citizen.
Died in Demopolis, 20th ult., Joseph Giles.
Died at Pollard, 23rd ult., Julius Jonas of Montgomery.
Died in Montgomery County, 23rd ult., W.G. Waller.

### Issue 3-8-1872

In Greene County a few days ago, Isham Haygood was killed by Ike Jolly, both negroes.

Died in Uniontown, 18th ult., Peter O. Terrell.
Died in Perry County, 26th ult., Andrew Heard.
Died in Mobile, 28th ult., Captain John McGrath.
Died near Mobile, 28th ult., Miss Catharine I. Donavan.
Died in Mobile, 28th ult., F.L. Barman.
Died in Mobile, 27th ult., Fannie, daughter of Cary W. Butt.
Died at Mount Sterling, 15th ult., Hon. G. Frank Smith, Representative from Choctaw County.
Died in Washington County, 17th ult., J.M. Boykin.
Died in Allenton, 16th ult., Dr. J.G. Bythewood.
Died in Conecuh County, recently, N.S. Piggott.
Died in Memphis, Pickens County, recently, Mrs. S.G. Coleman.

# THE SOUTHERN ARGUS - DEATHS - JUNE 1869 THROUGH JUNE 1874

Died near Monroeville, 27th ult., Mrs. Sarah M. Salter.
Died near Hale County, 25th ult., Mrs. William B. Drake.
Died in Memphis, Tennessee, 26th ult., Rev. Robert Frazer, at one time of Montgomery.
Died, Montgomery, 2nd inst., Kate McIntyre.
Died in this city, Friday evening last, Miss Ellen Goodwin.
Died near Plantersville the 28th ult., Ezzie?, infant son of H.G. and M.A. Lassiter.

Mike Fitzgerald of east Selma was burned Tuesday morning by a kerosene explosion.

Issue 3-15-1872

William Scott of Calhoun County was killed a few days ago by a kick from his horse.

Thomas Coyle of Mobile was found dead in Pascagoula the other day, under suspicious circumstances.

About two weeks ago, Penn Bedell, formerly of Montgomery, shot and dangerously wounded policeman Raspberry of Atlanta.

Henry Mack, on trial at Montgomery for the murder of Amos Harris, was found "not guilty" and discharged on the 2nd. Soon after his discharge he was arrested again on the affidavit of Maggie Reams, who swore that he had attempted to kill her with an axe.

Died in this city, Thursday last, Mrs. H. Ridgeway.

Charles Ligon of Columbus, Georgia, was shot and killed a few days ago by Dr. Colsey, toward whose daughter he had been guilty of improper conduct.

The wife of ex-Governor Bramlette of Kentucky is dead.

T.P.A. Bibb, a prominent Kentucky lawyer, is dead.

Issue 3-22-1872

Josie, daughter of Emile and M.L. Gilman of this city, died last Saturday.

# THE SOUTHERN ARGUS - DEATHS - JUNE 1869 THROUGH JUNE 1874

James Nobles, near Farriersville, Bullock County, was shot and killed one night about two weeks ago by unknown parties, supposed to be negroes.

On the 11th a little daughter of Mr. Eberhart of Barbour County was fatally burned by her clothes taking fire.

A few days ago a child, seven months old, son of Mr. Edgar Couch of Mobile fell in the fire, was terribly burned.

Joseph Ford of Cave Springs was killed at Rome, Georgia, the 9th inst. by a railroad accident.

Dr. S.A. Billings, an eminent physician in Columbus, Georgia, and formerly a resident of Alabama, died a few days ago.

## DIED IN ALABAMA

Died in Mobile, 8th inst., George W. Jennison.
Died in Madison County, 1st, Mrs. Sarah B. Roberts.
Died in the neighborhood of Hollow Square, 21st January, Stephen Wedgeworth.
Died in Conecuh County, recently, John Dudly Cary.
Died in Montgomery County, 9th inst., Mrs. N.A. Ray.
Died near Gadsden the 2nd inst., Mrs. Arabel Howell.
Died in Madison County the 4th inst., Alfred Hughes.
Died in Huntsville the 4th, Frank Gamble Boland, infant.
Died in Mobile the 5th, Louis H. Parkes.
Died in Linden the 1st, Charles Leslie Maupin, aged three years.
Died in Huntsville the 1st, Mrs. Matilda W. Venable.
Died in Hayneville the 5th, Albert N. Herbert.
Died in Washington County the 28th February, Rev. J.G. Rush.
Died in Enon, 25th ult., Dr. George W. Crymer.
Died in Florence, 4th inst., S. Hardy Smith.
Died in Lauderdale County, 28th ult., Rev. Andrew J. Falres.
Died in Limestone County, 28th ult., J.W. Qualls.
Died in Mobile, 7th inst., Edward Carlen.
Died in Calhoun County a few days ago, J.G.J. Whitesides.
Died in St. Landry's Parish, Louisiana, February 24th, Thomas H. Gordon, formerly of Alabama.
Died in Florence, 12th inst., Charles W. Karsner.
Died at Decatur, 12th inst., Dennis Dykous.
Died in Marengo County the 12th, Caleb Rembert Bryan.
Died in Mobile the 15th, R.H. Slough.
Died in Perry County the 12th, Mrs. Nancy Crawford.
Died in Limestone County, recently, Mrs. W.B. Morgan.

## THE SOUTHERN ARGUS - DEATHS - JUNE 1869 THROUGH JUNE 1874

Died at Virginia Military Institute, 22nd ult., J..D. Johnston, son of Capt. J.D. Johnston of Mobile.
Died in Mobile the 12th, Mrs. J.E. Covington.
Died in Huntsville the 9th, Morris Berney, infant.
Died in Greenville the 4th, Mrs. Elizabeth M. Caldwell.
Died in Butler County the 15th, Martin Peagler.
Died in Mobile the 11th, Robert T. Daily.
Died in Limestone County the 10th ult., John E. Davis.
Died in Mobile the 9th, Richard H. Redwood.
Died in New Orleans, 25th ult., John K. Collins, formerly of Mobile.
Died in Livingston the 2nd, J.W. Harriss.
Died in Mobile the 13th, Colonel Charles Forsyth.
Died in Jackson County, 28th ult., Mrs. Joab Crews.
Died in Lowndes County the 1st, Mrs. Nancy McKee.
Died near Eastaboga the 11th, William Montgomery.
Died in Coosa County the 9th, Mrs. Margaret Kelley.

Robert Summers, a Scotch gentleman visiting Florence, was seriously injured a few days ago by the accidental discharge of his gun while out hunting.

Alfred Gray, negro, was tried and acquitted in the Tuskegee Circuit Court last week for killing Jake Gordon, negro.

Colonel Charles Forsyth (son of Colonel John Forsyth), commercial Editor of the *Register* and secretary of the Mobile cotton exchange board, died in Mobile the 13th inst. Colonel Forsyth was the last Commander of the Third Alabama Infantry Regiment in the late war, and was widely known.

William E. Shelton's trial for murder was set for last Tuesday in the Macon Circuit Court.

G.W. Osborn was tried for murder in the Macon Circuit Court last week, and acquitted.

Warner L. Underwood of Bowling Green, an eminent Kentucky lawyer and politician, is dead.

Issue  3-29-1872

On Tuesday evening last in this city, George M. Rives, known as the "Indian Doctor", was shot and killed by Fred. J. Hooker.

Died at the residence of Frank L. Johnson, eight miles from this city, Wednesday morning last, Mr. B.A. Miller.

## THE SOUTHERN ARGUS - DEATHS - JUNE 1869 THROUGH JUNE 1874

Andrew J. Simpson was taken to the Mobile guard house on the 10th for having cut his own throat fearfully in an unavailing attempt to commit suicide the night before on the Mobile and Ohio Railroad.

Mrs. Fannie Gorman, mother of Capt. Dan Gorman of this city, died at Springfield, Massachusetts, the 6th inst.

Mrs. Drucie Patton, nee Heslep, who died in Shubuta, Mississippi, a few days ago, was a graduate of the Judson Institute at Marion.

Rev. Father Cornette, who died at Spring Hill, recently, aged fifty-three years, was a man of great learning...

Rev. E.B. Teague has been quite sick at his residence in this city.

Hans Whatley (negro) has been arrested in Chattanooga on the charge of murdering Jim Alexander (negro) in Jacksonville last fall.

Colonel Walter Drane, one of the oldest residents of Lowndes County, died in Pleasant Hill last Sunday on his way home from Selma. He was about seventy-six years old.

### Issue 4-5-1872

John Lemley was shot and killed a few miles south of Huntsville, March 23rd, by William N. Putnam.

Died on the morning of Saturday last at his residence about twenty-five miles below Selma, Dr. Benjamin E. Cobb, more than thirty years a citizen of Dallas County...

On Saturday last at the depot in South Selma, Captain Robert S. Hatcher, for many years a citizen of this county, fell between two cars of a moving train on the Selma and Gulf Railroad and was horribly mutilated and instantly killed...before the war, he had served his fellow citizens in both branches of the Legislature...

Sam Roesenan of Athens was on the 30th ult. very ill in New York.

Hon. Vanny Hall, an old citizen of Wills' Valley, was thrown from his horse a few days ago and seriously injured.

Sheldon Toomer, late Representative from Lee County, died in Opelika, March 26th.

## THE SOUTHERN ARGUS - DEATHS - JUNE 1869 THROUGH JUNE 1874

A.J. Wimberly and William Russell of Jackson County are both quite ill.

Lycurgus S. Welborn was fatally assaulted in his store in Eufaula the night of the 29th by some one supposed to be intent on robbery.
    Nelson James/Jaines (negro) has been arrested for the recent murder of Lycurgus S. Welborn in Eufaula.

Captain A. Pool, late of Cherokee County, died recently in Fitchburg, Massachusetts.

Emmett Hill of Benton was accidentally shot and killed Tuesday of last week.

### DIED IN ALABAMA
Died at Larkinsville, March 25th, Moses Manning.
Died at Bridgeport, March 29th, Jack O'Neal.
Died in Athens, March 26th, Mrs. Parthenia T. Higgins.
Died at Fairfield, March 4th, Johnnie T. Eddins.
Died in Havre, France, March 4th, Mrs. Amelia Phillippe, nee Hartel, formerly of Mobile.
Died in Louisiana, March 21st, Mrs. Eliza Case, formerly of Mobile.
Died in Mobile, March 26th, J.C. Morehead of Pickensville.
Died in Dadeville, March 10th, Rev. David Lowe Slaton.
Died in Perry County, March 21st, Sion Tubb, aged sixty-eight.
Died in Florence, March 11th, Mrs. Amanda B. Jenkins.
Died near Carpenter, March 10th, Mrs. Francis Griffin, aged ninety-four.
Died in Opelika, March 26th, Sheldon Toomer.
Died in Madison County, March 25th, Mrs. Mary E. Battle.
Died in Marshall County, March 20th, Lafayette Kinkle.
Died in Tennessee, 24th ult., W.F. Beutly/Bently, previous to 1843 a citizen of Greensboro.
Died in Tuskaloosa County, January 29th, Alexander Huffman.
Died in Colorado, 23rd ult., William H. Hendon, formerly of Bullock County.
Died in Butler County, 19th ult., Allen Rhodes.
Died in Montgomery, 22nd ult., John H. Robertson.
Died in Linden, 11th ult., Mrs. L.A. Woolf.
Died in Lauderdale County, 8th ult., E.J. Oliver.
Died in Mobile, 20th ult., Duncan McKerrell.
Died at Spring Hill, 20th ult., Rev. Father Cornette.
Died in Mobile, 18th ult., Mrs. Sallie E.A. Rone.
Died in Etowah County, 17th ult., John Croft.
Died in Etowah County, 11th ult., Mrs. John Croft.
Died in New York, 15th ult., Mrs. Angela Brewer, formerly of Mobile.
Died in North Port, 9th ult., Mrs. Amanda M. Powell.
Died in Jackson County, 16th ult., Camden Gentry.

## THE SOUTHERN ARGUS - DEATHS - JUNE 1869 THROUGH JUNE 1874

Died in Tuskaloosa County, 4th ult., James Dawns.
Died in Pickens County, 13th ult., Thomas S. McKinstry.
Died in Vienna, 7th ult., Mrs. Mattie J. Conuerley.
Died in Canton Bend, 22nd ult., Mrs. H. Robbins.
Died in Mobile, 22nd ult., Fina Holcomb Berry.
Died in Mobile, 21st ult., Mrs. Mary Meyer.
Died in Huntsville, 21st, John L. Halsey.
Died in Limestone County, 7th., Mrs. Sallie W. Morgan.

Issue 4-12-1872

Died near Harrell's Cross Roads, 26th, Mrs. Jennie, wife of Thomas Chisolm.

Dr. H.W. Heath of Gadsden has been quite sick.

Nelson James, negro, arrested for the murder of Wellhorn at Eufaula, has been discharged.

A few days ago in Eufaula, Frank McCollough, negro, killed Hill Strater, negro.

Marion Savage of Cherokee was seriously ill on the 4th.

Six miles east of Oxford a few days ago, J.G. Hudson shot and killed James Wood.

The wife of Hon. C.W. Raisler, the able and excellent Representative from Limestone, died a few days ago.

On the 3rd, Dr. R. L. Bliss of Lauderdale County was considered hopelessly ill.

A little child of Samuel Beall of Eufaula was badly burned a few days ago.

Captain George Graham of Mobile had his right leg terribly crushed the other day between the bumpers of two cars on the New Orleans Railroad.

Died in Arkansas, 29th ult., a child of W.L. Moore, formerly of Athens.

### DIED IN ALABAMA
Died in Athens, 30th ult., Mrs. C.W. Raisler.
Died in Limestone County the 2nd, Mrs. James L. Martin.
Died in Madison County the 3rd, Martin Cole, aged eighty-five years.

## THE SOUTHERN ARGUS - DEATHS - JUNE 1869 THROUGH JUNE 1874

Died in Louisiana, 21st, Douglas R. Roach of Camden.
Died in Sumter County the 4th, Colonel Charles R. Gibbs, aged eighty-six.
Died in Gainesville, recently, Robert Bradshaw.
Died in Perry County, 15th ult., Williamson Gray.
Died near Perryville, recently, Rev. Henry Ivey.
Died in Lowndes County, recently, Mrs. M.D. Robinson.
Died in Jackson County the 2nd, James Hawk.
Died at Bridgeport the 24th ult., William Layne.
Died in Florence, 29th ult., Charlotte, daughter of Dr. E.L. Hannum/Hanuum.
Died in Mobile the 2nd, John D. Ragland.
Died in Greenville, 30th ult., Mrs. Charlotte K. Cook.
Died in Mobile the 1st, Mrs. Mary Ellen Atkinson.
Died in Mobile the 2nd, D.R. Salter.
Died in Montgomery the 5th, Miss E.R. Jones.
Died in Talladega the 6th, Mrs. Martha Dawson Fetchner.
Died in Galveston, 1st ult., Frank Heflin, youngest child of Mark McElderry of Talladega.

John R. Tankersley, imprisoned for half a year past in Covington County Jail, for killing Sid P. Sellers of Wilcox, escaped a few nights ago and is at large.

John M. Russell of Limestone goes to Arkansas Hot Springs for his health's sake.

Mrs. Macon, wife of the Editor of the *Eufaula Times*, is recovering from a dangerous illness.

### Issue 4-19-1872

Died at his residence near Pleasant Hill the 13th inst., James G. Cowan, one of the oldest citizens of the county.

O.A.V. Rose was acquitted on Friday last in the Baker Circuit Court on the charge of murdering Giles Prince (negro) in this city some time ago.

Mrs. Y.E. Calloway, relict of the late Rev. C.C. Calloway and mother of D.M. Calloway and John W. Calloway of this city, died in Greensboro on Saturday last the 13th.

Moses Stephens of the Harrell's Cross Roads neighborhood in this county and a brother-in-law of William McCullom of this city was killed at Okalona, Mississippi the 23rd ult. by a Mr. Sanders.

## THE SOUTHERN ARGUS - DEATHS - JUNE 1869 THROUGH JUNE 1874

Pope Edwards of Opelika had a hand literally torn off the other day by being caught in his planing mill.

The negro who murdered Mrs. Files of Clarke County a short time ago has been sentenced to be hanged May 19th.

William Garrett of Greene County committed suicide last week by drowning.

Thomas H. Gordon, a native of this state but since 1865 a resident of Louisiana, died at his home on Atchafalaya River on the 24th of February last.

Old man Cook of Opelika committed suicide on the 8th by hanging.

At Kempville, Monroe County, a few days since, Ed Dennis was severely stabbed by Aaron Bradley.

H. Stewart of Morgan County has been tried before an examining court for killing G.W. Gladden the 19th ult. and discharged.

### DIED IN ALABAMA

Died in Marion the 10th, Mrs. Dr. W.T. McAlister.
Died in Madison County the 3rd, Martin Cole.
Died in Madison County the 7th, W.H. Wortham.
Died in Oxford the 9th, C.P. Samuel of Shelby County.
Died in Talladega the 6th, Mrs. Martha Fletchner.
Died in Talladega the 8th, Mrs. Mary Donahoo.
Died in St. Clair County the 1st, John Ash, aged eighty-nine years.
Died in Troy the 5th, Mrs. Jane Hudson.
Died in Florence the 4th, Dr. R. L. Bliss.
Died in Florence the 7th, Mrs. Urban Ozanne.
Died in Mobile the 7th, Colonel J.T. Walshe.
Died in Scottsboro, 30th ult., Mrs. Mary Rosson.
Died in San Jose, California, 31st ult., A.W. Murdock, formerly of Mobile.
Died in Limestone County the 2nd, Mrs. Jane L. Martin.
Died in Cherokee County the 6th, Washington Tomlin, child.
Died in Woodruff County, Arkansas, 10th ult., Mrs. Fannie Harrison, formerly of Limestone County.
Died in Helena, Arkansas, 29th ult., Stephen T. Nelson, formerly of Limestone County.
Died in Leighton the 4th, Samuel J. Leggett, infant.
Died in Jefferson County the 7th, Dr. James T. Jones.
Died in Mobile the 6th, Daniel Sullivan.

## THE SOUTHERN ARGUS - DEATHS - JUNE 1869 THROUGH JUNE 1874

Died in Greene County the 29th ult., George Willie, infant son of Mrs. Jane Marona.
Died in Little Rock, Arkansas, recently, Dr. Batt Peterson, formerly of Barbour County.
Died in Greenville, recently, Willie B. Worthen.

In an affray in Eufaula on the 8th, John Hartung was killed, and Adam Hartung and H.A. Scott were wounded.
    Dr. H.A. Scott is held in $2,000 to answer for killing John L. Hartung in Eufaula, recently.

Died in Los Angeles, California on Tuesday, March 19th, 1872, Jenkins Chapman, son of Wm. S. and Kate L. Chapman, aged nine years, ten months...

At Hollow Square some two weeks ago, J.T. Walsh killed a negro, who had assaulted him.

Issue 4-26-1872

A difficulty occurred at Scotland, Monroe County the 10th, between Aaron Bradley and Edward Dennis, resulting in the death of the latter.

Pierce Perry (negro) stabbed and killed Elijah Bell (negro) near ???? church in the northwestern portion of this county, Saturday last.

Peter G. VanWinkle, late United States Senator from West Virginia, died the 15th.

Mrs. Emily Lloyd of Leesburg, Virginia, is in jail charged with poisoning her husband, aunt, and four children.

Sunday of last week, at Chehaw, Macon County, Samuel Henry stabbed and killed William H. Thornton.

The Edgar murder case was tried at the recent term of the Washington Circuit Court, resulting in a verdict of guilty...

Old man Thacker died in South Carolina a few weeks ago, aged one hundred and thirty-eight years [sic].

Colonel John S. Scott, commander of the First Louisiana Cavalry in the late war, died in New Orleans on the 16th.

## THE SOUTHERN ARGUS - DEATHS - JUNE 1869 THROUGH JUNE 1874

W.H. Hope, an old newspaper man, the founder of the Star of Washington City, died in the city hospital at Louisville a few days ago.

Samuel Tepper of Wilcox left for England about two weeks ago to take possession of a fortune left by a brother amounting to near half a million dollars.

Andrew Pickens Calhoun, a grandson of the distinguished South Carolina statesman, died recently near Dalton, Georgia.

Marshall Black of Dadeville has been quite sick.

J.W. Butterfield, a policeman, died in Louisville the 18th of hydrophobia.

Professor J.L. Foster of Spring Hill was thrown from a buggy and seriously hurt a few days ago.

Deacon Hale Talbott of Troy is dangerously ill.

Dr. Guild of Tuskaloosa is recovering from a severe illness.

### DIED IN ALABAMA
Died in Hayneville the 12th, infant child of Lewis Belgart.
Died near Hayneville the 16th, Mrs. W.D. Sherman.
Died in Montgomery the 15th, Rev. Mr. Cary.
Died in Greene County the 12th, D. Hunnicutt.
Died in Limestone County the 5th, Mrs. Fannie James.
Died in Madison County the 11th, Benjamin Thompson.
Died in North Port the 10th, John D. Haly.
Died in Troy the 12th, Mrs. Sarah O. Park, aged eighty-four years.
Died in Jackson County the 10th, Mrs. Charity Stewart.
Died in Mobile the 18th, Mrs. Mary Ann Holt.
Died near Sumterville the 6th, James Hutchins, aged seventy-eight.
Died in Madison County the 7th, William H. Wortham.

### Issue 5-3-1872

John Black of the *Eufaula News*, one of the oldest publishers in the state, died at his residence in Eufaula, April 18th.

Died in Chester, Illinois, April 10th, Mrs. Mary A. Rice, formerly of this city.

General J.C. McFerrin of the United States Army died in Louisville the 25th ult.

## THE SOUTHERN ARGUS - DEATHS - JUNE 1869 THROUGH JUNE 1874

A German named Lauer died in Louisville the 26th ult. of hydrophobia.

Rev. Thomas Brown, an aged Presbyterian preacher, died at Philadelphia, Tennessee the 21st ult.

Rev. Joel K. Lyle, a prominent Presbyterian preacher of Kentucky, died on the 19th ult.

Died in this city, April 29th, William T., only son of John A. and Mary S. Doyle.

W.S. Munerlyn was drowned at Mobile last week.

Tribute of respect from Masonic Hall, Cahawba, Alabama, April 27th, 1872 upon the death of W. Turner Bell...that in the death of brother W.T. Bell this lodge has lost a good and zealous Mason, the community a good citizen, and the wife and children a good husband and father.

Mrs. Thomas H. Hobbs of Athens has been very ill.

Brownlow is at his home in Knoxville and the Tennesseans are not consoled by a hope of his speedy death.

### Issue 5-10-1872

Mrs. Sarah Montague died at the residence of Mrs. M.D. Bates, near Bellevue, on the 3rd inst.

B.F. Rowe, Fort Deposit, fell dead Tuesday of last week, while in the discharge of his duties as section master of the Mobile and Montgomery Railroad.

Major Charles Clarkson, a soldier of the War of 1812, died near St. Louis the 28th ult.

F.A. Vaughan of Dadeville is quite ill.

Edmund Whatley was kicked by a mule the 2nd, from the effects of which he died.

A son of J.W. Black, near Greenville, was shot and seriously wounded last week by a Mr. Myers, who mistook him for a wild turkey.

S.R. May of Cherokee has been dangerously ill.

## THE SOUTHERN ARGUS - DEATHS - JUNE 1869 THROUGH JUNE 1874

### DIED IN ALABAMA

Died in Tuscumbia, 23rd ult., Dennis Brown.
Died near Cherokee, 16th ult., John McL. Woodford.
Died in Tuscumbia, 14th ult., Walter Rogers McMahan, infant.
Died in Mobile, 25th ult., Rev. Joseph Steel of Middlebury, Vermont.
Died near Clayton, 12th ult., Mrs. Catherine McEachan, aged seventy-seven years.
Died in Clayton, 12th ult., James Clark, aged eighty years.
Died in Clayton, 17th ult., Charles L. Petty.
Died in Marion, 18th ult., Maggie Edmonds, aged fourteen.
Died in Marion, 21st ult., Estelle Randolph Fox, aged two years.
Died in Tuskaloosa County, 19th ult., Caroline Bagley, wife of Professor Joseph Griswold of the State University.
Died in Greene County, 22nd ult., Dr. William Patton, aged eighty.
Died near Coleraine, 17th ult., Windson Alabama Rabb, aged two years.
Died in Lowndesboro, 18th ult., Mrs. Margaret C. Hartwell, nee Irvin.
Died in Montgomery, 25th ult., Judge A.J. Walker.
Died in Birmingham, 23rd ult., Pressly Ashley.
Died near Farmersville, 29th? ult., Williams Cox.
Died in Tuscumbia, 27th ult., Lewis Linddeman, infant.
Died in Tuscumbia, 17th ult., Mary Russell Sargent, infant.
Died near Tuscumbia, 30th ult., Felix Sherrod, infant.
Died in Mobile the 1st, Peyton B. Mason.
Died 23rd ult., A.T. Owens.
Died in Madison County, 27th ult., Dr. Davis Moore, aged seventy-five years.
Died in Huntsville, 28th ult., Mrs. S.F. Darwin.
Died in Oxford, Mississippi, 30th ult., William H. Mitchell, Jr. of Florence, Alabama.
Died in Cincinnati, 19th ult., Maggie Fry, formerly of Florence, Alabama.
Died in Eufaula the 1st, little Robbie Bryan, infant.
Died in Coffeville, lately, J.D. Guy/Gay.
Died in Tuskegee, 25th ult., Mrs. Oppenheimer.
Died in New York, 26th ult., Mrs. Julius Norton, late of Montgomery.
Died in Pickensville, 27th ult., A.C. Lang.
Died in Edgecombe County, North Carolina, recently, Mrs. Nannie Speight, formerly of Huntsville.
Died in Athens, 25th ult., Major James B. Lockhart, aged ninety years.
Died in Prattville, 28th ult., James M. Hill.

### Issue 5-17-1872

Rienzi Baker (negro) was tried in the Dallas Circuit Court on Tuesday for killing William Stillings, some time ago in Marion, and convicted of manslaughter and sentenced to the penitentiary for one year.

## THE SOUTHERN ARGUS - DEATHS - JUNE 1869 THROUGH JUNE 1874

At Calera, on Sunday last, in a difficulty between John Lewis and Sol Schimerhorn, engineers on the South and North Railroad, the latter was shot and mortally wounded.

Bill Pittman committed suicide by hanging a few days ago near Roanoke.

B.F. Owen of Bridgeport is seriously ill.

Died on the 11th inst., Nora, daughter of James and Mary Allen, aged fifteen months.
Nora, infant daughter of James F. Allen, died in East Selma last Friday.

Tribute of respect from Masonic Hall, Cahaba, Alabama, May 5th, 1872, upon the death of Robert S. Hatcher.

Mr. Arnold and Miss Ada Powell, engaged to be married, died on the same day of meningitis, near Carrollton, Mississippi, recently.

James E. Moss, one of the oldest and best citizens of the county, died on the 13th, aged sixty-eight years.

The dead body of Isaac Marshall (negro), lately employed on Bat Smith's place four miles above the city, was recovered from the river near the ferry landing one day last week.

Colonel L. Hargove of Clayton is seriously ill.

Columbus Byrd was accidentally shot and seriously, though not dangerously, wounded at Eufaula a few days ago.

Gabe Cook was convicted of murder in the first degree at Opelika and sentenced to the penitentiary for ten years.

Mrs. J.R. Dowell of Opelika, who has been seriously ill for some time, is improving.

Issue 5-24-1872

Mrs. Laura Fair has asked to have a change of venue in her trail for killing Crittenden.

W.R. Wyatt, assistant superintendent of the Selma, Marion, and Memphis Railroad, is dangerously ill at Marion.

## THE SOUTHERN ARGUS - DEATHS - JUNE 1869 THROUGH JUNE 1874

Greene Barr, living in the southern portion of Marengo County, shot himself on the 7th inst.

Mrs. E.A. West of Centre was thrown from a buggy a few days ago and badly injured.

Daniel S. Grissit, living near Greenville, killed his wife the 15th, by cutting her throat.

W.W. Moore and J.W. McCasky of Bridgeport were thrown from a buggy the 8th inst. and severely injured.

General A.C. Jones of West Virginia and Calvin Sayre of Montgomery had a cane and knife fight in Washington City the 11th, in which both were badly hurt.

### DIED IN ALABAMA

Died in Evergreen, lately, Mrs. Sophronia Herrington.
Died in Stevenson the 5th, Mrs. Caroline Barber.
Died in Mobile the 9th, Ella W. Nason.
Died near Meridianville, March 29th, Mrs. M. Ford, aged sixty years.
Died at Rogersville, 26th ult., Virgiline Simmons, infant.
Died at Cecilia College, Kentucky the 1st, George Moore Jackson of Florence.
Died near Greenville the 1st, Wiley B. Hawkins.
Died in Greenville the 5th, Alex Black.
Died in Greenville, 13th, J.W. Buck.
Died near Eufaula, 18th, Mrs. Douglas, aged seventy years.
Died in Eufaula, 16th, Mrs. Sarah Brantly of Macon, Georgia.
Died in Madison County, 13th, Peter Weatherly.
Died in Huntsville, 13th, Mattie M. McBroom.
Died in Memphis, Tennessee, 9th, Frances Laura Buckalew, child, formerly of Huntsville.
Died in Huntsville, 10th, Mrs. Fannie Martin.
Died in Huntsville, 10th, Mrs. William Weaver.
Died in Athens, 9th, Edmund N. Lucas.
Died in Huntsville, 12th, Frank Drake.
Died near Opelika, suddenly, 8th, Mrs. Winslett.
Died in Wetumpka, 9th, William R. Samuels.
Died in Abbeville, 9th, Mrs. M.P. Harper.
Died in Eufaula, 11th, Mattie Daniel, infant.
Died in Carrollton, 5th, Dr. Benjamin Wilson.
Died in Whistler, 8th, Laura Cloudes McDougal.
Died in Jacksonville, recently, Mrs. Elizabeth Everett.

# THE SOUTHERN ARGUS - DEATHS - JUNE 1869 THROUGH JUNE 1874

Died in Calhoun County, 10th, John A. Findley.
Died in Oxford, 16th, Mr. Norton.

Henry Howard of Lowndesboro is recovering from his recent illness.

Issue 5-31-1872

W.H. Stearnes, living near Glennville, shot a negro in his employ last week, in self defence.

Mayor Baker of Evansville, Indiana is dead.

E.G. Collier of Centre is still confined to his bed.

John D. Lewis of Calera surrendered himself to the Sheriff for shooting S.K. Schemerhorn, had an examining trial, and was discharged.

W.R. Wyatt, assistant general superintendent of the Selma, Marion, and Memphis Railroad, whose illness was announced last week, died in Marion on, Thursday last. He was buried at Marion on Friday of last week...

The Governor has offered four hundred dollars reward for William Putnam, who killed John Lemley, near Huntsville, some time ago.

A Mr. Schneider was thrown from his wagon, in Mobile the 19th, and seriously hurt.

Joseph Clarke of Fackler is sick.

Jim Douglass, negro, living near Fort Deposit, shot and killed a four year old child one day last week.

A little daughter of M.A. Sanders of Eutaw had her leg badly crushed a few days ago while playing on a railroad turn table.

Henry Scroggins of Shelby County was thrown from a mule and killed on the 11th.

In a difficulty between Robert C. Clark and A.T. Hughes of Wetumpka a few days ago, the former was shot and dangerously wounded.

Mr. Milner, a section master on the Mobile and Montgomery Railroad, was killed Tuesday of last week by the falling of an engine.

## THE SOUTHERN ARGUS - DEATHS - JUNE 1869 THROUGH JUNE 1874

Primus Davis (negro) was shot and killed at Spring Hill, recently, by Reid Horton.

Bob Thornton (negro) was fatally stabbed in Mobile the 19th.

Captain James Roberts was drowned at Mobile, Wednesday of last week.

Jim Campbell, negro, was hung at Grove Hill the 17th.

Hon. John Gill Shorter, ex-Governor of Alabama, died at Eufaula on Wednesday last.

A dead body was found near Mobile a few days ago, but could not be identified. A due bill in favor of John Langdon was found in his pocket.

Johnny Carnes of Hayneville, broke his arm, recently, by falling from a tree.

John Chisholm near Centre was thrown from a mule last week and had his shoulder dislocated.

### DIED IN ALABAMA
Died in Marengo County the 18th, J.W. Mann.
Died in Greenville the 13th, J.W. Buck.
Died in Mobile the 15th, Hypolite Krebs, aged seventy-four years.
Died in Pickens County, recently, Mrs. Colson.
Died near Montevallo the 18th, Cora West, aged three years.
Died in Mobile the 23rd, Maud Seymour Chighizola, aged two years.
Died in Pike County, recently, Mrs. Amanda Barron.
Died in Barbour County the 15th, John Hough.
Died near Benton the 16th, Mrs. M.M. Cowling.
Died in Lauderdale County the 17th, Mrs. Lucy Stutts.
Died in Tallapoosa County the 12th, Captain Denson Crow.
Died in Dekalb County the 15th, John Cunningham.
Died in Demopolis the 21st, Dr. M.W. Creagh.
Died near LaFayette, recently, a daughter of Drayton Mills.
Died in Livingston the 22nd, William Lockard.

Mr. Davis Collins, a respected citizen of Spartanburg, who was tried before the United States Court at Raleigh, North Carolina, and sentenced to four years imprisonment, died in the Albany (New York) penitentiary recently.

Rev. W.C. Buck, a venerable and eminent Baptist preacher, died near Waco, Texas the 18th.

## THE SOUTHERN ARGUS - DEATHS - JUNE 1869 THROUGH JUNE 1874

Mrs. Sarah Colt, who established the first Sunday school in the United States in 1793, is dead.

Issue 6-7-1872

A personal difficulty occurred in Tuskegee last week between Bolling Reed and Colonel R.H. Abercrombie, resulting in the killing of the former.

Pat Shorter, negro, was drowned near Eufaula, Friday last.

Brister Williams (negro) shot and killed Anderson Heard (negro) at Calera the night of the 28th ult.

Policeman Lynch of Mobile was dangerously stabbed one night last week by a negro, who was attempting to release a prisoner from the hands of the officer.

Henry Thorn of Courtland had his arm badly crushed in a saw mill a few days ago.

A young man named Flanagan fatally stabbed a Mr. Pats in Colbert County, Saturday last.

Bud McGehee (negro) accidentally shot and killed himself in Eufaula, Friday last.

Miss Victoria Bolton of North Port was drowned Monday of last week in the Warrior River.

Hon. Porter King of Marion fell from a ladder last week and received severe injuries.

Colonel Williamson R. Hunt of Memphis, during the war on duty in this city, died the 28th ult.

John Presswood was hung the 24th ult. at DeKalb, Tennessee.

A brother of Horace Greeley is buried in Burke County, Georgia, and his grave was desecrated by Sherman's vandals.

A man named Brown attempted to commit suicide at Eufaula one day last week by taking laudanum.

## THE SOUTHERN ARGUS - DEATHS - JUNE 1869 THROUGH JUNE 1874

Issue 6-14-1872

Died in this city on the morning of the 9th, Ernest Graham, infant son of A.S. and Sallie H. Carroll.

Died in this city, Wednesday morning, June 12th at 7 1/2 o'clock, Thomas Strang, eldest son of A.E. and Mary H. Baker, aged twelve years, one month and five days.

Mr. L.W. Levy, an excellent gentleman who has made many friends here and was much beloved by them, died on Saturday last and was buried on Sunday by the order of B'--Breth and the Odd Fellows.

Henry Cassin, infant son of Horace and Rosa Holly, died Friday last.

Selwyn, a little son of Mr. and Mrs. C.L. Harrell, died Thursday evening last.

Edward Gale Collins was drowned at Mobile the 8th.

Dr. A. Martin of Abbeville has been seriously ill.

Mrs. L.H. Hawkins of the Union Female College, Eufaula, is dangerously ill.

Dr. Croxton, Athens, is quite ill.

### DIED IN ALABAMA

Died in Mobile, 25th inst., Francis R. Hacklander.
Died in Birmingham, 28th ult., H.G. Nabors.
Died in Shelby County, 27th ult., a little daughter of Mr. Davis.
Died near Bladon Springs, 20th ult., Mrs. Mary Harwell.
Died in Washington County, 25th ult., W.W. Bassett.
Died in Opelika, 18th ult., John Douson.
Died in Opelika, 18th ult., Carrie Elmore, child.
Died in Opelika, recently, Mrs. Elizabeth McNamce.
Died in Huntsville, 26th ult., Harriet Moore Rhett.
Died in Mobile, recently, George R. Newton.
Died in Mobile, 22nd ult., John Ellis West, infant.
Died near Columbiana, 9th ult., Mrs. Ellinor S. Anchors.
Died in Barbour County, 17th ult., Mrs. Amanda King.
Died in Mobile, recently, Alexander Short.
Died near Gadsden, 25th ult., William Simmons.
Died in Henry County, 1st, Mrs. Delilah Searcy/Scarey.
Died in Mobile, 9th, Mrs. Mary Gager.
Died in Butler County, recently, 29th ult., George S. Peagler.

## THE SOUTHERN ARGUS - DEATHS - JUNE 1869 THROUGH JUNE 1874

Died in Lowndes County, 1st, Captain S.S. Stakeley.
Died in Montgomery, 30th ult., Mrs. Sallie P. Kennedy.
Died in Tuscumbia, 31st ult., Peter Ohlman.
Died in Greeneville, 4th, W.W. Cook, aged seventy-two years.
Died in Lauderdale County, 25th ult., Mrs. Fanny Cochran.
Died in Lauderdale County, 30th ult., Mrs. Wilson English.
Died in Talladega, 7th, Cynthia Tennant Shouse, infant.
Died in Huntsville, 4th, Chamberlain Giles.
Died in San Francisco, California, 20th ult., Mrs. Louisa E. Inge, formerly of Greensboro.

Mr. Menke was thrown from a buggy in Birmingham a few days ago and severely hurt.

The city authorities of Mobile will allow the widow of police officer Lynch to draw his salary during the remainder of the municipal year.

Stephen Clay, negro, tried to fill a burning lamp in Stevenson a few nights ago. He will lose his eyesight.

John C. Johnson of Abbeville fell friday last, breaking his arm and badly bruising himself.

Turner D. Patterson, Marshall of Eufaula, was stricken down with paralysis one day last week.

### Issue 6-21-1872

R.H. Hart was drowned at Gadsden Wednesday night of last week.

John McKibbon and his little son of Silver Run, were badly injured a few days ago by being run over by a wagon.

An aged lady named Curry, living near Union Springs, was killed a few days ago by falling from a fence.

W.C. Stanley of Choctaw County was killed at Escatawpa the 6th.

Cadmus E. Tartt, who killed J.J. Little in Sumter County a few months ago, was arrested in Arkansas lately, and is now in the Livingston Jail.

Miss Emily Edwards, living near Gadsden, committed suicide the 6th.

Monroe Megginson, negro, was drowned near Grove Hill last week.

## THE SOUTHERN ARGUS - DEATHS - JUNE 1869 THROUGH JUNE 1874

Robert Smoke, living in the eastern part of this county, was so severely stung by bees a short time ago as to cause his death in a short time.

Died at the residence of his father in this county the 14th, Alphens E., son of Major G.W. and E.A. Mattison, aged thirteen years and six months.

Died in this city the 13th, Willie Bonnell, infant daughter of W.V.R. and Minnie L. Watson. (Pensacola, Florida; Syracuse, New York; and Newark, New Jersey papers please copy.)

T.M. Tart of Livingston was hooked in the mouth by a cow about two weeks ago.

A Mr. Burgess had his arm broken in Gadsden one day last week.

William Hendricks of Athens has recovered from a severe attack of rheumatism.

The 19th, near Scottsboro, Price Harris was run over by a train of cars and badly injured.

Issue 6-28-1872

A Mrs. Mary Vanderhook committed suicide in Mobile last week by taking arsenic.

Burwell E. Garner of Madison County was found dead Monday of last week, having accidentally shot himself while out hunting.

DIED IN ALABAMA

Died in Demopolis, 15th, H.D. Machen, aged seventy-two years.
Died in Lowndes County, 15th, Mrs. Matilda Grant.
Died in Lowndesboro, 15th, Walter Morris.
Died in Limestone County, 16th, Mrs. Elizabeth Gilbert.
Died in Tuscaloosa, 14th, Ella L. Hatten, infant.
Died in Eufaula, 16th, Elliott Thomas.
Died in Union Springs, 18th, Mrs. R.H. Powell.
Died in Talladega County, 13th, Mrs. Virginia C. Terry.
Died in Mobile, 18th, Clementina Barnewell.
Died in Monroe County, 2nd, Joseph W. Baas.
Died in Mobile, 20th, Mrs. E. Bevington.
Died in Tallapoosa County, 8th, Mrs. Sarah Stone.
Died in Hale County, 15th, William W. Britton.
Died in Demopolis, 19th, Richard Jones, Sen.

# THE SOUTHERN ARGUS - DEATHS - JUNE 1869 THROUGH JUNE 1874

Died near Glenville the 6th, Mrs. Cordelia Carter.
Died in Greenville the 12th, Mrs. Priscilla Reid.
Died in Madison County the 7th, Jefferson Eckels.
Died near Choctaw Corner the 8th, Bethel Phillips.
Died in Clarke County, recently, Jesse Smith.
Died in Tompkinsville, recently, William M. Fountaine.
Died in Grove Hill the 7th, Mrs. Caroline Reynolds.
Died in Barbour County the 14th, Goodwin Streater.
Died in Limestone County the 7th, James Williams, aged eighty-six years.
Died in Mobile the 10th, Oscar Chaudron.
Died in Opelika the 8th, Mrs. I.H. Vincent.
Died in Carrollton the 5th, Mrs. Charles D. Roberts.
Died in Barbour County the 7th, John W. Flournoy.
Died in Clopton the 4th, Mrs. A.J. Powell.
Died in Mobile the 12th, Lorenzo Gomez.
Died in Marion the 12th, James Rankin.
Died in Camden the 3rd, W.F.C. Martin, Jr., infant.
Died in Tuskegee the 7th, Mrs. G.B. Dryer.
Died in Tuskegee the 8th, George Schott.
Died in Lowndes County the 4th, John Hrabouski.
Died in Hayneville the 6th, Mrs. Cornelia Landingham Belgart.
Died in Tuskaloosa County the 8th, James Thompson Taylor.
Died in Tallassee the 9th, Mrs. Mary E. Jordan.
Died in Tuskaloosa the 8th, Professor S.F. Walter.
Died near Clayton the 11th, Emanuel Cox.
Died in Dadeville the 9th, Mrs. Mike Stone.
Died in Tallapoosa County the 7th, Arnold S.C. Herren.

Miss Stites of Louisville was burned to death on the 19th by a coal oil explosion.

Perry Gill of Cathage, Mississippi, recently shot and killed Katharine Hutchins, a young lady to whom he was to have been married the next day.

Issue 7-5-1872

DIED IN ALABAMA

Died in Gainesville, 13th ult., Judge Turner Reavis.
Died in Greenville, 8th ult., Mrs. Mary J. Potter.
Died in Dale County, recently, Exer Fain, child.
Died in Auburn, 12th ult., Rev. W.A. Dick.
Died in Madison County, 22nd ult., Richard Jainer.
Died in Oxford, 20th ult., William McLane, Senior.
Died near Forkland, 18th ult., Addie, infant daughter of W.A. Sorsby.

## THE SOUTHERN ARGUS - DEATHS - JUNE 1869 THROUGH JUNE 1874

Died in Cherokee County, 7th ult., E.G. Collier.
Died near Greenwood, 12th ult., John Rogers, aged seventy years.
Died near Bladon Springs, 15th ult., William Craig.
Died in Tuskaloosa, 25th ult., Emmett Lee Hatte, infant.
Died in Tuskaloosa, 23rd ult., Mrs. Millicent B. Battle.
Died in Marion the 1st, a little child of Rev. P.B. Lawson.
Died near Mount Willing, 20th ult., Elizabeth Smith.
Died in Perry County, 19th ult., Mrs. Rosannah Kynard.
Died in Henry County, 23rd ult., Captain W.W. Hare.
Died in Mobile, 29th ult., Mary Barnes.
Died in Florence, 22nd ult., Garrich T. Campbell.
Died in Florence, 22nd ult., Mrs. Josiah Pollock.
Died in Florence, 22nd ult., Mrs. Lucy Westmoreland.

Tuesday night of last week, two cousins named Whitt had a difficulty near Centre during which one was fatally stabbed.

Hon. F. S. Lyon of Demopolis has been quite ill since his return from the state convention.

Colonel Walden, Talladega, has been quite ill.

Issue 7-12-1872

Colonel Robert McKee:--We have a little band of independent reformers on Pea Ridge of about thirty members. Our aim is to aid in the great cause of temperance; and although we have been organized only two months, we have great cause to flatter ourselves on our success. Our wives, mothers, and sisters have no fears now when their husbands, sons, and brothers visit the city, of their returning home reeling under a load of strong drink.

We expected on the 19th of this month to have had a barbecue.....Mr. John Mixson, who is ninety-three years old and a residence of our neighborhood of more than seventy years, will not be with us but a few days at best, and through respect to him and his family, our barbecue has been postponed until the 8th of August, at which time we will be glad to see our friends and promise to entertain them to the best of our ability.

Died in this city the 3rd inst., after an illness of ten hours, Anna Edna, infant daughter of J.J. and V.R. Williams, aged eleven months and three days.

Died in this city the 7th inst., Willie R., only son of Mrs. E.J. Chambers.

Died in this city the 6th inst., Daniel, infant son of John and Margaret Shanahan.

## THE SOUTHERN ARGUS - DEATHS - JUNE 1869 THROUGH JUNE 1874

Captain R.B. Rhea shot and killed George James at Attalla the 1st inst.

Joe Bailey was stabbed during an affray between himself and two brothers named Weaver in Huntsville the 4th.

J.B. Neal of Atlanta is to be hung, August 18th, for murder.

Colonel William S. Phillips, who died in this city on Sunday last, in the sixty-seventy year of his age, was among the oldest citizens of Selma... Until he retired from the practice of law, he stood high in the profession he adorned.

Dr. J.W. Dunklin and Daniel Rast of Colerain were both dangerously ill last week.

John Lafan was found dead in a boat on the north bank of the Tennessee River near Bainbridge recently.

The 28th ult., John Martin, aged one hundred and nine years, died in Warren County, Tennessee.

Thomas Guthrie (negro) was hung for murder at Danville, Kentucky the 5th.

Died on the evening of the 29th ult. at the residence of her mother in Talladega County, Alabama, in the fullness of her youth and loveliness, Miss Cornelia Burt, aged twenty-one years. Jackson, Mississippi, Montgomery, and Nashville papers will please copy.

A Georgia Judge, who seventeen years ago sentenced John Dotton to be hung, last month performed the same office for John Dotton's son.

Rev. Robert Crassette, a well known----of the Congregational Church, died at his residence on College Hill, Cincinnati, recently.

Policeman Gibbons, Mobile, had his foot and hand badly crushed by a street car last week.

The guard house at Montevallo, together with a prisoner named Michael Cleary, were burned Monday night last week.

J.B. Neal of Atlanta is to be hung August 19th for murder.

William Smith, Editor of the *Cincinnati Price Current*, is dead.

Rear Admiral Crabbe is dead.

## THE SOUTHERN ARGUS - DEATHS - JUNE 1869 THROUGH JUNE 1874

B.S. Barker and family of Livingston were thrown from a buggy one day last week.

Issue 7-19-1872

Mr. E.A. Young, a well known citizen of East Perry, father-in-law of Mr. W.T. Airey/Alrey of this city, died the 12th inst., at the residence of his son-in-law, W.W. Smith near Perryville.

J.T. Smith, Tax Assessor for Greene County, was shot on the 6th, by Ham Thornton. The gun was loaded with squirrel shot.

Died at his residence on Pea Ridge on Sunday last, John Mixson, aged ninety-three years. Mr. Mixon had for more than half a century lived on the plantation on which he died and was perhaps the oldest citizen of Dallas County...

Henry Connerly of Vienna, Pickens County, hurt himself pretty badly a few weeks ago by falling from a tree which he was engaged in trimming.

An infant child of Pollard Crawford of Georgia was killed at Huntsville, Alabama, a few days ago by the falling of a shelter attached to the house.

Solomon Spurlock, who died in Barbour County the 9th, was several months over one hundred years old.

In Big Wills Valley the 4th, James Works was shot and wounded by Andrew Linn.

In Greenville the other day, Lizzie Trawick, negress, was shot and killed by Asa Moorer, negro.

Bill Wyatt is in the Madison Jail for shooting and wounding Shelly White.

General Baker, candidate for Congress at large, has been dangerously ill.

Messrs. Duffie and O'Brien, Montgomery policemen, were cut with knives while attemting to make an arrest on the 13th.

Harper Miles (negro) had his skull fractured in Hayneville the 10th by a brick thrown by another negro.

Sapphira Bentley of Limestone County recently hung herself.

## THE SOUTHERN ARGUS - DEATHS - JUNE 1869 THROUGH JUNE 1874

Near Livingston the other day, Tom Roy, negro, shot and wounded Ned Barbour.

Mrs. Sarah Davis, mother of Rev. J.C. Davis, Rector of St. James Church, Eufaula, died near Philadelphia a few days ago.

Jesse Drinkard was killed near Shiloh, Marengo County, recently by a negro.

On the 7th W.F. Bruce and F.M. Barrier had a shooting affray at Stevenson and both were wounded.

In Tuskaloosa the 7th, Moses Terrel, negro, was killed by another negro named Spanlard/Spanland.

Judge Linton Stephens of Georgia is dead.

There was a mistrial in the Stokes case for the murder of Fisk.

Died at Cobourg, Canada, on Tuesday last, Anna Parham, infant daughter of Major and Mrs. N.R. Chambliss of this city.

Died in this county the 12th inst., Mrs. Eliza F., wife of Hon. Ben Edwards Grey and daughter of the late Colonel Thornton B. Goldsby.

Dr. H.L. Densler, an old and respected citizen of Dallas, was drowned on Tuesday last in Mulbery Creek near Burnsville by the capsizing of a skiff.

Woodson Hendree, only son of Dr. and Mrs. J. Hendree of this city, was found dead in his bed on the morning of the 15th. He was aged twenty-one years and nine months. [see below]

Issue 7-26-1872

Mr. Boyd, near Forkland, Greene County, was dangerously ill a few days ago.

Henry Lockett of Marion, an estimable and promising young man, was fatally stabbed at Middleton, Tennessee, recently.

William Woodson Hendree. He departed this life on the night of the 14th inst., in the twenty-second year of his age....[see above]

Willie Murphy, who accidentally shot and killed himself recently, at Poughkeepsle, New York, was a native of Greene County.

## THE SOUTHERN ARGUS - DEATHS - JUNE 1869 THROUGH JUNE 1874

Near Calhoun, Lowndes County, the 15th, a man named Smith was shot and killed by Robert and George Rambo and George Coburn.

In Jackson County the 5th, Ambler Grubbs fell from a window of a mill and was instantly killed.

### DIED IN ALABAMA

Died in Eufaula, 6th, Mrs. Cordelia M. Carter.
Died in Suggsville, recently, Mrs. Eliza A. Odom.
Died in Talladega, 3rd, Mrs. Louis Bishop.
Died in Clayton, 29th ult., Hiram B. Hill.
Died in Mobile, 2nd, Mrs. John O'Brien.
Died in Lawrence County, 25th ult., Zach Leatherwood.
Died in Troy, 29th, Rochfort Parks, infant.
Died in Talladega County, 29th ult., Cornelia Bart/Burt.
Died in Mobile, 30th, Katie Westerfield, infant.
Died near Huntsville the 10th, George Jude.
Died in Huntsville the 10th, Miss Derby Ann Williams.
Died in Tuskaloosa the 1st, G. William Frye, artist.
Died in Mobile the 13th, Lewis McCoy.
Died in Birmingham the 4th, J.S. Thompson.
Died in Evergreen the 10th, Miss Eliza M. Rabb.
Died in Lynn, Massachusetts, the 4th, C.C. Farnham of Evergreen.
Died in Mobile the 12th, Mrs. Lizette D. Bromberg.
Died in Montgomery the 12th, W.H. Ogbourne.
Died in Montgomery the 11th, George Dawkins.
Died in Tuskegee the 6th, Robert L. Mitchell.
Died in Tuskegee the 8th, Mrs. P.P. Carlos.
Died in Madison County, 29th of March, Jason M. Brazelton.
Died at Tuskaloosa the 7th, Col. B.I. Harrison.
Died near Pleasant Ridge, 25th ult., Abner A. Steele.
Died in Barbour County the 9th, Elisha Davis.
Died in Barbour County the 9th, Solomon Spurlock.
Died in Eufaula the 7th, Andrew Womble.
Died in Opelika the 3rd, Isham Dorsey.
Died in Chambers County the 7th, Laurance Fedder.
Died near Montevallo, 30th ult., Mrs. C.E. Fancher.
Died in Mobile, recently, Richard Drummond of Dayton.
Died in Mobile the 2nd, Cornelius McCarthy.
Died near Bridgeville, 28th ult., James Duncan.
Died in Pickens County, 27th ult., little Willie Jones.
Died in Jackson the 1st, Mrs. E.A. Wainwright.
Died in Eufaula the 10th, Caleb Driggers.
Died in Greenville the 8th, Mr. Register.

# THE SOUTHERN ARGUS - DEATHS - JUNE 1869 THROUGH JUNE 1874

Died in Barbour County the 10th, Jimpsey Cox.
Died in Jackson County the 5th, Ambler Grubbs.
Died in Mobile the 17th, Frederick Tones.
Died in Lawrence County, 30th ult., Mrs. George Atwood.
Died in Jackson County the 12th, Mrs. Elizabeth Willis.
Died in Eufaula the 10th, Mary Eugenia Cameron, infant.
Died in Wetumpka, recently, Samuel Stonaker.
Died in Mobile the 14th, Mary Elener Shaw, child.
Died in Barbour County the 9th, Elisha Davis.
Died in Mobile the 15th, William Stewart Glover, child.
Died in Mobile the 15th, Marino Martin.
Died near Mobile the 13/15th?, William Wisdom.
Died in Madison County the 6th, Mrs. Sarah Butler.
Died near Forkland the 1?th, Mrs. David Bragg.
Died in Indianapolis the 17th, M. Carmelich of Mobile.
Died in Talladega the 16th, Mr. Harrison.
Died in Gadsden the 13th, child of A.L. Woodliff.
Died in Greenville the 18th, Mrs. M.J. Bailey.
Died in Eutaw the 10th, Mrs. Elizabeth J. Head.
Died in Texas, 5th ult., Mrs. Annie P. Stewart, formerly of Greene County.
Died in Eufaula the 17th, infant son of E.B. Young.
Died in Livingston the 7th, Mrs. Corrinna Cnsack/Cusack.

James Works, shot by Andrew Linn on the 4th in Etowah County, is dead.

A little son of B.J. Fort, at Marion Junction, died Monday last of diphtheria.

Hugh Ferguson, a sprightly little son of Dr. Russell McCord of Rio Janeiro, while playing in the yard of his grandmother's (Mrs. Hugh Ferguson) residence in this city Tuesday last, fell into a kettle of boiling syrup, and was so burned that he died in a few hours.

Mr. Roberts, Editor of the *Opelika Locomotive*, has been quite ill.

General Alphens Baker is getting well, though he is quite weak.

Rev. M.B. DeWitt of Huntsville is in bad health and is visiting Tennessee.

Died on the "Colby Place" near this city on Monday last Major Robert Swann

### Issue 8-2-1872

Mr. Amsden, who graduated at Dartmouth College with Daniel Webster, died in the Augusta, Georgia hospital last week.

## THE SOUTHERN ARGUS - DEATHS - JUNE 1869 THROUGH JUNE 1874

Herman Jordan, a Private in an Artillery Company at Fort Pulaski, Savannah, Georgia, was deliberately shot and killed by Sergeant Carr a few days since.

Lewis Ash (negro) was drowned in the Tennessee River, at Whitesburg the other day.

During the recent floods, John Bookout, wife and daughter, living six miles from Springfield, were drowned in their house, which was washed away at night.

A few days ago in Birmingham, a man named Duncan was shot and wounded by his brother-in-law, a lad of sixteen.

Died in Fayette, Missouri, a few days ago, Eddie V. Wills, son of Rev. J.C. Wills, formerly a professor in the Southern University at Greensboro.

Mr. Connolly, living near Demopolis, lost a little son by drowning one day last week.

Dr. A.F. Watson, formerly of Mobile, died in Brownsville, Texas the 2nd ult.

In Mobile the 27th ult., Annie Johnson was killed by lightning.

Died in East Selma, Wednesday last, Richard Clark, infant son of W.H. and Elizabeth Harwell.

The accomplished wife of Mr. S.W. John is seriously ill at Colonel Woolsey's residence in this city.

Died in this city, suddenly, Saturday night last, a Mr. Farnham, from Maine, who had been here about three months.

One of the Lowry outlaws in North Carolina has been killed.

Mr. M.J. Williams has been seriously indisposed since his return from the mountains of Virginia.

Issue 8-9-1872

Died in this county on the morning of the 26th of July, Caroline Hamilton Smith, infant daughter of G. Waring and Charlotte E. Smith, aged two years and five months.

Judge Fera M. Wood of Eufaula has been seriously ill.

## THE SOUTHERN ARGUS - DEATHS - JUNE 1869 THROUGH JUNE 1874

Frank Brown was drowned in Troy Creek, Cherokee County, the 19th ult.

Mrs. Mary Dillard was killed by lightning in Opelika the 30th ult.

The 24th ult., in Mobile a negress named Annie Johnson was killed by lightning.

Ellis E. Hill, formerly of Lawrence County, was murdered at Hot Prairie, Texas on the 15th ultimo.

In a difficulty at Brownsboro, 20th ult., between Mead Hewlett and his son Tom on one side, and Ben Sublett and his two sons on the other, the two Hewletts received severe wounds with sticks on the head, and the two young Sublett's were cut very severely with a knife.

### DIED IN ALABAMA
Died in Montgomery, 20th ult., Mrs. Rose Cunningham.
Died in Mobile, 22nd ult., Mrs. Elizabeth M.R. Ulrick.
Died in Mobile, 21st ult., Mary E. Marsh.
Died in Birmingham, 4th ult., Miss Emily Worthington.
Died near Birmingham, 12th ult., Mrs. Louisa Hickman.
Died near Elyton, 18th ult., Mrs. Jap Anderson.
Died in Cherokee County, 22nd ult., George W. Williams.
Died in Athens, 15th ult., Mrs. Mattie Boggan.
Died in Jackson County, 12th ult., Mrs. Elizabeth Willis.
Died in Birmingham, 3rd ult., Thomas Scott Tate, infant.
Died at McKinley, 12th ult., Alvin Borden Armstrong, infant.
Died in Dadeville, 19th ult., Eula Johnson, infant.
Died near Scottsboro, 21st ult., Benjamin Snodgrass.
Died at Calvert, Texas, 1st ult., Mrs. Mary Jane Aycock, formerly of Greene County.
Died at Pleasant Ridge, 4th ult., Lizzie Steele Murphy, infant.
Died in Sumter County, 8th ult., Maggie Lou McKerall, child.
Died at Mt. Hebron, June 16th, Marion T. Morgan, child.
Died near Uniontown, 6th ult., Mrs. M.L. Evans.
Died near Forkland, 14th ult., Mr. Boyd.
Died near Huntsville, 23rd ult., Cora Lee Nichols, infant.
Died in Calhoun County, recently, Mrs. Winney Vandiver.
Died near Rehoboth, 15th ult., Pettie K. Tidwell, child.
Died in Brooklyn, recently, William Haessell.
Died in Evergreen, 26th ult., Miss Susan J. Rabb.
Died in Mobile, 30th ult., Mrs. Mary Bryant.
Died in Talladega County, 25th ult., W.Y. Bailey / Balley
Died in Talladega, 28th ult., Mrs. R.A. Reed.

# THE SOUTHERN ARGUS - DEATHS - JUNE 1869 THROUGH JUNE 1874

Died in Opelika, 30th ult., Mrs. Mary Dillard.
Died in Abbeville, 20th ult., Curtis Elizabeth Price, infant.
Died in Mobile, 27th ult., Benjamin Smoot, child.
Died in Texas, 20th ult., Colonel J.T. Montgomery.
Died in Greene County, 14th ult., Wm. B. Bridges.
Died near St. Stephens, 13th ult., Mrs. Mary Harris.
Died near Mooresville, 22nd ult., Mattie McClellan, child.
Died in Eutaw, 29th ult., James C. Ustick.
Died in Greene County, 10th ult., Mrs. Elizabeth Bragg.
Died in Hale County, 29th ult., Mrs. Priscilla Hatter.
Died in Wetumpka the 3rd, Clarence Leslie Luckett, child.
Died in Tuscumbia, 27th ult., Edward Mandley.
Died in Colbert County, 28th ult., Ella Burns Pearsall.
Died near Florence, 24th ult., Mrs. Lou R. McCoritin.
Died near Florence, 24th ult., Willie Martin, infant.
Died in Lauderdale County, 21st ult., Miss Mary Jones.
Died in Demopolis, 29th ult., Mrs. A.A. Grote.
Died in Cartersville, Georgia, 20th ult., Mrs. N. McGhee, late of Cherokee County.
Died in Gadsden, 30th ult., Rev. A.M. Spalding.
Died in Mississippi, recently, Prof. C.F. Gayle of Pickensville.
Died in Florence, 30th ult., Eddie Hooks, infant.
Died in Mississippi, recently, Peter Armstrong, formerly of Camden.
Died in Wilcox County, recently, Elijah Hanks.

Tribute of respect from the Planters' Association at Burnsville upon the death of James E. Moss, a pioneer, who for half a century has been an industrious, upright, and esteemed citizen of Dallas County... We tender to his sister and bereaved relatives our deep sympathy.

Jack Hollingworth of Limestone County killed a negro, name unknown, the 26th ult.

J.S. Harwell, Mayor of Demopolis, has been sick.

## Issue 8-16-1872

Died in East Selma, Friday last, a child of P.H. Murphey.
Died near Orrville, Saturday last, John B., child of W.E. and S.F. Beaird.

Milt. Malone, formerly of this city, in Atlanta the 10th, killed a Mr. Frank Phillips.

# THE SOUTHERN ARGUS - DEATHS - JUNE 1869 THROUGH JUNE 1874

Perry Abbott of Talladega County was bitten by a rattle snake a few days ago.

Died Saturday the 10th near Marion Junction, infant daughter of Mr. and Mrs. F.E. Harrell.

Henry Bender (not the cotton warehouseman) yard master at the Alabama Central Railroad Depot, in attempting to get upon an engine while in motion, Wednesday last, was thrown under the wheels and his left leg was crushed so as to render amputation necessary.

Died at her residence near Selma on Sunday last, Mrs. Martha Wilson, aged about sixty years.

Died at her residence, four miles west of Selma, Sunday, August 11th, Mrs. Martha Wilson, consort of the late Elijah Wilson, aged seventy-two years.

Mr. and Mrs. W. H. Bell of Marion Junction have the hearty sympathy of the entire community in the afflictions which have fallen upon them. On the 1st inst., their daughter Fannie, and the 6th their daughter Ila, sweet and promising children, died. Only a few days previous, Mrs. Bell had lost a little brother, son of B. J. Fort, Esq.

Major Blake Little has returned to his old home in Livingston, enfeebled by age and in delicate health.

James F. Aldridge and daughter of Marengo were thrown from their buggy, which the team was running away with, on the 4th, and Mr. Aldridge was badly hurt.

B. D. Murphee of Troy was badly injured a short time ago by the running away of his mules.

Mr. Bledsoe, an old gentleman of Pike County, was the other day thrown from his horse in Troy and seriously injured.

George Thomas (negro) was stabbed and killed in Clarke County the other day by Henry Evans (negro)

Issue 8-23-1872

Daniel Fitzgibbon died in this city last Saturday.

Died in this city on Monday last, Maud, daughter of J H Robbins

## THE SOUTHERN ARGUS - DEATHS - JUNE 1869 THROUGH JUNE 1874

Died near Harrell's Cross Roads the 18th, Miss Maggie Chestnut.

Archie Hall had his hand so badly lacerated by a saw at Mobile last week that amputation of three fingers and part of the thumb was necessary.

In East Selma, Saturday night last, an old man named Wilson was shot twice and seriously wounded by one of his sons.

A difficulty recently occurred at Cokerville between two men named Mooney and Joiner in which the latter was killed.

Richard Desharo of Shelby County was killed one day last week at Melner's Mill by a piece of timber falling on him.

Hon. David Read, Probate Judge of Lee County, died very suddenly on Friday night the 9th. Disease supposed to be a apoplexy.

Mrs. Whatley and Mrs. Levison of Dadeville are both suffering from paralysis.

William A. Avery, living near Greensboro, was dangerously stabbed by a negro in his employ one day last week. The negro escaped.

Edward Burfield/Barfield was drowned at Mobile, Thursday of last week.

### DIED IN ALABAMA

Died near Pollard, 26th ult., W.M. Johnson.
Died at Whistler the 1st, Willie Shinault.
Died in Mobile the 7th, J.M. McGovern.
Died in Tuskegee the 3rd, Mrs. Mary Moulton.
Died in Tuskegee the 3rd, W.W. Williams.
Died in Cross Plains, 19th ult., child of T.C. Stevenson.
Died in Barbour County the 2nd, Calvin Teal.
Died in Eufaula the 6th, Ellis W. Jenkens.
Died in Barbour County the 5th, Mrs. Charlie F. Massey.
Died in Eufaula the 5th, child of Mr. Smart.
Died at Pollard, 22nd ult., child of R.E. Corry.
Died near Sparta, 19th ult., Mrs. Frances Crosby.
Died in Huntsville the 3rd, Mrs. Ann C. Lanford.
Died in Philadelphia, 19th ult., Libbie Davis, daughter of Mrs. S.J. Allen of Mobile.
Died in Mobile the 5th, Mrs. S.E. Tuomey.
Died in Huntsville, 30th ult., Mrs. Eliza R. Pooser.
Died in Huntsville, recently, Mrs. G.W.F. Price.
Died in Talladega County, 20th July, E. Williamson.

## THE SOUTHERN ARGUS - DEATHS - JUNE 1869 THROUGH JUNE 1874

Died in Carrollton the 5th, Terry, child of E.D. Willett.
Died near Pickensville, 29th ult., Fannie G. Lang.
Died in Greenville, South Carolina, 25th ult., John Brooks, formerly of Lowndes County, aged eighty-four years.
Died in Greenville, South Carolina, 26th ult., Mrs. J.W. Brooks, formerly of Lowndes County.
Died in Butler County the 7th, Frederick Boan.
Died near Jonesboro the 6th, Rev. W.B. Moore.
Died near Jonesboro the 7th, Mrs. W.B. Moore.
Died near Radfordsville, 23rd ult., Eulalle Smith.
Died in Marion, recently, Miss Mattie H. Whitsett.
Died in Marion the 5th, Ellen Gray Brown, child.
Died in Marion the 3rd, Columbus W., child of Knox Lee.
Died near Marion the 1st, Mrs. Mary Sullivan.
Died in Perry County, 20th ult., Dr. John Seawell.
Died in Marion the 6th, Rose Araminta, child of W.C. Ward.
Died in Mississippi, 10th ult., W.J. Sims, formerly of Hale County.
Died in Madison County, 25th ult., Nancy Allison.
Died in Camden, 31st ult., Stella Jones, child.
Died in Montgomery, 10th inst., Samuel David Finley, child.
Died in Limestone County, 1st, Mrs. Mary C. McElzia.
Died in Opelika, 12th, Mrs. Ann W. Wilkerson.
Died in Brock's Gap, 5th, Mrs. Mary E. Brown nee Perry.
Died in Lee County, 9th, David Read.
Died in Cherokee County, 11th, Judge J.R. Lowe.
Died near Knoxville, Greene County, 3rd, William E. McCracken.
Died near Springfield, July 28th, Lela Falson, infant.
Died in Tuskegee, 4th, Mamie Sue Parker, infant.
Died in Dadeville, 11th, F.S.C. Sommerkamp.
Died in Dadeville, 11th, Miss Jesse Bunckley.
Died in Sumter County, July 20th, Mrs. Bettie Monette McKerrall.
Died near Troy, 3rd, Amanda J. Jones, infant.
Died near Elmore, 2nd, S.A. Michael.
Died in Gadsden, 7th, Jammie M. Thrash, infant.
Died in Etowah County, 8th, John Shephard.
Died in Camden, 9th, Mrs. Catherine Martin.
Died in Hayneville, 11th, Mrs. Charity Garrett.
Died in Lowndes County, 9th, Miss Mary Moss.
Died in Lowndes County, recently, Mr. Guthrie.
Died near Courtland, 15th, R. Gibson.
Died in Leighton, 4th, S.J. Leggett.
Died in Montgomery, 11th, Judge Tilman Leake.
Died in Mobile, 17th, M. Wagenbrener.
Died in Mobile, 17th, F. Maumme.

## THE SOUTHERN ARGUS - DEATHS - JUNE 1869 THROUGH JUNE 1874

At Mt. Royal, Limestone County, 9th, W.S. Todd was shot and killed by T.A. Stewart.

Tribute of respect on the death of Daniel Fitzgibbon, St. Patrick's L&B Association.

Frank Gibson of Troy was injured recently by the running away of a horse.

W.H. Troy of Troy, who has been quite sick, is improving.

Rev. Mr. Cobbs of Greensboro is visiting the mountains of Virginia for his health.

The health of R.B. Waller of Greensboro who is at St. Clair Springs, is improving.

Rev. Dr. Thomas E. Bond, an eminent Methodist preacher and editor, died the 19th.

D.T. Bradley of Opelike was thrown from a mule one day last week and had his shoulder broken.

Issue 8-30-1872

A personal difficulty occurred in Lawrence County last week between Tom Davidson and a Mr. Redding, during which Davidson was severely stabbed.

A negro named Henry Weems was accidentally shot and killed in Mobile one day last week.

A negro named Pleas was killed at Demopolis by the cars one day last week.

Saleta, daughter of J.K. White was buried here yesterday evening.

Mr. W.B. Gill is reported quite sick at Yellow Sulphur Springs, Virginia.

A little child of Mrs. Jane Day, formerly of Marion, was buried here Tuesday last.

Died near Barnsville the 27th, Miss Eddie, daughter of Mr. J.L. Claughton, aged twenty-one years.

### DIED IN ALABAMA
Died in Lawrence County, 18th, William McKay.

# THE SOUTHERN ARGUS - DEATHS - JUNE 1869 THROUGH JUNE 1874

Died in Lauderdale County, recently, G. Jacobs.
Died in Mobile, 23rd, John Graham.
Died in Athens, 18th, Mrs. Annie Hobbs.
Died in Montgomery, 24th, Daniel Boyle.
Died in Chambers County, 15th, Joseph W. Phillips.
Died in East Tennessee, 15th, H.C. Hooten of Union Springs.
Died in Gadsden, 15th, Minna Augusta Disque, infant.
Died in Bullock County, 13th, Mrs. Nancy Collins.
Died in Opelika, 20th, Jimmie McNermee, infant.
Died in Mobile, 19th, Frank Johnson.
Died in Mobile, 30th, L.F. Aurieres.
Died in Philadelphia 11th, Sarah E. Campbell, formerly of Mobile.
Died in Prattville, 19th, Mrs. Mary Ann DeBardelaben.
Died in Marion, 25th, Miss Florence Potts.
Died in Leighton, 4th, Colonel S.J. Leggett.
Died in Fair Haven, Connecticut, 21st, John E. Brey of Eufaula.
Died near Evergreen, 18th, Mrs. Julia Locke.
Died in Tuskaloosa County, recently, W.R. Quarles.
Died in Tuskaloosa County, 11th, Mary Emma Prince, infant.
Died in Marion, 18th, Willie Verdot Craig, child.
Died in Colbert County, 19th, Mrs. James Jackson.
Died in Madison County, 17th, Mrs. Jennette Swasy.
Died in Talladega, 9th, Austin Mayfield, aged ninety-eight years.
Died in Memphis, Tennessee, 15th, Thomas J. Dill, formerly of Talladega.
Died in Opelika, 15th, "Little Fay" Shell, infant.
Died in Pickensville, 5th, Moses F. Hearren.
Died in Eutaw, 8th, George, son of Ellen and M.J. Cole.
Died in Eutaw, 10th, Mrs. Samuel Frenkel.
Died in Greene County, 17th, Alonzo D. Fason.
Died in Forkland, 11th, John Hughes.

George Queen (negro) was committed to the Eufaula Jail last week on the charge of poisoning three negro children.

Mr. M.J. Williams, who has been seriously ill at his residence in this city, had sufficiently recovered on Tuesday last to leave for Shelby Springs.

Dr. Semple, surgeon in the United States Army, died in a sleeping car on the westward bound train on the Alabama Central Railroad, Tuesday last of apoplexy.

## THE SOUTHERN ARGUS - DEATHS - JUNE 1869 THROUGH JUNE 1874

Thomas Timms, who keeps a grocery near the Box Spring, on the Alabama and Chattanooga Railroad, was shot and seriously wounded, and the store robbed of a gold watch and $400 in money by a negro man, on the night of the 16th.

Bion Leftwich of Tuskaloosa was thrown from a horse cart last week and seriously injured.

Tom Sanky (negro) killed another negro by the name of Martin in Montgomery County a few days ago.

At Waterloo, a few days ago, an escaped prisoner named Tom Terry, shot and mortally wounded a Mr. Humphrey.

Issue 9-6-1872

Died Monday last in this city, Mary, infant daughter of Dr. George H. and Mrs. Lenoir.

We regret to hear that Judge P.G. Wood is quite sick at his residence in this city.

The infant of Thomas H. and Mrs. M.E. Hopkins died in this city on Friday last.

Died in this city Thursday morning the 5th inst., Thomas L. Mitchell, late of Marion, aged about twenty-seven years.

Died in this city the 3rd, Rosa Lee, infant daughter of Mr. W.H. and Mrs. R.V.E. Hicks.

Rev. Mr. Foster of Troy is quite ill.

A little daughter of Mrs. Taylor in Mobile was run over by a dray one day last week and severely injured.

### DIED IN ALABAMA

Died in Bladon Springs, 25/26th ult., Sanford Lewis.
Died in Athens, 26th ult., Eddie Russell, infant.
Died in Lowndes County, 26th ult., Edward Burford.
Died in Lowndes County, 25th ult., Thomas Polly.
Died near Mt. Willing, recently, Mr. Jay.
Died in Huntsville, 27th ult., Willie A. Jones.
Died in Birmingham, 22nd ult., W.H. Tilford.

## THE SOUTHERN ARGUS - DEATHS - JUNE 1869 THROUGH JUNE 1874

Died near Glenville, 30th ult., a son of Michael McGuire.
Died in Jefferson County, 12th ult., William Ellard.
Died at Shades Mountain, 2nd ult., John Ritter.
Died in Birmingham, 22nd ult., Mrs. Ophelia J. Graham.
Died in Crenshaw County, 17th ult., John Littleton Welch.
Died near Choctaw Corner, 14th ult., Mrs. Grunby Deaton.
Died near Fort Deposit, 10th ult., Laird Kirkpatrick.
Died in Hale County, 23rd ult., E.L. Kimbrough.
Died in Mesopotamia, 23rd ult., Joseph Hall, infant.
Died in Greene County, 8th ult., Bessie Fitzgerald, infant.
Died in Huntsville, 24th ult., Hudson Allen.
Died near Huntsville, 23rd ult., Mrs. Nancy L. Schrimsher.
Died in Tallapoosa County, 20th ult., Seaborn J. Thomas.
Died in New Marlboro, Massachusetts, recently, Edmond S. Sheldon, formerly of Mobile.
Died in Sheldon, Vermont, 13th ult., S. Bartlett Waring of Mobile.
Died in Tuskaloosa County, 7th ult., J.M. Hall.
Died in Florence, 23rd ult., George Sholl.
Died in Cherokee County, 20th ult., S.M. Hargue.
Died in Cherokee County, 27th ult., Mrs. Amanda Green.
Died near Collinsville, 19th ult., W.W. Pruitt of Attalia.
Died near Marion, recently, Alice Martin, aged five years.
Died in Lauderdale County, 22nd ult., Jeremiah Dowdy.
Died at Bailey Springs, 25th ult., Colonel Williams of Bartlett, Tennessee.
Died in Opelika, 24th ult., Mrs. Isabella Leverson.
Died in Lee County, 23rd ult., A. Pringle.
Died in Lee County, 15th ult., Sallie Carter, infant.
Died in Mobile, 25th ult., Dr. Kelly.
Died in Washington County, 23rd ult., Mary Cox Wilson.
Died in Madison County, 22nd ult., John Sandford.

Tribute of respect from Selma Fraternal Lodge #27 F.A.M. on the death of Madison Jackson Williams.

The funeral ---? of Mr. M.J. Williams, on Friday last, were the most imposing ever witnessed in the city. The business houses were all closed; and the entire population turned out to do honor to the memory of one so useful and so beloved. The Masons of the several lodges, the Odd Fellows, the Firemen of the different companies, the city council, the officers and members of the Presbyterian Church.....to the church and hence to the grave...

Jim Todd (negro) fell off a hand car near Union Springs a few days ago, and was badly hurt.

## THE SOUTHERN ARGUS - DEATHS - JUNE 1869 THROUGH JUNE 1874

Mr. Humphrey of Waterloo who was shot by young Terry, will recover.

W.H. Loomis of Gadsden was thrown from his horse one day last week and severely bruised.

Owing to the illness of his wife, Dr. Groce declines making the race for Representative in Talladega.

Issue 9-13-1872

Near Lowndesboro the 31st ult., William Rugely (negro) was killed by his wife, whom he had undertaken to whip.

Died August 27th, in the 21st year of her age, Edwina [Eddie] daughter of J.L. and S.E. Claughton. She with her twin sister professed religion and have been members of the church five years...parents, brothers and sisters...

Peterson Tanner, a prominent, citizen of Athens, was run over by the cars on the 6th, and mortally injured.

On the 4th, Monroe Byrd, a brakeman on the Montgomery and Eufaula Road, fell from a car and was run over by the train and killed.

Died in Richmond, Virginia, 24th ult., Mrs. Ellen A. Jarvis of Huntsville.
Died in Jackson County, recently, Henry Halsey.
Died in Lowndes County, recently, E. Bozeman.
Died in Mobile, 5th, Mrs. Janet Cumming.
Died in Montgomery, 6th, Miss Mary P. Houghton.
Died in Randolph County, 1st, L.R. Lawler.
Died near Greensboro, 29th ult., W.P. Hughes.
Died near Hollow Square, 22nd ult., E.L. Kimbrough.
Died in Perry County, 19th ult., Ida Alice Herron, child.
Died in Perry County, 23rd ult., Milton Foster Herron, child.
Died in Perry County, 24th ult., Mattie Felton Herron, child.
Died in Athens, 7th, Peterson Tanner.
Died in Tuskaloosa County, 1st, Dr. Bedee.
Died in Sumter County, 1st, Miss Lena Ball.
Died in Livingston, 1st, W.K. Ustick.
Died in Montgomery, 5th, Louisa Nickel.
Died in Montgomery, 8th, Annie Laura Hodgson, infant.
Died in Mobile, 4th, Benjamin Forcheimer, child.
Died near Garland, 17th ult., John Robertson, child.
Died in Tuskegee, 4th, N.K. Holt.
Died in Eufaula, 4th, Sallie Berry, child.

# THE SOUTHERN ARGUS - DEATHS - JUNE 1869 THROUGH JUNE 1874

Died in Barbour County, 2nd, Colquitt C. Ingram.
Died in Opelika, 30th ult., Elenore R. Cameron, infant.
Died in Perry County, 31st ult., Miss Georgia Crawford.
Died in Perry County, 29th ult., Mrs. Susan Hogue.
Died in Perry County, 28th ult., Jennie Matthews, child.
Died in Barbour County, recently, Charles Butts.
Died in Marion, 10th, L.C. Tutt.

Some two weeks ago, John Anthony Carr of Clay County committed suicide by shooting himself.

In Opelika a few days ago, little Lee Collins attempted to get on a car while it was in motion, slipped and fell under it, and had a leg horribly crushed.

In memoriam: Died at his residence in Lowndesboro, August 25th, Mr. Thomas Polly, aged about fifty-eight years. The deceased was an honorable, upright and respected citizen of Lowndes, who leaves one son and daughter... The deceased was born in South Carolina and emigrated in early life to this state, where his family now reside. Shortly after coming to Alabama he married a daughter of Mr. Thomas Abercrombie of Perry County, Alabama, who died at Lowndesboro in the year 1839? 1859? 18?9..

Died August 4th, 1872, in the thirty-third year of her age, Mrs. Sirena Hornbeak, wife of E.M. Hornbeak, and fifth daughter of J.K. and N.S. Callen. She had been a consistent member of the Presbyterian Church at Valley Creek for a number of years; was an exemplary christian; a devoted wife; a faithful daughter and affectionate sister.... Since her marriage, her aged father-in-law has been a constant inmate of her home, and none could have been more tender and thoughtful of him....

Death has been busy among us lately. We have another to add to the list of his victims. George C. Phillips, Jr., died at the family residence in this city, on Friday last in the twenty-seventh year of his age. Mr. Phillips was the son of the late Colonel W.S. Phillips whose death was recorded but a few months ago, and a nephew of Colonel G.C. Phillips, to whose memory and virtues we paid a tribute only last week...But disease months ago marked him for its victim...

On the 5th at Allenton, William Albritton was stabbed, but not fatally, by E. Craig.

We regret that Sidney Herbert, an industrious conscientious, painstaking, and capable editor, has found it necessary, on account of his health, to retire from the *Troy Messenger*.

## THE SOUTHERN ARGUS - DEATHS - JUNE 1869 THROUGH JUNE 1874

Since the death of Mr. Williams, Merritt Burns has associated with John B. White, a very capable and excellent man, with him in the real estate business.....

Issue 9-20-1872

Died in this city, Sunday morning last, George P. Duncan.
Died in this city Friday last the 13th, Mrs. Frances D. Holley.
Died at Marion Junction, Saturday last, a little son of Mr. L.C. Litesey.
Died at Orrville the 3rd inst., Mrs. Althea C. Brown, wife of J.R. Brown.
Died near Ha?rch's Cross Roads the 12th, Estelle, infant daughter of Rev. J.A. Lowrey.

E.H. McDuffie was thrown from his buggy in Gadsden last week and badly bruised.

Died in Portland the 14th instant, Mrs. R.D. Boykin, in the thirty-seventh year of her age.

Died in this city the night of the 11th inst., Mrs. Fannie Louisa, wife of Dr. Thomas M. Logan.

On Wednesday of last week, Dr. John Blevins of this County lost by death a little daughter, and on Friday thereafter his mother-in-law died.

Adeline Rugely (negro) killed her husband near Greenville the night of the 7th.

A negro named Hamp killed his father-in-law in Butler County the 8th.

John Flynn attempted to cut his wife's throat in Mobile the other day.

Frank Humphrey (negro) was stabbed and instantly killed by Peter Points/Pointe (negro) in Madison County the 10th.

James Gibson of Eufaula accidentally shot himself a few days ago.

Abram, a negro man living near Greensboro died a few days ago, aged about one hundred years.

Frank Adams of Cherokee County has been dangerously ill.

Newton Humes was accidently shot in Huntsville the 11th.

## THE SOUTHERN ARGUS - DEATHS - JUNE 1869 THROUGH JUNE 1874

In South Selma, Sunday evening last, a negro man named Andrew Tipton was shot and killed by Mr. R.J. Fowler who had caught him in an act of theft.

Richmond Thomas, a negro employed in the shops of the Alabama Central railroad, was killed in one of the cars on the westward bound train on that road Monday morning last, by his head, which had been thrust out of a window, coming in contact with the timbers of Valley Creek bridge.

Willis Pitts accidentally shot himself a few days ago in Dadeville.

Mr. Cooley, a butcher in Montgomery, was shot and seriously wounded by a negro named Bob Pelham a few days ago.

Mrs. Britton, who died near Fayetteville the 10th of June, was in the eighty-eighth year of her age, and had been a member of the Baptist Church for more than half a century.

A little daughter of Frank Newberry of Eufaula fell off the bluff at that place, a few days ago and was seriously hurt.

To the Editor of the *Argus* on the death of George Crawford Phillips: The sad announcement in your last issue of the death of Colonel G.C. Phillips carried me back forty years when I knew him as a boy in the University of Alabama, in which I was at the time professor of Ancient languages... The friendship which we then formed continued till his death, and although I saw him but seldom, our intercourse was kept up by his confiding to my care the education of his younger brother John, his three sons, and two of his nephews. His father, Dr. Phillips, was a member of the board of trustees, and one whom Dallas County delighted to honor... H.T., Greene Springs, Alabama, Sept 11th.

Captain Little of Tuscumbia was slightly burned last week by the explosion of some kerosene.

### DIED IN ALABAMA
Died in New Orleans, 9th, Charles W. Linn, formerly of Montgomery.
Died in Mobile, 9th, Emelia Herman.
Died near Talladega, 9th, Edmund Welch.
Died near Eastaboga, 9th, William Montgomery.
Died in Tuskaloosa County, 7th, Wilkerson V. Ward.
Died in Tuskaloosa County, 8th, Elias Barton.
Died in Tuskaloosa, 9th, Emma Back.
Died in Tuskaloosa, 5th, Mrs. Jennie Hays.
Died in evergreen, 5th, Agnes Reed, infant.

## THE SOUTHERN ARGUS - DEATHS - JUNE 1869 THROUGH JUNE 1874

Died in Florence, 8th, Hattie Gray.
Died in Lauderdale County, 4th, Melvina G. Deason.
Died in Pickensville, 3rd, Charlie Beard Morehead, infant.
Died in Lawrence County, 5th, Emmet Abernathy.
Died in Hale County, 6th, Miss Jennie Clements.
Died near Macon Station, 2nd, James C. Collins.
Died in Washington County, 3rd, Fannie Johnson, infant.
Died in Mobile, 16th, Henry Chrystal.
Died in Jefferson County, 10th, William Barrett.
Died in Mobile, 14th, Louis Meyers.
Died in Huntsville, 7th, Adeline Mosely.
Died in Mobile, 8th, John Booth, aged eighty-six years.
Died in Greenville, 5th, Marion Oscar Seawright, infant.
Died in Livingston, 10th, Mrs. Hannah Hyden.
Died in Greene County, 3rd, John Thomas McAlpine, infant.
Died near Pleasant Ridge, 7th, Mrs. Elizabeth P. Mobley.
Died at Oxford, Mississippi, 8th, Alice Garland, formerly of Tuskaloosa.
Died in Mobile, 12th, Henry Ledyard Gwinn, infant.
Died in Dadeville, 30th ult., Mary Leoline Kyle, infant.
Died in Cherokee County, 5th, Anderson White.
Died the 26th ult., Mrs. Aurelia, widow of the late ex-Governor Fitzpatrick.
Died in Tallapoosa County, 13th ult., Mrs. Sarah E. Washburn.
Died in Tallapoosa County, 16th, child of B.S. Washburn.
Died near Uniontown, 28th ult., Thomas Walthall Hardie, infant.
Died at Brierfield, 11th, Laurie Whitfield McMain, child.
Died in Demopolis, 11th, Mrs. A.F.J. Watkins.
Died near Demopolis, 11th, Miss Ella McRee.
Died at Spring Hill, 11th, Mrs. Lemuel Sledge.

Mr. Zach Drummond of Mobile was killed by lightning Monday of last week.

Died at Liberty Hill, Dallas County, April 17th, 1872, Charlie Antoinet, eldest son of Dr. F.G. and Nettie Wilson, aged three years and nine months.... mentions deceased mother.

In an alternation in East Selma Monday night last between Charles Schafer (white) and Nathan Lee (negro), both d--ymen, the latter was shot and painfully wounded. Schafer was required to give $2,000 bond to answer at the next term of the criminal court for an assault with intent to murder.

Issue 9-27-1872

Died in Cambridge, Dallas County the 24th, Mr. W.A. Cochran.
Died in Dallas County the 23rd, Robert Hinton, aged seventy-two years.

# THE SOUTHERN ARGUS - DEATHS - JUNE 1869 THROUGH JUNE 1874

Died in this city the 23rd, Charles Fahs, infant son of G.W. Morris.
Died in Cahaba, Sunday evening the 22nd, Ida Belle, infant daughter of W.L. and C.F. Kirkpatrick.

In Sherman, Texas some time ago, Frank P. Reed, recently of this city, shot and killed a man named Thompson.

James Meenan and Major Hannon were thrown from a buggy in Mobile one day last week.

Osce, son of Willis Roberts of the Shelby Guide had his foot and ankle so badly mashed by being run over by a locomotive the other day as to make amputation necessary.

Died in this city the night of the 20th, Ida, daughter of C.G. and A.H. Helmer, aged two years and eight months.

Miss May Bradfield, living at Helena, was burned to death one day last week by the explosion of an oil can.

Elias Weaver and Charles Mason, brothers-in-law, became engaged in a fight at Columbiana the 17th, during which Weaver was shot and seriously wounded.

Thomas J. Coleman stabbed and killed Joseph Cunningham, Jr. in Pickens County last week.

Mrs. Hawthorne, who died recently in Greenville, was the mother of General Hawthorne, and of Rev. J. B. Hawthore, formerly of this city.

William Shelton has been convicted of manslaughter for the murder of O.D. McCluskey in Tuskaloosa and sentenced to the penitentiary for seven years.

## DIED IN ALABAMA

Died in Athens, 17th, Mrs. Elizabeth Elliott.
Died in Marion, 22nd, J.P. Graham.
Died in Mobile, 19th, Mrs. M. Fallon.
Died in Montgomery, 23rd, Dr. J.G. Scott.
Died in Montgomery, 23rd, Mrs. Sarah A. Chapman.
Died in Montgomery, 23rd, Mary M. Adams, infant.
Died in Huntsville, 18th, William Cunningham.
Died in Morgan County, recently, Rev. J.D. Robinson.
Died near Hollow Square, 22nd, Joseph Chapman.
Died in Greensboro, 22nd, H.W. Watt.

## THE SOUTHERN ARGUS - DEATHS - JUNE 1869 THROUGH JUNE 1874

Died in Gadsden, 13th, Mattie M.A. Collins, infant.
Died in Mobile, 17th, William Batcheller Arnold.
Died in Troy, 9th, Augusta Isbell Gardner, infant.
Died in Shelby County, 16th, Ransom Ramie.
Died near Montevallo, 7th, Josephine Hardin.
Died in Madison County, 14th, William Matkin.
Died in Tuscumbia, 15th, Fannie Simpson Keller, infant.
Died near Tuscumbia, 5th, William Wilson, infant.
Died in Huntsville, 18th, Lucien T. Matthews.
Died near Eufaula, 20th, Mrs. Mary P. Lillienstein.
Died in Eufaula, 20th, Clifford Pope Macon, infant.
Died in Greenville, 16th, Mrs. Martha Hawthorne.
Died in Greenville, 15th, an infant son of Comer Knight.
Died Fort Deposit, 14th, Robert Walker.
Died in Hayneville, 16th, James Sheehan.
Died in Hayneville, 16th, Logan Griffin, infant.
Died in Lowndes County, 13th, Mrs. Rebecca Adams.
Died in Tuscaloosa, 12th, Mrs. Martha C. Skelton.
Died in Tuskaloosa, 14th, Gertrude Seed, infant.
Died in Tuskaloosa County, 15th, S.F. Moses.
Died in Camden, 12th, Emma Moore, child.
Died in Atlanta, Georgia, 18th, Colonel James A. Turner, formerly of Lowndes County.
Died in Dayton, 6th, William T. Brame.
Died in Dayton, 8th, Annie Bailey, child.
Died in Linden, 10th, Alexander W. Dunn.
Died near Marion, 15th, Mrs. Nancy McLaughlin.
Died in Lowndes County, 12th, Jo Owens.
Died in Gadsden, 15th, an infant child of Mr. Hull.
Died in Gadsden, 14th, Andrew Fletcher.
Died near Gadsden, 14th, Mrs. Sarah Tatum.
Died near Midway, Texas, August 17th, Julia M., wife of Dr. J.C. Braton; eldest daughter of E.G. and Lucy J. Wagner, formerly of Autauga County.

Mark Dickinson (negro) broke the skull of Henry Norwood (negro) at Greenville last week.

Henderson Brooks (negro) was drowned at Mobile a few days ago.

James M. Malone and daughter were thrown from a buggy near Athens one day last week and severely bruised.

Dr. B.W. Maclin and W.R. Pryor of Athens are sick.

# THE SOUTHERN ARGUS - DEATHS - JUNE 1869 THROUGH JUNE 1874

Thornton M. Baugh and Dr. W.K. Jones of Union Springs cared for an unknown man found sick near that place until he died.

A white man named Hunt, living near Forkland, was badly beaten a few days ago by a negro.

Issue 10-4-1872

John Gage, a well known citizen of Mobile, accidentally shot and killed himself Wednesday of last week.

Ben Williford, near Eufaula, had his left arm so badly cut by a cotton gin as to necessitate amputation.

Wm. Prescott Smith of Baltimore, an eminent railroad man, is dead.

Charles F. Harvey and Robert Forsythe had a shooting match in Louisville a few days ago in which both were badly hit.

A man named Odum was shot near Greenville a few nights ago while stealing corn.

Colonel Morgan Johnson, near Union Springs, has lost two children lately by meningitis.

Henry Brown (negro) was thrown from a wagon and killed at Livingston one day last week.

Rev. Peter Cartwright of the North Methodist Church, is dead.

## DIED IN ALABAMA

Died at Bridgeville, 12th ult., Edward Eugene Duncan, infant.
Died at Sipsy Mills, 13th ult., Mrs. McAlilly.
Died in Greene County, 12th ult., Samuel Archibald.
Died in Memphis, Alabama, 3rd ult., Mrs. Mary E. Rogers.
Died at Sandy Ridge, Lowndes County, 2?th ult., William Payne.
Died in Huntsville, 21st ult., Harriet Eliza Phelps, infant.
Died in Cherokee County, 22nd ult., Frank Adams.
Died at Shades Mountain, 24th ult., Mrs. E.R. Mitchell of Montgomery.
Died in Birmingham, 21st ult., Miss Hattie Watkins.
Died in Pike County, 18th, James G. Cook.
Died in Marion, 21st ult., Hon. J.P. Graham.
Died in Opelika, 22nd ult., Mr. Alexander.
Died in Eufaula, 21st ult., Charles Hall.

## THE SOUTHERN ARGUS - DEATHS - JUNE 1869 THROUGH JUNE 1874

Died near Linden, 17th ult., "Uncle Jimmy" Moore.
Died near Birmingham, 19th ult., James Edward.
Died in Athens, 20th ult., William A. Elliott.
Died near Hollow Square, 22nd ult., Joseph Chapman.
Died in Greensboro, 2nd ult., Hugh W. Watt.
Died in Hale County, 23rd ult., Mrs. Ben Griffin.
Died in Greene County, 13th ult., Walter Abner Fason, infant.
Died in Greene County, 11th ult., Mrs. Rebecca F. Fason.
Died in Eutaw, 13/15th ult., Katie Elvise? Cunningham.

George Spigner was thrown from a buggy in Rockford the 26th ult. and killed.

A man by the name of Riley committed suicide in Birmingham the 20th ult.

John H. Huff of Ozark was killed by the cars near Union Springs one day last week.

A little son of J.B. Taylor of Wetumpka was bit last week by a rattlesnake.

At 4:30 Tuesday morning last, an accident occurred on the South and North Road, about twenty miles north of Birmingham, in which James M. Smith of St. Louis, formerly of Montgomery, and C.C. McLemore of Greensboro were killed and others were seriously wounded.

Dave Lony (negro) has been sentenced to the penitentiary for twenty years from Perry County for murder.

General William Harrow, Indiana, was killed by a railroad accident the 27th ult.

Issue 10-11-1872

In Limestone County a few days ago, William Edmondson was stabbed seriously by a Mr. Watkins.

In Sumter County the other day, Daniel Polnitz (negro) was fatally shot by Bill Wells (negro).

In Sumter County the 23rd ult., John L. Dees was shot and killed by John E. Dees.

We regret to learn that on Friday last, Mr. L.B. Parker, the conservative candidate for the Legislature in Autauga County, lost by death a most interesting and lovely child.

# THE SOUTHERN ARGUS - DEATHS - JUNE 1869 THROUGH JUNE 1874

In West Lowndes a few days ago, Betsey Dudley was stabbed and killed by Betsey Williams, black.

In Dadeville the 30th ult., Hansen Henderson was fatally, and Addison Turner seriously, shot.

### DIED IN ALABAMA

Died in Lowndes County, 9th, Dr. J.W. Danklin.
Died in Autauga County, 4th, Lazarus B. Parker, child. [see below]
Died in Tuscumbia, 3rd, Mrs. Sue E. Simpson.
Died in East Perry, 23rd ult., Thomas Muse.
Died in Mobile, 2nd, Mrs. Mary A. Mervin.
Died in Greenville, 1st, Dr. J.M. Jennings.
Died in Mobile, 1st, Thomas Gretofull.
Died near Talladega, 26th ult., Louise Boby/Roby McClellan, infant.
Died in Louisiana, 19th ult., D.A. Long.
Died in Florence, 30th ult., Mary Rigg Lindsay, child.
Died in Dale County, 24th ult., Rev. J.L. Oliver.
Died in Opelika, 22nd ult., Mr. Alexander.
Died in Montgomery, 27th ult., Richard Gill.
Died near Linden, 17th ult., James S. Moore.
Died in Tuskaloosa, 15th ult., Mrs. Julia A. Dearing.
Died in Birmingham, 17th ult., Miss Hattie Watkins.
Died in Autauga, 20th ult., P.H. Whetstone.
Died in Mobile, 26th ult., James Frazer.
Died in Mobile, 28th ult., W. Cusick.
Died in Madison County, 27th ult., Henry Cochran.
Died in Montgomery, 20th ult., Annie Glenn Billinglsea.
Died in Madison County, 3rd, Mrs. Ann E. Hinds.
Died near Huntsville, recently, Mrs. Pheebe Hamblett.
Died in Huntsville, 5th, Colonel Geo. A. Gordon.
Died in New York, 5th, E.H. Caldwell of Mobile.
Died in Mobile, 4th, William Affron.
Died in Montgomery, 5th, Mrs. J.D. Bunting/Banting.
Died in Marion, 7th, Miss Kate Huckabee.
Died in Camden, 24th ult., Dr. J.H. Pressly.
Died near Macon Station, 17th ult., Mrs. Kate McClusky.
Died on Friday evening the 4th inst., Lazarus B., son of Lazarus B. and B.M. Parker of Autauga County, aged five years. [see above]

Capt. J.M. Macon of the *Eufaula Times* has been dangerously ill.

## THE SOUTHERN ARGUS - DEATHS - JUNE 1869 THROUGH JUNE 1874

Another good man has passed away! Henry Crawford Hatcher died at his residence four miles west from Orrville, October 5th, 1872, aged [?7] years eight months and seven ? days... wife and children...

Obituary. Colonel George Crawford Phillips was born in Madison County, Alabama, on the 2?th day of May, 1815, and departed this life at his residence, near Selma in Dallas County, Alabama, on the 30th day of August 1872. For fifty-two years he was a resident of Dallas County. He was twice a member of the Legislature of the state. He was for nineteen years a member of the Commissioners Court of the County... devoted husband and father... deacon in Presbyterian Church... born Madison County, we believe...

Issue 10-18-1872

C.C. Skillman was thrown from a horse at Eufaula a few days ago and badly injured.

### DIED IN ALABAMA
Died in Greenville, 8th, Joseph Goodman.
Died in Huntsville, 12th, William Wells.
Died near Allenton, 7th, James P. Williams.
Died in Wilcox County, recently, R.K. Middlebrooks.
Died in Pickens County, 16th ult., John Evans.
Died in Lauderdale County, 25th ult., Mrs. Martha A.F. Alexander.
Died in Florence, 7th, Robert A. Campbell, infant.
Died in Florence, 3rd, Rev. William H. Mitchell.
Died in Cherokee County, 22nd ult., Frank Adams.
Died in Montgomery, 12th, Dr. James H. Taylor.
Died in Huntsville, 9th, Miranda Hook.
Died in Tuscumbia, 2nd, Mrs. Sue E. Simpson.
Died in Birmingham, 27th ult., Mrs. M.S. Hughes.
Died in Henry County, 7th, Henry P/ F/ I.? Reynolds.
Died in Mobile, 25th ult., Mrs. Elizabeth Forbes Burgwin Clitherall Hall.
Died in Huntsville, 4th, Mrs. Pheebe Hamlet.
Died in Marion, 5th, Mrs. Catherine Baxter.
Died in Marion, 7th, Ira Dunkin, boy.
Died in Perry County, 2nd, John J. Herron, child.
Died in Texas, recently, Nathaniel Terry, formerly of Limestone.
Died in Henry County, 7th, Henry T. Reynolds.

In Columbia, Henry County, the other day, J. J. Grimsley was shot and slightly wounded by Norman McLeod.

Ex-Congressman Deming of Connecticut died the 9th.

## THE SOUTHERN ARGUS - DEATHS - JUNE 1869 THROUGH JUNE 1874

James R. Spaulding, one of the original proprietors and editors of the New York World, died the 11th.

Judge J. W. Brooke, formerly of Greene County, Alabama, died at Meridian the 9th.

Mrs. Greeley's health is slowly failing and her death may be expected at any time.

A little son of Joseph Dickens of Henry County died a few days ago from the effects of a snake bite.

On the 7th, E. Howard McCaleb and R. B. Rhett, Jr., both of New Orleans, fought a bloodless duel.

W.H. Seward was in the seventy-second year of his age when he died.

In Savannah the 11th, David R. Dillon was shot and killed by his son, Alexander Dillon.

George, infant son of C. Heinz, died the 1?th in East Selma.

Captain Macon of the Eufaula Times is recovering from his recent illness.

Dr. C.M. Howard has declined the nomination for State Senator from the Autauga District on account of ill health.

The Florence Journal appeared last week in mourning for the death of Rev. W.H. Mitchell, President of the Florence Female College.

Issue 10-25-1872

Died in this city, Sunday last, Miss Tim Rains.
Died in this city the 22nd after a long illness, Mr. Isaac Sterne....

John T. Stocks of Cherokee County was dangerously ill the 17th.

Robert Allen of DeKalb County was run over and killed by a train a few days ago.

Rev. Mr. Winkler, who has but recently taken charge of the Baptist Church in Marion, has the sympathies of a large community in the recent death of a promising child.

# THE SOUTHERN ARGUS - DEATHS - JUNE 1869 THROUGH JUNE 1874

M.A. Bridges is held in a thousand dollar bond to answer for the killing of B.W. Hammett in Jefferson County.

### DIED IN ALABAMA
Died near Eutaw, 13th, George W. Roberts.
Died in Greenville, Walter Montgomery Grace, child.
Died in Lowndes County, 10th, W.H. Johnson.
Died in Lowndes County, recently, Robert Davis, aged one hundred seven years.
Died in Lowndes County, 12th, Samuel Johnson.
Died in Hayneville, 14th, Mrs. H. Schwabacher.
Died near Hayneville, 11th, John Witcher.
Died near Hayneville, 17th, Benjamin Meadows.
Died in Lowndes County, 16th, Mrs. G.R. Haigle.
Died in Choctaw County, 16th, Agnes Trice, child.
Died near Mooreville, 4th, Emma High, child.
Died in Lee County, 15th, Mr. Whitten.
Died in Montgomery, 2_th, Juliet Berney, infant.
Died in Montgomery, 20th, Mrs. Rosanna Hopkins.
Died in Opelika, 13th, Plant S. Purnell, infant.
Died near Birmingham, 5th, Benjamin Wesson.
Died in Tuskaloosa, 10th, Tommy Ferrell.
Died in Marion, 13th, Annie Winkler.
Died at Artesia, Mississippi, 14th, Charles S. Perkins, formerly of Marion.
Died in Mobile, 13th, Jefferson Davis Walthall, infant.
Died near Triana, 10th, James P. Springer.
Died in Montgomery, 13th, Edward F. Goode.
Died near Prairieville, 18th, Mrs. Charles Collins.
Died in Mobile County, 19th, A. Royster.

A little son of Captain James Hopkins of Mobile was killed by the accidental discharge of a shot gun on the 16th.

A difficulty occurred in Elyton a few days ago between Bose Simpson and a Mr. Hewitt, during which the former was shot and killed.

Near Talladega on the night of the 17th, William Walker shot and killed W.R. Linebaugh.

Right Reverend Michael O'Connor, late Catholic Bishop of Pittsburg, is dead.

Right Reverend Alexander Goss, Catholic Bishop of Liverpool, is dead.

## THE SOUTHERN ARGUS - DEATHS - JUNE 1869 THROUGH JUNE 1874

Rev. Merle D'Aubigne, the celebrated historian of "The Reformation," died at Geneva the 21st.

Issue 11-1-1872

Died in Dallas County the 13th ult., Bessie, child of Mr. Joel Gibson.
Died in this city, Tuesday last, Annie, daughter of Mr. and Mrs. M. Monteaboro.
Died in this County, 25th ult., Colonel Samuel M. Hill, aged sixty-four years.
Died at Day's Mill, Bibb County, the 19th ult., Mrs. A.J. Day, a native of Dallas County.

A son of J.B. McMullan, living near Greensboro, was killed last week by being caught in the wheels of a cotton gin.

Cadmus E. Tartt of Sumter County has been acquitted on the charge of murder for killing J. J. Little.

Wyley Jones of Marengo County has been arrested, charged with shooting a negro man and negro woman near Shiloh the night of the 22nd ult.

Sheriff Malone of Limestone County has been quite sick.

G. W. Cain has been appointed Treasurer of Limestone County, vice Mr. Tanner, deceased.

Died in Griffin, Georgia, recently, Mrs. DeVotie, formerly of Montgomery.
Died in Louisville, Alabama, 11st [sic] ult., Mrs. Anna Norton.
Died in Jackson County, 7th ult., Mrs. Mary Dodson.
Died in Jackson County, 10th ult., Henry Kelton.
Died in Florence, 8th ult., Rudolph D. Rice, infant.
Died in Tuskegee, 21st ult., Mrs. G.B. Slaughter.
Died in Montgomery, 24th ult., Mrs. Ellen O'Keefe.
Died in Hale County, 10th ult., Julina Ardella Stringfellow, infant.
Died in Hale County, 18th ult., Mrs. Lou Collins.
Died in Montgomery, 25th ult., William A. Elam.
Died in Lowndes County, 21st ult., Reverend Samuel Rives of Texas.
Died in Lowndes County, 19th ult., William Pullum.
Died in Lowndes County, 22nd ult., Mrs. Todd, aged eighty years.
Died near Wedowee, 22nd ult., Edgar Latimer.
Died in Pickens County, 21st September, Mrs. Margaret McAuley.
Died in Butler County, 18th ult., W.P. Routon.
Died in Florence, 18th ult., Theo. Allen Jones.
Died in Camden, 18th ult., Henry Boltz.

# THE SOUTHERN ARGUS - DEATHS - JUNE 1869 THROUGH JUNE 1874

Died in Montgomery, 26th ult., Mamie Burton, infant.
Died in Marion, 27th ult., Enoch R. Pollard.
Died in Marion, 27th ult., Miss Annie Lockhart.

Issue 11-8-1872

We regret to learn that Miss Minnie McCall, an accomplished and lovely young lady of this city, is almost hopelessly ill at Franklin, Tennessee.

Near Pinetucky, a few days ago, a son of Israel Jones accidentally shot himself through the upper part of the left arm, terribly shattering the bone. The resection of the shoulder joint was performed by Dr. Royston and the patient is getting well.

Tribute of respect from Selma Fraternal Lodge F.A.M. held on Monday, November 4th, 1872, on the death of Isaac Sterne... [mentions wife, children] From the *Daily Times*: Mrs. Maggie M. Lowery, wife of Rev. W.J. Lowery, died at her home on Saturday at 8 A.M., in her thirtieth year. She was born in Starkville, Mississippi, was early left an orphan, and was reared under the care of a loving aunt, Mrs. Montgomery. When sixteen years old, she made profession of her faith in Christ, by uniting with his church. Shortly after this, she went to Columbia, Tennessee, where she completed her education in 1860, when she returned to her home in Mississippi. In August 1861, she gave herself in marriage to him whom death has now so bereaved, and they together moved to Wilcox County, Alabama, where Mr. Lowery was then preaching. From there they moved to Selma, in 1866, where she has since resided... [condensed]

Rev. W. J. Lowry, the beloved pastor of the Presbyterian Church, has the deep and heartfelt sympathy of this entire community in the terrible affliction which has befallen him in the death of Mrs. Lowry.

Wiley Oliver (negro) killed his brother, John Wiley (negro), in Hayneville a few days ago.

Murdered in cold blood by highway robbers, while returning home near Hamburg, in Ashley County, Arkansas, Robert Edwin Weaver, son of William C. Weaver of Perry County, Alabama. Also at the same time and place, mortally wounded and robbed, H.P. Weaver, formerly of Perry County, Alabama, and son-in-law of said William C. Weaver. Also at the same time and place, fired upon several times, Joe Weaver, brother to said H.P. Weaver, but providentially made his escape unhurt. Also, on Wednesday, 16th, following, near the same place, while returning home from a professional visit to H.P. Weaver, a Dr. McCoin was shot dead from his horse. Three of the murderers are now in jail in Hamburg, Arkansas.

## THE SOUTHERN ARGUS - DEATHS - JUNE 1869 THROUGH JUNE 1874

Died in Hartford, Connecticut the 31st ult., Alice, daughter of W.R. Bill of this city, aged four years.

Died at the residence of his father near this city yesterday (Thursday) morning, Wright Griffin, a gentleman raised here, well known in all this section, and highly esteemed by a large circle of acquaintances.

In Guntersville the other day Pleas. Nichols was shot and killed by Spence Thomas.

R.H. Wilson has been appointed Register in Chancery in Madison County, vice W.B. Figures, dead.

On the 1st, Mrs. Walls, wife of a merchant of Columbiana was accidentally and fatally burned.

John Pratt of Centre had his hand caught in the machine of a cotton gin a few days ago and badly crushed.

Capt. J.M. Macon of the *Eugaula Times* has got well.

Issue  11-15-1872

Died near White's Bluff the 6th, Mr. L. E. Lenoir, in the 32nd year of his age.

Died at her residence in East Selma on the 8th inst., Mrs. B.E. Shearer, aged seventy-five years.

In this city, Sunday night last, Frank Barron (negro) accidentally shot and seriously wounded his wife.

Henrietta March (negress), who died here on Sunday last, is the last kerosene oil victim we have to report.

On Monday last in this city, Berry Ford (negro) shot and terribly, probably fatally, wounded Sam Young (negro).

Eli Walkins (negro) shot and killed his wife near Decatur last week.

A woman named Betty Rasher died suddenly in Mobile one night last week.

William J. Walton of Hale County was kicked to death by his horse the other day.

## THE SOUTHERN ARGUS - DEATHS - JUNE 1869 THROUGH JUNE 1874

The dead body of Ransom Sherman was found on the Reed place near Gordonsville on the 6th.

Holman Perry of Jackson County accidently shot himself the 5th.

John S. Greene of the editorial staff of the *Mobile Register*, died the 8th of congestion of the brain.

### DIED IN ALABAMA

Died in Calhoun County, 16th ult., T.J. Caver.
Died in Macon County, 28th ult., Miss Anna B. Fannin.
Died in Henry County, 21st ult., Rev. J.D. Morris.
Died near Wetumpka, 10th ult., W.C. Perrick.
Died in Jackson County, 19th ult., Mrs. Hannah Boone.
Died in Mobile, 27th ult., Orlean Emma Sibley, infant.
Died in Whistler, 2?th ult., Martha Ainchbacker/Alnchbacker, child.
Died in Montgomery, 29th ult., Mrs. T.A. Madigan.
Died in North Port, 2?th ult., Mrs. Loa T. Brown.
Died in Mobile, 30th ult., Adam Prichard.
Died in Union Springs, 25th ult., James H. Thompson.
Died in Evergreen, 23rd ult., George V. Rabb, infant.
Died in Eufaula, 31st ult., Alfred H. Dickson, Sr.
Died in Monroe County, 9th ult., Miss Dora E. Hurry.
Died in Monroe County, 9th ult., little Dickie Hurry.
Died in Suggsville, 24th ult., Thomas W. Denny.
Died in Tuscumbia, 25th ult., Mrs. Mary P. Inman.
Died near Tuscumbia, 29th ult., John Ritter.
Died in Cherokee County, 28th August, Mrs. Margaret Darrell.
Died in Cherokee County, 28th September, Mrs. Mary Jane Chastain.
Died in Mobile the 2nd, Sidney Antoine Charborinet, child.
Died in Dayton, 27th ult., Joel S. Jones.
Died in Linden, 27th ult., Albert Sidney Glass, child.
Died in Oxford the 2nd, Lena Rosenberger.
Died in Montgomery, 2nd, William B. Benson.
Died in Limestone County, 28th ult., Abner Robertson. [see below]
Died in Elyton, 27th ult., Florence Walker, infant.
Died in Birmingham, 28th ult., Chipman Pierce, infant.
Died in Birmingham, 28th ult., Gertrude Clemens, infant.
Died in Limestone County, 28th ult., Abner Robinson. [see above]
Died in Madison County, 30th ult., Robert M. Lyne.
Died in Huntsville, 5th, Augustus Bliss, infant.
Died in Greene County, 2nd, Charles E. Spencer.
Died in Tuskaloosa, 5th, Wm. Barnes, child.
Died in Greensboro, 4th, James Cox.

## THE SOUTHERN ARGUS - DEATHS - JUNE 1869 THROUGH JUNE 1874

Died in Greensboro, 4th, Clarence May.
Died near Hillsboro, 4th ult., Mrs. Melissa Williams.
Died in Lawrence County, 20th ult., Mrs. Henry Thorn.
Died in Talladega County, 9th, Giles Pitts.
Died in Mobile, 8th, J.S. Greene.
Died in Perry County, 4th, Dr. S.R. Blakewood.
Died in Marion, October 18th, Eugene Reid, child.
Died in Marion, 10th, H. Norman Lockhart.
Died in Perry County the 19th, John Boyd.

Edward McMahon was accidentally drowned at Mobile the 5th.

Joseph W. Gilmore of Bullock County has been acquitted on charge of murder for shooting his niece some months ago.

Mrs. S. H. Sedbury of Centre is dangerously ill.

Captain Berney, Editor of the *Eutaw Whig*, has been sick.

William J. Walton of Hale County was kicked to death by his horse the other day.

A fight occurred at Garrett's Ferry last week, during which Mart Roberts was stabbed and a Mr. Oliver was shot.

A negro attempted to murder a Mrs. Miller, living about seventeen miles from Mobile, last week. The woman escaped but the negro robbed the house of everything valuable.

Issue   11-22-1872

Mr. A.G. Maynes, the accomplished master mechanic of the Selma, Rome, and Dalton Railroad, has had a dispatch informing him of the death of a brother, killed by a railroad accident a few days ago.

Paty, accused of killing his wife and child and burning their bodies, is in the Cleburne Jail.

Chandler Maddox, aged ninety-six, and his son, William Maddox, aged seventy-eight, are both citizens of Tuskaloosa County, father and son, and are now each drawing pensions, as soldiers in the War of 1812. The old man's wife, Margarette, is still living, aged ninety-six.

## THE SOUTHERN ARGUS - DEATHS - JUNE 1869 THROUGH JUNE 1874

Ike Denman, yard master at the Mobile Depot of the Mobile and New Orleans Railroad, was run over by a switch engine, a few days ago, and had both legs horribly mutilated.

### DIED IN ALABAMA

Died near Meridian, recently, Dr. Peyton King, formerly of Pickens County.
Died in Tennessee, 26th ult., Mrs. Mollie Lucas, nee Ragland, formerly of Florence.
Died near Livingston, 8th, James Branch.
Died in Tuskaloosa, 8th, Robert T. Harris.
Died at Spring Hill College, 14th, Reverend Father Lespes.
Died at Coleraine, 3rd, Daniel F. Rabb.
Died in Lowndes County, 8th, Lennie Edwards, child.
Died in Haynesville, 9th, James H. Jarrett.
Died in Greensboro, 13th, Adie Bayol, child.
Died near Newbern, 14th, Willie Hagins, child.
Died near Newbern, 14th, Minnie Hagins, child.
Died near Gadsden, 9th, James Smith.
Died in Attalla, 5th, Eddie Orr, child.
Died in Mobile, 13th, Mrs. E.B. Kirkbride.
Died in Marion 3rd, Mrs. Emeline E. LeVert.
Died in Marion, 7th, Mrs. Kate Kilfoil/Kilfoll.
Died in Mobile, 13th, Katie Dane.
Died in Georgiana, 10th, Ira W. Stott.
Died in Monroe County, recently, J.M. Davidson.
Died in Talladega County, 9th, Miss Kate Turner.
Died in Talladega, 8th, Giles C. Pitts.
Died in Shelby County, recently, G.R.C. Harless.
Died in Mobile, 9th, David Fowler.
Died in Texas, recently, W.H. Boswell, formerly of Eufaula.
Died in Wedowee, 29th ult., James Bennet.
Died in North Alabama, recently, Robert C. Robinson.
Died in Mobile, 3rd, Mrs. Susan Girard.
Died at Grove Hill, 31st ult., P.J. Keane.
Died in Lauderdale County, 1st, Mrs. Sarah Butherick.
Died in Tuscumbia, 3rd, James H. Gordon.
Died in Tuscumbia, 11th, Mrs. M. Demasters.

Rev. S.R. Freeman, late President of Howard College, died in Jefferson, Texas, the 19th.

At Roanoke the 9th, J.H. Davis, Jr. was shot and wounded by Jesse Reaves.

## THE SOUTHERN ARGUS - DEATHS - JUNE 1869 THROUGH JUNE 1874

B.G. Norwood of Shiloh, while conveying an escape convict to jail at Linden, was pulled from his horse and murdered.

William King, a lad living near Eufaula, fatally shot himself while out hunting a few days ago.

Mrs. Martin H. Smith has been dangerously ill.

George Melton has been dangerously ill.

Died in this city, Wednesday last, Mrs. Hydrick.

Judge Milton J. Safford has been seriously indisposed.

Miss Minnie McCall of this city, who has been dangerously ill at Franklin, Tennessee, is getting well.

Walker, charged with shooting Linebaugh, was arrested at Rome, Georgia, and is in the Talladega Jail.

                  Issue   11-29-1872

Died in this city the 21st inst., Samuel Chesnut.

Mike Dukes (negro) was run over by a train on the Selma and Gulf Railroad, Saturday last, and instantly killed.

Died at the residence of her brother, Colonel J.M. Dedman, on Wednesday last, Mrs. Jane C. Strawbridge.

We regret to learn that our valued fellow-citizen, Albert G. Mabry, Jr., is dangerously ill at the residence of his father in this city.

Mat Williams (negro) is in the Opelika Jail for killing Cain Blackmon (negro).

Harrison Hays (negro) is in the jail at Mobile for killing Dare Kidd (negro).

On Friday last, Jake Kornegay, Joe Jones, three women, and two children (all negroes) started to come down the river from the Kornegay place, two miles above, to the city, in a leaky canoe, which soon sunk, and all except Jake Kornegay were drowned,

On the 20th near Lowndesboro, Jim Smith (negro) was killed by Luke and Bill Jennings (negroes).

## THE SOUTHERN ARGUS - DEATHS - JUNE 1869 THROUGH JUNE 1874

Joe Patey of Cleburne was not hung by a mob as reported, but is safe in the Calhoun Jail.

In Greene County the other day there was an affray in which a Mr. Ray was fatally shot by a Mr. Perry. Mr. Perry was stabbed, a Mr. Knott was shot by a younger Ray, and the latter in turn was badly wounded.

The *Bladon Herald* says: "Joshua Morse, the assassin of Newell E. Thomas, is dead."

In Madison County a few days ago a young man named Turner was shot and killed by his brother-in-law, Howard.

In Jackson County, 17th, O.A. Moody was shot and killed by Thomas Moody.

### DIED IN ALABAMA
Died near Livingston, 11th, Thomas A. Johnson.
Died in Tuskaloosa, 15th, Fannie Collins Sullivan.
Died in Union Springs, 1st, Kate Leak, infant.
Died in Union Springs, 16th, Mrs. Mary Peebles.
Died in Hale County, 3rd, Dr. W.S. Nesmith.
Died in Marion, 16th, John C. Lowry.
Died in Covington County, 12th, little Adrid Reid.
Died in Mobile, 22nd, A.E. Rouse.
Died in Portland, Maine 22nd July, Abba Trask, daughter of the late B.K. Seawell of Mobile.
Died in Portland, Maine, 26th ult., Ellen Day, daughter of the late B.K. Seawell of Mobile.
Died in Pennsylvania, recently, James A. Hooper, formerly of Mobile.
Died near Lowndesboro, recently, infant son of Rev. Mr. Butt.
Died in Hayneville, 16th, Mrs. Brightman.
Died near Landersville, August 12th, Mrs. M. (F. or P. or R.?) C. Willis.
Died in Tennessee, 17th ult., P.W. Stephenson, formerly of Moulton.
Died in Huntsville, 17th, Lillian DeWitt Searcy.
Died in Arcola, 20th, Samuel Strudwick, Sr.
Died at Scottsboro, 16th, Willie Watson.
Died in Eufaula, 18th, Sigismund Oppenheimer, infant.
Died near Union Springs, 11th, Mrs. Henry R. Dawson.
Died near Wedowee, 20th, Bryant Gibbs.
Died in Montgomery, 25th, Elizabeth Adam/Adams.

Dr. Costly of LaFayette and the Marshall of the town were both shot one day last week by Dr. Carter of Tallapoosa County.

## THE SOUTHERN ARGUS - DEATHS - JUNE 1869 THROUGH JUNE 1874

John Morrow, an old and well-known citizen of Selma, was thrown from his buggy last Saturday, and seriously, but not dangerously, hurt.

Issue 12-6-1872

Dave Falconer (negro) was accidentally shot and killed by Crawford Hill (negro) in Greene County a few days ago.

As we write (Thursday noon) there appears to be little hope that Albert G Mabry, Jr. will live through the day.

Willie Buford of Eufaula fell from a tree the other day and was seriously injured.

From Barbour County, Frank McCullough (negro) goes to the penitentiary for forty years for killing Hill Streater (negro).

Dr. Scott of Eufaula, under bail to answer for the killing of John Hartung, failed to appear at the late term of court.

A little child of Mr. Jones of Tuscumbia fell on a knife a few days ago and was badly cut.

### DIED IN ALABAMA
Died in Mobile, 23rd ult., David Parsons.
Died in St. Clair County, 17th ult., Mrs. Susan Seale.
Died at Fayette C.H., 18th ult., Mrs. Leona Moore.
Died in Macon County, 15th ult., T.B. West.
Died near Prattville, 25th, M.D. Moore.
Died in Marion, 25th ult., Frankie Waddell, child.
Died in Mobile, recently, Mrs. Hall of Lowndesboro.
Died near Tuskaloosa, 3rd ult., George Garner, child.
Died in Limestone County, 24th ult., Lizzie Hayes.
Died near Jonesboro, 25th ult., Rebecca McFalls, child.

John H. Crease, for many years Treasurer of Arkansas, is dead.

James H. Cox, one of the editors of the *Memphis Avalanche* is dead.

Issue 12-13-1872

In Eutaw, 29th ult., Lucy Alexander (negress) was burned to death.

## THE SOUTHERN ARGUS - DEATHS - JUNE 1869 THROUGH JUNE 1874

Tribute of respect from the Dallas Bar on the death of Albert G. Mabry, Jr. Our young friend and professional brother and associate, Albert G. Mabry, Jr. departed this life at his father's residence in this city on Thursday the 5th day of December, 1872...[condensed]

In Jackson County the 26th ult., Robert Nichols was struck with a rock and killed by his stepson, Hop Cox.

The boiler in the mill of Mr. Copeland, in Chambers County, exploded one day last week, killing a small son of the proprietor.

Dr. Costly of LaFayette, who was shot some weeks ago, is recovering.

A little daughter of Mr. Gilley of Dale County was accidently burned to death a few days ago.

A body of a man, supposed to have been murdered, was found near Trinity Station, Madison County, recently. A book in his pocket was marked A.B. Andre.

### DIED IN ALABAMA

Died in Clay County, 4th, Wyatt W. Worthy.
Died near Larkinsville, 28th ult., William Shelby.
Died in Tuscumbia, 28th ult., P.N. Sutherlin.
Died in Mobile, 6th, Mrs. Eliza DeWitt Evans.
Died in Mobile, 6th, Mary E. Cherry, infant.
Died in Mobile, 27th ult., Elizabeth Buckley, infant.
Died in Mobile, 27th ult., Randolph Heustis.
Died in Mobile, 28th ult., Evie Greene, infant.
Died in Mobile, 30th ult., Mrs. M.A. Fowler.
Died in Mobile, 28th ult., Margarett Welsh.
Died in Mobile, 26th ult., Elias Spicker.
Died in Mobile, 27th ult., Phillip Harold.
Died in Mobile, 28th ult., William Shaw.
Died in Mobile, 28th ult., Isaac Durham.
Died in Mobile, 29th ult., Mary Olivia Murray.
Died in Mobile, 29th ult., Charles H. Stephenson.
Died in Mobile, 30th ult., Mary Hyland.
Died in Mobile, 2nd, J. DeF. Richards.
Died in Mobile, 3rd, Elizabeth Robertson.
Died at Wetumpka, 12th ult., Dr. A.W. Jones.
Died in Mooresville, 24th ult., Lizzie Lane Hayes.
Died in Montgomery, 4th, James T. Rencan/Reneau/Renean?
Died in Madison County, 26th ult., P.B. Peebles.

## THE SOUTHERN ARGUS - DEATHS - JUNE 1869 THROUGH JUNE 1874

Died in Coosa County, 4th, Daniel Crawford, Jr.
Died at Stonewall Institute, November 3rd, Willie Sorsby.

On Saturday last, Alexander Baker (negro) was fatally crushed between two cars of the Alabama Central Railroad, which he was in the act of coupling.

Levi Pennington of Sanford County was thrown from his wagon a short time ago near Columbus, Mississippi, and killed.

At Cornwall Iron Works the 30th ult., Charles Fulton was shot and killed by Taylor Full.

George Harrison, late Deputy Sheriff and Jailor of Shelby County, killed a prisoner in the jail of that county on the 23rd ult.

Frederic Small (negro) escaped from the jail at Opelika a short time ago after being shot and wounded by the Jailor.

Issue  12-20-1872

Died in this city the 16th, Mrs. Mary Elizabeth Shearer, relict of the late William Shearer.

Rev. A.A. Porter, once pastor of the Presbyterian Church in this city, died in Augusta, Texas, the 8th inst.

In St. Clair County the 13th, John Ewing was badly stabbed by William McCoy.

Died on Saturday last at the residence of her son-in-law, Major S.J. Saffold, in this city, Mrs. Virginia Caldwell Molette, relict of the late John U. Molette of this city, in the fifty-third year of her age.

Died in Eutaw, Friday night last, John Monroe, in the seventy-fourth year of his age. This venerable and honored man was the father of Mr. W.O. Monroe, proprietor of the *Eutaw Whig*, and of Frank A. Monroe, an estimable employee of this office, and was widely known in Greene and adjoining counties.

The estimable wife of our distinguished townsman, W.J. Norris, was seriously, but happily not fatally hurt in an accident on the 4th to the northward bound train on the South and North Railroad, a few miles south of Birmingham. Mrs. Norris is now with her daughter, Mrs. D.M. Scott, in Tuskaloosa, but she is still, we believe, confined to her room.

## THE SOUTHERN ARGUS - DEATHS - JUNE 1869 THROUGH JUNE 1874

In Henry County, recently, William Grantham was badly cut by Ridley Cummius/Commlus.

### DIED IN ALABAMA
Died in Pickens County, 20th ult., John T. Forstelle.
Died in Shelby County, 20th ult., Pomple Cross, child.
Died near Camden, 8th, William A. Carter.
Died in Union Springs, 22nd ult., Pierre Beaumont.
Died near Hollow Square, 5th, T. Monette.
Died in Mobile, 7th, Captain W.B. Drake.
Died near Gadsden, 7th, Mrs. McDuffie.
Died in DeKalb County, 2nd, James P. Newman.
Died in Montgomery, 12th, James T. Andrew.

### Issue 12-27-1872

Mr. B. Stiefiel of Montgomery was dangerously stabbed by some unknown party the night of the 24th.

Dr. Rushing of Elba was seriously hurt a few days ago by the kick of a horse.

Died in Montgomery, 19th, Henry Potts.
Died in New York, 17th, John Reed, Sen. of Mobile.
Died in Mobile, 17th, Joseph Casal, Jr.
Died in Huntsville, 14th, David T. Knox.
Died in Limestone County, 8th, Mrs. Charles B. Haygood.
Died in Athens, 7th, Miss Caroline Elliott.
Died in Limestone County, 7th, P.H. Sandefur.
Died in Eufaula, 16th, Thomas L. Hardman.
Died in Birmingham, 14th, Albert Malakoff.
Died in Birmingham, 10th, Mrs. R.B. Ryan.
Died near Kymulga, 9th, Miss Maggie Nickols.
Died in Talladega, 16th, Mary DeFreese.
Died in Macon, Georgia, 15th, Miss Mary McIntosh.
Died in Mobile, 18th, Sister Jane Williams.
Died in Texas, September 25th, Rev. J.D. Teague.
Died in Lauderdale County, 12th, Thomas Massey.
Died in Florence, 16th, John S. Karsner.
Died in Mobile, 20th, Mike Faith.
Died in Huntsville, 13th, Mrs. M.A. Tolbett.
Died in Choctaw County, 5th, J.G. Slater.
Died in Montgomery, 24th, Judge John L.C. Danner.
Died near Union Springs, 19th, Judge Daniel A. McCall.

## THE SOUTHERN ARGUS - DEATHS - JUNE 1869 THROUGH JUNE 1874

Issue 1-3-1873

At the burial of Mrs. Palmer in Etowah County the other day, three of her children, triplets, nearly fifty years old, were present.

Mr. E. A. Heidt of the *Marion Commonwealth* has been quite sick.

A few days ago, Jake Marshall, negro, fell from the steamer Lotus at Nannahubba bluff and was drowned.

The *Greensboro Beacon* of the 24th ult., said: "Professor Lupton, President of the State University, advises us that the stomach of Mr. R. L. Bennett, who died suddenly in Montgomery, was not sent, as we stated, to a northern city for examination, but to him; and further, that after a thorough analysis 'no indication, whatever, of poison was found.'"

In Mobile the 27th, Robert Bassford was severely, perhaps fatally, cut by a man named Lefevre.

Died at Roseland in Marengo County on Thursday the 26th December at about half past two in the morning, Walter Fitts, son of the late Samuel A. and S.E. Fitts, aged eleven years, eleven months and seven days.

Issue 1-10-1873

Professor Stafford of Tuskaloosa has been confined to his rooms for several weeks by a lingering, but not alarming, illness, originating in the infirmities of advancing age.

Robert J. Emerson of this city died on Saturday last from congestion of the brain.

Died the 7th near this city, Charles English, son of Mrs. Sarah English, aged fourteen years.

Died Tuesday the 7th inst., Henry Arthur Nicoll, son of Robert A. and Mary M. Nicoll, in the twenty-fifth year of his age.

The clothes of Miss Carrie Rogers, daughter of Dr. Lewis Rogers of Lewisville, caught fire the 29th ult. and she was fatally burned.

William Killiard, wife, and child, were carried over the dam at Moragne's Mill in Etowah County the 28th ult. and drowned.

## THE SOUTHERN ARGUS - DEATHS - JUNE 1869 THROUGH JUNE 1874

Joe Simmons (negro) was frozen to death in Eufaula some two weeks ago.

The 20/29th? ult. in Mobile, a child of Louis Bauerlien was run over and killed by a street car.

A few days ago, a negro on Mrs. John Lee's place, near Marion, was shot and killed by another negro.

The night of the 21st ult., Charles Wright (negro) froze to death in Limestone County.

The Rev. Mr. Watson, who murdered his wife in London last year, has been sent from Pentonville to the prison in the Isle of Wright for his health.

### DIED IN ALABAMA

Died in Henry County, recently, Mrs. Jane Wilkins.
Died in Henry County, 24th? ult., Mrs. Thomas Armstrong.
Died in Mobile, 5th, W.H. McGovern, child.
Died in Mobile, 4th, Mrs. Martha Lewis.
Died in Greensboro, 2nd, Angele Whelan, child.
Died in Greensboro, 2nd, Major W.B. Inge.
Died in Tuskaloosa County, 18th ult., Mrs. Elvira Q. Mabarry.
Died in Florence, 12th ult., Thomas Massey.
Died near Marion, 28th ult., W.H. Johnson.
Died in Limestone County, 26th ult., Miss D.N. Holt.
Died in Hayneville, 30th ult., Charles Beasley.
Died in Mobile, 20th ult., Mrs. Eliza E. Bass.
Died near Gadsden, 30th ult., Josephine McGlathery.
Died in Butler County, 2nd, James T. Oglesby.
Died near Terry's Mills, 31st ult., Mrs. Sarah Russell.
Died in Georgia, 31st ult., A.S. Hardman, late of Eufaula.
Died in Huntsville, 29th ult., Lena Anna Conne, child.
Died in Sumter County, 2nd ult., Anna McDowell.

Colonel Thomas W. Riley, a prominent Louisville lawyer, is dead.

Issue 1-17-1873

The family of the late W.H. Johnson of Perry County passed through this city on Tuesday last carrying with them to their old Kentucky home his remains. Mr. Johnson was the brother of Madison C. Johnson, the most eminent lawyer of Kentucky, and of the late Provisional Governor George Johnson of that state, who fell so heroically at Shiloh on the 7th of April 1861. He had resided near Marion since 1864.

## THE SOUTHERN ARGUS - DEATHS - JUNE 1869 THROUGH JUNE 1874

We regret to learn that Mr. E. K. Carlisle, Sr., the head of the firm of Carlisle, Jones & Co., is seriously ill at his residence at Mr. McConnico's on Broad Street. We are happy to hear that he is not regarded as in immediate danger, and we hope to have the pleasure next week of announcing his convalescence.

Near Boyd's Switch, Jackson County, a man named Kennemore was recently dangerously stabbed by one Pruett.

Near Mobile a few days ago, George Hosfeldt was fatally gored by an ox.

Sam. T. Johnston is a candidate for Legislature in Tuskaloosa County to fill the vacancy occasioned by the death of Mr. Whitfield.

B.M. Avent of Wilcox has died of the wound inflicted upon him on the 4th by Barvin Haddox.
 Barvin Haddox of Wilcox, now over seventy years old, is held in bail of $2,500 to answer for mortally wounding B.M. Avent.

The *Birmingham Independent* says the railroad has provided for the education of the children of a Mrs. Hughes, who was accidentally killed recently on its track.

In Mobile, Thursday last, James Real was shot and killed by his brother-in-law, Warren Cannon.

A preliminary trial at Eutaw resulted in the acquittal and discharge of Ross Ward for killing Nat Harrison.

Governor Lindsay has had a slight attack of paralysis.

In Mobile the 9th, Alfred Blacand(?), fifteen years old, was seriously stabbed by Willie Sampson, aged nine.

### DIED IN ALABAMA
Died in Louisville, Kentucky, 3rd, Mrs. W.H. Davis of Florence.
Died in Lauderdale County, 25th ult., Mrs. Nancy Waters.
Died in Montgomery, 9th, Holt A. Clanton.
Died in Montgomery, 9th, Mrs. Emily W. Finley.
Died in Butler County, 8th, Dr. A.R. Sheppard.
Died in Cherokee County, 29th ult., James Harwell.
Died in Eutaw County, 31st ult., Lewis E. Varnum.
Died in Eufaula, 3rd, George W. Whipple.
Died near Eufaula, 8th, Mrs. L.F. Johnson.

## THE SOUTHERN ARGUS - DEATHS - JUNE 1869 THROUGH JUNE 1874

Died en route for Texas, recently, James Alley of Dale County.
Died in Dale County, recently, a daughter of Green Willis.
Died in Jackson County, 23rd ult., Richard Kirby.
Died in Jackson County, 22nd ult., Mrs. Harrison.
Died in Jackson County, 1st, W.P. Young.
Died in Camden, 7th, Pauline Jones, child.
Died in Camden, 4th, B.M. Avent.
Died in Birmingham, 2nd, Mrs. Bettie Constantine.
Died in Birmingham, 30th ult., Mrs. Delilah J. Hawkins.
Died in Lowndes County, recently, Jacob Stanwood.
Died in Lowndes County, recently, Bradley B. Wilson.
Died near Benton, recently, N. Mealing Howard.
Died near Benton, recently, Frank Walker.
Died in Montgomery, 11th, Willie Preiss.
Died in Montgomery, 13th, John Brame.
Died in Montgomery, 13th, John B. Jewell.
Died in Greene County, 18th ult., John B. Watson.
Died near Huntsville, 7th, Daniel F. Street.
Died in Montgomery, Texas, 22nd ult., J.C. Davis, formerly of Perry County.

A young lady in Savannah, Miss Elizabeth Spencer, died of heart disease in church on Christmas during the ceremony of her confirmation.

Mrs. Elizabeth Patterson, who was married to Jerome Bonaparte, the youngest brother of Napoleon Bonaparte, on the 24th of December, 1803, is now lying at the point of death in Baltimore. She is about eighty-eight years old.

### Issue 1-24-1873

The death of E.K. Carlisle in this city on Sunday evening last surprised and shocked and grieved this entire community and carries regret and sorrow to a wide circle of acquaintances and friends to other cities and counties. Mr. Carlisle was born in Lincoln County, Georgia, and was sixty-four years old. He came to Perry County when quite a boy and except while in Mobile, that was the residence till his death. For probably twenty-five years he was in business in Mobile.... Nearly three years ago, he identified himself with the business interests of Selma.... [condensed]

In Birmingham the other day, Mr. Eaves was shot and wounded by Mr. Poyner.

The remains of William King Acklen of Huntsville, who fell in the seven days' fight around Richmond and was buried in Hollywood Cemetery, were re-interred in Huntsville the other day.

## THE SOUTHERN ARGUS - DEATHS - JUNE 1869 THROUGH JUNE 1874

Jeff. Becham (negro) was killed by some unknown person at Moyler's store, in Clarke County the 8th.

Capt. J. E. Goodwin of Tuscumbia has been very ill with pneumonia.

Mrs. James W. Huston and Miss Laura Hogan, both of Tuscumbia, were among the injured by the recent accident on the Louisville and Nashville Railroad.

Old man Turner, living at Lamb's Ferry, Lawrence County, was murdered at few weeks ago by two men named Hickerson, who were staying all night in his house.
    The citizens of Courtland have offered a reward of $1,500 for the arrest of the murderer of old man Turner.

Policeman Prescott of Montgomery was shot the evening of the 16th and dangerously wounded by Charles Ford, whom he was in the act of arresting.

Woodson Allen, living in Dudleyville, was shot and mortally wounded by some unknown person the night of the 11th.
    Woodson P. Allen of Chambers County was murdered in his own house by some unknown party the evening of the 11th.

In Montgomery the 18th, Joseph Solomons was severely stabbed by T. F. Thomason.

Elisha Jones of Pickens County is missing under circumstances indicating foul play.

Near Fayetteville, 25th ult., William Satterwhite was accidentally shot and killed while out hunting.

W. J. Gilmore, Senator from Sumter County, died in Montgomery the 20th.

### DIED IN ALABAMA
Died in Perry County, 9th, William Moore.
Died in Eufaula, 12th, Ed. L. Sporman, infant.
Died in Cherokee County, 10th, Martin Coffee.
Died in Cherokee County, 29th ult., Jas. Harwell.
Died in Birmingham, 10th, Mrs. Calvin Brown.
Died in Montgomery, 14th, Nat C. Jewell, child.
Died in Montgomery, 14th, Sigismund Steiner, child.
Died in Jefferson County, 5th, Jesse W. Williams.
Died in Limestone County, 7th, Charles McCormick.

## THE SOUTHERN ARGUS - DEATHS - JUNE 1869 THROUGH JUNE 1874

Died in Eufaula, 18th, William G. Ryalls.
Died in Limestone County, 12th, Mrs. Mary E. Eggleston.
Died in Waco, Texas, 9th ult., Mrs. Margaret L. Wallace, formerly of Lawrence County.
Died in Falls County, Texas, October 27th, Mrs. Jane McGhee, formerly of Lawrence County.
Died near Courtland, 9th, Mrs. Thomas Lightfoot.
Died in Jonesboro, 11th, Mrs. William Jones.
Died in Abbeville, 3rd, Col. W.H. Owens.
Died in Wedowee, 12th, Mrs. Elizabeth Heflin.
Died in Dadeville, 11th, John Bostock.
Died near Warsaw, 30th ult., Joseph Rogers.
Died near Warsaw, 26th ult., J.I. Windham.
Died near Warsaw, 10th, A. Irby.
Died near Warsaw, 14th, Miss Mary E. Cunningham.
Died near Letohatchie, 11th, Abner Jarrett.
Died in Montgomery, 18th, Miss Ann Lloyd.
Died in Montgomery, 18th, Miss Julia Sparrenberger.
Died in Montgomery, 20th, Rev. J.B. Taylor.
Died in Lowndes County, 20th, John Caffey.
Died in Montgomery, 20th, Mrs. T.A. Means.
Died in Montgomery, 20th, W.J. Gilmore.
Died in Montgomery, 19th, J.G. Hardaway.
Died in Montgomery, 17th, daughter of Jacob Ruppenthal.
Died in Perry County, 19th ult., Robert Carlisle.
Died in this city the 17th after a prolonged sickness, Mrs. A.R. Heawood.
Died near Liberty Hill, 13th, Captain Charles I. Pegues, a well known, greatly respected and useful citizen.

Miss Anne Crane Seemuller, nee Crane, author of "Emily Chester" and other novels of unusual merit, died in ?

Father Ryan of Mobile is dangerously ill at Milan, Italy

Issue 1-31-1873

Died in this city, Tuesday last, Mrs. Anna Fitch, relict of the late Dorastes Fitch of Vermont, and mother-in-law of Mr. William Rothrock, aged seventy-five years.

J. W. Bridgeforth of Limestone County was thrown from his horse recently and badly hurt.

## THE SOUTHERN ARGUS - DEATHS - JUNE 1869 THROUGH JUNE 1874

Rev. Early Bruce of DeLalb County has lost one eye from disease and the other is endangered.

Dr. Edward Gage, for nine years a resident of Mobile, died in Boston the 10th.

Monroe Donaho, democrat, is elected to the Legislature from Tuskaloosa County, vice Mr. Whitfield, dead.

DIED IN ALABAMA
Died in Montgomery, 22nd, James G. Smith.
Died in Eufaula, 21st, Henry Barr.
Died in Eufaula, 20th, Mrs. Emily S. Paullin.
Died in Pickens County, 13th, James Gibson.
Died in Pickensville, 31st ult., Miss B.M. Nance.
Died in Birmingham, 15th, Mrs. A.E. Fuller.
Died in Birmingham. 17th, Miss Lemie C. Bates.
Died in Birmingham, 18th, infant son of S.T. Harris.
Died near Montevallo, 29th ult., Sylvestr Ambrose.
Died near Seale Station, 28th ult., Mrs. R.E. McGehee.
Died in Perry County, 21st, Owen Tubb.
Died near Scottsboro, 1?th, Mrs. John Metcalf.
Died in Tuskaloosa, 14th, Mrs. Ann Teresa McAuliffe.
Died in Montgomery, 25th, Miss Minnie Williams.
Died in Montgomery, 26th, B.W. Norris.

Charles Hoope, an employee of the Mobile and Ohio Railroad, had both legs crushed between two cars in Mobile the 21st.

Issue 2-7-1873

Custis Jordan of Mobile, in jail for the murder of Stephen Brannon, has been admitted to bail.

Clayton Lewis, formerly a citizen of Huntsville, died in Denver, Colorado, recently.

Mrs. J. M. Denson was badly hurt the other day in getting off the train at Columbiana.

Frank Spencer, who has been in jail in Mobile on charges of murder and arson, has been released on bail.

## THE SOUTHERN ARGUS - DEATHS - JUNE 1869 THROUGH JUNE 1874

Dr. Hagood, an eminent physician of Barnwell Courthouse, South Carolina, is dead.

James H. Greene writes from Woodstock, Tuskaloosa County, to the *Tuskaloosa Times*, as follows: "A somewhat unusual circumstance occurred in this neighborhood during last week in the death of four old citizens: On Thursday the 16th inst., Andrew Hays, aged eighty-five, and John McAllister, aged seventy-eight, died; on Friday the 17th, John White, aged seventy-two died; on Saturday the 18th, John Edmunds, a soldier of the War of 1812-15, died, aged ninety-three."

Died in Dallas County, Friday night last, Samuel M. Hill, Jr.

We regret to learn that Judge Brooks is seriously ill at his residence in this city.

Dr. William A. Cochran of this County, a citizen of high character and large acquaintance, died on Saturday last.

Rev. James L. Cotten, for many years a citizen of this County, and for nearly a quarter of a century a member of the Alabama Methodist Conference, died at Durant, Mississippi, the 4th instant.

An election in Sumter for Senator to fill the place of Gilmore, deceased, has been ordered for the 25th.

The 26th ult. in Mobile, W. B. Heitman was cut and severely wounded in the head by Otto Aschenbaum.

A short time ago in Lauderdale County a tree fell upon Jehu Simons and killed him.

In Dale County, recently, two men named Dean and Chancy got drunk and then exchanged a few shots in which both were wounded.

It was Henry Creed, a section master of the Montgomery and Eufaula Railroad, who died on the Mobile and Girard train at Linwood, Pike County, a few days ago.

Tom Martin (negro), a fireman on the North and South Road, was left at Athens the other day with his skull fatally fractured.

## THE SOUTHERN ARGUS - DEATHS - JUNE 1869 THROUGH JUNE 1874

Mrs. Lucy Spencer, who died recently in the poor house of Pickens County, where she had been for twenty-five years, was once possessed of a fine property and was the belle of the county.

Squire Brooks (negro), the assassin of Woodson P. Allen of Chambers County, has been arrested.

### DIED IN ALABAMA
Died near Eufaula, 30th ult., W.S. Bradley.
Died in Mobile, 2?th ult., James S. Conway.
Died in Evergreen, 26th ult., Thompson Kindell.
Died near Talladega, 26th ult., Mrs. Martha Albright.
Died near Notasulga, 11th ult., Barham Calloway.
Died in Marion, 20th ult., Harry Rodding/Redding, child.
Died in Perry County, 22nd ult., Johnson McAuley.
Died in Mobile, 28th ult., Lawrence P. Hill.
Died in Mobile, 26th ult., Edward L. Smith.
Died in Mobile, 27th ult., Mrs. Charlotte Storer.
Died in Chambers County, recently, Mrs. Eliza Davis.
Died in Randolph County, recently, Harrison Crow.
Died in Butler County, 22nd ult., Josiah Roads.
Died in Allenton, recently, Jacob Kahn.
Died in Clarke County, recently, Daniel McLeod.
Died in Birmingham, 21st ult., Miss Julia Evans.
Died in Mobile, 30th ult., Mrs. Mary B. Newbold.
Died in Tuskaloosa, 25th ult., Mrs. Mary McNally/McNully.
Died in Bennett's Cove, 24th ult., Mr. Sutton.
Died near Letocatchie, recently, Mrs. Pinkney Bayne.
Died in Montgomery, 25th ult., Willie Whitman.
Died in Huntsville, 23rd ult., W.H. Kirk.
Died in Huntsville, ?? ult., Joseph Ward.
Died near Woodstock, 1?th ult., Andrew Hayes.
Died near Woodstock, 1?th ult., John McClister.
Died near Woodstock, 17th ult., John White.
Died near Woodstock, 18th ult., John Edmonds.
Died in Tuskaloosa, 2?th ult., Geo. F. Grass, child.
Died near Marion, 3rd inst., Miss Amela Edwards.

Issue 2-14-1873

Mrs. N. W. Roberts, widow of the late Lorenzo Roberts of this County, died in Marengo County a few days ago.

General Mahone is convalescent from a serious illness.

## THE SOUTHERN ARGUS - DEATHS - JUNE 1869 THROUGH JUNE 1874

B.R. Gilbert, a Boston banker, is dead.

Colonel James Collier, lawyer and politcian, died at Steubenville, Ohio, the 2nd.

Willie McIntosh, son of Rev. W.H. McIntosh, late of Marion, and grandson of Dr. James Guild of Tuskaloosa, died of meningitis in Macon, Georgia, 25th ult.

Near Ashville, 24th ult., Gabe Jones (negro) was shot and wounded by some unknown person.

The 12th? ult., William Perryman of Talladega County had his arm broken by a fall from his horse.

The widow of the late Edwin M. Stanton, Secretary of War, is said to be in rapidly declining health.

In Jackson County, recently, a daughter of a Mr. Smith was caught in a gin and fatally mangled.

Miss Charlotte Cushman was too sick to fill her engagements in Montgomery and Mobile.

Near Mobile, Sunday was a week ago, Mrs. Louisa Steiner committed suicide.

Gaines Whitley of Fayette County, a lad of seventeen, was killed a few days ago by a fall from a mule.

Mrs. Sanford, living near Vaughn's Mill in Macon County, committed suicide a few days ago.

Mr. William Huntington of Marion is convalescent from a serious illness.

In Cherokee County, 30th ult., a difficulty occurred between a Mr. Cothran and a Mr. Smith, in which the former had an arm and jawbone broken, and the latter was shot through the breast.

### DIED IN ALABAMA

Died in Mobile, 2nd, James McAdory.
Died in West Point, Mississippi, 26th ult., John Crowell, formerly of Pickens County.
Died in Morgan County, 28th December, Mrs. Nancy Morrow.

## THE SOUTHERN ARGUS - DEATHS - JUNE 1869 THROUGH JUNE 1874

Died near Wedowee, 29th ult., Elliot J. Reeves.
Died in Henry County, 3rd, E.H. Thomas.
Died in Clarke County, 25th ult., James F. Singleton.
Died in Tallapoosa County, recently, Wm. Britton.
Died near Eutaw, 26th ult., Joseph Elliott.
Died near Clinton, 25th ult., Jason Scears.
Died near Greenville, 30th ult., Pickens McKellar.
Died in Nashville, recently, E.W. Parker, formerly of Morgan County.
Died in Livingston, 28th ult., Robert Johnson.
Died in Mobile, 31st ult., John F. Yeend.
Died in Mobile, 31st ult., Kate Byrd Roberts, infant.
Died in Colbert County, 25th ult., Daniel Walters.
Died in Tuscumbia, 27th ult., Charles Henry Downs, child.
Died in Colbert County, 26th ult., Robert H. Hogan.
Died in Cherokee County, 28th ult., Mrs. Dory Dupree.
Died near Cedar Bluff, 27th ult., William James.
Died near Lee'sburg, 2nd, Miss Eleanor Patterson.
Died in Henry County, 28th ult., Hosea Smith.
Died in Montgomery, 5th, Kate Norton.
Died in Mobile, Dr. J.F. Paton.
Died in Washington County, 28th ult., George F. Salle.
Died in Linden, 31st ult., James A. Young.
Died near Larkinsville, 31st ult., Mr. Igou.
Died in Stevenson, 2nd, Mrs. Mary Longacre.
Died near Larkinsville, recently, Peter Davis.
Died in Limestone County, 30th ult., Irene Proctor Hayes, infant.
Died in Jefferson County, 28th ult., James Potts.
Died in Birmingham, 6th, Miss Alice Scott.
Died in Wilcox County, 2nd, Mrs. Addie Paine Dumas.
Died in Greene County, 2nd, Mrs. Jinsey Elliott.
Died in Sumter County, 2nd ult., Henry H. Rogers, child.
Died in Montgomery, 24th ult., Mrs. Isabel Gilmore.
Died in Butler County, 27th ult., Levi Davis.
Died in Mobile, 5th, Mrs. Zeline Guesnard.
Died in Wetumpka, 28th ult., Leander Bryan.

J.C. Thompson, a Nashville lawyer, died the 2nd.

Rev. James Holmes, D.D., died at Covington, Tennessee, the 4th.

General Mahone is convalescent from a serious illness.

# THE SOUTHERN ARGUS - DEATHS - JUNE 1869 THROUGH JUNE 1874

Issue 2-21-1873

Mrs. Sanford, living near Loachapoka, committed suicide the 8th.

On the 7th, Pat McDonald was run over by his own ray [dray?] and fatally hurt.

David Porter, the oldest man ?? one in Greene County, died the 25th ult. from a broken thigh received in a fall from his horse.

James T. Smith, Tax Assessor of Greene County, was thrown from his horse recently and had his arm dislocated.

John Holland, a Private in Troop D 5th United States Cavalry, died in Opelika the 3rd.

In Madison County the ?th, Mrs. Marion Turner fell in the fire and was fatally burned.

Thomas Dillahunfy?, ran over by a train on the New Orleans Road, died in Mobile the 14th.

Died in Mississippi, 28th ult., Mrs. Ella Basken, nee Sherrod, formerly of Greene County.
Died near Clinton, 8th, J.W. Coates.
Died near Knoxville, Greene County, 25th ult., David Porter.
Died in Greene County, 8th, Mrs. Elizabeth Merriweather.
Died in Greene County, 8th, John Parker of Wetumpka.
Died in Stephenville, Texas, recently, Mrs. Brockett, nee Fisher, formerly of Hayneville.
Died near Letohatchie, 3rd, Wilson Knox.
Died near Letohatchie, recently, Mrs. Sue Sanderson, nee Morrison.
Died in Decatur, 2nd, Mrs. Elizabeth A. Hoxter.
Died near Bragg's Store, recently, Nelson Moorer.
Died near Bragg's Store, recently, Mrs. John Dudley.
Died near Bragg's Store, recently, John Dudley.
Died near Manack, recently, Edgar Rupel Haigler, child.
Died in Lowndes County, 3rd, Mrs. George W. McQueen.
Died in West Point, Georgia, recently, B. Richards, formerly of Lowndes County.
Died in Clarke County, recently, Thomas Jordan.
Died in Clarke County, recently, William A. Morris.
Died in Clarke County, recently, Larkin Foreman.
Died in Eufaula, 8th, Frederick Wallace, child.

## THE SOUTHERN ARGUS - DEATHS - JUNE 1869 THROUGH JUNE 1874

Died in Florence, 1st, Julian Clanton Price, child.
Died in Calwell County, Texas, 10th ult., Mrs. Eliza Ann Barr, formerly of North Alabama.
Died in Opelika, 6th, Maggie Roberts, child.
Died in Mobile, 10th, Charles W. Dorrance.
Died in Chicago, 4th, Miss Addie Burton, whose parents are supposed to live in Alabama.
Died in Limestone County, 16th ult., H.T. Wiles.
Died in Virginia, 12th, D.C. Williams, formerly of Greene County.
Died in Meridian, 30th ult., Miss Amelia G. Millingham, formerly of Hale County.
Died in Cherokee County, 27th ult., Wm. James.
Died in Cherokee County, 2nd, Miss Eleanor Patterson.
Died in Huntsville, 8th, Mrs. Joseph Ward.
Died in Limestone County, 22nd ult., Miss Mary Starkey.
Died in Limestone County, 26th ult., James Leslie.
Died in Robinson County, Tennessee, recently, John Mingea, formerly of Athens.
Died near Wedowee, 30th ult., Mrs. M.A. Edwards.
Died in Montgomery, 11th, child of Charles Rosenstiel.
Died in Montgomery, 10th, Mrs. Samuel Norton, Jr.
Died in Dadeville, 8th, Jos. B. Johnson.
Died in Brundidge, 8th, Dr. O.F. Knox.
Died in Butler County, 29th ult., Mastin B. Pugh.
Died in Memphis, 5th, Mrs. Simpson, formerly of Tuscumbia.
Died in Mobile, 12th, Melville C. Butt.
Died in Marion, 7th, Miss Mollie Mickelboro.
Died in Gadsden, 30th ult., Charlie Brown.
Died in Choctaw County, 26th ult., Major F.Y. Gaines.

Tribute of respect from Fulton Lodge #98 held February 3rd, 1873, on the death of fellow brother Dr. William A. Cochran. (mentions aged father, mother, widowed wife)

Christopher Cockrell of the Missouri Legislature is dead.

Issue 2-28-1873

Near Marion the other day, John Underwood (negro) was run over and killed by the down train on the S., M., & M.R.R.

In Florence a few days ago, Mason Phillips accidentally shot himself in the leg, inflicting a wound which made amputation necessary.

## THE SOUTHERN ARGUS - DEATHS - JUNE 1869 THROUGH JUNE 1874

Charles Lewis, son of W.H. Lewis of Gainesville, committed suicide in New York the 11th.

Near Mobile the 17th, William Baldwin was drowned from the Swan.

John Haynes of Clay County was killed a short time ago by the falling of a tree.

The 22nd ult. near Whistler, Mike Daily was killed in attempting to get from the cow-catcher of an engine on which he had got without permission.

At Mobile, 19th, Charles Shreve was badly, but not fatally, crushed between two cars.

William Hughes was murdered by negroes near Batesville, Mississippi, the 14th ultimo.

Died in Mobile, 20th, Mrs. Sarah A. Thomas.
Died in Dadeville, recently, Mrs. John W. Johnston.
Died in Montgomery, 21st, Henry P. Conley.
Died at Stockton, 11, James W. Shackleford.
Died in Clarke County, 16th, William R. Gwynn.
Died in Clarke County, recently, John Bumpers.
Died in Huntsville, 15th, Joseph Smith Certain, infant.
Died in Huntsville, 18th, Mattie Sue Dement, infant.
Died in Mobile, 21st, Miss Alabama A. Deering.
Died in Lowndes County, recently, G.W. Holman.
Died in Benton, 14th, Miss Mollie Ernest.
Died in Montgomery, 16th, Dr. S.J. Shrewsbury.
Died in Eufaula, 22nd, Thomas Berry.
Died in Henry County, 8th, James Pynes.
Died in Gordon, 17th, Mrs. Nancy Register.
Died in Tuskaloosa, 18th, Mrs. Martha Ann Marrast.
Died in Tuskaloosa, 15th, infant child of John and Caroline Pritchett.
Died in Mobile, 18th, W.H. Baldwin.
Died in Mobile, 18th, Mrs. Mollie B. Spear.
Died in Claiborne, recently, Miss C.C. Henderson.
Died near Talladega, 1?th, Mrs. Martha A. Lackey.
Died in Etowah County, 10th, Mrs. A.B. Horton.
Died near Oxford, recently, I.M. Ford.
Died near Munford, recently, Mrs. Foggy.
Died in Mobile, 17th, John Duff.
Died in Claiborne, recently, T.C. Brewer.
Died in Camden, 12th, infant child of Frank Green.

## THE SOUTHERN ARGUS - DEATHS - JUNE 1869 THROUGH JUNE 1874

Died in Lauderdale County, 2nd, Samuel Richardson.
Died in Lauderdale County, 9th, Fountain Rogers.
Died in Lauderdale County, 10th, George Simmons.
Died near Florence, 6th, Mrs. Isabella Harvell.
Died in Colbert County, 3rd, Mrs. M. Davidson.
Died in Eutaw, 18th, Nelson Hughes.
Died at Boligee, 5th, Dr. Ezra Fisk Bouchelle.
Died in Ashville, 16th, Alemeth Byers.
Died in Northport, 14th, Miss Mary Emily Fisher.
Died in Talladega County, 16th, Mrs. William R. Stone.
Died in Jefferson County, 18th, Joel Blackburn.
Died in Birmingham, 19th, Mrs. R.H. Roberts.
Died in Pennsylvania, recently, D. Eben Ormesby, formerly of Autauga County.
Died in Tuskaloosa, 19th, Prof. S.M. Stafford.
Died in Montgomery, 9th, Mrs. Jeania B. Norton.
Died in Lawrence County, 17th, two children of Rev. W.S. Whitten.
Died in Tuscumbia, 5th, Major John Goodwin.
Died in Mobile, 23rd, John F. Beroujon.
Died in Mobile, 21st, William J. Mathews.
Died in Mobile, 24th, Thomas Henry Jordan.
Died in Tampa, Florida, 13th, Micah Taul.
Died in Pickens County, 10th, William Stuckey.
Died in Mobile, 19th, Mrs. Martina T. Roberts.
Died near Bowden, Georgia, recently, Mrs. Brown, formerly of Randolph County.
Died near Wedowee, recently, Mrs. Teal.

Colonel R.P. Price, a brother of the late General Sterling Price, died in Galveston, Texas, a few days ago.

W.H. McNairy of Nashville died the 14th.

Edward Green of Clark County, Kentucky, committed suicide the 15th.

Rev. J.S. Vallandingham, brother of the late C.L. Vallandigham, died in Cincinnati the 13th.

James A. Nesbitt, a prominent Georgian, is dead.

The wife of Judge Hop Price of Louisville died a few days ago.

Recently a little child of Mr. Hardwick of St. Clair County fell into a tub of hot water and was fatally injured.

## THE SOUTHERN ARGUS - DEATHS - JUNE 1869 THROUGH JUNE 1874

Aaron McLeon (negro) was accidently killed at Shelby Iron works a few days ago.

Issue 3-7-1873

Died in this city, Tuesday last, Mrs. Joseph Harwell.
Died in Dallas County, 22nd ult., John Brantly Lott, aged nineteen years.

In Russell County, recently, Mack Halliday was shot and killed by a negro named Walker.

George W. Smith of Eufaula fell from a scaffold on which he was working, a few days ago, and seriously injured himself.

A Mrs. Mitchell, who recently lived near Glennville, was burned to death, near Carthage, Texas a few weeks ago.

Thomas H. Jones of Lawrence County has been tried for killing D.T. Galley, and acquitted.

Died in Geneva, 15th ult., Robert Henson, infant.
Died in Pike County, 26th ult., F. Westbrooks.
Died in Troy, recently, Walter Daniel, child.
Died in Eufaula, 6th ult., Howell C. Burtz.
Died in Abbeville, recently, Mrs. Patterson.
Died in Talladega, 25th ult., Mrs. Warwick.
Died in Florida, 23rd ult., C.C. Young of Opelika.
Died in Shelby County, 7th ult., Mrs. Sallie A. Dunlap.
Died in Mobile, 25th ult., Rev. Father Vaur.
Died in Mobile, 25th ult., Sister Mary Michaella.
Died at Ramsey's Station, 16th ult., W.O. Simms.
Died in Montgomery, 28th ult., John Murray.
Died in Tupelo, Mississippi, 19th ult., Mrs. Martha Crosswell of Alabama.
Died in Barbour County, 27th ult., Daniel Nolan.
Died near Ashville, 20th ult., E.M. Montgomery.
Died in Ashville, 25th ult., infant child of Geo. H. Cather.
Died in Elmore, 15th ult., George M. Howle.

Joseph Redmon committed suicide in Lexington, Kentucky, the 26th ult.

Rev. Dr. Hamilton of Tuskaloosa wants information of John Haughey?, who died about twenty years ago somewhere in Alabama, possessed of a large property; or of John Wilson and wife, relatives of Haughey/Hanghey/Hanghy, who inherited his property and died soon after.

## THE SOUTHERN ARGUS - DEATHS - JUNE 1869 THROUGH JUNE 1874

Tribute of respect from the students of Stonewall Institute, held February 26th, 1873, on the death of John B. Lott, who died at home, February 23rd, of disease contracted during the Christmas holidays...

General Edward Johnson, who recently lay ill several weeks at the St. James Hotel in this city, died in Richmond, Virginia, the 2nd.

In Cherokee County, recently, G.M. Crouch shot at what he supposed [to] be a chicken thief and fatally wounded his own son.

Mr. Moat's residence in Russellville was burned recently, and two children perished in the flames.

John Redding of Hale had his hand badly injured a few days ago by the accidental discharge of a gun.

Issue 3-14-1873

Thomas Anderson committed suicide in Mobile, 27th ult.

Dr. Deason of Elyton is, we regret to learn, seriously ill.

C.A. Strong of Madison County was thrown from his horse recently and badly injured.

Larry Sullivan died in Hunstville the other day from the effects of an injury received in the yard of the Memphis and Charleston Railroad.

Jerome Pillow has got a verdict against the Memphis and Carleston Railroad for $14,000 for damages received several years ago.

In Gadsden, 1st, Charlie Ross, a lad of sixteen, accidently shot himself with a pistol.

The 28th ult., Tom Locket (negro) was hung in Linden for the murder of B.F. Norwood.

Disappointed in love, William Jackson (negro) of Sumter suicide a few days ago by throwing himself into a hole of muddy water.

Died in Jackson County, 25th ult., Mrs. Louisa S. Eckles.
Died in Northport, 27th ult., William V. Burns.
Died in Marengo County, recently, S.B. Davis.
Died in Eutaw, 27th ult., Mrs. Mary J. Hickman.

# THE SOUTHERN ARGUS - DEATHS - JUNE 1869 THROUGH JUNE 1874

Died in Greene County, 1st, David B. Phillips.
Died in Amelia, Virginia, 12th ult., D.C. Williams, formerly of Greene County.
Died near Seale, recently, J.M. Reese.
Died in Mobile, 7th, W.B. Robinson, infant.
Died in Albany penitentiary, 14th ult., J.D. Young of Tallapoosa.
Died near Belton, 6th ult., Mrs. Elizabeth Treadwell.
Died in Montgomery, 7th, Robert Barron.
Died near Bellefonte, 1st, J.W. Holland.
Died in Prattville, 3rd, Henry Hunt.
Died in Autaugaville, recently, Mrs. Mary M. Stoudenmire.
Died in Mt. Hilliard, 12th ult., John McCreless.
Died in Montgomery, 6th, Henry R. Greenwood.
Died in Montgomery, 6th, Caroline Hinderer, infant.
Died in Montgomery, 5th, Miss Lillie Belle Molton.
Died in Mobile, 3rd, Mrs. Josephine S. Stephens.
Died in Rome, Georgia, 27th ult., Aaron Webb, formerly of Cherokee County.
Died in Cherokee County, 26th ult., Mrs. Nancy Hardwick.
Died in Clay County, 10th ult., Mrs. Holland Cox.
Died in Etowah County, 2th ult., James Burson/Barson.
Died in Mobile, 4th, James S. Moreland.
Died in Troy, 28th ult., Mrs. Tucker.
Died in Mobile, 4th, Ruth J. Cox.
Died in Mobile, 4th, Mrs. Alice E. McCormick.
Died in Choctaw County, 26th ult., Mrs. Henrietta Bruster.
Died in New Orleans, 26th ult., Henry Alfred Cload, a native of Mobile.
Died in Greenville, 25th ult., Miss Sallie Taylor.

Robert W. Dacus of Hayneville has been seriously ill.

A reward of $1,000 is offered for the arrest and conviction of the person who murdered William Kinghorne on the 1st.

The 28th ult. in Salisbury, Maryland, George Hall, aged eighteen, shot and killed Amelia Shinkley, aged fourteen, who had rejected him.

Issue 3-21-1873

Colonel Weyer of the Federal Army has been very sick at Livingston.

John Hollingsworth recently in the Limestone Jail for killing a negro, has been declared insane and sent to the asylum.

E.S. Gossett formerly of Shelby was sent to the insane asylum from Blount County a short time ago where he died.

## THE SOUTHERN ARGUS - DEATHS - JUNE 1869 THROUGH JUNE 1874

Died in this city, Friday last, Annie, daughter of Mrs. J. W. Moore.

Charlie Crowder, for many months a well known and popular conductor on the Selma and Montgomery Railroad, died at Montgomery, Tuesday night last.

William Alley, formerly of Tuskegee, shot and killed himself in Mobile the other day.

The hearts of a large circle of acquaintances and friends are saddened by the knowledge that Mrs. Richard E. Baker, daughter of the late Colonel W.S. Phillips, is lying at the point of death, with scarce a hope that she may be spared even a few days longer to her afflicted husband and family.

William Kinghorne, an old citizen of seventy-two, was shot and killed by negro thieves the night of the 1st, on the Bay Road, near Mobile.

Died in Etowah County, 3rd, Mrs. Sarilda Treadway.
Died in Gadsden, 8th, Amos Curry.
Died in Greensboro, 10th, Samuel W. Inge.
Died in Arkansas, recently, H.W. Barnett, formerly of Lauderdale County.
Died in Lauderdale County, 8th, Mrs. M.G. Denson.
Died in Mobile, 13th, Dr. Edward Byrne.
Died in Calhoun County, 10th, William Greene.
Died at Whistler, 12th, William S. Parmlee.
Died in Greene County, recently, M.D. Kimbrough.
Died in Greene County, recently, Mrs. A.M. Pippen.
Died in Arkansas, recently, Dr. W.H. Yarbrough, formerly of Limestone County.
Died in Limestone County, 9th, Gideon Huston.
Died in Opelika, 3rd, Mrs. W.M. Snow.
Died in Dale County, 20th ult., Earnest Melton, child.
Died in Springville, 3rd, L.W. Herring.
Died in Perry County, 1st, Mrs. Mattie King Scott.
Died in Newbern, recently, John F. Reynolds.
Died in Greenville, 9th, Wesley Kendrick.
Died in Jackson County, Arkansas, 22nd ult., Francis F. Tisdale of Limestone County.
Died in Union Springs, 11th, Mrs. Pedie Roberts.
Died in Mobile, 11th, Captain Fred Sheffield.
Died in Mobile, 10th, Mrs. Elizabeth G. Mayberry.
Died in Montgomery, 12th, Edwin Allen.
Died in Montgomery, 12th, Willie Maxwell, child.
Died in Mobile, 9th, Thomas E. Bass.

## THE SOUTHERN ARGUS - DEATHS - JUNE 1869 THROUGH JUNE 1874

Died in Talladega County, 9th, W. Ogletree.
Died in Autauga County, 16th, Mrs. M.J. Whetstone.
Died in Thomasville, Georgia, Albert Williams of Montgomery.
Died in Mobile, 6th, Mrs. W.E. Lloyd.
Died near Huntsville, 12th, Robert Fearn.
Died in Carrollton, 10th ult., infant of Mr. and Mrs. A.W. Latham.
Died in Pickens County, 6th, Mrs. Frances Haynie.
Died in Missouri, 4th, Mrs. Emily K. Croxton of Carrollton.
Died near Athens, 26th ult., S.W. Chapin.
Died in Elyton, 13th, Dr. G.T. Deason.
Died in Livingston, 6th, Miss Lizzie Houston.
Died in North Port, 12th, James Haley.
Died near North Port, 11th, Henry Jordan.

His many friends here and elsewhere will regret to learn that Captain Ed. Cooper is dangerously ill at his residence in this city.

C.J. Spurlock, a prominent lawyer of McMinnville, Tennessee, died 28th ult.

Dr. Trammell of Cusseta had a finger sawed off in his lathing mill a short time ago.

Stokes is not to be hanged this spring anyhow.

Issue 3-28-1873

Horace Frank Thurber, telegraph operator at Stevenson, was drowned the 13th in Reservoir Creek.

L.V.B. Martin of Tuskaloosa has been dangerously ill.

William Jordan is in the Pike Jail for the murder in November last of Mrs. Elizabeth Collier.

B.D. Rogers, near Mann's Landing, Marengo County, was shot and killed the 21st by his brother-in-law, J.G.M. Luther.

Died in Greenville, 14th, J.B. Henry, infant.
Died in Butler County, 12th, Ezekiel H. Pickens.
Died in Attalla, 16th, Commodore Farrand.
Died in Gadsden, 15th, Dr. J.S. Petty.
Died in Huntsville, 17th, Mrs. Susan Bridges.
Died in Huntsville, 17th, W.B. Lloyd.
Died in Clay County, 9th, Jonathan Baker.

## THE SOUTHERN ARGUS - DEATHS - JUNE 1869 THROUGH JUNE 1874

Died in Union Springs, 3rd, Charles E. Baugh, infant.
Died in Nashville, Tennessee, 16th, Erwin Tait of Wilcox County.
Died in Tuskegee, 19th, Mrs. M.A. Caldwell.
Died in Montgomery, 19th, Emelle Sparrenberger.
Died at Guntersville, 18th, Charles L. Dill.
Died in Tuskaloosa County, 13th, J.W. Prewitt.
Died in Tuskaloosa County, 15th, Annie Hays Bolton, infant.
Died in Pickens County, 13th, Walker W. Speed.
Died in Sumter County, 11th, Martin Rumly.
Died in Eutaw, 13th, John Victor McGee, child.
Died in Morgan County, recently, Mrs. Ed. Rusk.
Died in Clay County, 11th, Isaac Hannah.
Died in South Carolina, 30th, Mrs. Hattie Figures Hallinguist, formerly of Huntsville.
Died in Mobile, 25th, Judge Jos. F. Johnson.
Died in Etowah County, 11th, M.L. Abbott.
Died in Jackson County, 17th, J.A.B. Williams.

Joseph Chamberlain, one of the pioneers of Louisville, died the 17th.

Talladega County sends a man named Walker to the penitentiary for manslaughter.

Issue 4-4-1873

Died in this city, Sunday last, after a lingering illness, Mrs. Richard E. Baker, daughter of the late Colonel W.S. Phillips.

Died in Marion, 28th ult., Mrs. Fannie C. Fox, daughter of Mr. J.W. Crenshaw of that city, and wife of Dr. J.O. Fox, late of Selma.

Columbus Wood of Fayette County was recently shot by the Sheriff whom he was resisting.

The morning of the 20th ult., a son of James Gidley of Etowah County, aged twelve, hanged himself, accidentally it is supposed.

In Sumter County a few days ago, Frank Harper (negro) shot another negro named Gilbert, severely wounding him.

Montgomery sentences George Rivers (negro) to twenty-five years in the penitentiary for killing Caesar Reese (negro).

Died in Sumter County, 27th ult., Henry Pipkin.

# THE SOUTHERN ARGUS - DEATHS - JUNE 1869 THROUGH JUNE 1874

Died in Tuskaloosa, 22nd ult., L.V.B. Martin.
Died in Tuskaloosa, 22nd ult., Alvey W. Miller.
Died in Lauderdale County, 7th ult., Mrs. Nancy Blanton.
Died in Lauderdale County, ?6th February, W.C. Mitchell.
Died in Henry County, 22nd ult., Quincy Fulmore.
Died in Eufaula, 27th ult. Miss Julia L. Brannon.
Died in Chambers County, 15th ult. Effie Jones, infant.
Died in Etowah County, 18th ult. Mrs. Thomas Hughes.
Died in Mt. Vernon, recently, A. McD. Lumsden.
Died in Greensboro, 22nd ult. Edwin Nutting.
Died in Hale County, 21st ult. R.K. Smith.
Died in Lawrence County, recently, Mrs. Martha Sims.
Died in Montgomery, 23rd ult. G.B. Holmes, child.
Died in Eufaula, 21st Mrs. S.B. Evarts.
Died near Russellville, 16th ult. William Skinner.
Died in Pickensville, 25? 15th? Miss Jane Newell.
Died in Pickens County, 15th ult. Joe D. Cameron.
Died in Pickens County, 15th ult. John W. Garner.
Died in Carrollton, 30th ult. James T. Garner.
Died in St. Clair County, 21st ult., Minnie Brown, child.
Died in Limestone County, 21nd(?) ult., Mrs. Levica McWilliams.
Died in Bullock County, 23rd ult., E.B. Penick.
Died in Randolph County, recently, Mr. Lovelace.
Died in Randolph County, recently, Mrs. Leagan.
Died in Montgomery, 26th ult., Mrs. Catherine L. Benson.
Died in Mobile, 23rd ult., Mrs. Mary E. Deane.
Died in Mobile, 31st ult., Dr. J.C. Nott.

P.C. Wester offers two hundred dollars for the arrest and delivery to the Sheriff of St. Clair County of John Stapp and Taylor Hobbs, murders of James Wester.

A Mr. Walden in Sanford County has small-pox.

Richard S. Watkins of Russellville has been appointed Chancellor of the Northern District, vice Skinner, deceased.

The *Bigee News* says: Extremely foolish is one conductor on the A. & C. Railroad to shoot another 4 or 5 times with a pisto; in order to kill him and thereby endanger his own neck. All he had to do was let him alone. A few trips over that road would have effectually done the work without gunpowder.

Capt Estis, one of the superintendents of the A & C Railroad was shot and wounded the 23rd ult. in Tuskaloosa by Jack Guthery, night operator there.

# THE SOUTHERN ARGUS - DEATHS - JUNE 1869 THROUGH JUNE 1874

Issue 4-11-1873

In Union Springs the 30th ult., Bob Thomas (negro) was fatally beaten by Thomas Ramsey, who fled at once.

Mrs. E.H. Rolie/Rolfe of Huntsville was badly burned the 30th ult. by the bed clothes taking fire from a lamp.

J.A. Palmer, who was a policeman in Huntsville during reconstruction rule, died in jail at Edwardsville, Illinois, recently.

Jack Gary (negro) made a murderous assault on Edmond Alexander in Lowndesboro the other day.

A son of the late George S. Mason was drowned in the Coosa River, at Wetumpka the 17th ult.

Mrs. McBryde was drowned recently in One Mile Creek, near Mobile.

Mrs. Freeman of Abbeville fell down a pair of steps, recently, and broke a collar bone.

Dr. J.E. Pouncey has been tried for killing a negro in Barbour County some time ago and acquitted.

Dr. Josiah C. Nott died on his sixty-ninth birthday.

At Cross Plains, recently, Hugh Vincent was badly, perhaps fatally, cut by a negro.

A man named Hughes, living in the north eastern part of Perry, was killed on the 1st by a falling tree.

In Gainesville, 29th ult., Hut Lipscomb was shot and killed by Harrison Manly.

Died at Six Mile, Bibb County, last week, Wm. E. Thomas.
Died in Jacksonville, 24th ult., John D. Hoke.
Died in Tuskegee, 29th ult., Jas. G. Peterson.
Died in Dadeville, recently, Miss Sue Allen.
Died in Opelika, 30th ult., Mrs. John M. Slaughter.
Died in Marion, 5th, Governor A.B. Moore.
Died in Greensboro, 31st ult., Thomas Rainey.
Died in Conecuh County, 25th ult., W.M. Bradley.
Died in Butler County, 31st ult., P. Jordan, formerly of Mobile.

## THE SOUTHERN ARGUS - DEATHS - JUNE 1869 THROUGH JUNE 1874

Died in Tallapoosa County, 31st ult., Daniel Davis.
Died in Centre, 25th ult., Mrs. Lovi Potts.
Died near Gayleville, 23rd ult., infant of Robert Harton.
Died in St. Clair County, 18th ult., Mrs. Arminta Beason.
Died in Montgomery, 2nd, G.A. Cushing.
Died in Choctaw County, 26th ult., C.P. Mills.
Died in Birmingham, 26th ult., Mrs. Ida Allen.
Died in Henry County, 23rd ult., Henry Champion.
Died in Henry County, 23rd ult., W. Barnett.
Died in Claiberne, 25th ult., Eva Langdon Harris, child.
Died in Mobile, 29th, F.H. Reynolds.
Died in Mobile, 5th, S.U. Fosdick.
Died in Livingston, 13th ult., Dr. Blake Little.
Died in Livingston, 31st ult., Mrs. Tempie M. Scruggs.
Died in Livingston, 22nd ult., Mrs. Patience Arrington.
Died in Columbia, Louisiana, 9th ult., Stephen D. Tillman, late of Perry County, aged forty-six years.

In Monroe County the 29th ult., Joseph Martin was killed by William Parton.

Died in this city, Tuesday last, John M. DeYampert, son of the late Thomas J. and H.J. DeYampert.

Died in this County the 26th ult., Mrs. H. Emma Jones, wife of C.O. Jones, and daughter of Mark H. Petway of Wilcox County.

Escambia County sends Sol Murphy (negro) to the penitentiary for life and Louis Ashford (negro) for ten years for killing Jack Jones (negro) in Butler County some time ago.

Rev. Dr. Sprangler, pastor of the Methodist Church at Uniontown, was stricken down with paralysis, while in the midst of his sermon Sunday night was a week ago.

Charles Burrows is seriously ill at Eufauia with rheumatism.

C.D. Henderson, a Deputy Sheriff of Lee County was dangerously ill the 2nd.

### Issue 4-18-1873

Little Mary Clark, daughter of Colonel and Mrs. John W. Davis, died in this city on Monday last.

## THE SOUTHERN ARGUS - DEATHS - JUNE 1869 THROUGH JUNE 1874

Died in East Selma, Monday last, Mrs. Laura Kennard, daughter of Mr. J.W. England of Perry County.

Reverend H.C. Harris, formerly of Alabama, recently committed suicide in New Orleans.

In Talladega County, two weeks ago, Bob Fain (negro) murdered his wife.

Miss Sallie Davis, who died at Eufaula the 11th, committed suicide it is believed.

Eugene Smith, indicted in the Bullock Circuit Court for killing Reese Bird last fall, has been admitted to bail in the sum of two hundred dollars.

S.J. Tisdale, a pedler of patent medicines, was murdered on the night of the 4th inst. in Hale County near Macon Station.

Mrs. Marlowe of Calhoun County, lately released from the insane hospital, committed suicide a few days ago.

Magaret Dabney, lunatic, was accidentally burned to death in Randolph County, recently.

Died in DeKalb County, recently, Mrs. Sallie Smith.
Died near Birmingham, 5th, Mrs. Josephine Hall.
Died in Montgomery, 9th, William Hendrix.
Died near Columbia, 8th, John Scofield.
Died in Evergreen, 30th ult., Wilbur Reed, child.
Died in Eufaula, 12th, Lewis F. Johnson.
Died in Eufaula, 9th, Leonard Ross, infant
Died in Tuskaloosa, 4th, H. Kulper.
Died in Greene County, 10th ult., Mrs. Laney E. Reeves.
Died in Eufaula, 11th, Miss Sallie Davis.
Died in Pickens County, 24th ult., Miss Minnie Stringfellow.
Died in Fayette County, 17th ult., James McCollum.
Died in New Orleans, 9th, R.H. Gayle, formerly of Alabama.
Died in Stevenson, 7th, Louis Cargile, aged one hundred eight.
Died in Greensboro, 6th, A.A. Sneed.
Died in Calhoun County, 4th, Mrs. Mary E. Ea???/Eaths
Died in Mt. Sterling, 8th, Miss Annie E. Prince.
Died in Henry County, 4th, Thomas Collins.
Died in Henry County, 8th, Thomas Gamble.

Robert Fountain of Montgomery committed suicide the 10th.

## THE SOUTHERN ARGUS - DEATHS - JUNE 1869 THROUGH JUNE 1874

At Wayne Furnace, recently, John A. West of Limestone County was killed by the caving of an ore bank.

Hugh Vincent of Cherokee County was badly stabbed by a negro some weeks ago.

Henry Evans goes to the penitentiary for twenty years, from Clarke County, for murder in the second degree.

In an accident on the Alabama and Chattanooga Railroad near Woodstock the 6th, Reverend Thomas Davenport had his collar bone broken.

On the 5th, Mrs. R.B. Woodson of Gainesville was thown from a buggy and seriously hurt.

Dr. Erwin of Wilcox who has been sick is convalescent.

Issue 4-25-1873

The Hale Circuit Court acquitted Thaddeus T. May, charged with killing Jack Ellis, in December last.

Stephen Smith of Clay County was run over by his wagon and killed the 13th.

William Jordan (negro), confined in the Pike Jail for the murder of Mrs. Collier, has been released because the grand jury did not find a true bill against him.

Eli Fike of East Perry, and not Mr. Hughes, was killed in the storm on the 1st.

On the 18th, Dr. J.D. Malone of Athens was dangerously ill with meningitis.

Daniel P. Pratt has been seriously ill at his residence in Prattville.

Died in Decatur, 15th, M. Gavin.
Died in Morgan County, 15th, Joe Gunn.
Died in Chickasaw, 12th, T.F. Buchanan.
Died in Colbert County, 10th, Mrs. B.F. Gaston.
Died in Greene County, 10th, John W. Powers.
Died near Livingston, 26th ult., Mrs. E.M. Rhodes.
Died in Gainesville, 2nd, Mrs. Henrietta Mobley.
Died in Tuskaloosa, 10th, Mrs. Jane O. Coleman.
Died in Tuskaloosa, 15th, John S. Debardelaban.
Died in Tuskaloosa, 12th, little Earle H. Bristow.
Died in Elyton, 15th, Mrs. M.E. Morrow.

## THE SOUTHERN ARGUS - DEATHS - JUNE 1869 THROUGH JUNE 1874

Died in Walker County, 11th, J.M. Stanley.
Died in Hale County, 6th ult., Mrs. A.R. Auderson.
Died in Columbiana, 14th, L. Webster.
Died in Greenville, 10th, Albert Metcalf, child.
Died in Montgomery, 17th, Florence Gerson, child.
Died in Perry County, 10th, Jacob Kynerd.
Died in Talladega, 27th ult., G.W. McGaha.
Died in Pike County, 13th, Mrs. Eugenie Haley.
Died in Pike County, 14th, Hines Holt Goode.
Died in Athens, recently, Lawrence Cannon.
Died in Decatur, 8th, Maggie Taylor Rather, child.
Died in Montgomery, 12th, Mrs. David Campbell.
Died in Choctaw County, 16th, S. Averytt.
Died in St. Stephens, 17th, Mr. Williams.
Died in Athens, 15th, F.G. Crenshaw.
Died at Monterey, 16th, Mrs. M.A. Yeldell.
Died in Butler County, 14th, Rutledge Hatcher.
Died in Montgomery, 22nd, Mrs. F.E. Alford.
Died in Clayton, 20th, Bennie Smart.
Died in Mobile, 20th, Brown R. Sherwood.
Died in Nashville, 17th, W. Hy. Smith, formerly of Huntsville.
Died in Louisiana, recently, Thomas J. Robertson, formerly of Lowndes.
Died in Limestone County, 10th, Mrs. Margaret Smith.

In Opelika, recently, Lewis Coleman and Jesse Lockhart were severely wounded by an accidental pistol shot.

At the late term of the Chambers Circuit Court, Squire Brooks was sentenced to be hung for the murder, recently, of Woodson P. Allen.

### Issue 5-2-1873

Tribute of respect from Selma Fraternal Lodge #27, Selma, Alabama, April 28, 1873, upon the death of Nathaniel Monroe. One of the oldest residents of this city; almost reached the age three score and ten; a copy of this record to be sent to his family in Baltimore...

Mrs. Henrietta Pettigrew of Eutaw had her arm broken about ten days ago.

M.A. Sanders of Eutaw recently hiccoughed for seven days without intermission.

Dr. J.D. Malone of Athens is convalescent, having been dangerously ill.

## THE SOUTHERN ARGUS - DEATHS - JUNE 1869 THROUGH JUNE 1874

J.B. Ollis, engineer of the Gulf City Paper Mills near Mobile, was caught in the machinery a few days ago and instantly killed.

The Calhoun Circuit Court sentenced Hans Whatley (negro) to the penitentiary for ten years for the murder of Jim Alexander (negro).

In Loachapoka the 22nd, John Reynolds was shot and killed by Robt. Owens.

Died in Jasper, 18th ult., Sallie Gamble, child.
Died in Tuskegee, 24th ult., Mrs. Dr. Jones.
Died in Tuskegee, 20th ult., Mrs. H.D. Moore.
Died in Birmingham, 2?th ult., Miss Mary T. O'Connor.
Died in Savannah, Georgia, 22nd ult., R.H. Henley.
Died near Auburn, 23rd ult., Addison Frazer.
Died in Pike County, 20th ult., Mrs. Serenthe Wren.
Died in Pickens County, 20th March, Clarence Beard, infant.
Died in Pickens County, 17th ult., O.H.P. Windham.
Died in Pickens County, 14th ult., Ambrose Sanders.
Died in Pickens County, 30th March, Mrs. Dr. E. Sanders.
Died in Pickens County, 17th ult., Mrs. Mary Mustin.
Died in Pickens County, 9th ult., Mrs. Julia Strickland.
Died in New Lexington, 12th ult., Dr. R.B. Watts.
Died in Florence, 22nd ult., Mrs. E.W. Allington.
Died in Gaylesville, 13th ult., David Bolling.
Died in Oxford, 1st ult., James K. Hamilton.
Died in DeKalb County, recently, Abraham Horton.
Died in Etowah County, 17th ult., Wm. McMahan.
Died in Clarke County, 6th ult., Mrs. C.E. Turner.
Died in Talladega, 22nd ult., Mrs. Jane Harris.
Died in Tuscumbia, 19th ult., Sallie Goodwin Hunter, child.
Died near Huntsville, 19th ult., Louis Johnson.
Died in Huntsville, 18th ult., Mrs. Mary Howard.
Died near Gilmerville, recently, Joseph Gunn.

Bledsoe, accused of shooting Nathan Scruggs in Huntsville, will be examined before Mayor Erwin, tomorrow.

In Morgan County, recently, a little son of Pulaski Lawrence was accidentally shot by his brother and killed.

Garrett Smith of Perry County committed suicide the 20th ult. by cutting his throat.

## THE SOUTHERN ARGUS - DEATHS - JUNE 1869 THROUGH JUNE 1874

Two of the murderers of old man Turner in Colbert County some time ago have been captured in Texas and are now in jail at Tuscumbia.

On the 19th in Pickens County a man named Reynolds was killed by the accidental discharge of his gun.

Daniel Pratt is recovering from his recent illness.

Issue 5-9-1873

Dr. Malone of Athens died of meningitis.

Died in this city one day last week, Bessie, daughter of Mr. and Mrs. F.S. Brown.

A little son of John Turnipseed of Pickens County was thrown from a mule and killed on the 28th ult.

Two weeks ago, Mrs. Bell of Fayette Court House took morphine by mistake for quinine causing death in a few hours.

Squire Brooks, the negro who killed W.P. Allen, is to be hung in Lafayette on the 6th of June.

Wm. Park is in jail at Scottsboro for killing Steele some time ago.

Judge P.G. Woods has been presiding in the circuit court this week, vice Judge Saffold, sick.

Dr. D.C. Smyly of Pleasant Hill, who has been very sick, is convalescent and was in the city yesterday.

A short time ago, John Appling, son of Judge Appling of Henry County was badly bitten by a dog.

Dr. William McElrath of Cherokee County has recovered from a dangerous illness.

In Baldwin Circuit Court, James T. Flanagan was found guilty of manslaugter in the second degree and sentenced to twelve hours imprisonment in the county jail.

Sheriff Bryan of Loundes County was kicked by a mule a short time ago and badly hurt.

## THE SOUTHERN ARGUS - DEATHS - JUNE 1869 THROUGH JUNE 1874

John Maloney is in jail at Eutaw for killing an Irish lavorer at Boligie Depot, Alabama and Chattanooga Railroad.

Joseph Boggs, convicted of murder in the second degree in Randolph County and sentenced to the penitentiary for ten years, only remained there three or four months when a new trial was ordered with a change of venue to Chambers County, where he was tried and acquitted.

At Hook's Station, Alabama and Chattanooga Railroad the 29th ult., J.P. Lyles, a fireman on the northward bound train, was run over and killed.

Died in Auburn, 25th ult., James T. White.
Died in Opelika, 26th ult., Mrs. I.T. Morgan.
Died in Mobile, 1st, Alexander Revault.
Died at Fayette Court House, 17th ult., Mrs. Bell.
Died in Fayette County, 15th ult., Richard Olive.
Died in Montgomery, 1st, Miss C. Raymur.
Died in Tuskegee, 27th ult., Dr. W.M. Menifee.
Died in Chambers County, recently, Jas. R. Marsh.
Died in Vicksburg, Mississippi, 15th ult., Gales S. Patridge, formerly of Marion.
Died in Athens, 26th ult., Dr. J. David Malone.
Died in Tennessee, 8th ult., Mrs. Malica Stewart, formerly of Limestone County.
Died near Wedowee, 27th ult., Mrs. Rice.
Died in Morgan County, recently, Mr. Mitchell.
Died in Etowah County, 22nd ult., John McMahan.
Died in Etowah County, 28th ult., Mrs. J.W. Garner.
Died in Etowah County, recently, Mrs. Sanson.
Died in Etowah County, 28th ult., E.L. Appling.
Died in Dekalb County, 24th ult., Jack Frazier.
Died in Trussville, 30th ult., Mary Ella Morrow, infant.
Died in New York, 29th ult., Mrs. Annie Scott, formerly of Mobile.
Died in Mobile, 26th ult., O.B. Joseph.
Died in Dale County, recently, Mrs. Daniel Bolton.
Died in Wilcox County, 30th ult., William F. Wheeler.
Died near Gordonsville, recently, Miss Paralie Coney.
Died in Texas, 26th March, Dr. R.M. Whitman, late of Lowndes County.

Tribute of respect to the memory of Hon. Andrew B. Moore by his brethren of Perry County bar.

## THE SOUTHERN ARGUS - DEATHS - JUNE 1869 THROUGH JUNE 1874

Issue 5-16-1873

Peter Shenfessle died in Estill County, Kentucky, the other day, aged one hundred ten years.

George Lea was hung at Yanceyville, North Carolina, a few days ago, for murder.

Dr. Hoffman of Athens has been quite sick.

In Mobile the 11th, James Simons, drunk and jealous, shot his wife severly, and shot himself, it is thought fatally.

Mrs. Sallie Hudson, daughter of Mr. James D. Craig, and wife of Dr. H.S. Hudson of this city, died at her residence on Tuesday last. Mrs. Hudson was a native of this county, and grew up, married, and died among those who mourn her death...

Bob McDaniel (negro) recently shot and killed Alf Speake (negro) in Lawrence County.

Assessor McRae of Loundes County has been absent from home two months and it is not thought he will return.

W.D. Humphrey has been appointed a commissioner in Choctaw County, vice Avcrytt/Averytt, dead.

Mrs. James E. Saunders of Courtland was thrown from her horse and severly hurt on the 2nd.

Mrs. Sanson of Etowah County was erroneously reported dead last week.

Robert D. Irwin, formerly of Athens, was drowned near Columbus, Mississippi, a few weeks ago.

James Spurlock of Butler County was drowned in Rockey Creek the 10th.

John M. Minter, a native of Dallas and widely known in the county, died at his residence near Benton on Friday evening last, in the forty-fourth year of his age.

On Tuesday last, Mr. C.D. Armstrong of this city, uncle of Mr. J.P. Armstrong, was drowned near the mouth of Beach Creek by the capsizing of a boat in which he was fishing. He leaves a large family.

## THE SOUTHERN ARGUS - DEATHS - JUNE 1869 THROUGH JUNE 1874

Burrel Johnson has been appointed tax collector for Hale, vice Nutting, dead.

In Mobile, last Sunday, John Simons, formerly of Selma, in a fit of jealousy shot and badly wounded his wife, whom he married here, and then shot himself through the head, inflicting a wound that will probably prove fatal.

Died in Henry County, 8th, Hickman Davis.
Died in Henry County, 8th, Mrs. J.W. Blow.
Died in Mobile, 8th, Mrs. Catharine Jackson.
Died in Morgan County, 24th ult., C.P. Rally.
Died in Athens, 3rd, Captain R.C. David.
Died near Bragg's, 6th, Mrs. John Hanna.
Died in Montgomery, 10th, W.H. English.
Died in North Port, 7th, Dr. J.A. Carraway.
Died in Huntsville, 3rd, Oliver D. Sledge.
Died in Cherokee County, 4th, Mrs. Lonan Adrain.
Died in Pickens County, 4th, Geo. W. Basinger.
Died in Montgomery, 8th, William H. Crozier.
Died in Talladega, 7th, Thomas Hood.
Died at Citronville, 2nd, Miss Mary H. Bickly.
Died in Mobile, 5th, Leonard C. Lindsey.
Died at Clayton, 29th ult., Buckner Williams.
Died in Stevenson, 2nd, S.W. Foster.
Died in Jackson County, recently, J.W. Holland.
Died in Jackson County, recently, Peter T. Hurt.
Died in Moulton, 2nd, W.A. Pickens.
Died in Tuscumbia, 4th, Jimmie Jones Halsey, infant.
Died in Jackson County, recently, W.W. Campbell.
Died in Louisiana, 13th ult., Mrs. Helen Moore, formerly of Lowndes.
Died in McMinnville, Tennessee, 2nd, Mrs. Jennie Chadwick Whatson/Whitson, formerly of Huntsville.

### Issue 5-23-1873

Died in this city, Wednesday last, Maggie, daughter of Mr. C.A. Tinch.

Harry Augustus Jordan, formerly of Selma, died in Los Angeles County, California, the 26th ult.

The body of Mr. C.D. Armstrong, who drowned on Tuesday of last week, was recovered on Saturday last and interred in the cemetery.

An infant child of Mr. Meyer, Birmingham, was giving a dose of morphine instead of quinine a few days ago and died from the effects of the same.

## THE SOUTHERN ARGUS - DEATHS - JUNE 1869 THROUGH JUNE 1874

A son of Dr. Wingo, residing near Tuscumbia, was thrown from a mule a few days ago and his skull badly fractured.

Mr. A. Herd of Eutaw fell from a porch a few days ago and was seriously injured.

A son of Mr. Lem. Wilson of the Spring Villa Lime Company was caught in the band of a saw mill and instantly killed Tuesday of last week.

Dr. D.N. Richardson of Athens, is confined to his bed by sickness.

Miss Ada Nichols of Decatur is quite ill.

In Perry County, Hen Cole (negro) stabbed Moses Holifield (negro) one day last week.

A little son of Alfred Scott of Greenville accidentally cut one of his eyes out last week.

Dr. William B. Hall of Loundesboro, who has been confined to the house since November, is slowly recovering.

Died in La Fayette, 12th, little Robert Quillar.
Died in Henry County, 10th, A.J. McAllister.
Died in Greenville, 13th, Mrs. H.M. Jones.
Died in Birmingham, 11th, Mrs. M.E. Alexander.
Died near Clinton, 1st, Mrs. Sallie Clara Handley.
Died near Loachapoka, 5th, infant son of Mr. L.B. Stroud.
Died in Greensboro, 14th, John J. Denton.
Died at Jonesboro, 5th, Mrs. Sarah Wade.
Died in Tuscumbia, 4th, Jemmie Jones Holsey, infant.
Died in Conecuh County, April 20th, Edmund Joiner, aged ninety-six years.
Died in Shreveport, Louisiana, 12th, Mrs. Mary Martin, formerly of Evergreen.
Died in Shelby County, 9th, Daniel Gardner.
Died in Decatur, 9th, Captain W.H. Nichol.
Died in Courtland, 4th, Mrs. Talitha Goode Sherwood.
Died in Courtland, 8th, Robert Morris.
Died near Jacksonville, 9th, Mrs. Mary Ann Moragne.
Died in Birmingham, 14th, Ada Archer, infant.
Died in Mobile, 7th, Andrew Jay Cook, infant.
Died at the residence of her father in Bibb County on the 4th instant, Miss Mattie, daughter of Hon. J.W. Suttle, aged sixteen years...

# THE SOUTHERN ARGUS - DEATHS - JUNE 1869 THROUGH JUNE 1874

Issue 5-30-1873

Died in this city, last Tuesday, Mr. S. Dunbar, a freight conductor on the Selma, Rome and Dalton Railroad.

Lewis R. Davis, for many years a resident of Summerfield and prominent citizen of the county, died on the 13th inst. at Rolling Fork, Issaquena County, Mississippi, to which place he had recently removed from Edward's Depot, Mississippi. Mr. Davis was well and widely known in Dallas...

Sam Anderson (negro) was drowned in Lauderdale County last week.

Meredith Wilson of Clarke County accidentally shot and killed himself about two weeks ago.

A Mr. Moore died in Opelika about two weeks ago under circumstances that indicated foul play.

A serious difficulty occurred in Randolph County the 12th between two men named McMurry and a Mr. Alsebrook, during which the former was shot and the latter hit with an axe.

Charlie Freeman was badly stabbed a few days ago by a young Mr. Skipper, both of Abbeville.

Doc Bailey, near Childersburg, stabbed and killed Lewis McGee (negro) few days ago.

Sheriff Hudson of Florence is quite sick.

John McDonald was stabbed twice with a sword cane by Capt. Van B. Gunnison the night of the 23rd in Mobile.

Rev. Mr. Williams of Seale is recovering.

## TEXAS NEWS

Mrs. W.F. Hamilton of Smith County is dead.

Rev. B.F. Hall of Denison is dead.

Colonel John Boyd, an old citizen of Limestone County, is dead.

Harvey Smith, an old citizen of Bell County, is dead.

## THE SOUTHERN ARGUS - DEATHS - JUNE 1869 THROUGH JUNE 1874

John Williamson was accidentally killed in Fannin County, recently.

A man named Phillips has been arrested in Grimes County, charged with killing a man in 1867, in Alabama.

Colonel George S. Massey of Grayson County is dead.

In the burning of Rev. R.P. Chisholm's house in Kauffman County, two children perished, and Mrs. C. broke both ankles in jumping from a window.

A son of Mrs. Cook of Hempstead was badly burned the other day with kerosene.

John D. Hooper killed Thomas Phillips in Opelika the 22nd.

### DIED IN ALABAMA
Died in Sumter County, 5th, Lemuel B. Hall.
Died in Talladega, 18th, Mareus Rowden/Bowden McElderry.
Died in Pike County, 17th, Josiah Davis.
Died in Linwood, 1st, Mary Henry Wren.
Died in Mobile, 20th, Kate Dubroca.
Died in Tuskegee, 15th, David M. Ford.
Died in Tuskegee, 18th, Miss Mattie Motley.
Died in North Port, 6th, Dr. James A. Carraway.
Died in Tuskaloosa County, lately, F.J. Naughan.
Died in Eutaw, 11th, Adolphus W. Jarvis.
Died in Chambers County, 6th, William F. Swint.
Died in Courtland, 11/ 14th?, Lizzie R. Machin.
Died in Limestone County, 11th, Charles Anderson.
Died in Baldwin County, April 30th, Mrs. Endora C. Greenwood.
Died in Pensacola, Florida, 23rd, Margaret LeBarron, nee Holmes, of Mobile.
Died in Tuskaloosa County, 15th, Mrs. Carrie E. Cribbs Farmer.
Died in Lauderdale County, lately, Mrs. A.S. Claiborn.
Died near Carrollton, Georgia, 10th, Harris Russel, formerly of Clay County.

Issue 6-6-1873

### DIED IN ALABAMA
Died in Gadsden, 21st, Mrs. William Gardner.
Died in Cherokee County, 19th ult., Rev. Mr. Hood.
Died in Greensboro, 20/29th? ult., W.S. Cowin.
Died near Greensboro, 25th ult., Clare Avery, child.
Died in Livingston, 3rd ult., James P. Kennard.
Died near Ozark, 17th ult., Samuel S. Grace.

## THE SOUTHERN ARGUS - DEATHS - JUNE 1869 THROUGH JUNE 1874

Died near Ozark, 19th ult., Morgan B. Grace.
Died near Athens, 23rd ult., James Harrison.
Died in Marion, 27th ult., Miss Abbie F. Godden.
Died in Eufaula, 30th ult., Courtney Baker.
Died in Tuskegee, 18th ult., Mattie Motley.
Died in Tuskegee, 23rd ult., Mrs. Nancy Breedlove.
Died in Greenville, 22nd ult., J.F. Turner.
Died in Talladega, 24th ult., William Y. Hendrick.
Died near Roanoke, 22nd ult., Emily J. Stiker.
Died near Athens, 23rd ult., James Harrison.
Died in Greensboro, lately, Charles Johnson Jones, infant.
Died in Montgomery, 20/29th? ult., Minna Donaldson, child.
Died in Clarke County, 26th ult., F.O. McMillan of Demopolis.
Died in Bladon Springs, 25th ult., Joseph Wolf of Camden, Mississippi.
Died in Fayette County, 16th ult., infant child of R.S. Abernathy.
Died in Limestone County, 14th ult., Major Charles D. Anderson.

Messrs. E. Gillman and Jack Hinton will not leave for Vienna until the 11th, their departure having been delayed, we are sorry to learn, by the illness of one of Mr. Gillman's children.

Rev. John Early, President of Georgetown College, is dead.

Mrs. Heddin, a respectable elderly lady of Hawsville, Kentucky, committed suicide the 27th ult.

In the course of an altercation between a Mr. Karny and a Mr. Dignon in Gainsville the 23rd ult., the latter was severely stabbed.

A negro woman named Eliza Moody died in Tuskaloosa County last week under circumstances indicating poison.

Adam Gully (negro) was killed by lightning near Snow Hill the 28th ult.

Governor Lewis offers a reward of two hundred dollars for the arrest of William Parton charged with killing Josiah Martin in Monroe County a few weeks ago.

A young man named Charley Heron was killed by lightning while ploughing his field in Choctaw County last week. His horse was also killed.

Mrs. Sarah A. English, relict of the late Thomas J. English, died at her residence four miles west of this city on Tuesday last.

## THE SOUTHERN ARGUS - DEATHS - JUNE 1869 THROUGH JUNE 1874

The wife of Rev. W.H. Armstrong of Decatur is quite ill.

Dr. Bass of Ashland has recovered from an attach of pneumonia.

TEXAS NEWS

Gus Currier was murdered in Dallas the night of the 16th ult.

In Houston the 21st, Alexander Detz shot and dangerously wounded his wife.

A man named Fowler was drowned at Pace's Ferry near Hempstead recently.

Mrs. Margaret Jemison, one of the oldest settlers in Texas, died in Brenham the 18th ult.

In Brownwood the 10th ult., a man named Atkins was shot by a man named Fielder with a Spencer rifle and badly wounded.

William Bonner died in Tyler the 16th ult.

Mrs. Mary G. Lytle, an old resident of San Antonio, is dead.

In Dallas County, Robert R. Johnson was shot recently and killed.

Mrs. Martha Brennan, the oldest American resident of Cameron County, is dead.

A son of Mr. Clarity in Dallas County was killed by lightning a few days ago.

A little son of Judge J.W. Ferris of Waxahachie was killed a few days since by the accidental discharge of a gun.

Fayette County sends Daniel Gains and William Cole to the penitentiary for murder.

Rev. Father Theis, Catholic priest at Springfield, Ohio, was thrown from his buggy and killed the 29th ult.

Issue 6-13-1873

Died in this city, Tuesday last, Miss Mattie Wilson.

Miss Adelia Chapman of Grove Hill, Clarke County, died in Summerfield in this County the 8th inst., in the seventeenth year of her age.

## THE SOUTHERN ARGUS - DEATHS - JUNE 1869 THROUGH JUNE 1874

Dr. Clint. Parmer of Greenville has been confined to his bed by sickness.

Lon Grant of Jacksonville has been sick.

Squire Brooks (negro) was hanged at Lafayette the 6th for the murder last January of Woodson Allen.

Charley Hearon, living near Choctaw Corner, was killed by lightning about two weeks ago.

Henry Hickson (negro) was drowned near Grove Hill week before last.

Henry F/E. Hadson, United States District Attorney, died at Memphis the 4th of cholera.

In Augusta, recently, E.D. Meyer was shot and killed by his son, August Meyer.

Martin Lawson of Lauderdale County had his leg broken a few days ago.

### TEXAS NEWS

Near Corsicana, recently, Captain W.M. Love was murdered by Alexander Barrackman.

In the neighborhood of Hill's Store, Collin County, Mrs. Garrett and a boy, unnamed, have recently been killed by lightning.

Samuel Bargliss, formerly of Jefferson, was shot and killed the other day by a man named Buck Wilson.

James McGuire, formerly Marshal of Austin, is dead.

Near Pilot Knob, recently, a Mr. Woods was killed by lightning.

Mrs. Elizabeth Hufford, George Wistenhunt, and Steven Shelton, all old citizens of Van Zandt County, are dead.

Judge Thomas H. Stribling of Bexar County is dead.

Mrs. Crisp, the actress, has been very ill in Waco.

The residence of Thomas Davis in Clarkesville was struck by lightning recently, and his little son was killed.

## THE SOUTHERN ARGUS - DEATHS - JUNE 1869 THROUGH JUNE 1874

Phillip Strans/Straus, an old Houston merchant, recently committed suicide in New York.

Major Thomas H. Lightner, living near Clayton, committed suicide last Friday by taking laudanum.

James McDonald fell from the railroad bridge over Shoal Creek in Lawrence County the 19th ult., and was instantly killed.

The wife of Rev. Nathan P. Smith of Greene County committed suicide the 28th ult. by cutting her throat.

Charles Werner, a member of the band of the second United States Infantry, at Mobile, committed suicide last week by taking laudanum.

An old man named A. Graham died in his chair on the steamer *Annie*, last week at Mobile.

### DIED IN ALABAMA

Died in Florida, 23rd ult., Ettie J. Holmes LeBaron, Jr. of Mobile.
Died in Livingston, 1st, Henry Otto Voss.
Died in Liberty, Missouri, 16th ult., David Barnum.
Died in Gadsden, 28th ult., James Monroe Hail, infant.
Died in Camden, 2nd ult., F.S. McGuire.
Died at Cedar Bluff, 28th ult., Mrs. Lucinda Bogan.
Died in Jefferson County, Georgia, 25th ult., Mrs. M.E. Hines, formerly of Evergreen.
Died near Lockhart, Texas, lately, Dr. William L. Hamner, formerly of Greenville.
Died in Greenville, 29th ult., John F. Turner.
Died near Greenville, 1st, Mrs. Jane Davis.
Died in Lowndes County, 1st ult., Mrs. E.R. Donelson.
Died in Randolph County, 28th ult., Alexander McCain.
Died in Randolph County, 26th ult., Mrs. Shaw.
Died in Randolph County, 29th ult., John R. Green.
Died in Birmingham, 2nd, Mr. Stellers, late of Huntsville.
Died in Memphis, Tennessee, 13th ult., Goodloe Malone of Colbert County.
Died in Iuka, Mississippi, 29th ult., Henry A. David of Limestone County.
Died in Coffee County, 31st ult., Thomas Frazier.
Died in Perote, 31st ult., Mrs. Dr. William Bryan.
Died near Macon, Georgia, 30th ult., Professor Robert C. Smith, formerly of Alabama.

## THE SOUTHERN ARGUS - DEATHS - JUNE 1869 THROUGH JUNE 1874

Enoch Jefferson (negro) was killed by Ike Herschfelder in Escambia County the 30th ult.

A little son of Mr. Tisdale of Crenshaw County accidentally killed his sister a few days ago by hitting her on the head with a stick.

The Pension Bureau will this week issue the first certificates of pensions arising from the Modoc War in favor of the widow of Lieutenant Thomas.

The remains of Bishop John Henry Hopkins, first Bishop of Vermont, will be removed to their new resting place at Rock Point on the 10th prox.

At Binghampton, New York, Mrs. Canning is charged with the murder of her mother.

Issue 6-20-1873

James Brown (negro) will be hung in Richmond, Virginia, 11th July, for killing Mrs. Jones and Mrs. Dozier.

Mr. Marks, an aged citizen of Rome, Georgia, was fatally burned a few days ago.

### TEXAS NEWS

At Eagle Lake, 8th ult., Captain W.D. Wynn was shot and killed by Nat. Morris.

### ALABAMA NEWS

Two weeks ago last Wednesday, near King's Landing in this County, King Sails (negro) was murdered by Allen Harris (negro), who is now in jail.

Died in Summerfield the 17th instant of dysentery, Mrs. Florence Fuller, daughter of Dr. John Taylor of Forkland, Greene County, and sister-in-law of Rev. D.C.B. Connerly of Plantersville.

The Eufaula Bar has passed a series of resolutions upon the death of Judge Cochran.

Rad McKissack, who lived in Henry County, starved himself to death lately, dying one day last week.

Dan Williams (negro) was killed at Opelika, the 7th, by an officer who was attempting to arrest him.

## THE SOUTHERN ARGUS - DEATHS - JUNE 1869 THROUGH JUNE 1874

John Connelly of Mooresville, Limestone County, the 6th, shot and killed his step-mother, a most estimable woman. The murder has been put in irons in the Athens Jail.

A young son of A.W. Henderson of Morgan County was thrown from a horse and killed about three weeks ago.

Mr. Knight, a stranger, is quite ill at the residence of Mr. Hill in Trinity, Morgan County.

H.F. Crawford of Decatur is quite ill.

Mrs. J. Nichols of Decatur had a congestive chill last week.

Miss Mollie Tanner of Athens has been very sick but is now recovering.

Benjamin Marriott and Elijah Williford of Eutaw are dangerously sick.

Rev. Mr. Galland of Abbeville has been quite sick but is now improving.

J.D. Powers of Mobile was found dead near Bladon Springs a few days since.

### DIED IN ALABAMA
Died in Cherokee County, 5th, Mrs. Rosa Chestnut.
Died in Tuskaloosa, 10th, Miss Lou Williams.
Died in Walker County, 6th, Judge Moses Camak.
Died in Montgomery, 11th, Mrs. John B. Fuller.
Died in Limestone County, 13th, James B. Lentz.
Died in Tuskaloosa, 10th, James O'Day.
Died in North Port, 10th, Dr. Matthew Thompson.
Died in Greensboro, 10th, Henry Boardman.
Died in Sandford County, 4th, Judge Morton.
Died in Montgomery, 13th, William J. Nelson.
Died in Henry County, lately, Mrs. Spann.
Died in Huntsville, 10th, Benjamin Jolley.
Died in Tuskaloosa, 8th, Lucy Perrine Harris, infant.
Died in Clark County, 1st, Joseph D. Powers of Mobile.
Died at Ringgold, Georgia, 4th, Mrs. Martha Woods, mother of Colonel Mike Woods of Birmingham.

Young Wigginton, who killed Reid in Franklin County, has been transferred to the Tuscumbia Jail.

## THE SOUTHERN ARGUS - DEATHS - JUNE 1869 THROUGH JUNE 1874

Issue 6-27-1873

On the 4th inst., J.W. Clyde, Editor of the *Times*, died at Chicot City, Arkansas, of cholera.

The wife of Genral Robert Lowry of Mississippi died the 18th.

In Waldo County, Maine, the 16th, Alman Gordon, his wife, and their child, were murdered by Gordon's brother.

E.W. Adams, an old citizen of Nashville, is dead.

TEXAS NEWS

Major J.A. Hawkins died recently at Canton.

Captain Randall Jones, a "veteran," died at Houston the 1st.

At Austin, recently, Mr. A. Starrett was accidentally killed.

James T. Miller of McLennan County has been held in a $1,000 bond to answer a charge of being implicated in the recent murder of Seth Miller.

Smith Kellum of McLennan County was murdered on the highway on the 7th.

DIED IN ALABAMA

Died in Dadeville, 12th, Richard C. Wade.
Died in Dadeville, 13th, William McLendon.
Died in Eufaula, 18th, R.E. Lee Sporman, child.
Died in Union Springs, 17th, Mrs. Emily C. Rea.
Died in Huntsville, 16th, Samuel Coltart.
Died in Russell County, 12th, Mrs. Annie Michell.
Died in Shelby County, 13th, Mrs. Louisa Holmes.
Died in Tuskaloosa County, 13th, John Robertson.
Died in Green County, 14th, W.A.G. Clements.
Died in Greenville, 15th, Dr. D.C. Parmer.
Died near Huntsville, 17th, Mrs. Susannah Pollard.
Died in Wetumpka, 12th, Miss Willie Thompkins.
Died in Pickens County, 12th, Nathan B. Arendale.
Died in Mobile, 21st, DeVaubencey Tell, infant.
Died in Barbour County, 16th, J. DuBose.
Died near Clayton, 17th, Mrs. John Bell.
Died in Evergreen, 17th, Mrs. Dr. A.A. McKittrick.
Died in Chambers County, 14th, Hon. Toliver Towles.
Died in Russell County, 19th, Dr. Thomas H. Dawson.

## THE SOUTHERN ARGUS - DEATHS - JUNE 1869 THROUGH JUNE 1874

Died in Arkansas, 16th, Mrs. Mary Jarman, formerly of Tuscumbia.
Died in Barbour County, 18th, Mrs. Peter Cunningham.
Died in Montgomery, 24th, Loomis Giovanna, infant.
Died in Barbour County, 20th, Major John L. Williams.

A little son of Mr. Hamilton, living near Fatama, Wilcox County, was killed the 13th by the falling of a sack of corn.

William Simpson (negro) is in prison at Mobile on suspicion of murdering his wife.

S.T. Bradly was murdered at Madison, Limestone County, the 11th.

Elijah Williford of Tuscumbia County is recovering from an attack of typhoid pneumonia.

Anthony King (negro) was drowned near Marion, Monday of last week.

The 14th at Birmingham, Mr. Mann shot a Mr. Smith.

Miss Eula Roop of Decatur is quite ill.

A little son of Peter G. Rowell, formerly of Montgomery County, was drowned a few days ago near Versailles, Kentucky.

A young son of Colonel Penn Yonge, near Opelika, was crushed to death in a mill the 17th.

Colonel Banks and S.T. Wert of Decatur are quite ill.

Eddie Buhler, son of Mr. and Mrs. E.A. Buhler, died in this city, Monday last.

Died in Kentucky the 5th inst., Mrs. Mary M. May, formerly Mrs. Krout, of Cahaba.

John D. Hooper of Opelika has been admitted to bail in the sum of $5,000 for the killing of Mr. Phillips some time ago.

Horace F. Clark, an eminent railroad and business man, died in New York.

All the business houses in Eufaula were closed during the burial ceremonies of Judge Cochran.

# THE SOUTHERN ARGUS - DEATHS - JUNE 1869 THROUGH JUNE 1874

Ram Keys, engineer on the Mobile and Ohio Railroad, was badly burned at whistler a few days ago by the explosion of a kerosene lamp.

Dr. W.S. Palmer of Carrollton has been seriously ill.

General Seth Mabry of Clayton has been confined to his room by sickness.

Issue 7-4-1873

Jacob Holley of Dadeville is dangerously sick.

T.J. Walker of Oxford fell from a mill dam a few days ago and was seriously hurt.

George Cockburn was thrown from a wagon in Tuscumbia a few days ago, and one wheel ran over him.

Hiram Thomason, Tony Thomason, Alexander Rice, and Bud Wilson are all on trial at Lafayette, charged with being implicated in the murder of Bird Kitchens, near Roanoke, a few days ago.

## DIED IN ALABAMA

Died in Jasper, 17th ult., Levi Sides.
Died in Walker County, lately, Elias Steedman, Jr.
Died in Portsmouth, Virginia, 17th ult., George Harry Ellison, infant, of Mobile.
Died in Mobile, 26th ult., James Pinkey McCormack.
Died in Seale, 22nd ult., little Mary Allen.
Died in Havana, 24th ult., Mrs. Mary M. Sheldon.
Died in Tuskaloosa, 21st ult., Mrs. McGee.
Died in North Port, 22nd ult., Ira Lee Powell, infant.
Died in Tuskaloosa County, 23rd ult., Elijah Williford.
Died in Greene County, 14th ult., Williamson A. Glover.
Died near Citronnelle, 27th ult., John Parker.
Died near Greensboro, 27th ult., Bessie Melton of Mobile.
Died in Chambers County, recently, Leonard H. Young.
Died near Huntsville, 21st ult., Dr. George R. Wharton.
Died in Huntsville, 22nd ult., James M. Venable.
Died in Birmingham, 27th ult., John Burnett.
Died in Tuskaloosa, 25th ult., William J. McKerrall of Sumter County.
Died in Morgan County, 25th ult., Mrs. Hence Breedlove.
Died in Mobile, 23rd ult., Sarah Kendall, infant.
Died in Pensacola, Florida, 15th ult., Mrs. Mattie Booth Fife Gonzalez, formerly of Greensboro.
Died in Etowah County, 17th ult., Mrs. Mary Cash.

## THE SOUTHERN ARGUS - DEATHS - JUNE 1869 THROUGH JUNE 1874

Died in Smith County, Texas, 9th ult., Mrs. Hattie Reynolds, late of Lee County.
Died in Talladega County, 22nd ult., Mrs. Elizabeth Billen.
Died near Fayette Court House, 14th ult., J.E. Lavender.
Died in Fayette Court House, 16th ult., infant son of W.L. Jones.
Died in Montgomery, 28th ult., Mrs. Elizabeth Follansbee.
Died in Montgomery, 28th ult., infant son of Samuel E. Norton, Jr.
Died in Hamburg, Perry County, 29th ult., Isaac Schwarz, aged five years.
Died at Hamburg, Perry County, 30th ult., Annie Schwarz, aged three years.
Died in Jefferson County, 30th ult., A.W. Hawkins.
Died in Birmingham, 30th ult., W.T. Straub.
Died in Huntsville, 28th ult., Stephen Murphy.
Died in Talladega, 1st, James M. Skaggs.
Died in Hayneville, 27th ult., Eugene Inge Pritchett, infant.
Died in Montgomery, 30th ult., infant of Mr. and Mrs. W.R. Taylor.
Died in Montgomery, 1st, Mrs. Henrietta Lawrence.
Died June 29th, 1873, near Harrell's Cross Roads, Mrs. N.J. Cochran, wife of James Cochran.

The only child of Mr. and Mrs. Charles F. Brown of this city, an infant, died at Newbern on Friday evening last.

Rev. S.A. Goodwin of Greenville is recovering from his recent illness.

Captain Gus Blackwell of Decatur is still quite sick.

A Mr. Loper of Pike County was killed by lightning the 22nd ult.

Ran Keys, the engineer burned at Whistler a few weeks ago, has since died.

Jonathan Ware's horse run away with his buggy in La Fayette a few days ago, throwing John S. Love out and injuring him considerably.

George Morrow (negro) was drowned in Shoals Creek, Madison County, last week.

Mrs. M.C. Wade of Decatur has been quite ill.

Frank Young killed a man named Patterson at Cherokee a few days ago.

George Fields, a negro criminal of Augusta, Missouri, has been hanged by a mob.

# THE SOUTHERN ARGUS - DEATHS - JUNE 1869 THROUGH JUNE 1874

Colonel T.T. Hill, brother of General A.P. Hill, died suddenly at Culpeper Court House, Virginia, a few days ago.

Edward S. Mosely, State Treasurer of Connecticut in 1867 and 1868, died recently at the age of sixty years.

The *Opelika Observer* says "We rejoice to announce that the statement in our last issue that a son of Colonel Penn Yonge had been crushed to death in the machinery of a grist mill was incorrect."

Master Willie Christian of Centre was thrown from a mule last week.

A.N. Smith was hanged at Springfield, Massachusetts, the 27th ult. for murder.

Oran Webb of Greene was snake bit Tuesday of last week.

## TEXAS NEWS

On the 9th near Silver Creek, Peter R. Smith was killed by Dallas Logan.

Dr. A.H. Parish of Austin died the 18th ult.

Major B.A. Calhoun died in Grimes County the 9th ult.

A young man named Mangold was drowned in Grayson County.

Dr. Brown died in Dallas the 8th ult.

Wilbur Cherry, one of the founders of the *Galveston News*, died recently.

Fuller Millsap of Weatherford committed suicide the 7th ult.

Dr. William R. Smith died recently in Galveston.

A man named Stanley was drowned in Montgomery County some weeks ago.

Dr. Steiner, formerly of Austin, died in Marietta, Georgia, a few weeks ago.

Issue 7-11-1873

## TEXAS NEWS

William Ferguson died at Denison the 23rd ult.

Abraham Fain, an old citizen of Parker County, died the 18th ult.

## THE SOUTHERN ARGUS - DEATHS - JUNE 1869 THROUGH JUNE 1874

Samuel Kerr of Collin County was recently drowned in Elm Creek.

Governor Davis offers $700 reward for the arrest of Secundo Alisando, who recently murdered Adams, Grayson, and Perry near Bonham.

Alexander Arbucle, one of the murderers of D.C. Applewhite, whose death caused martial law in Limestone, was convicted on the 11th ult. and sentenced to the penitentiary for life.

Robert Parks has recently died in Fayette County of hydrophobia.

G.B. Andrews was drowned in the San Jacinto near Baytown, recently.

In Bryan, recently, George Deaton was dangerously stabbed by J.A. Woods.

Mrs. George Wade of Polk County, Georgia, was killed by lightning the other day.

Henry Miller of Murfreesboro, Tennessee, was killed recently by an unknown assassin.

James Mullins, late Congressman from Tennessee, died in Shelbyville the 26th of cholera.

Died near Pleasant Hill, ?nd/3rd? inst., L./V? F., daughter of J.V.F. and F.A. Walker.

Mr. W.H. Boswell of this city is quite sick on his plantation near Harrell's Cross Roads.

Miss Lou Webster, sister-in-law of Mr. L.A. McMillan of this city is dangerously ill at Dr. O.F. Harrell's near Bellevue.

Died at Maplesville, the 5th, Mary Louise, daughter of H.V. and A.V. Bierly of this city, aged five years and four months.

Mr. W.A. Sorsby, formerly of this county, but at the time of his death a citizen of Birmingham, died at Blount Springs the 7th of cholera.

The *Gadsden Times* learns that one Peevey, a revenue officer, formerly of that section, was killed in Tennessee a few weeks ago.

A negro was caught at Hathechubbee, a few days ago, who killed Berry McMichen (negro) at Seale about four years ago.

# THE SOUTHERN ARGUS - DEATHS - JUNE 1869 THROUGH JUNE 1874

John Sullivan of Jefferson County was shot and killed last week by Columbus Robins.

James A. Meeks of Nashville is quite sick at Centre.

Augustus Girard of Mobile was drowned a few days ago.

Windolin Werdle is under arrest at Dalton, Illinois for wife murder.

John W. Branch of Dale County was dangerously hurt one day last week by being thrown from a wagon.

In Tallapoosa County, last week, Gus Green stabbed to death George Kimbal (negro).

George Brown, the negro burglar of Eufaula, has been shot and killed.

A blind man named Melton living in Madison County has disappeared very mysteriously.

Frank Mastin of Huntsville fell from a second story window the night of the 29th, and received injuries which caused his death.

Two men named Coleman were killed by lightning in Marshall County a few days ago.

## DIED IN ALABAMA

Died in Florence, 26th ult., Mrs. Jordan, relict of Rev. W.H. Jordan.
Died in Barbour County, 2nd, Mrs. Rebecca Thornton/Thornston?.
Died in Birmingham, 1st, Charles Hale, infant.
Died in Jefferson County, lately, James Vann.
Died in Birmingham, 28th ult., Mrs. Virginia Mitchell.
Died in Birmingham, 27th ult., John Bennett.
Died in Jasper, 27th ult., Anna Eugenia Green, infant.
Died in Greene County, 27th ult., Katie Brown, infant.
Died in Greene County, 25th ult., Benjamin Marriott.
Died in Gallatin, Tennessee, recently, John W. Walton, formerly of Greensboro.
Died in New Orleans, 2nd, Frank Daily of Eutaw.
Died in Marshall, Texas, 20th ult., Mrs. Nora W. Staton, nee Jones, formerly of Greensboro.
Died near Sawyerville, 3rd, Annie Love, infant.
Died in Union Springs, 1st, Edgar H. Foster.
Died in St. Clair County, 24th ult., Wm. O'Neal.
Died in Blount County, 26th ult., Mrs. G.T. Oglesby, late of Greenville.

## THE SOUTHERN ARGUS - DEATHS - JUNE 1869 THROUGH JUNE 1874

Died in Cherokee County, 30th ult., Mrs. J. Clinton.
Died in Montgomery, 3rd, William Duggan.
Died in Huntsville, 28th ult., Stephen H. Murphy.
Died in Montgomery, 2nd, George W. Clough.
Died in Pickens County, 30th ult., Jackson Acker.
Died near Huntsville, 2nd, John H. Swift.
Died in Huntsville, 3rd, Sewell P. Jordan.
Died in Hayneville, 30th ult., Rufus Wiley Dacus.
Died in Moulton, 20th ult., T.M. Morris.
Died in La Fayette, recently, Mrs. Elizabeth Burke.

Mrs. Lyster, aged ninety-one, was buried at Graysville, Indiana, last week, in the wedding garments which she wore seventy-three years ago. They were of linen, spun and woven by herself.

W. Kennedy, a prominent merchant of New Brighton, Pennsylvania, committed suicide the other day.

Joseph G. Wilson, member of Congress from Oregon, died at Marietta, Ohio, the 2nd.

A difficulty occurred near Brooklyn, Conecuh County, a few days ago, between William Turk and William Wade, during which the latter was badly cut.

Issue 7-18-1873

### TEXAS NEWS

A young man named Taylor was recently killed at San Felipe.

A man named Smith was recently murdered between Granbury and Fort Worth.

John J. Smith, an old citizen of Bastrop County, is dead.

Theodore Dorset, the murderer of Marcellus Speight at Bolivar Point in 1868, has been arrested in Galveston.

George Martin, who shot and killed Captain Stubblefield, on the steamer Ida Rees, at Hall's Bluff, some two years ago, has been arrested at Vicksburg, Mississippi.

Near Waco the 29th ult., Mat Wallace was taken from his house by a mob and hung.

# THE SOUTHERN ARGUS - DEATHS - JUNE 1869 THROUGH JUNE 1874

Sidney E. Mosely died in Austin the 2nd.

### DIED IN ALABAMA
Died in Tuskegee, 2nd, Penelle J. Eich, infant.
Died in Tuskegee, 8th, Clara E. Stevens.
Died in Eufaula, 12th, William Brantley Brannon.
Died in Montgomery, 12th, Catherine Barham.
Died in Montgomery, 7th, James Maloney.
Died in Montgomery, 10th, Peachy R. Grattan.
Died at Wood's Station, 6th, Mrs. Bridget Friel.
Died at Wood's Station, 9th, Hugh Friel.
Died at Birmingham, 9th, Mrs. Charles Douglas.
Died at Elyton, 9th, Captain W.M. Nabors.
Died in Pickens County, 1st, Mrs. Phoebe Shepherd.
Died in Birmingham, 4th, J.G. Chambers.
Died in Birmingham, 4th, Miss Laura Hagood.
Died in Birmingham, 1st, Mrs. Catherine A. Bean.
Died in Troy, 4th, La Boma Wilson, infant.
Died in Troy, 6th, Colonel J.F. Rhodes.
Died in Cherokee County, 3rd, Reuben T. Comer.
Died in Marion, 7th, Mrs. L.L. Childs.
Died at Trussville, 9th, daughter of I.L. Davis.
Died in Tuscumbia, 6th, Dr. B. M. Croxten.
Died in Birmingham, 10th, Willie Powers, child.
Died in Birmingham, 10th, son of Mr. Worthington.
Died in Lauderdale County, 3rd, T.W. Carter.
Died in Jefferson County, 11th, Mrs. M.F. Hale.
Died in Birmingham, 11th, Mrs. John O'Brien.
Died in Birmingham, 11th, child of Mr. Hughes.
Died in Livingston, 5th, Laura Brown, child.
Died in Birmingham, 3rd, Mrs. W.L. Kennedy.
Died in DeKalb County, 11th, David Sibert.
Died near Hickman's, recently, David Jones.
Died at Birmingham, 13th, E.W. Smith.
Died at Birmingham, 14th, E. Linn.
Died at Birmingham, 14th, Mrs. Terry.
Died in Montgomery, 7th, Mary, daughter of John A. Young.
Died in Birmingham, 5th, Eliza Curtis Oxford, child.
Died in Athens, 10th, little daughter of Mrs. Colin R. Hobbs.
Died near Birmingham, 10th, child of Peyton G. King.
Died in Coahoma, Mississippi, June 1st, R.W. Lawler, formerly of Sumter County.
Died in Birmingham, 6th, Miss Grace Cummings of Tuskaloosa.
Died in Hansboro, Mississippi, 6th, Mrs. Anna Sedberry of Centre.

## THE SOUTHERN ARGUS - DEATHS - JUNE 1869 THROUGH JUNE 1874

Died near Kymulga, 29th ult., Mrs. Lockey Ann Baker.
Died in Talladega County, 27th ult., David Garrigas.
Died in Dallas County, 25th ult. of congestion, Rebecca, youngest child of Mrs. William Cunningham.

J.D. Duncan is again on the streets in Eutaw after a dangerous illness.

Mrs. A.M. Wooten, a most estimable and excellent lady, died in this city on Friday last of consumption.

Mrs. Tina U. Huston, wife of Thos. A. Huston of Shelby County, formerly of Dallas, died near Wilsonville on Sunday last the 13th inst.

Mr. and Mrs. A.C. Oxford, formerly residents of this city, where they have many friends who sympathize with them in their bereavement, lost their little daughter, Eliza Curtis, at Birmingham on the 5th of cholera.

A white man named Roberts, who was lying asleep on the track of the Mobile and Girard Railroad at Union Springs, was recently run over by an extra train and badly injured.

On account of bad health, John Frazer has resigned the office of Treasurer of Montgomery.

Mr. Mathews, one of the editors of the *Birmingham Independent*, had cholera, and the publication of his paper was temporarily suspended.

A little daughter of Joe Sturges in Eufaula was badly burned the 6th by kerosene.

Augustus Girard, an old citizen of Mobile, was drowned the 29th ult.

A son of Richard Barnes of Montgomery was drowned in the river last Sunday.

Rev. P.A. Pitts has been sick in Tuskaloosa.

Miss Grace Cummings, who died at Birmingham of cholera the 6th, had just graduated at the Methodist Female College in Tuskaloosa.

T.W. Carter left Birmingham for his home in Limestone County and died of cholera before he reached his destination.

## THE SOUTHERN ARGUS - DEATHS - JUNE 1869 THROUGH JUNE 1874

In Pickens County, recently, Tom Seaymer (negro) was killed by Dick Edwards (negro).

E.H. Foster, who died at Union Springs the other day, was a cadet of the State University.

Lauchlin McLean is dangerously ill at Eufaula.

Died on pulmonary consumption on the 12th inst. at the residence of Mrs. Martha Jones of Summerfield, Alabama, David Laws, a native of North Carolina and for some years past a citizen of Alabama and resident of Summerfield...

Died near Orrville in this County on the 6th instant, Blanche, daughter of Isaac W. and Margaret E. Lenoir, aged eight months and twenty-one days.

Eliza Curtis, daughter of A.C. and A.A. Oxford, died in Birmingham, Alabama, on the 4th day of July, 1873, aged two years, four months, and eight days. "Daisy" was always a delicate child and when the dread cholera, which had for the past few weeks been raging in our city, laid hold upon this tender little plant, it could not survive the dreadful shock...

Issue 7-25-1873

### TEXAS NEWS

At Sherman, recently, E.D. Picard was thrown from his buggy and fatally injured.

Captain W.F. Ford of Austin died in Mier, Mexico, June 20th.

A little daughter of Mr. McWharton of Hood County was burned to death a few weeks ago.

Joe Davis was murdered near Waco some time since by unknown parties.

Fred Hase died in Fort Worth recently.

W.L. Davenport of Marlin died recently.

John Rice fell from a train of cars on the 2nd near Dallas and was fatally injured.

J.F. Pills, Post Master at Palestine, has been arrested for murder.

## THE SOUTHERN ARGUS - DEATHS - JUNE 1869 THROUGH JUNE 1874

Mr. A.H. McGuire, a brother of Mrs. Robert H. Baker of this city, died in Mobile on the morning of the 21st inst.

Mr. A.B. Griffin, a native and long a resident of Dallas but for five years past a prominent citizen of Mobile, died at Blount Springs of consumption on the night of the 17th inst., aged about thirty-five years.

On the plantation of Colonel S. Ruffin in Choctaw County, recently, a negro man killed his wife.

Wm. Watts of Carrollton was badly injured on the 8th by a fall from a ladder.

The *Greensboro Beacon* believes the reported death of John W. Walton, late of Hale County, at Gallatin, Tennessee, is incorrect.

A little child of James B. Crook of Greene County was recently drowned in a well.

Dr. Dick Fletcher of Athens has been sick.

Esquire Tanner of Athens, eighty-six years old, is in very feeble health.

Rev. W. Jacob Parker of Grove Hill has been very sick.

At Larkinsville the 12th, J.M. Gullatt was stabbed seven times by Sanford Carden.

Wilks Davidson of Colbert County recently shot and wounded himself.

In Russell County the 12th, Thomas Rainey inflicted a dangerous injury upon a Mr. Floyd by striking him with a billet of wood.

Moran Burns of Chambers County recently committed suicide by shooting himself.

Jake Marrast (negro) drowned himself at Tuskaloosa recently.

Rev. W.S. McDiarmid, well-known in Eastern Alabama, was drowned at Lumberton, North Carolina, the 26th ult.

### DIED IN ALABAMA
Died near Birmingham, 1st, Mrs. Albert Roebuck.
Died in Talladega, 19th, Miss Mary Walden.
Died in Talladega, 20th, infant of J.T. Adams.

## THE SOUTHERN ARGUS - DEATHS - JUNE 1869 THROUGH JUNE 1874

Died in Montgomery, 22nd, Dr. M.L. Gilmer.
Died in Birmingham, 21st, child of Mr. Cavett.
Died in Dale County, 13th, James War.
Died in Dale County, 13th, two children of James War.
Died in Marion, 19th, Mrs. Young Tarrant.
Died in Greene County, 3rd, Mrs. Eleanor R. Steele.
Died in Demopolis, 11th, infant of Mrs. McMillan.
Died in Birmingham, 19th, John Patrick.
Died in Birmingham, 19th, child of Mr. Austin.
Died in Montgomery, 16th, Mrs. Catharine Shelby.
Died in Choctaw Corner, 7th, Wilson Jowers.
Died in Birmingham, 18th, Mrs. S.J. Rudd.
Died in Conecuh County, 13th, John Ellis.
Died in Carrollton, 12th, Mrs. Willis J. Moore.
Died in Huntsville, 13th, Miss Julia Smith.
Died in Huntsville, 15th, A.J. Tannock.
Died in Birmingham, 17th, W.G. Bird.
Died in Jefferson County, 21st, Mrs. Holland of Birmingham.
Died in Clay County, 10th, infant of J.E. Upchurch.
Died in Arkansas, recently, Mrs. Sally, formerly of Lowndes County.
Died in Eufaula, 18th, Annie Lou, infant of Mr. and Mrs. B.C. Ford.
Died in Madison County, 11th, Samuel Pleasants of Huntsville.
Died in Tuskaloosa, 12th, Mrs. Margaret C. Shortridge.
Died in Tuskaloosa, 15th, Guy Maxwell Jesper, infant.
Died near Dudleyville, 19th, Mrs. Elliza E. McLendon.

Colonel W.D. Bowie of Maryland is dead.

Dr. Wm. Layton has been appointed by the Governor of Kentucky assistant superintendent of the lunatic asylum in Lexington, vice Dr. T.P. Dudley, deceased.

Issue 8-1-1873

M.C. Riggs, a prominent citizen of Houston (Texas), died the 7th ult.

James Martin, who killed Chapman, has been held to bail in fifteen hundred dollars.
On Friday last at the Dew Drop saloon, John Lewis Chapman, recently steward at the St. James Hotel, was shot through the head and killed by James Martin.

## THE SOUTHERN ARGUS - DEATHS - JUNE 1869 THROUGH JUNE 1874

Mr. W.E. McGehee, one of the heirs of a Mr. Smith, who died in Montgomery we believe, some years ago, has brought suit in the Dallas Chancery Court for certain valuable lots on Broad, Washington, and Alabama Streets in this city, which it is alleged the said Smith disposed of when non compo mentis.

Near Glennville, recently, Henry Butt was struck on the head by a negro, with a hoe, and seriously injured.

Colonel W.D. Hays was, the 25th ult., dangerously ill at his residence near Athens.

Mrs. Sallie Brown of Conecuh County is one hundred and four years old, and is in good health and quite active.

Mr. Meeks of the *Gasden Times* has had an attack of bilious fever.

The following white citizens of Birmingham and vicinity died of cholera outside of the city: Mrs. H. A. Hale, Mrs. Gardner Hale, A.W. Hawkins, child of Mr. Davis, W.A. Sorsby, son of Peyton G. King, Mr. Carter, Mr. Holland and wife, and Mrs. Kelly.

Rev. J.D. Anthony, Editor of the *Mountain Eagle* at Jasper, had an attack of cholera, which he contracted in Birmingham.
    Rev. J.D. Anthony is again at home in the office of the *Mountain Eagle*, after an absence of three weeks.

Miss N.C. Stewart has been tried in Gadsden for insanity and acquitted.

Calvin Brown of Gadsden, who has been dangerously sick, is convalescent.

On the 25th ult., Robert Brewer, living near Scottsboro, was dangerously ill.

Gater Glasscock of Jackson County was recently thrown from his horse and killed.

L.J. Bryan, the Sheriff of Lowndes, who has been ill for some time past, has been taken to Montgomery for treatment.

The lower limbs of Victor W. Flint of Bladon Springs are paralyzed.

Near Elkmont, Limestone County, the 18th ult., Jim Eaves crushed in John Locke's head with a hoe.

William Fulton was drowned at Mobile the other day.

## THE SOUTHERN ARGUS - DEATHS - JUNE 1869 THROUGH JUNE 1874

In Mobile, 27th ult., Wyatt R. Pryor, twelve years old, fell from a window and was killed.

The following are the names of the white persons who died in Birmingham of cholera: Mr. Stellars, Mr. Bennett, Mr. Stroub, Mrs. Bennett, Mr. Hughes and two children, Mrs. W.L. Kennedy, Eliza C. Oxford (child), J.G. Chambers, Mrs. C. Douglas, Mrs. J.T. Terry, infant of J. Worthington, infant of Mr. Houghan, Miss Laura Hagood, child of N.F. Miles, Mrs. O'Brien, Miss Gracie Cummings, W.M. Nabors, Mr. Sheehan, E.W. Smith, Mr. Henly, Mrs. Hurst, Edward Linn, S.A. McLaughlin, Mr. Weidman and child, child of Mrs. Kelley, white man name unknown.

William Christopher of Gadsden has had a dangerous attack of something like cholera.

Mr. S.A. Thornton of Gadsden is suffering with dropsy.

On the 19th ult., near Waterloo, Lauderdale County, O.P. Whitten was seriously, perhaps fatally, cut by W. Hill.

In a recent affray in Russell County, Nat Wilkinson was stabbed in the side, Robert Wilkinson was cut in the arm, and Charles Harvey was slashed in the hand.

In Montgomery the other day, George Johnston, while drunk, badly cut his sister-in-law, Miss Hilliard, with a bowie-knife.

Died in Issaquena County, Mississippi, July 2?th, at 6:30 a.m., Wm. B. Padleford, son-in-law of the late L.R. Davis. Mr. Padleford was born in Holmesville, Pike County, Mississippi, November 6th, 1845, lived for several years near Raymond, Hinds County, Mississippi, and removed thence to Issaquena County last winter. He was married to Miss Luella Davis about eighteen months ago; and now leaves her widowed...Mr. Padleford had been a consistent member of the Methodist Church about a year...

Died of billious remittent fever on the 2nd day of July, 1873 at McDowell's Station, Sumter County, A.J. Arendale, aged twenty-two years. Andrew had been a consistent member of the Christian Church at Rocky Springs, Jackson County, almost from childhood. He was, at the time of his death, in the employment of the Alabama Central Railroad, as bridge carpenter.....

Tribute of respect from Masonic Hall, Fulton Lodge, Orrville, Alabama, July 13, 1873 on the death of Frank L. Milhous, who died in this place July 11, 1873, aged forty-six years.....

## THE SOUTHERN ARGUS - DEATHS - JUNE 1869 THROUGH JUNE 1874

### DIED IN ALABAMA

Died in Choctaw County, 23rd ult., James Wright.
Died in Montgomery County, 15th ult., Mrs. Mary Finch.
Died in Troy, 17th ult., Julia Barron, infant.
Died in Pickens County, 19th ult., Jed G. Seaymer.
Died near Hamburg, 22nd ult., I.N. Steele.
Died in Eutaw, 20th ult., John Daly.
Died in Eutaw, 19th ult., John Watson.
Died in Clarke County, recently, D. Garick.
Died in Demopolis, 24th ult., Miss Maggie McMillan.
Died in Demopolis, 22nd ult., L.R. Holland.
Died at Bailey Springs, 16th ult., Samuel B. Hudson.
Died in Pickens County, 21st ult., Dr. W.S. Palmer.
Died in Pickens County, 21st ult., Mrs. Hicks B. Chappelle.
Died on steamer for Europe, 10th ult., Thomas T. Bonner, formerly of Pickens County.
Died in Talladega, 20th ult., Melville Adams, infant.
Died in Talladega County, 11th ult., Esquire McClung.
Died near Mayport, Florida, June 9th, Haywood H. Hunter, formerly of Greene County.
Died near Greensboro, 10th ult., Alice J. Mellown, child.
Died in La Fayette, 20th ult., Mrs. Josephine Robinson.
Died in Linden, recently, child of Mr. and Mrs. A. Northrop.
Died in Forkland, 21st ult., Maggie Patterson, child.
Died near Perryville, 23rd ult., George Pope Harris, infant.
Died at C.C. Smith's, Perry County, 26th ult., Mrs. Equilla Hopper, aged seventy-seven.

Issue 8-8-1873

### TEXAS NEWS

A son of Mr. Ragden, near LaGrange, only ten years old, hung himself the 1?th ult.

Colonel Leman, an eminent lawyer, for nearly a quarter of a century solicitor of the middle circuit, is dead.

George Moore was recently drowned in Lamar County.

If Mrs. Applewhite, widow of D.C. Applewhite, who was killed on the 14th of October 1871 by state police at Groesbeck, Texas, will call on I.W. Pickens, Sheriff of Caddo Parish, Louisiana, she will receive information which may prove of considerable pecuniary advantage to her.

## THE SOUTHERN ARGUS - DEATHS - JUNE 1869 THROUGH JUNE 1874

S.R. Wheeler of Bell County was recently dragged to death by his pony.

The 7th ult., a Mrs. Williams was murdered in Brown County by Indians.

Burke Yarbrow died in Tyler recently. He was formerly of St. Clair County, Alabama.

Lambert Hopkins, an ex-Alabamian, died in Milam County, July 8th.

Daniel Dean, formerly of Butler County, Alabama, died in Anderson County the 14th of July.

Captain Harry Bedell, an ex-Alabamian, was thrown from his buggy four months ago and had his ankle dislocated and broken so badly that he has ever since been confined to his bed.

Henry E. Perkins of Houston at one time grand master of Odd Fellows, died recently.

In Galveston the 23rd ult., I. DeBendetti stabbed and killed Charles A. Hugenard.

Robert P. McGibbin, formerly Colonel in the United States Army, died in Galveston a few days ago.

Mrs. E. Terry, an old resident of Fort Worth, is dead.

W.J. Dorsey committed suicide at Hearne the 22nd ult.

Charles A. Russell was hanged in San Francisco the 25th ult.

A Mr. Harrison was quite ill last week at the hotel in Evergreen.

Near Paint Rock the other day Miss Lily Jones died of burns received from kerosene oil.

G.B. Avery of Corn House, Randolph County, has been very sick.

Near Carter's Store, Randolph County, the 22nd ult., Jesse Burns shot and badly wounded John White.

A. Dudley Lewis has been appointed Sheriff of Lauderdale, vice Hudson, deceased.

## THE SOUTHERN ARGUS - DEATHS - JUNE 1869 THROUGH JUNE 1874

Thomas Kenan Graham, a gentleman of good family, of exemplary character, and of fine promise, died in this city on Monday last after a long and painful illness, in the 23rd year of his age. He was a native of Dallas, and for several years had been a citizen of Selma, where he had made many friends ...

W.H. Denson of La Fayette has been employed to prosecute Heard for killing Jennings.
At Dudleyville the other day, Mr. Jennings was fatally stabbed by James Heard.
Mr. Heard of Tallapoosa has been held in a $5,000 bond to answer for the killing of Mr. Jennings.

Mrs. W.W. Mason of Norcross, Georgia, formerly of Tuskegee, has been very ill.

Miss Gillam, daughter of John Gillam of Tuskaloosa County, was recently killed by a limb blown from a tree.

William Leigh of Florence was very sick the 30th ult.

A young man named Wesson was recently run over near Florence by a pair of frightened horses and badly bruised.

L.E. Hill, formerly of Lauderdale County, was recently accidentally killed on the railroad near Pulaski, Tennessee.

S.B. Hughes has returned to Gadsden from Arkansas with his brother Mack, who has been very sick.

Mrs. J.L. Bozeman of Hale County has been very sick.

Cadet Penniss of Illinois was drowned at West Point the 23rd ult.

A man named Mathews was stabbed in Tuskaloosa, recently, by James Burchfield.

Mr. William Comegys lies hopelessly ill at the residence of his brother-in-law Thomas B. Slade in Tuskaloosa.

### DIED IN ALABAMA
Died in Birmingham, 27th ult., Mrs. D.A. Walker.
Died in Lauderdale County, 18th ult., Caleb Stafford.
Died in Florence, 17th ult., William Amonett.
Died in Tyler, Texas, recently, Burke Yarborough, formerly of St. Clair County.

# THE SOUTHERN ARGUS - DEATHS - JUNE 1869 THROUGH JUNE 1874

Died in St. Clair County, 22nd ult., Miss J.E. Reese.
Died in Opelika, 27th ult., Mrs. S.W. Bloodworth.
Died in Etowah County, 20th ult., Elias Reed.
Died in Talladega County, 11th ult., Mrs. Ann Eustace Welch.
Died in Greensboro, 18th ult., D.J. Powers.
Died in Birmingham, 29th ult., P. Newman.
Died in Montgomery, 30th ult., Miss Fannie Hunter.
Died in Chambers County, 25th ult., Mrs.. D.H.B. Abernathy.
Died in Madison County, 22nd ult., child of C.H. Humphrey.
Died in Clinton, 26th ult., J.F. Strother.
Died in Uniontown, 14th ult., Mrs. Fannie Waldrom.
Died in Sanford County, recently, Joseph Pennington.
Died in Fayette Courthouse, 24th ult., Mrs. Mary Amanda Phillips.
Died in Tuscumbia, 30th ult., Hugh Kearney, child.
Died in Prattville, 30th ult., B.F. Smith.
Died in Huntsville, 25th ult., James B. Campbell.
Died in Huntsville, 28th ult., Mrs. Jane Callighan.
Died near Paint Rock, recently, Miss Lilly Jones.
Died in Jackson County recently, Thomas V. Province.
Died in Jackson County, recently, Moses Jones.
Died in Somerville, 17th ult., Robert A. Stuart.
Died near Decatur, 19th ult., Joseph T. Evans.
Died near Moulton, 17th June, Rev. R.D. Hardin.
Died in Courtland, 27th ult., Mary Sue Puryear, infant.
Died in Jasper, recently, Della Floyd Guttery, child.
Died in Columbiana, 29th ult., Mrs. Margaret Johnson.
Died in Texas, 8th ult., Lambeth Hopkins, formerly of Perry County.
Died in Perry County, 13th ult., Mary Anna Hopkins.
Died in Athens, 27th ult., infant of Ike Boseman.
Died in Limestone County, 28th ult., Mrs. Lucy Holt.
Died in Eufaula, 30th ult., Hattie Edmenson, infant.
Died in Greenville, 28th ult., A.C. Green.
Died in Texas, 11th ult., Daniel Dean, formerly of Butler County.
Died in Girard, recently, W.B. Martin.
Died near Larkinsville, 28th ult., John Isbell.
Died near Scottsboro, 20th ult., Robert Brewer.
Died in Greene County, 20th ult., John Watson.
Died in Tuskaloosa County, 20th ult., Benjamin Rosser, Sr.
Died in Tuskaloosa County, 12th ult., Miss Mary E. Jennings.
Died in Montgomery, 2nd, Lee Barnett Ledyard, child.
Died in Lowndes County, 31st ult., Willie Bell, infant.
Died in Birmingham, 1st, Mrs. Louisa King.

R.A. Childress of Tuskaloosa was, on the 31st ult., very sick.

# THE SOUTHERN ARGUS - DEATHS - JUNE 1869 THROUGH JUNE 1874

Issue 8-15-1873

James E. Elam, Mayor of Baton Rouge, is dead.

S.P. Dorsey, son of L.L. Dorsey of Jefferson County, Kentucky, jumped from a hotel window in Cleveland, the 3rd, and killed himself.

Captain James Safford was gored by a bull on Saturday last and seriously, but not fatally, hurt.

While he was in this city on Wednesday, Mr. M.O. Marshall of Bellevue was stricken down with a congestive chill and for a few hours he was in a critical condition.

Chancellor Clark, recently quite sick at Birmingham, has returned to Eutaw convalescent.

John Allen, living near Owensboro, Kentucky, was killed, and his uncle, Robert Allen, was wounded the night of the 6th by a band of assassins who attacked their house.

Monday of last week, John M. Talbott of North Middletown, Kentucky, was shot and fatally wounded by Joe Harris.

Rev. Mr. Osborn died at Gallatin, Tennessee, the 2nd.

Herman Hirsch of Seale has been very sick.

Thomas Burke, charged with the murder of Austin Barnes (negro), has been arrested in Crenshaw County.

Mr. K. Tims, living near Arbacooche, accidentally shot and killed himself a few days ago.

Near White Hall a few days ago, Newman M. Ruff badly and perhaps fatally cut the throat of a Mr. Jones.

The heirs of the late J.H. Smith of Lowndes are suing for the recovery of some valuable property in Montgomery.

Rewards aggregating $3,500 have been offered for the arrest of Joe Harris who killed Talbott at Midolton, Kentucky the 14th.

# THE SOUTHERN ARGUS - DEATHS - JUNE 1869 THROUGH JUNE 1874

The wife of Rev. E.C. Gordon of Huntsville has been sent to the lunatic asylum at Tuskaloosa.

### DIED IN ALABAMA

Died in Greenville, 3rd, infant of A.C. Green.
Died in Talladega County, 2nd, Jeremiah Collins.
Died in Randolph County, 1st, L.G. Hicks, child.
Died in Demopolis, 4th, Miss Fanny Roby Jones.
Died in Lowndes County, 5th, Elbert Harrell.
Died in Elmore County, 4th, Mrs. Howell Rose.
Died near Moulton, 5th, Mrs. Rebecca Garrison.
Died in Benton, 2nd, Hugh Lundy, child.
Died at Collirence, 26th ult., Dunklin Rast, child.
Died in Choctaw County, 1st, Mrs. Sarah L. Horn.
Died in Calhoun County, 7th, William Dale.
Died in Montevallo, 5th, Grandson Galloway.
Died near Wilsonville, 29th ult., A.B. Nelson.
Died in Montgomery, 2nd, Lee Barnet Ledyard.
Died in Decatur, 5th, infant of J.W. Oglesby.
Died in Athens, 8th, Miss Martha Ann Turrentine.
Died in Greene County, 1st, Mrs. Samuel O. Gordon.
Died in Tuskaloosa, 1st, W.C. Comegys.
Died in Choctaw County, 23rd ult., James Wright.
Died in Madison County, 4th, Hamilton G. Bradford.
Died in Huntsville, 2nd, Miss Mary F. Coler.
Died in Florence, 31st ult., Rev. Wm. Leigh.
Died in Birmingham, 6th, Miss Agnes Mader.
Died in Troy, 4th, infant of Mr. T.M. Murphree.
Died in Troy, recently, Johnnie Townsend.
Died near Montgomery, 4th, Richard H. Taylor.
Died near Stevenson, 3rd, Thomas Carlton.
Died in Montgomery, 7th, Lizzie O'Brien, infant.
Died in Pickens County, 3rd, little George Lynch.
Died at Butler Springs, recently, Charles, son of Ike Cook of Hayneville.
Died in Butler County, 4th, child of Harris H. Wilson.
Died in Florida, 30th ult., J.W. McQueen, formerly of Lowndes County.
Died in Canton, Mississippi, 6th, John F. Bosworth, thirty-five years ago of Eufaula.
Died in North Port, 20th ult., Mrs. Martha Raymond.
Died in North Port, 30th ult., infant of W.L. Christian.
Died near Evergreen, recently, daughter of James Greene.
Died in Jackson County, 22nd ult., Mrs. Sarah Wallace.
Died in Montgomery, 7th, child of Mr. P.J. Anderson.

## THE SOUTHERN ARGUS - DEATHS - JUNE 1869 THROUGH JUNE 1874

Died in Norcross, Georgia, recently, Mrs. Matilda Mason, formerly of Tuskegee.

Died in Tuskaloosa County, 12th ult., Miss Mary E. Jennings.

Issue 8-22-1873

TEXAS NEWS

Lipscomb, shot at Hearne, died the 7th . Mr. Lipscomb was accidentally shot and dangerously wounded in Hearne the 6th.

Dr. T.A. Harrison died in Harrison County the 30th ult.

Harry Williams, a stranger, committed suicide at Bremond the 8th.

Mr. DuTour, late a clerk in the land office, was drowned near Austin the 3rd.

Annie Carter, about eleven years old, recently committed suicide by hanging, near LaGrange.

W.H. Brown, an Englishman, committed suicide at Waco the 6th.

Colonel Charles Progay? died in Fannin County the 29th ult.

Mrs. E. Yost died in Wilkesbarre, Pennsylvania, the 12th, aged one hundred five years.

Judge William F. Pierce, who died at Eutaw the 11th, had cholera, contracted, it is thought, at Blount Springs, from which he had just returned, or Birmingham, through which he had passed.

At Cowles Station the 11th, Ed. Walker shot and killed Wm. Clark.

Moses Melson of Dublin beat was killed by lightning one day last week.

Died on Saturday last, near Orrville the 16th, child of Mr. J.E. Kennedy.

Mr. G.S. Thompson of New York City died at the St. James Hotel the 19th of typhoid fever.

General W.J. Hardee has been seriously ill at the Montgomery White Sulphur Springs.

## THE SOUTHERN ARGUS - DEATHS - JUNE 1869 THROUGH JUNE 1874

Mrs. Watts, wife of Col. E.T. Watts, for many years of this city, now of Eagle Lake, Texas, died at the residence of her sister, Mrs. Wa??, near Carlowville, in this county, on Wednesday morning last the 20th.

Bob Carson (negro) has been sentenced by the City Court of Greenville to be hanged for the murder of an Irishman named Taylor.

A son of Alexander Steele of Shelby County accidentally shot and wounded himself a few days ago.

### DIED IN ALABAMA

Died in Montgomery, 1st, A.L. McLemore, child.
Died in Eutaw, 11th, Judge William F. Pearce.
Died in Randolph County, 1st, James O. Stone.
Died in New Market, 6th, Alice Ruth Hambrick.
Died in Madison County, 3rd, Rhoda E. Drake.
Died in Madison County, 3rd, Sam A. Trotman.
Died in Huntsville, 8th, Hugh Easley.
Died in Limestone County, 7th, Miss Cornelia Love.
Died in Limestone County, 7th, W.B. Hayes.
Died in Lowndes County, 12th, Mrs. Jesse Robertson.
Died in Lowndes County, recently, Mrs. Hinson.
Died in Greensboro, 13th, Estelle Nutting, infant.
Died in Bladon Springs, 11th, Emma Tabb, child.
Died in Eutaw, 9th, Roberta Perrin, infant.
Died in Jefferson, Marengo County, 26th ult., Mrs. Tanner.
Died in Jefferson, 20th ult., Miss Rosa Peteet.
Died in Jefferson, 30th ult., Mary Aldridge, child.
Died in Jefferson, 4th, Malcolm Nickerson.
Died in Jefferson, 4th, Miss Mollie Williams.
Died in Eufaula, 14th, Mrs. Matilda Daniel.
Died in Montgomery, 18th, Thomas G. Jones, infant.
Died in Montgomery, 18th, Otto Lehing.
Died near Uniontown, 17th, Mrs. Kittie Pitts Hudson.
Died at Blount Springs, 17th, Hon. James B. Clark.
Died in Talladega County, recently, Baker Dulaney.
Died in Pike County, 12th, Rev. William McCarra.
Died in Eutaw, 9th, Major J.G. Pearce.
Died at Blount Springs, 12th, William Walker.
Died at Hamburg, 9th, Rosa Estelle Blackburn, child.
Died in North Port, 8th, Willie C. Andrews.
Died in Pickens County, 6th, Mrs. Mary Fowler.
Died in Carrolton, infant of James L. Land.
Died in Carrolton, 2nd, Kate Celestia Gibson, infant.

## THE SOUTHERN ARGUS - DEATHS - JUNE 1869 THROUGH JUNE 1874

Died in Tuscumbia, 12th, Mrs. Mary Ann Barclay.
Died in Opelika, 7th, Miss Lizzie Slaughter.
Died near Stevenson, recently, Joseph Jennings.
Died in Bladon Springs, 25th ult., Mrs. B.M. Conner.
Died near Birmingham on the 10th instant, little Peyton, infant son of Peyton G. and Allie King, aged one year and nine days....

Issue 8-29-1873

TEXAS NEWS

At Brooklyn, recently, Erasmus Griflin killed Dan Valentine.

John Parks died recently in Anderson County.

Rev. Mr. Goodwin of the Greenville Baptist Church has been quite sick.

Mr. James B. Head, who has been very sick at Blount, is convalescent.

Bob Carson (negro) is to be hung at Greenville, March 13th, 1874, for murder.

Chancellor Clarke did not die of cholera.

Mr. William Smaw recently returned to Eutaw from Blount Springs very sick with bilious fever.

Died on the 19th at Harrell's Cross Roads, W.T. Oswalt, aged sixty years.

Mrs. H.A. Herbert, who was very ill at Blount Springs, has recovered.

Mr. E.P. Legg, an old and respectable citizen, died in Pleasant Hill on Wednesday last the 27th.

Mr. P.H. Ulmer, a venerable and honored citizen of Dallas, died near Richmond one day last week.

Ned Gilkey, negro, is in the Pickens Jail for complicity in the murder of an infant near Memphis the 15th.

Mr. E.L. Whipple is lying at his home near Hayneville in a very feeble condition.

On the 21st, the *Blade* reported the following persons very sick in Tuskaloosa: Mrs. Norfleet Harris, Mrs. E.H. King, and Mrs. J.A. VanHoose.

## THE SOUTHERN ARGUS - DEATHS - JUNE 1869 THROUGH JUNE 1874

We learn that Mr. James Smiley died at the residence of one of his sons, near King's Landing a day or two ago.

Miss Hannah Goldsmith of Mobile died in this city the 28th at the residence of her uncle, Mr. J.S/B. Schuster, at whose house she was visiting at the time of her fatal illness.

William Hunt of Athens was recently badly bruised by a railroad accident.

W.E. Douglas and his wife of Tuskegee, both of whom have been dangerously sick, are now recovering.

Dr. McLean of Bladon Springs was very sick a week ago.

Samuel Murry, son of Captain John Murry, was drowned the 13th in the Alabama River, near Earle's woodyard.

Judge Merrill Ashurst, who died lately in Santa Fe, was a brother of Colonel R.T. Ashurst, and an uncle of Honorable J.F. Ashurst, both of Tallapoosa County.

### DIED IN ALABAMA

Died in Barbour County, 9th, Miss Addie Davis.
Died in Demopolis, 18th, Mrs. J.P. Deford.
Died in Washington County, 11th, P. Ball.
Died in Rayville, Louisiana, 16th, Mrs. H.M.M. Phillips, formerly of this state.
Died in Gadsden, 14th, James Petty, child.
Died in Gadsden, 16th, Franklin Pope, child.
Died in Gadsden, 16th, Wm. Lafayette Epping, child.
Died in Barbour County, 19th, infant of C.J. Jones.
Died at Chandler Springs, 16th, Miss Theodosia Renfroe of Talladega.
Died near Talladega, 18th, Clement Arthur Bingham.
Died near Clinton, 15th, Annie Fason, child.
Died in Villula, 20th, Miss Laura Turk.
Died in Seale, 14th, Mrs. Emma Corbitt.
Died in Hurtville, recently, Mrs. Rivers.
Died in Talbott County, Georgia, recently, Mrs. Fannie Pitts of Russell County.
Died in Seale, 15th, Mrs. Emma S. Martin.
Died in Abbeville, 16th, Mrs. Emeline Kincey/Kineey?.
Died in Abbeville, 16th, Miss Mollie Ward.
Died in Memphis, Pickens County, 17th, Guy Pruitt, child.
Died in Memphis, Pickens County, 17th, infant of J.D. Purnell.
Died in Birmingham, 19th, Edna Webb, infant.
Died in Sumter, recently, James B. Ivey.

## THE SOUTHERN ARGUS - DEATHS - JUNE 1869 THROUGH JUNE 1874

Died in Jacksonville, 19th, Miss Ella Laird.
Died in Clarke County, 13th, Rev. R. Hickson.
Died in Clarke County, 13th, E.W. Glen.
Died in Limestone County, 19th, Mace H. Gilbert.
Died in Pensacola, 18th, Rev. P.H. Lundy, formerly of Lowndes.
Died at Fort Deposit, 20th, Mrs. Lucy Gilmer.
Died in Montgomery, 19th, Bessie Buell, child.
Died near Scottsboro, 16th, W. Walton.
Died at Decatur, 10th, Daniel Gilbert.
Died in Arkansas, 10th, Miss Thenia Rossen of Scottsboro.
Died in Montgomery County, 18th, Daniel Meadows.
Died in St. Clair County, 15th, Miss Mollie C. Robinson.
Died in Birmingham, 14th, Julian Harris, infant.
Died in Jefferson County, recently, Rev. Joseph Byers.
Died in Jefferson County, 15th, Mrs. Nancy Menzer.
Died in Gadsden, 12th, Arthur Baxter Farley, child.
Died near Mt. Meigs, 26th, Mrs. Lafayette Murdock.
Died in Lowndes County, 26th, Benjamin Harrison.
Died in Galveston, Texas, 15th, Matthew Toulmin English of Mobile.
Died in Birmingham, 24th, Eliza Simmons.
Died at Montvale Springs, 19th, Sandy Flournoy of Montgomery.
Died in Limestone County, 15th, Mrs. John A. Johnson.
Died on Sand Mountain, recently, child of Red Chisenhall.
Died in Santa Fe, New Mexico, recently, Merrill Ashurst, formerly of Montgomery.
Died in Mobile, 22nd, infant of Andrew C. McLean.
Died in Louisiana, 16th, Mrs. Margaret Ann Quinlan, formerly of Mobile.
Died near Marion, recently, Henry L. Chapman.

### Issue 9-5-1873

Captain Edward Halbrook, an eminent Louisvillian, is dead.

Dr. Mendenhall of Cincinnati was struck with paralysis the 28th ult.

Judge Carter Campbell of Madison, Georgia, died the 28th ult.

William Campbell was hanged for murder at Cairo, Illinois, the 29th ult.

General J.F. Benjamin of Shelbina, Missouri, was shot and killed the 25th ult.

Honorable James P. Holcombe of Virginia died at Capon Springs, in that state, the 22nd ult.

## THE SOUTHERN ARGUS - DEATHS - JUNE 1869 THROUGH JUNE 1874

Mrs. Elizabeth Hunt of Greene County, Georgia, died the 27th ult., aged one hundred two years.

Judge Mears of Clarksville, Arkansas, was assassinated the 27th ult.

William R. Boyce, President of the First National Bank of Lynn, Massachusetts, committed suicide the 27th ult.

General J.F. Benjamin of Shelbina, Missouri, was shot and killed the 25th ult.

J.H. Rosenquest, cashier of the First National Bank of Tarrytown, New York has committed suicide.

### TEXAS NEWS

Mrs. C.C. Gillaspie died at Houston the 7th ult.

Jim Miller was assassinated at Tehuacana the 19th ult.

In Barnett [Burnet] County, Clay Stinnett killed Andrew Danly.

W.S. Wimberly has been killed near Tyler.

A young man named Jones has been murdered in Johnson County.

In Lamar County, Henry Vickers was killed by lightning a few days ago.

A Mr. Savage, recently from Georgia, was murdered on the 4th ult. on Ripley Creek, ten miles from Mt. Pleasant.

Major Thomas L. McCarty died at Bryan the 20th ult.

Died of diphtheria, near Orrville, August 16th, James E. Kennedy, son of J.E. and Julia M. Kennedy, aged two years, five months and twenty days.
    Died of diphtheria, near Orrville, August 23rd, E?ander/Evander? A. Kennedy, son of J.E. and Julia M. Kennedy, aged five years and twenty-five days.

Mrs. Fannie Keeble the young and accomplished wife of Mr. Henry C. Keeble of this city, died on Saturday last at Lebabon, Kentucky, where, at the time, she was visiting relatives.

## THE SOUTHERN ARGUS - DEATHS - JUNE 1869 THROUGH JUNE 1874

Mr. H.P. Ulmer, who died in Warrenton last week, was seventy-one years old; Mr. James Smyly, whose death occurred the 25th ult., was seventy-one years old; and Mr. E.P. Legg, whose death took place the 26th ult., was seventy-six years old. They had long been honored citizens of Dallas, and were generally known by all the older people of the county.

Stephen Jones, brakeman on the Mobile and Ohio Railroad was killed at Citronelle last Saturday.

Dr. D.P. Davis of Pickens County was recently fatally injured by a fall from his horse.

Last week, Dr. Smith was very ill at Jas. McGhee's in Cherokee County.

Last week, John A. Thompson of Florence was dangerously ill.

George Roberts, a lad of sixteen, near Gadsden, was fatally kicked by a horse the 18th ult.

Frank A. Duvall of Birmingham came near bleeding to death the other day by the brusting of an atery in his nostril.

### DIED IN ALABAMA

Died in Montgomery, 28th ult., C. Cox.
Died in Clarke County, 23rd ult., John Creighton.
Died in Montgomery, 27th ult., Daniel H. Savage.
Died in Hayneville, 28th ult., Willis Brewer, infant.
Died in Gordonville, 25th ult., child of Mr. Bell.
Died in Tuskaloosa County, 23rd ult., Dorcas Sloan.
Died in Tuskaloosa, 26th ult., John Thomas.
Died in Huntsville, 20th ult., Mrs. Mary J. Bailey.
Died in Birmingham, 27th ult., R.M. Orme.
Died in Montgomery, 20th ult., Jos. Wyatt Wilson.
Died near Wetumpka, 22nd ult., Rufus Greene.
Died in Montgomery, 27th ult., Mrs. M. Lobman.
Died in Troy, 26th ult., infant of N.W. Griffin.
Died in Pickens County, 17th ult., Frank Gates.
Died in Pickens County, 18th ult., W.R. Fullerton.
Died near Gordo, recently, Dr. D.P. Davis.
Died in Eutaw, 22nd ult., Mrs. Henrietta Pettigrew.
Died near Hickman, 24th ult., James G. Ussery.
Died near Gadsden, 18th, George Roberts.
Died in Gadsden, 20th ult., E.A. Mosely, child.
Died in Eufaula, 26th ult., Mrs. H.H. Herring.

## THE SOUTHERN ARGUS - DEATHS - JUNE 1869 THROUGH JUNE 1874

Died in Talladega County, 20th ult., F. Ledbetter.
Died in Talladega, 25th ult., George Miller.
Died in Marion, 15th ult., H.E. Bailey, child.
Died near Marion, 15th ult., John Morrison.
Died in Florence, 13th ult., Nannie McLarin, child.
Died in Jefferson County, 25th ult., W.F. Bell.
Died in Camden, 26th ult., John Dannelly.
Died in Mobile, 29th ult., Mrs. Catherine Laurence Lavretta.
Died near Farmersville, Lowndes County, Willie Gilbert, child.
Died in Greenville, 25th ult., Arthur Whitehead, child.
Died in Tallapoosa County, 24th ult., son of Tarp Taylor.
Died in Morrisontown, New Jersey, ??th ult., Mrs. Dr. Bozeman, formerly of Montgomery.
Died near Evergreen, 25th ult., Miss Hettie Cary of Pensacola.
Died in Memphis, 19th ult., Dr. A. Lopez, formerly of Mobile and Selma.
Died in Carrollton, 27th ult., Annie Slaughter, child.
Died in Perry County, 24th ult., Emmet Blackburn, child.
Died in Perry County, 26th ult., William Curb, child.
Died in Tuscumbia, 24th ult., Sarah Moore Winston, infant.
Died in Philadelphia, 27th ult., George Johnson of Mobile.
Died in Elyton, 26th ult., Edward Lee Davidson, infant.

Issue 9-12-1873

J.B. Hartley died of flux in Madison, Indiana, the 2nd. He was a celebrated horse trainer and veterinary surgeon in New Orleans and Mobile, and known all over the south.

Hon. D. Ringo, the first Chief Justice of the State of Arkansas and for twelve years United States Judge of the Eastern District of Arkansas, died the 2nd at Little Rock, aged seventy-five years.

### TEXAS NEWS

Colonel L.W. Groce died in Hempstead the 29th ult.

Champe Carter, Sr., died at Chappell Hill, 17th ult.

G.A. Gibson, Deputy Sheriff of Bexar County, is dead.

Recorder Ed. L. Leonhart of Houston died on the 23rd ult. of an enlargement of the heart.

Mr. D.J. Blair has been appointed Sheriff of DeWitt County to fill a vacancy occasioned by the death of Jack Helm.

## THE SOUTHERN ARGUS - DEATHS - JUNE 1869 THROUGH JUNE 1874

John K. Ryan was recently waylaid and shot in Liberty County.

In Lamar County, recently, Bob Little was shot and killed by Mrs. John D. Dickerson.

Captain Patterson of the Army died at Fort Davis the 28th ult.

General J.E. Harrison had a stroke of paralysis at Harrison Station the 28th ult.

Dr. John Daniel was recently shot and killed in Lamar by Steve Tyler.

Judge John G. Scott died in Austin the 24th ult.

Joe Brown is in jail in Quitman for the recent murder of Harris Hammond at Minneola.

### DIED IN ALABAMA
Died in Mobile, 26th ult., Edwin Percy Vanghan, child.
Died near Florence, recently, Simon Reesgraff.
Died at Florence, 31st ult., E.A. Allison of Chattanooga.
Died in Georgiana, recently, Edward Lee.
Died in Rayville, Louisiana, 2nd, Alice, child of Wiley P. and Fannie Mangham, formerly of this state.
Died in Barbour County, 6th, C.P. Long.
Died in Huntsville, 20th ult., Birdie Lawler, child.
Died at Nanafalia, 26th ult., William Russell.
Died in Clay County, 31st ult., Matthew Stewart.
Died in Tuskaloosa, 1st, Mrs. Norfleet Harris.
Died in Eutaw, 2nd, Horton Shedecor, infant.
Died in Washington County, 9th ult., Parker Ball.
Died near Gunthersville, 27th ult., Mrs. Corvin.
Died in Marshall County, 27th ult., J.C. Collier, child.
Died in Conecuh County, 29th ult., Mrs. James P. Myers.
Died in Monroe County, 30th ult., Miss Maggie Fore.
Died in Monroe County, 1st, Mrs. Mary Stainton.
Died in Conecuh County, 29th ult., Felix Sullivan.
Died in Springville, 26th ult., Miss Emma Tress(?).
Died in Troy, 30th ult., infant of Mr. and Mrs. L. B. Soles(?).
Died in Demopolis, recently, Mrs. Ada B. Jones.
Died in Eufaula, recently, Mrs. Haily.
Died in Carrolton, 1st, Mrs. Elizabeth Watts.
Died in Pickens County, 30th ult., Mr. Bridges.
Died in Carrolton, 31st ult., infant of Mr. and Mrs. E.D. Willett.

## THE SOUTHERN ARGUS - DEATHS - JUNE 1869 THROUGH JUNE 1874

Died in Pickens County, 16th ult., Miss Spruill.
Died in Pickens County, 17th ult., Mrs. Goree.
Died in Pickens County, 31st ult., Mrs. Susan Daniel.
Died in Pickens County, 31st ult., Mrs. Isham Buckhalter.
Died near Oxford, 1st, Michal Gorman, said to have been one hundred three years old.
Died near Centre, 31st ult., W.L. Munford, infant.
Died in Tallapoosa County, 16th ult., Miss Maggie J. Smith.
Died in Lincoln, 21st ult., Miss Ebedocia Knox.
Died in Gadsden, 30th ult., Robert Rian, infant.
Died near Gadsden, 29th ult., May Vann, child.
Died in Gadsden, 30th ult., Ada Eliza Condon, child.
Died in Gadsden, 31st ult., Joseph Ralls, child.
Died in Eufaula, 4th, Mrs. Carrie Berry.
Died in Winston County, 22nd ult., Orrin Davis.
Died in Tuskaloosa, 25th ult., John Thomas.
Died in Greenville, 31st ult., Lena Mastin, child.
Died in Chunnennuggee, recently, Mrs. Matilda Vann.
Died at Woodstock, 18th ult., Maria H. Sasman.
Died in Tuskaloosa, 27th ult., Ettie Burn, child.
Died at Blount Springs, 30th ult., Roberta, infant of Dr. and Mrs. Garnett.
Died near Tuskaloosa, 20th ult., Gertrude Garner, child.
Died in Arkansas, 1st ult., John Yerby, formerly of Tuskaloosa.
Died in Dale County, 30th ult., Mrs. W.J. Ward.
Died in Dale County, 30th ult., Miss Herring.
Died in Dale County, recently, child of G.F. Thompson.
Died in Dale County, recently, child of B.A. Lanier.
Died in Ozark, 31st ult., Amariah Stubbs.
Died in Russell's Valley, 18th ult., Mrs. Mary East.
Died in Decatur, 27th ult., little daughter of F. Bell.
Died near Wetumpka, recently, Rufus Greene.
Died in Hayneville, 29th ult., Ellen Seatal.
Died near Mt. Willing, 31st ult., Mrs. Mattie Gardner.
Died in Benton, 28th ult., Nellie Farley, child.
Died in Jackson County, recently, Enoch Hill.
Died in Montgomery, 31st ult., infant of Mr. and Mrs. M.J. Farrow.
Died in Tuscumbia, 30th ult., infant of J.D. Rather.
Died in Montgomery, 1st, Mrs. Thomas H. Watts.
Died in Montgomery, 4th, Mary, daughter of Rev. D.W. Gwin.
Died in Jackson County, 2nd, W.R. Grantham.
Died in Jackson County, 5th, a child of Mr. Clem.
Died in Mobile, 7th, Dr. Samuel Wolff.
Died in Mobile, 7th, Miss Lenora Hawthorn.
Died in Mobile, 7th, John Horlock.

## THE SOUTHERN ARGUS - DEATHS - JUNE 1869 THROUGH JUNE 1874

Died in St. Louis, 1st, Dr. J.L. Collins of Mobile.

The 29th ult., below Jonesboro, a man named McAlister was killed by another named Wilson.

Drake Dolbear of Clarke County was accidentally shot and badly wounded by a negro a short time ago.

Caezar Coleman (negro) was recently killed by Charles Cates (negro) in Montgomery.

John Horlock, an old citizen of Mobile, was accidentally shot and killed last Sunday morning.

James Hadley, negro, died near Choctaw Corner, July 17th, aged one hundred and fifteen years.

Died near Lebanon, Kentucky, her former home, on a visit to visit to her friends and relatives, Mrs. Fannie Keeble of Selma, Alabama, on Saturday, August 30th, 1873... [mentions little Bessie]. For several years she was a member of the Baptist Church... while convulsed with cholera to which she was a victim.

J.E. Cahall had a leg crushed recently in the Chicasabogue paper mill.

In Pickens County, 23rd ult., Stephen Fowler was shot and killed by Doc. Hyde.

The 27th ult., Mr. Bell was horribly mangled by the saw of Smith & Massey's mill, near Newton, Dale County.

In Decatur, recently, Sam Weaver was shot and killed by Hamp Crenshaw of Athens.

The infant son of Dr. and Mrs. G.H. Lenoir died in East Selma last Friday.

Died in this city, Wednesday, September 3rd, infant son of Mr. and Mrs. James S. Jacob.

Died in this city, Thursday night of last week, Charles, son of Colonel and Mrs. Martin H. Smith.
    Died in this city, September 4th, 1873, in the seventh year of his age, Charlie, son of M.H. and H.C. Smith....

## THE SOUTHERN ARGUS - DEATHS - JUNE 1869 THROUGH JUNE 1874

Thomas Jenkins of East Selma committed suicide Thursday night of last week by taking laudanum.

Felicia, daughter of Steptoe Pickett of Madison County, recently swallowed a bead with a small wire attached, with fatal results.

Issue 9-19-1873

TEXAS NEWS

Henry Croshever died in Bastrop recently.

Henry McGuire died in Hopkins County the 18th ult.

Miss Julia A. Reese died in Waco the 2nd.

Died in Waco, 23rd ult., J.W. Riley.

In Austin, recently, Thomas E. Sneed was badly cut by Sam Wright.

Died in Austin, 31st ult., Mrs. Margaret R. Bledsoe.

Died near Austin, 27th ult., Mrs. Elizabeth A. Giles.

T.H. Hargraves died in Galveston of yellow fever the 4th--the first case there.

A young man named Watkins was accidentally killed in Denton County, recently.

At Mt. Pleasant, Titus County, a Mr. McCartney was murdered by H.W. Jones and Reub. Read.

James B. Edwards died recently in Denton County.

In Lamar the 27th ult., Hugh Armstrong was killed by George Nichols.

An old man named Siemens was recently burned to death in Waco.

Bill Dixon and his father-in-law were recently killed by the Sheriff of Lampasas and his posse, whom they were resisting.

Our friend, Mr. H.C. Keeble, was called to Lebanon, Kentucky, on Tuesday last, by the sudden and serious illness of his child, who since the recent untimely death of its mother has been there in charge of its aunt. [see issue 9-12-1873]

## THE SOUTHERN ARGUS - DEATHS - JUNE 1869 THROUGH JUNE 1874

Tribute of respect: Providence in His mysterious wisdom, took from the Dixie Sabbath School on the 28th of August last, by death, Ida Macon, aged nine years......

Obituary: Died at Bladon Springs, August 11th, 1873, Emma Tabb, aged two years eight months and three days, also August 17th, John C. Tabb, aged four weeks and one day, children of Edward and Hattie N. Tabb.

### ALABAMA NEWS
E. H/ N.? Sawyer was last week lying very ill at Shelby Iron Works.

Colonel J.A. Reeves of Centre has been very ill.

### DIED IN ALABAMA
In Elyon, 10th, Ora Covington, child.
In Fayette County, 30th ult., Robert Miles.
In Cherokee County, 7th, Ezekiel Mathews, aged ninety six?/Ninety five?
At Ladiga, 9th, Charles Farmer/Parmer, child.
In Walker County, 6th, Rev. Sam'l Rutledge.
In Mobile, 10th, Asa Holt.
In Tuscumbia, 5th, Mary Warren, child.
In Covington County, recently, Jacob Ramer.
In Kushla, 9th, William Neville Forbes, child,
In Mobile, 10th, Mrs. Eugenia E. Kennedy.
In New Orleans, 8th, W. Kay, formerly of Mobile.
In Ashville, 3rd, Alta Robinson, infant.
In Clinton, 7th, Mrs. Phoebe Pascal.
In Hale County, 10th, infant of T. D. Webster.
In Tuskaloosa, 9th, Annie Horan Ralph, child.
Near Gainesville, 3th?, Miss Emma E. Eddins.
In Carrollton, 9th, Annie Nabers Stone, child.
In Calhoun County, 26th ult., W.R. Hubbard, Jr.
In Sumter County, 6th, Mrs. Hetty Nixon.
In Abbeville, 10th, child of J.F. Scale? Scade?
In Troy, 10th, Mrs. Ann Thompson.
Died in Columbia, Henry County, 30th ult., Mrs. Sarah McGriff.
Died in Meriden, Connecticut, 30th ult., Hiram Butler, formerly of Talladega.
Died Cincinnati, recently, F.R. Lord, formerly of Talladega.
Died in Talladega County, 30th ult., J.M. Ledbetter.
Died near Bellefonte, 9th, Mrs. Martha Edds.
Died in Jackson County, 10th, child of Robt. Estes.
Died in Prattville, recently, Mel. Frazer.
Died in Shreveport, Louisiana, 16th, of yellow fever, Walton W. McCain, formerly of Selma and Talladega.

## THE SOUTHERN ARGUS - DEATHS - JUNE 1869 THROUGH JUNE 1874

Jacob Ramer of Covington was recently killed by a fall from his horse.

Mrs. Mike McCarver of Gadsden has been taken to the asylum at Tuskaloosa.

Archie, son of Mr. Virgil Irwin of this county, a promising lad of about sixteen years, died the night of the 16th.

Bayless Moton, Marshal of Tuscumbia, the 9th, shot and wounded Mr. Henderson, a farmer of Colbert County.
    Marshall Moton of Tuscumbia has been held in $500 for wounding Mr. Henderson.

W.A.B. Falkner, circuit clerk of Russell, has been very sick.

                    Issue 9-26-1873

In East Perry on Friday last, Mr. W.E. Massey was shot and instantly killed by Dr. M.H. Daniel.

In the Lawrence Circuit Court, Schuyler Parshall was tried for killing conductor Oats in April 1869 and acquitted.

Rev. Thomas Wallace of Cleburne County died the 11th of snake bite.

In Clarke County the 1st, J.? Walter Malone cut and killed George C. Clements.
    A Clarke County examining court discharged Malone who killed Clements.

Died near Farmersville the 18th, Mrs. Betsy M. Cox.

John Martin of Waterloo, Lauderdale County, recently fell into a burning brick-kiln and was badly injured.

Albert Duke of Burnt Corn, was recently thrown from his horse and badly hurt.

Colonel Hundley of the *North Alabama Reporter* has been sick.

Preston Hesterly, a refugee from Georgia for a murder committed in 1865, was recently found in Lauderdale County but resisted arrest, and, though twice shot, succeeded in getting away from the officers.

Died in this county the 10th of "yellow disease," Mr. John Roller, an old, well known, and honored citizen.

## THE SOUTHERN ARGUS - DEATHS - JUNE 1869 THROUGH JUNE 1874

The DeKalb Circuit Court sends John Long to the penitentiary for life for the murder of Blevin Taylor.

Recently, in Conecuh County, Anderson Smith was shot through the arm by F.R. Lynch.

Col. J.P. Jones, late of this city, has had yellow fever at Pensacola.

Miss Kate Evans, daughter of Judge and Mrs. J.L. Evans, a young lady of lovely temper and rare accomplishments, "the idol of a large circle of friends and relatives, died in this city on Friday last the 10th inst.

### TEXAS NEWS
A Mrs. Hill and her three daughters, women of bad repute, living near Springtown, were murdered last month by unknown parties.

The 22nd ult., a woman and three men, all of bad repute, entered Springtown, Parker County, and without provocation, shot a Mr. Laird.

### Issue 10-3-1873

### TEXAS NEWS
The murderer Chassart was recently taken from the jail at Castroville and hung by a mob.

At Brenham, 17th ult., James Parrot was shot and killed by Thomas Alcorn.

Captain W. Hendley, an old Galveston merchant, is dead.

R.S. Morrow was recently assassinated in Montague County.

Colonel Battle's family in Waco were lead poisoned recently, and one child died.

### DIED IN ALABAMA
Died in Sumter County, 22nd ult., William Little.
Died near Gainesville, August 17th, James B. Ivy.
Died in Calhoun County, 20th ult., Mrs. E.A. Browning.
Died in Oxford, 21st ult., Mrs. Robert Thompson.
Died near Kymulgee, 3rd ult., Mrs. Eliza E. Nicholls.
Died in Mobile, 22nd ult., John Johnson.
Died in Gaylesville, 19th ult., Miss Alabama T. Senter.
Died in Cross Plains, 25th ult., Lela Craig, child.
Died in Cross Plains, 25th ult., Josie Sharp, child
Died in Cross Plains, 26th ult., Bettie Caldwell, child.

## THE SOUTHERN ARGUS - DEATHS - JUNE 1869 THROUGH JUNE 1874

Died in Decatur recently, Mrs. Ballew.
Died in Gadsden, 18th ult., Agnes Moody, child.
Died in Cherokee County, 17th ult., Ezekiel Matthews.
Died in Gadsden, 18th ult., Stella McCarver, child.
Died in Gadsden, 19th ult., Robert Slack, child.
Died in Coat's Bend, 14th ult., Cornelia Thornton, child.
Died in Coat's Bend, 16th ult., Julia Thornton, child.
Died in Gadsden, 22nd ult., Miss Lee Johnson, child.
Died in Marion, 22nd ult., Annie Delia Hawley, child.
Died in Somerville, Tennessee, recently, John Nicholls, formerly of Montgomery.
Died in Montgomery, 25th ult., Timothy McCarty.
Died at Fort Decatur, 16th ult., Lizzie Wagner, child.
Died in Montgomery County, 20th ult., Campbell Jones, child.
Died in Lawrence County, recently, Mrs. William Johnson.
Died in Lawrence County, recently, J.C. Roberts.
Died in Pickens County, 15th ult., Benny Gunter, child.
Died in Memphis, Alabama, 21st ult., Francis Price McCarty.
Died in Pickens County, 12th ult., infant of W.D. Allen.
Died in Mobile, 27th ult., Francis Webster.
Died in Mobile, 27th ult., William Boinkman.
Died at Beaver Meadow, 25th ult., C.P. Clarke.
Died in Demopolis, 24th ult., Mrs. E.H. McFarland.
Died near Ashland, 23rd ult., Oscar Bonner, child.
Died near Ashland, 24th ult., Ella Cole, infant.
Died in Montgomery, 24th ult., Mrs. Elizabeth Holland.
Died in Montgomery, 24th ult., S.T. Agner.
Died at Kingston, New York, 23rd ult., Lehman Marks of Montgomery.
Died in Montgomery, 26th ult., W.F.L. Morgan.
Died near Montgomery, 26th ult., C.R. Hubbard.
Died in Montgomery, 26th ult., George Becker/Beeker.
Died in Montgomery, 26th ult., child of George W. Harris.
Died at Mt. Willing, 23rd ult., Mrs. Mary Coleman.
Died in Mobile, 26th ult., Archy Benson.
Died in Mobile, 26th ult., George Cornavilla, child.
Died in Mobile, 25th ult., D.W. Henderson.
Died in Tuskaloosa County, 13th ult., W.C. Tieree.
Died in Sanford County, 13th ult., Mrs. Mary Box.
Died in Walker County, 18th ult., Mrs. Catherine Boshell.
Died in Greenville, 23rd ult., Wesley McLain.
Died at Pennsacola Junction, 21st ult., Samuel Christian.
Died in Mobile, 23rd ult., Mary Hays.
Died in Mobile, 23rd ult., Frank Mosely.
Died in Aberdeen, Mississippi, 17th ult., Mrs. David Clark of Mobile.

## THE SOUTHERN ARGUS - DEATHS - JUNE 1869 THROUGH JUNE 1874

(the following were in type for last week's paper and were crowded out only by other matter)

Died in Eufaula, 18th, H.M. Streater.
Died in La Fayette, 9th, Mrs. Hardaway.
Died in Montgomery, 20th, Miss Mary Frances Morgan.
Died in Shreveport, recently, Mrs. Springfellow, formerly of Montgomery.
Died in Shreveport, recently, Mrs. Wilson, formerly of Montgomery.
Died in Mobile, 19th, John Young.
Died in Butler County, 14th, Mrs. Edith Stephens.
Died near Wood's Station, 16th, infant daughter of Mr. and Mrs. James Wilson.
Died in Decatur, 12th, Mrs. W.E. Willard.
Died in Courtland, 9th, Mrs. Schuyler Parshall.
Died in Pond Spring, 4th, infant of Captain R.M. Clark.
Died in Opelika, 17th, Mrs. Sallie J. Beale.
Died in Columbus, Georgia, 11th, John A. Ramsey, late of Pike.
Died at Braggs, 14th, William Watson.
Died at Braggs, 14th, W.J. Underwood.
Died near Farmersville, 8th, Walter Bozeman.
Died in Mobile, 17th, Patrick Hamilton.
Died at Whistler, 15th, child of James Templeton.
Died in Hollow Square, 17th, W.G. Saddler.
Died in Greensboro, 15th, Gussie, son of A.H. Stollenwerck.
Died at Mobile, 18th, Sister Regina of the Sisters of Charity.
Died in Mobile, 18th, daughter of Michael Jordan.
Died in Mobile, 17th, Sarah Reitts, child.
Died in Mobile, 16th, W.H. Rapier.
Died in Opelika, 15th, Mrs. Dr. Hodge Drake.
Died near Choctaw Corner, 10th, Miss Fannie Waddell.
Died in Gainstown, 7th, Dr. W.W. Wilson.
Died at Jones' Bluff, 13th, child of D.W. Mitchell.
Died near Bennett's Station, 5th, infant of W.T. Jarman.
Died in Tuscumbia, 17th, Sammy Morgan.
Died in Mobile, 21st, James Bartee.
Died in Mobile, 21st, John F. Pagles.
Died in Mobile, 21st, J.R. Eastburn.
Died at Benton, 21st, Mrs. Young.
Died at Leighton, 15th, H.C. Leeky.
Died at Oak Level, 11th, Rev. T. Wallace.
Died near Moulton, 7th, W. Watkins.
Died near Courtland, 17th, Mrs. Martha Tallaferro.
Died in Cherokee County, 13th, Mrs. Mattie Sandlin.
Died in Greene County, 8th, Josephine E. Brown, child.

## THE SOUTHERN ARGUS - DEATHS - JUNE 1869 THROUGH JUNE 1874

Died in Lauderdale County, 12th, Francis W. Irvine.
Died in Gadsden, 10th, Sallie Letson, child.
Died in Gadsden, 10th, son of Mr. J.C. King.
Died in Decatur, 17th, James Sandlin.
Died in Mobile, 15th, Mrs. Ellen M. Grimes.
Died in Pot??l, Missouri, Mrs. Anne E. Hall, daughter of the late Governor Bagby.
Died at Hamburg, 9th, Rosa Estelle Blackburn, child.
Died in Lawrence County, 6th, Daley E. Hall.
Died in Ashland, 10th, John M. Bunn.
Died in Montgomery, 15th, Joseph H. Bradford.
Died in Montgomery, 15th, Mrs. A.E. James.
Died near Blount Springs, 14th, Mrs. Elizabeth McDonald.
Died in Mobile County, recently, Henry Wiggins.
Died in Montgomery, 11th, Mrs. Mary A. Farris.
Died in Montgomery, 12th, Mrs. C.L. Horton.
Died in Montgomery, 12th, John G. Schau.
Died near Pine Level, 4th, Mrs. Elizabeth Jackson.
Died in Jackson County, 8th, Mrs. Jemima Davis.
Died in Letohatchie, 6th, daughter of B.F. Dean.
Died near Mt. Willing, 11th, William Carnes.
Died in Lowndes County, 8th, Lula McQueen, child.
Died near LaFayette, 6th, A.R. Etchison.
Died in Pickens County, 10th, Mrs. Martha F. Noland.
Died in Pickens County, 11th, Mrs. Jennings.
Died in Montgomery, 20th, Miss Mary Frances Morgan.

Died Selma, Alabama, on the 3rd September, 1873, Captain A.N. Porter.... in the sleep that knows no mortal waking, the last remains of Archibald Newton Porter. A native of Mississippi, at an early age of his childhood he was, by the death of both his parents, left an orphan. Taken in charge by his uncle, Hon. Thomas A. Walker of Calhoun County, he was brought to Alabama and reared in the family of Judge Walker - by his unselfish kindness and affectionate disposition, early endearing himself to that now bereaved circle.....
Of precocious intellect and rare preparation in one so young, at an early age he was entered a student at the University of Alabama, where he made easy and rapid advancement in learning... 5th Alabama Battalion... resigning for the time the profession of the law..

John Roberts is in the Madison Jail for the murder of Charlie Boyd in 1871.

Dr. W. McElrath of Centre has been seriously ill.

## THE SOUTHERN ARGUS - DEATHS - JUNE 1869 THROUGH JUNE 1874

Near Montgomery the 24th ult., J.T. Agner was killed by Herbert A. Jones, in self defence.

The wife of Dr. M.W. Francis of Jacksonville was dangerously ill last week.

Baily Griflin, formerly of Calhoun County, was recently killed by a fall from a mule, in Lincoln County, Tennessee.

Major Miller, near Gadsden, was very ill a week ago.

Dr. W.M.A. Mitchell of Dadeville was struck with paralysis a few days ago.

On the 14th near Gadsden, one Ables was fatally stabbed by a man named Medcalf.

A week ago, John G. Means of Gadsden was sick.

John Newson, City Treasurer of Memphis, is dead of yellow fever.

Died in this city, 26th ult., Maggie Buhler, aged two years.

### Issue 10-10-1873

### TEXAS NEWS

Solomon White died from hydrophobia in San Antonio, Texas a few days since.

In Lamar County, recently, Dr. John L. Daniel was shot and killed by Stephen Tyler.

Died near Bryan, 10th ult., Edward A. Dudley, formerly of Lowndes County, Alabama, and son of J.L. Dudley.

At Denison, recently, Colonel T.C. Lipscomb shot and killed Colonel Fitzhugh.

H.H. Walker and his son Henry were murdered by Indians at Little Salt Creek, September 13th.

Mr. Goldsten of Grayson County and his wife recently perished in a well from foul air, the latter in trying to rescue her husband.

Died in Emory, 11th ult., Joshua L. Martin, a native of Tuskaloosa.
Died at Spring Station, Harrison County, 25th ult., Celsus L. Gayle, formerly of Mobile.

## THE SOUTHERN ARGUS - DEATHS - JUNE 1869 THROUGH JUNE 1874

Died in Gatesville, 24th ult., Mrs. J.H. Allen.
Died in Belton, recently, Dr. P.P. Alexander.
Died in Gatesville, 19th ult., Dr. J.M. Longmire, formerly of Alabama.

In Paris, 15th ult., one Williams shot and killed his brother-in-law, Pearson.

Died in San Antonio, Cornelius Hartnett.
Died in Belmont, 16th ult., T.D. King.

Frank C. Puett died in San Antonio the 18th ult.

Rev. G.J. Malone, a visitor from Brenham, died in Austin on the night of the 17th ult. of typhoid fever.

Arthur Bolles, a young gentleman residing in Marshall, was killed on the 17th ult. by being thrown from his horse.

Fred. McFarland, a son of Judge McFarland, died of congestive fever in Brenham on the 19th ult.

Dr. Dudley Bush of Lexington, Kentucky, is dead.

Hon. John B. Baldwin of Virginia died at Staunton the 30th ult.

Captain Jack and three other Modocs were murdered by hanging, last Friday.

Colbert County sends Green Clements to the penitentiary for ten years for killing Thos. Walker.

By a premature blast in a well, near Jones' Lane, Limestone County, an old man named Raines and a negro were killed.

Marshal Moton of Tuscumbia has been tried for shooting Henderson and acquitted.

Vincent Henry committed suicide in Mobile the 1st.

Mrs. A.B. McEackin and Mrs. E.H. King of Tuskaloosa are recovering from recent sickness.

Colonel DuBose, who recently died in Clarke, represented that county in the Legislature in 1826.

## THE SOUTHERN ARGUS - DEATHS - JUNE 1869 THROUGH JUNE 1874

Near Parton's Station, Thomas Walker was killed recently by Green Clements.

In Colbert County, Green Clements killed Thomas Walker the 24th ult., and was tried and sentenced to the penitentiary for it the next Wednesday.

The 27th ult., the locomotive of the down train on the Alabama and Chattanooga Railroad went through a trestle near Stewart's Station and Aleck Angell, engineer, was killed.

The wife of Rev. J. McLeroy, living near Harpersville, died the 27th ult. from injuries received by being thrown from her buggy.

The infant of Mr. Virgil Weaver died in this city Thursday morning.

Levi Stone, an old well-known, and greatly respected citizen of Dallas County, died in this city on tuesday last at the residence of Colonel B.M. Woolsey.

### DIED IN ALABAMA

Died in Shelby County, 26th ult., A. Garrett.
Died in Shelby County, 27th ult., Mrs. Missouri Foust.
Died near Harpersville, 27th ult., Mrs. McLeroy.
Died in Greene County, 16th ult., Miss Eugenie Roberts.
Died in Greene County, 24th ult., T.P. Horn.
Died in Mobile, 3rd, Mary E. Cosgrove.
Died in Mobile, 2nd, Mrs. Ann Scully.
Died in Athens, 27th ult., Mrs. Robert Love.
Died in Pickens County, 24th ult., infant of A.D. Howard.
Died in Lowndesboro, recently, child of Clarence Douglas.
Died in Lownesboro, 27th ult., child of Edmund Alexander.
Died in Lowndes County, 28th ult., Allen Powell.
Died in Decatur, 1st, infant of A. Maderia.
Died in Morgan County, 2nd, A.S. Blackwell.
Died near Brooklyn, Alabama, 24th ult., Morgan P. Johnson, child.
Died in Troy, 27th, Mrs. H.C. Wiley.
Died in Troy, 10th ult., "Aunt" Ann Thompson.
Died in Bullock County, 26th ult., Matthew Hall.
Died in Lauderdale County, 26th ult., Miss Mary Virginia Rowell.
Died in Mobile, 1st, Richard Jones.
Died in Mobile, 1st, John Hartley.
Died in Mobile, 2nd, Ellwood McCann.
Died in Mobile, 1st, Vincent Henry.
Died in Mobile, 1st, Benjamin Berry.
Died in Mobile, 21st ult., Mrs. Hannah E. Roberts.

## THE SOUTHERN ARGUS - DEATHS - JUNE 1869 THROUGH JUNE 1874

Died in Butler County, recently, Mark Franklin.
Died near Georgianna, recently, Dr. Harrison.
Died in Clarke County, recently, Elias H. DuBose.
Died in Madison County, 25th ult., Samuel Frotman.
Died in Mobile, 28th ult., Thomas Nugent.
Died in Mobile, 29th ult., Simon Weekes.
Died in Mobile, 29th ult., Holman R. Bidgood.
Died in Mobile, 29th ult., Carrie, infant of C.W. Murrills.
Died in Montgomery, 3rd, Putnam Larkins.
Died in Montgomery, 2nd, child of Mr. Caminade.
Died in Wetumpka, recently, Mrs. O. Kyle.
Died near Wetumpka, 4th, C.M. Cabot.
Died in Montgomery, 4th, Bryant Cunningham.
Died in Chambers County, 29th ult., Martin Hammonds.
Died in Montgomery, 6th, Henry B. Bray.
Died in Lowndes County, 6th, W.R. Powell.
Died in Montgomery, 5th, Mrs. Julia Ware.
Died in Tuskegee, 5th, Mrs. Glover of Montgomery.
Died in Mobile, 3rd, J.H. Taylor.
Died in Mobile, 3rd, Jennie Caroline Glover.
Died in Mobile, 26th ult., Miss Virginia Reins.

Issue 10-17-1873

### TEXAS NEWS

Captain Thomas McKinney died near Austin the 2nd.

Lewis C. Phillips was drowned in the flood that swept away a part of Lampasas the 27th ult.

Near Lampasas the 27th ult., Judge W. Garrett and one child and a Mr. Jones and two children were drowned in trying to escape from the flood in Burleson and Sulphur Fork Creeks.

Seven miles below Pilot Point, Lige Townly was recently killed by John Whittaker.

In Jefferson the 29th ult. Dick Brooks was killed by Joe Lane.

Dr. M.H. Daniel, charged with killing W.E. Massey in Perry County, has been held in a $10,000 bond.

A little boy aged six years, son of Mr. William Langston, living nine miles north of Marion, was smothered to death in a pile of cotton on the 6th.

## THE SOUTHERN ARGUS - DEATHS - JUNE 1869 THROUGH JUNE 1874

In the Etowah Circuit Court a verdict was given in favor of the county in a suit by Mrs. Lee for $5,000 for the killing of her husband by disguised parties.

Died in Shreveport, Louisiana, of yellow fever on the 26th of September, Julius Ormand(?) formerly of Greenville, Alabama. Montgomery and Greenville papers will please copy.

Died near Warrenton on Monday night last the 13th inst., Mrs. E.W. Wade.

Died in this city Monday last, Thomas C., son of Mr. and Mrs. Joseph S. Brooks.

About two weeks since, Mr. W.B. Harper of the firm of Shackelford & Harper of this city lost by death an interesting child of eleven months.

The child of Dr. T.O. Summers of Greensboro died of diphtheria.

### DIED IN ALABAMA
Died in Dale County, 4th, Nettie Dowling, child
Died in Auburn, 7th, John S. Pollard.
Died near Rocky Mount, 6th, Rev. Wiley Lloyd.
Died in Opelika, 9th, Thomas Mizell.
Died in Opelika, 4th, son of George Smith.
Died in Tuscumbia, 8th, Robbie Moton, child.
Died near Bridgeville, 29th ult., Mrs. Martha A. Hood.
Died in Pickens County, 26th ult., Mrs. B.E. Henry.
Died in Mobile, 7th, Robert D. Post.
Died in Mobile, 7th, Dr. Frank M. Stone.
Died near Mt. Hilliard, 24th ult., William Boswell.
Died in Bullock County, 26th ult., Thomas Barker, child.
Died in Bullock County, 2nd, Eva Lee Barker, child.
Died in Evergreen, 2nd, Chesley Sampey, infant.
Died in Evergreen, 3rd, Wilson Kendall.
Died near Burnt Corn, 1st, Lawrence Taff.
Died in Mobile, 9th, J.S. Secor.
Died in Greensboro, 3rd, son of Dr. and Mrs. T.O. Summers.
Died in Eutaw, 28th ult., Fannie, infant of Mr. and Mrs. J.D. Steele.
Died in South Carolina, 9th ult., only child of J.P. Little of Greene County.
Died in Wilcox County, 16th ult., W.W. Sheffield.
Died in Choccolocco Valley, 2nd, John Borders.
Died in Meridian, 1st, Feister Foy, one of the old settlers of Sumter County.
Died in Tuskaloosa County, Ben Massingale.
Died in Marion, 4th, Mary Binion, child of Mr. and Mrs. J.B. Cooke.
Died near Gaylesville, 2nd, Mrs. Cartledge.

## THE SOUTHERN ARGUS - DEATHS - JUNE 1869 THROUGH JUNE 1874

Died in Gaylesville, 4th, George C. McConnell, child.
Died at Long View, Texas, 18th ult., R.L. Mackey, formerly of Cherokee County.
Died in Montgomery, 11th, R.B. Ryan.
Died in Montgomery, 10th, W.F. Moncrief.
Died in Montgomery, 10th, Elsey Myers.
Died in Macon County, 8th, B.F. Foster.
Died in LaFayette, 3rd, Charles McLendon, infant.
Died in Abbeville, 4th, Dora Stokes, child.
Died in Texas, 18th August, John A. Murphy, formerly of Henry County.
Died recently, Mrs. Henry Worthy Wiley of Pike County.
Died at Whistler, recently, Thomas Lewis.
Died in Montgomery, 9th, Benjamin F. Burton.
Died at Cunningham Station, 7th, James Farley.
Died in Montgomery, 10th, John W. Parker.
Died in Montgomery, 9th, Charles A. Harris.
Died in Montgomery, 9th, child of John C. Scott.
Died in Montgomery, 9th, Mr. McKittrick.
Died near Pensacola, ?th, Mrs. Mary C. Falconer, formerly of Montgomery.
Died in Montgomery, 14th, John Tyler Tisdale.
Died in Montgomery, 13th, Henry Sparrenberger, child.
Died in Montgomery, 13th, Mrs. Sarah Booth.
Died in Montgomery County, 14th, Dr. G.M. Merriwether.
Died in Barbour County, 5th, Miss Mary Williams.
Died in Mobile, 9th, Mrs. Eugenia E. Kennedy.
Died in Montgomery, 12th, Samuel Fight.

Issue 10-24-1873

Pat Ragland, Secretary of State, died in Jackson County the other day.

T.R. Terry, manager of the Southern and Atlantic telegraph line, died the 20th about thirty miles east of Montgomery.

D.V. Gregory has been elected city clerk of Birmingham, vice R.B. Ryan, dead.

The reported death at Waco, Texas of Geo. Tankersly, Wallace Varner and Bethel Varner, ex-Alabamians, was unfounded.

Mr. C.H. Williams, formerly of this city, was killed by a negro on a plantation near Linden on Tuesday last; but no particulars have been received here.

## THE SOUTHERN ARGUS - DEATHS - JUNE 1869 THROUGH JUNE 1874

At Brooklyn the 11th, W.D. Kennedy was shot and dangerously wounded by A. Leonard.

Mrs. Sumter Lea, who has been dangerously ill, is better today, and we trust sincerely will soon be restored to health.
    Died at the residence of Mr. J.D. Hill in Dallas County on Monday last, Fannie, daughter of Mr. and Mrs. Sumter Lea of Selma, aged two years and nine months; and their infant son died at their residence in the city on Wednesday last.

### TEXAS NEWS

The following were the deaths in Calvert the 12th and 13th: Mrs. Dr. Gilson, Mrs. Baker, Miss E. McCarkle, Mrs. Stamp, Mr. Brooks, photographer, Mr. McDaniels, railroad agent, J. Lipke, servant of Mr. Montgomery, and three blacks.

The 25th ult. unknown persons murdered W. Reps Crowder about fifteen miles below Gatesville.

Died in Gatesville, 23rd ult., Mrs. Jeffersonia Allen, formerly of Lawrence County, Alabama.

Dr. W.B. Field, Mr. C.A. McDaniels, and Mrs. C.A. McDaniels are among the recent dead in Calvert.

Miss Annie, youngest daughter of Judge Edwin Waller of Waller County, is dead.

Died at Richmond the 28th ult., Max Franklin, an old citizen.

Mr. C. Fink, an old citizen of La Grange, is dead.

Tribute of respect from the teachers of Dallas Academy, October 20, 1873, on the death of fellow-teacher, Miss Kate E. Evans...

Near Harpersville the 11th, Thomas Nelson killed a negro named Randall Scott.

In Cherokee County the 11th, Henry Allread was killed by James Westmoland, Jack Kidd, and Fell Daniel.

Mr. J.A. Bilbro of the Opelika Locomotive has been very sick with typhoid fever.

# THE SOUTHERN ARGUS - DEATHS - JUNE 1869 THROUGH JUNE 1874

## DIED IN ALABAMA

Died in Bladon Springs, 11th, Mrs. Lottie P. Long.
Died near Benton, recently, Charles W. Hartwell.
Died in Montgomery, 16th, John Yung.
Died in Montgomery, 17th, child of William Owen.
Died in Montgomery, 17th, James T. Jewell.
Died near Montgomery, 17th, infant of J.R. Adams.
Died in Montgomery, 17th, Jacob Holzer.
Died in Decatur, 15th, infant of J.J. Woodall.
Died in Union Springs, 12th, M.A. Baldwin.
Died in Wills?? Valley, 10th, Mrs. Missouri Crump.
Died in Gadsden, 12th, child of James T. Sutton.
Died Near Bridgeville, 11th, Miss Alice Duncan.
Died In Tuscumbia, 14th, Mrs .H.C. Harrington.
Died In Limestone County, 7th, Dr. Hal C. Bibb.
Died in Ambersom, 5th, Sallie R. White, child.
Died in Tuskaloosa County, 1st, Presley Matthews.
In Greensboro, 11th, James E. Griggs.
Died in Greensboro, 13th, Mrs. Eliza Hobson.
Died in Tishabee, 11th, Robert A. Tucker.
Died near Cuba Station, recently, Miss Eliza Lynn.
Died in Evergreen, recently, child of E.W. Martin.
Died in Opelika, 9th, Emmet Mizel.
Died in Montgomery, 15th, Francis Widmer.
Died in Cherokee County, 8th, child of J.M. Wilson.
Died near Centre, 12th, daughter of J.F. Wester.
Died in Marion, 13th, John Burnett.
Died in Marion, 12th, Henry Raphael, child.
Died in Marengo County, 8th, David Espy.
Died in Courtland, 10th, Mrs. Eliza Weatherford.
Died in Pickens County, 12th, Mrs. M.A. Clarke.
Died in Mobile, 14th, D.G. Turner.
Died in Mobile, 19th, infant of Rev. J.W. Rush.
Died in Mobile, 20th, Mrs. Ira H. Ricker.
Died in Ozark, Dale County, 11th, Wiley Balkum.
Died in Ozark, Dale County, 15th, Joshua T. Hood.
Died at Gordon, 14th, Dempsey Harrel/Harvell.
Died in Montgomery, 20th, Miss Fanny Stewart.
Died in Montgomery, 20th, Gains Kibbie.
Died in Montgomery, 18th I.N. Hard/Hurd
Died in Montgomery, 18th, H.H. Booth, child.
Died in Montgomery, 18th, Geo. E. Coupee.
Died in Montgomery, 19th, Harriett Hereford.
Died in Montgomery, 15th? 16th?, Mrs. Ella S. Berrs/Beggs

## THE SOUTHERN ARGUS - DEATHS - JUNE 1869 THROUGH JUNE 1874

Died in Montgomery, Richard Diamond.
Died in Montgomery, 19th, child of R.B. Ryan.
Died in Marion, 15th, Gideon E. Nelson.
Died in Marion, 16th, Robert Kennon.
Died in Marion, 19th, _____ Baker of Louisiana.
Died in Jackson County, recently, Pat Raglan.
Died in Montgomery County, 20th, T.R. Terry.
Died in Pensacola, 10th, Calvin Knight of Tallapoosa County.
Died in Lowndes County, 14th, infant of John Hagood.
Died in Montgomery County, 16th, Murdoch Mitchell, child.
Died in Sumter County, 5th, Fannie Lee Stanton, child.
Died in Montgomery County, 30th ult., Bessie Roughton, infant.
Died in Madison County, 23rd ult., child of J.W. Travis.
Died in Philadelphia, 10th, Henry M. Richards of Mobile.
Died in Cahaba Valley, 25th ult., Major William McDuff.
Died in Arkansas, 1st, Lawson Withers, late of Madison County.
Died in Little Rock, 13th, Joseph Keith, son of Hon. S.D. Hale of this state.

Issue   10-31-1873

Dr. S.B. Beresford, who died recently in Hartford, is said to have owned the finest gallery of paintings in Connecticut.

### TEXAS NEWS

Ed. Rosenau was recently found dead in the road ten miles from Brenham.

From September 27th to October 15th, the following white persons had died in Calvert:---Mrs. Haynes, Phil Taylor, Mr. Marks, Mrs. Williams, Mr. Williams, Miss Bettie Girard, Mr. Wicks, Mr. Knapp, Dr. Wilson, Sam Bergman, S. Harrell, boy, Mrs. Montgomery, James Cassdes, Mr. Girard, Lee Rector, Herman Hammen, J.A. Moore, Johnny Cain, infant, Mrs. A. Glass, Joe Wright, Julius Hermann, Dr. W.B. Fields, Mary Shirley, Mrs. McDaniel, Mrs. Gibson, Mrs. H. Wicks, John Watson, Mrs. Keeze, a child of the street, Miss Emma Barnes, Alex Montgomery, Mr. Wicke, Tom Williams, Mrs. Stamp, Wm. Regensberger, Major Tillman, child of H. Wicks, J. Schmeidler, child of Mrs. Chevalier, Mr. Brooks, Mr. McDaniel, Mrs. W. Baker, Mr. Lipke, and Miss Ella McCarkle.

Dr. Attaway, an old citizen of Rusk County, died the 10th.

Professor Thomas Baker died in Austin the 13th.

John Eaton, charged with the murder of Isham Bullard, has been jugged in Wood County.

## THE SOUTHERN ARGUS - DEATHS - JUNE 1869 THROUGH JUNE 1874

A special from Galveston, the 22nd, to the *New Orleans Picayune*, says the fever is very bad at Columbus and that among the dead were J.W. Harcourt and Hon. G./O/ C. W. Smith.

### ALABAMA NEWS

B.F. Ashley of Ashville has been dangerously ill.

In Evergreen, 15th, Elijah Bone was shot and killed by Marion Wood. The farm of J.R. Lowe, deceased, on Coosa River in Cherokee County, recently sold for $19,000.

Dr. McGhee's residence near Fayetteville was burned the 21st; his wife had died the day before from the effects a burning received while attempting to fill a lighted kerosene lamp.

Westmoland is in the jail at Centre for the murder of Allread a few weeks ago.

Miss Ida Woodliff of Gadsden, who has been very sick, is convalescing.

### DIED IN ALABAMA

In Montgomery, 22nd, Miss Mollie Sparrenger.
In Montgomery, 20th, Mrs. Dr. Hereford.
In Montgomery, 23rd, Miss A. Barthelot.
In Montgomery, 22nd, G.H. B. Matthews.
In Mobile, 20th, C.C. Colton.
In Baltimore, 21st, Rev. F.R. Hanson of Demopolis.
Near Greensboro, 17th, Alfred Thigpen.
In Newbern, 19th, Katie Hatch, child.
At Arcola, 22nd, son of Alfred Hatch.
Near Greensboro, 18th, infant of Benjamin S. Evans.
Near Greensboro, 23rd, child of B.S. Evans.
Near Montevallo, 21st, Mrs. Benjamin Randall.
In Gadsden, 18th, child of R. O. Randall.
Near Fayetteville 20th, Mrs. Dr. McGhee.
In Brooklyn, 21st, James N. Strange.
In Sumter County, recently, L.V. Underwood.
In Gadsden, 19th, child of J.P. Cooper.
In Montgomery, 23rd, Mrs. Mary G. Booth.
In Montgomery, 23rd, Mrs. Sarah Winter.
In Columbus, Georgia, 22nd, S.F. Miller, formerly of Tuskaloosa.
In Dale County, 18th, Wiley Strickland.
In Dale County, 19th, Mrs. Wiley Strickland.
Near Rockey Head, recently, Old Mrs. Trant.
Near Patsalaga, 9th, Mrs. Sarah Saunders and two infants.

## THE SOUTHERN ARGUS - DEATHS - JUNE 1869 THROUGH JUNE 1874

In Butler County, 15th, Benjamin Griswold.
Near Roanoke, 21st, D.C. Worrell.
In Opelika, 21st, Miss Cecilia Alford.
In Tuskaloosa, 16th, infant of B.B. Lewis.
In Talladega, 22nd, infant of I. Knox Albright.
In Tuskegee, 18th, infant of Mr. M.R. Scullins.
In Tuskegee, 16th, William Miller.
In Montgomery, 22nd, Mrs. H.G. Hille.
In Montgomery, 22nd, Lou A. Wilson.
In Cropwell, 21st, John W. Jones.
Near Scottsboro, 26th, Mrs. Lucy V. Garland.
In Scottsboro, 27th, Mrs. Ellis.
In Jefferson County, 27th, Timothy Neaves.
In Montgomery, 27th, Miss Ruth Brittan.
In Montgomery, 24th, Emmet Brittan.
In Montgomery, 27th, Jacob Marks.
In Montgomery, 26th, Pedro Caminade.
In Montgomery, 26th, Mrs. Fannie Shields.
In Montgomery, 24th, John Links.
In Montgomery, 27th, John B. Jones.
In Montgomery, 24th, Jessie R. Jones.
In Montgomery, 25th, John C. Jones.
In Montgomery, 27th, Miss Emma Berthelot.
In Montgomery, 26th, Mary Ann Padgett.
In Montgomery, 26th, A.F. Fawcett.
In Montgomery, 27th, Sarah Mass.
In Mobile, 18th, infant of Rev. J.E. Foust.
In Mobile, 11th, Alexander Shedden.
In Greenville, 24th, J.K. Munchus.
Near Benton, 18th, Quintillia Grumbles, child.
Near Benton, recently, Charles Hartwell.
Near Farmersville, 14th, Susan Wheeler, child.
Near Farmersville, 26th, Edward Dudley, Sr.
In Lawrenceville, 26th, Rev. John Cassaday.
Near Scottsboro, recently, Franklin Watts was badly stabbed by Thomas Howard.

In a recent family fray in Sanford County, John Pennington killed his father-in-law, mortally wounded his brother-in-law, and dangerously stabbed his mother-in-law.

Obituary. Died on the 20th of October 1873, Mrs. Emma B. Higgins, in her twenty-fifth year, of bronchitis, at the residence of her father, Mr. John T. Bender of Pleasant Hill, Dallas County, Alabama.

## THE SOUTHERN ARGUS - DEATHS - JUNE 1869 THROUGH JUNE 1874

Only a little more than two years have passed since I wrote the following:- "Married, in Pleasant Hill, Alabama, June 19th, 1871, at the residence of the bride's father by the Rev. Mr. Ware, Mr. Geo. Y. Higgins to Miss Emma Bender......A friend...

Mrs. Higgins had been for about nine years and was at the time of her death a -----member of the Presbyterian Church, and was the mother of an interesting little girl of about fourteen months when the love and will of her Heavenly Father said, "Come up higher"... a devoted child, sister, wife, mother, friend.

Died in Liberty Hill, Sunday morning, October 12th, Pattie B., daughter of the late Mr. A.E. and Mrs. K.L. Bayol, aged fourteen years.

Died in East Selma, Sunday evening last the 26th, Miss Nannie Law.

The *Hayneville Examiner* says:--By the death of Mr. Riggs of Louisiana, Dr. Kendall of Benton, and a sister of the deceased in Dallas, are said to inherit property valued at about $40,000.

Near Scottsboro, recently, Franklin Watts was badly stabbed by Thomas Howard.

Neander H. Rice of Launderdale has been appointed secretary of state, vice Pat Ragland, dead.

Issue 11-7-1873

TEXAS NEWS

The following deaths were reported at Calvert for the 19th and 20th ult.:--- Mrs. Farrand/Earrand, Mrs. Schrigner, Charles Solomon, Frank Maddox, John McDaniel, L. Wickel, Miss Bailey, Mr. Allard, Mr. Mendez, Miss Grillo.

Henry Dougall recently died near Tyler.

Dr. Russell of Weston recently died in Denison.

Judge H.L. Stuart died in Smith County the 14th ult.

Beverly K. Johnston, an eminent lawyer, died in Abingdon, Virginia, 23rd ult.

Heenan, the prize fighter, died of consumption.

Died in this city, Thursday, October 30th, Robert H. Wellington.

## THE SOUTHERN ARGUS - DEATHS - JUNE 1869 THROUGH JUNE 1874

The death of Mr. J.E. McCraw on Wednesday evening last struck from our social circles a brilliant light, and took ?? the ranks of our business men one of the most capable and faithful of the --nger? ones of their number.

Mrs. Sarah Hall, aged one hundred three years, died in Conceuh the other day.

Jack Cole of Coffee County was recently killed by Tom Nobles.

M.F. Coker of Tuskaloosa has been very sick and is getting well.

Dr. Fars, who has been dangerously ill, is convalescing.

We regret to state that General Hardee is in a worse health than for some months past, and that his friends here entertain the greatest apprensions [sic] of the result of his illness. Colonel and Mrs. Roy left here yesterday morning for his bedside in Wytheville, Virginia; and he will probably arrive at home today on a special car fitted up for his use. There is still room to hope that the fears of this community, exaggerated it may be by the general interest in his welfare and the universal affection borne him, may not be realized and that he will still be spared to us who honor him so much and love him so sincerely.

### DIED IN ALABAMA
In Tuskaloosa County, 23rd ult., John Vanzant.
In Montgomery, 28th, W.T. McCutchen.
In Cropwell, 25th ult., John W. Jones.
In Shelby County, 25th ult., Samuel Baker.
In Montgomery, 20th ult., Charles E. Stewart.
In Etowah County, 23rd ult., John Shepherd.
In Etowah County, 23rd ult., Josephine Fergarson, child.
In Gadsden, 21th ult., Carrie Belle Bowen, child.
In Gadsden, 26th ult., Emma L. Kyle, child.
In Mobile, 28th ult., Mrs. Gates.
In Walker County, 23rd ult., Perilee Richardson, child.
In Brooklyn, 20th ult., H.M. Blow, child.
In Huntsville, 27th ult., Mrs. Kate McDonald.
In Conecuh County, 26th ult., Mrs. Sarah Hale.
In Conecuh County, 26th ult., Leonidas Hale.
In Hale County, 24th ult., Lemuel Wilson.
In Hale County, 10th ult., Ransom Day.
In Uniontown, 29th ult., Dr. G.N. Ware.
In Lowndes County, 20th ult., Jesse Perdne.
In Lowndes County, 23rd ult., John Ritchey.

## THE SOUTHERN ARGUS - DEATHS - JUNE 1869 THROUGH JUNE 1874

At Braggs, 27th ult., child of M.R.P. Moorer.
Near Auburn, 27th ult., John Brown.
In Montgomery, 30th ult., Mrs. Sarah Slorah.
In Montgomery, 30th ult., Edward Haley.
In Montgomery, 30th ult., James Alexander.
In Italy, July 17th, Anthony M. Barelli, formerly of Mobile.
In Montgomery, 2nd, E. Carroll.
In Montgomery, 2nd, Miss Fannie Smith.
In Montgomery, 2nd, Mrs. Wise.
In Montgomery, 3rd, Miss Adele Hanson.
In Montgomery, 2nd, Lillie Winter.
In Montgomery, 1st, Hannah Mason.

Issue 11-14-1873

William Gordon of Lowndes County was run over by a passing train at Brierfield Iron Works, recently, and instantly killed.

In the case of Hooper for killing Phillips, a change of venue has been taken to Russell County.

In Lowndes County, recently, Joseph Mastin was shot and badly wounded by Julius Middlebrooks.

Died at her residence near Pleasant Hill on the evening of the 7th inst., Mrs. Mattie Powell Saffold, wife of Dr. A.H. Saffold.

William Parton is in the Monroe Jail for killing a man named Martin some time ago.

Owing to the bad health of its proprietor, Captain J.M. Macon, the *Eufaula Times* will be sold at public outcry December 1st if not previously sold.

Tribute of respect on the death of Lieutenant-General William J. Hardee. The impressive funeral services at St. Paul's Church...

Robert McQueen of Hayneville is sick.

### DIED IN ALABAMA

At Hoboken, 25th ult., W.W. Cowan.
Near Hoboken, 30th ult., J.W. McMillian.
In Lawrence County, recently, Mrs. T. Perry.
In Lauderdale County, recently, Mrs. Jones.
In Moorsville, 30th, Robert B. Peebles.

## THE SOUTHERN ARGUS - DEATHS - JUNE 1869 THROUGH JUNE 1874

In Athens, 30th, W.S. Peebles.
In Colbert County, 27th ult., Christian Snidow.
In Tuskaloosa, 1st, M.F. Coker.
In Claiborne, 28th, Felix Chaudron.
In Mobile, 7th, Mrs. Jacobina Steidel.
In Montgomery, 7th, W.J. Howard.
At Fort Deposit, 1st, D.J. Rivers.
In Lowndes County, 3rd, Jack Neeley.
At Brierfield, recently, Wm. Gordon.
Near Eufaula, 1st, J.B. Burnley.
Near Clayton, 4th, Asa Blakey.
Near Mt. Andrew, 4th, Lewellen Earp.
In Mobile, 4th, Miss Elizabeth Jane Crowe.
In Mobile County, 4th, Mrs. Mary Wootan.
In Montgomery County, 5th, D.S. French.
In Montgomery, 5th, Michael Harkins.
In Montgomery, 6th, Philip O'Dwyer.
In Greenville, 4th, Mrs. P.B. Waters.
In Montgomery, 4th, Wm. C. Waller.
In Montgomery, 3rd, Mrs. S.D. Walker.
In Montgomery, 3rd, Miss Frances E. Smith.
In Montgomery, Luther Swank.
In Conecuh County, Mrs. Fannie Cobb.
In Walker County, 25th ult., Daniel Burket.
In Perry County, 2nd, Robert Underwood.
In Eufaula, 5th, E.C. Ellington.
In Mobile, 7th, Mrs. V. Hurtel.
In Mobile, 7th, Aristede Bouillemet, infant.
In Montgomery, 8th, Miss Rose Robinson.
In Montgomery, 9th, B.F. Mitchell.
In Montgomery, 10th, Reeve Lewis.
In Montgomery, 10th, Leroy Taylor.
In Pickens County, 2nd, William A. Gaskin.
In Pickensville, 1st, John David Johnson.
In Lawrence County, recently, Mrs. Mary E. Holland.
Near Luther's Store, 2nd, child of J.S. Norred.
In Lawrence County, recently, Miss Temple Johnson.
Near Olney, recently, George Summerville, formerly of Pickens County.
In Mississippi, 25th ult., Andrew Norris, formerly of Tuskaloosa County.
In Montgomery, 5th, Mrs. Eliza Jane Chappell.
In Sherman, Texas, recently, Dr. Jo Fennet, formerly of Pickens County.

## THE SOUTHERN ARGUS - DEATHS - JUNE 1869 THROUGH JUNE 1874

Tribute of respect from Meridian Sun Lodge #88, F and A.M., convened at Shiloh Church, on Saturday the 26th of October, 1873 on the death of Levi Stone, who died in the city of Selma on the 7th inst....stricken widow and children.

Issue 11-21-1873

TEXAS NEWS

Bannister, recently convicted of murder in Houston, has been granted a new trial.

Henry McDougall, near Tyler, was caught in the running gear of his gin and fatally injured.

Tom Faulkner is to be hung at Fort Mason for the murder of a man named Howling.

Died in Austin, 31st, W.C. Tomlinson.

Eight hundred dollars reward is offered for the apprehension of the murderer of John P. Fries, late Sheriff of Kenney County.

Died in Tyler, 4th inst., Larkin C. Selman, formerly of Alabama.

Judge Dotty died at Columbus the 7th.

DIED IN ALABAMA

In Eufaula, 9th, Mrs. Sarah Clayton.
In Eufaula, 9th, Mrs. Sarah Clifford Macon.
In Montgomery, 14th, infant of Mrs M.J. Parker.
In Talladega, 17th, Mrs. Mary Curry.
In Eutaw, 8th, Miss Sallie A. Dunlap.
Near Centre, 5th, Jimmie Henson, child.
In Tuskaloosa, 7th, Mrs. Sarah J. Burn.
In Tuskaloosa, 6th, Corla Lee Henry, child.
In Pickens County, 9th, Martin Holley.
In Pickens County, 9th, John Nations.
In Union Springs, 10th, A.M. Williams.
In Mobile, 10th, Miss Lela Agnes Dunn.
In Etowah County, 17th ult., Thomas L. Hester, child.
In Etowah County, 30th ult., Sallie Gay, child.
In Etowah County, 4th, Della Gay, child.
In Etowah County, 10th, Margaret Gay, child.
In Gadsen, 6th, Mollie Lafaulette, child.

## THE SOUTHERN ARGUS - DEATHS - JUNE 1869 THROUGH JUNE 1874

In Waterloo, 6th, P.H. Cunningham.

Little Rosa Clanton Burns, daughter of John F. Burns, a child wonderfully intelligent and precocious, the idol of her parents heart, died last Friday.

Dr. C.F. Fars/Fahs, one of our eminent citizens, one of our most distinguished physicians, died in Griffin, Georgia, Monday evening last. As a man, he was upright, conscientious, faithful in every position, and diligent in the discharge of every learning. In his profession he united great learning, long experience, and the finest abilities. He was loved and honored and trusted by all who knew him and this community deplores his loss as a public calamity.

Judge Brickell has been very ill in Huntsville.

The wife of Hon B.H. Epperson died in Marion County a few days ago.

Tuskloosa Circuit Court sends Cates to the penitentiary for eight years for murder.

In the Tuskaloosa Circuit Court, Wade (negro) was convicted of rape and will be hung.

In the Madison Circuit Court, Henry Beasley, for killing Joe Todd in Limestone County, was sentenced to the penitentiary for eleven years.

The lands of the estate of John Ritters of Sumter County, were sold last week at $5,771/2 an acre.

An old man named Shearer was run over at Opelika, recently, by a railroad train and killed.

Richard Cary, a freight conductor on the Memphis and Charleston Railroad, was knocked off a car, recently, near Tuscumbia, and killed.

The estimable wife of Capt. J.M. Macon of the *Eufaula Times* is dead.

Issue  11-28-1873

TEXAS NEWS

Died in Bellville the 3rd, James Foster Cochrane.

Mrs. Cruchfield died in Dallas the 12th.

C.C. Waters died recently in Paris.

## THE SOUTHERN ARGUS - DEATHS - JUNE 1869 THROUGH JUNE 1874

Isaac Coleman, Alderman of Houston, died the 14th.

Monroe Robert (negro) of Marion County has been assassinated by other negroes because he was a democrat.

The following is a complete list of those who died of yellow fever during the recent epidemic in Calvert: Dr. Wilson, Mrs. T.C. Glass, Mrs. Haynes, Phil Taylor, John Marks, H.E. Williams, John Knapp,Mrs. Emma Williams, C. Wicke, Miss Bettie Girard, Sam Bergman, child of Sam Harrel [,] James Castles, Thomas Girard, L.? Rector, Herman Hammon, J.A. Moore, Johnnie Cain, Joseph Wright, child of R.E. Kamp, J.A. Watson, Mrs. Andrew Glass, Mrs. Kessee, Dr. W.B. Field, Miss Shirley, Mrs. McDanniel, Jules Herman, Miss Ella McCorkle, J.W. Brooks, Mrs. W.C. Gilson, Mrs. Wicke, H. Wicke, Mrs. Stump, Mrs. W.A. Baker, Ada Wicke, Miss Emma Barnes, W.A. Baker, T.J. Williams, miller, Colonel Tillman, Alex. Montgomery, L. Schmeidler, W. Regensburger, Sam Harred, Dr. W.C. Gilon, Mrs. Rowell, Freddie Haldeman, Charley Wallace, George F. Randolph, Curtis George, Mrs. T.J. McHugh, C. Solomon, George W. Brown, Mrs. Ihringer?, Mrs. George W. White, Louis Wicke, Miss Rosa Forsander, H.A. Morel, Miss Lottie Parker, L.H. Bailey, Miss Lottie Marks, J.C. Sabin, child of C. Lazard, Frank Maddox, Mortimer Allard, George Menses, Amelia Sterling, John McDanniel, Mrs. George Jefferies, Mrs. McCarthy, Mrs. H. Bergman, Mr. Bemuth, Mrs. Henry Hust, A.D. Leonard, Miss Bettie Lovett, Mr. Estes, D.B. Schnebley, Mrs. Peevey, Dr. R.A. Crawford, Miss Dunlap, Miss May Haynes, Richard Blake, child of Mr. Street, Z. Rowell, Phinney Bergman, Mrs. Z. Rowell, Charles Childers, John Volle, George Couter/Conter, James Bush, child of Stricker, L. Elkins, Mrs. Joseph Strupper, Mrs. Hodge, Captain J. W. Beard, Mr. Alexander, child of Kaiser, Mrs. Allard, Mrs. Thomas Girard, Eugene Hymas, Richard Schmeidler, Isaac Einstein, child of Henry Hust, Spencer Lahue, Captain A.C. Read, Mrs. Love, Mrs. Ashe, Owensville: Charles Lipke, W.F. Hughes, refugee from Shreveport: Mrs. J.S. Montgomery, Mr. McDanniel, railroad agent, child of Mrs. Chevelier, Roll Lundy, nurse, of Galveston.

### ALABAMA NEWS

Louisa Snyder, a German woman, committed suicide a few days ago in Mobile.

The wife of P.T. Barnum died the 20th.

Ex-Senator John P. Hale of New Hampshire is dead.

S.P. Watson, now of St. Louis, formerly of Eutaw, accidently shot and badly wounded himself in the latter place on the 19th.

## THE SOUTHERN ARGUS - DEATHS - JUNE 1869 THROUGH JUNE 1874

In Walker County the 15th, John Miller was fatally cut by J. Romine.

At Fitzpatrick's station the 19th, Ed. Napier and Clarke Thompson shot and wounded each other.

R. H. McKevy of Moulton has been very sick.

DIED IN ALABAMA

In Uniontown, 20th, Mrs. Spangler.
In Randolph County, 27th ult., child of W.B. Nicholls.
In Calhoun County, 16th, Mrs. Daniel Boozer.
In Eufaula, 18th, Owen Sherry.
In Eufaula, 18th, infant of G.W. Barfield
In Hayneville, 21st, Rob Carson.
In Litohatchie, 13th, Crawford Grant.
In Hayneville 18th, infant of Mrs. Sheehane
In Butler County, 11th, Sarah Virginia Wood, child.
In Limestone County, 17th, child of D.R. Echerberger.
Near Livingstone, 18th, Mrs. Mary A.V. Sprott.
In Limestone County, 18th, John Black.
In Pike County, 13th, E.S. Owen.
In Pike County, 13th, infant of A.H. Owen.
In Hale County, 13th, Mrs. B.H. Dorroh.
In Hale County, 13th, Lutie Ola Sample.
In Eutaw, 16th, Mrs. Honoria Braune.
In Eutaw, 19th, Mrs. Annie Perkins.
In Tuskaloosa, 17th, T.S. Johnson.
In Etowah County, 17th, Mrs. Sarah Leek.
Near Gadsden, 14th, Miss Cassie Owens.
In Gadsden, 16th, Elijah Powell.
In Montgomery, 19th, infant of James McManus.
In Mobile, 18th, Mrs. L.E. Bond.
In Pensacola, 13th, C.E. Elmore, formerly of Alabama.
In Mobile, 18th, Michael C. Stevens.
In Ashville, 17th, infant of John Nelson.
Near Marion, 4th, Willie Dedlake.
In Perry County, recently, Mr. Tidwell.
Near Georgiana, recently, Mr. Little.
In Baldwin County, 15th ult., William T. Anderson.
In Gordon, 20th, J.D. Leslie.
In Wilcox County, 10th, Nathan Gerald.
In Mobile, 24th, Mrs. Mary Lynch.
In Mobile, 23rd, Major R.F. Knott.

## THE SOUTHERN ARGUS - DEATHS - JUNE 1869 THROUGH JUNE 1874

Issue 12-5-1873

### ALABAMA NEWS

R.A. Kennedy of Seale died the other day of small-pox contracted at the Macon fair. [see below]

The night of the 23rd ult. in Florence, Robert White was badly stabbed by William Barnes.

At Iron Mountain Iron works the 19th, a man named Gates shot and wounded one Williams and also his (Gates's) wife.

Life insurance decision, circuit court, W.E. Tait, et al, Heirs of Doctor Samuel Bond, deceased vs. New York Life Insurance Company...

Rev. Dr. Hamilton of Tuslakoosa is, we regret to learn, in bad health.

A son of Mrs. Jernigan near Brewton, recently accidentally shot and wounded his little sister.

Vandy Hearn of Lee County was thrown from a wagon recently and killed.

Jos. McGhee, Jr. has been dangerously sick at Lebanon, Dekalb County.

Mrs. C.A. Shives, moving from North Carolina to Mississippi, was thrown from her wagon in Walker County the 20th ult., and killed.

Tribute of respect from Pea Ridge Grange on the memory of E.S. Owens, a member of that grange.

### DIED IN ALABAMA
In Seale, 23rd ult., R.A. Kennedy. [see above]
In Greenville, 10th/19? ult., Mrs. Rosina Beck.
In Wetumpka, 14th ult., Mrs. L.S. Greene.
In Cherokee County, 20th ult., J.W. Rains.
Near Oxford, 19th ult., Miss Essie Allen.
In South Butler, 22nd ult., Rev. S.F. Piily.
In Wilcox County, recently, John McLean.
At Whistler, 29th ult., Mrs. Kate E. Powers.
In Gordon, 22nd ult., Mrs. Caroline Smith.
In Gordon, 23rd ult., Clara Britt, child.
In Eufaula, 27th ult., Mrs. H.F. Courie.
In Montgomery, 1st, D.L. Whetstone.
In Madison County, 9th ult., John M. Lynch.

## THE SOUTHERN ARGUS - DEATHS - JUNE 1869 THROUGH JUNE 1874

In Madison County, 22nd ult., J.M. Cochran.
In Portland, Maine, 14th ult., Miss Lucretia Day Sewad, formerly of Mobile.
In Texas, recently, Dr. H.L.M. Kennon, formerly of Dale County.
In Barbour County, 24th ult., William Williams.
In New York, 17th ult., W.R. Acton, father of Dr. Acton of Oxford.
Died in Butler County, 20th ult., infant of W.H. Shell.
In Walker County, 22nd ult., son of S.M. Gunter.
In Jackson, Mississippi, 23rd ult., Mrs. Jane Grey Hitzheim, nee Bradford, formerly of Huntsville.

Issue 12-12-1873

### TEXAS NEWS

Died in Smith County, 11th ult., wife of Rev. Mr. Burgamy.
Died in Dallas, 15th ult., Mrs. Frances E. Crutchfield.
Died in Navasota, 5th ult., Mrs. Augusta Eliza McCaslan.
Died in Navasota, recently, Rev. E.D. Johnson.
Died in Jefferson, 19th ult., James Durr, Junior.
Died in Kendall County, October 23rd, W.W. Stigler.
Died in San Antonio, 16th ult., Judge Thomas Whitehead.

Judge Fowler, formerly of Denton, has been appointed Judge of the Tenth Judicial District, vice Judge Scott, dead.

Tom Sankey, negro, is to be hung in Montgomery for murder.

The 4th ult., William Brewster, formerly of St. Clair County, was killed in Mississippi.

Gabriel Boyce of Limestone County died recently in the Albany penitentiary, whither Busteed sent him a year ago as a Ku Klux.

In a recent affray in Tuskegee, John G. Graham was shot and mortally wounded by Robert Keeling. [see below]

A Mr. Acre, cut in a recent difficulty at Rutledge, Crenshaw County, by a Mr. Benbow, has died.

### DIED IN ALABAMA

In Cherokee County, 29th ult., W.D. Glen.
In Tuskegee, recently, John G. Graham. [see above]
In Mobile, 3rd, Mrs. H.J. Davidson.
In Madison County, 20th ult., G.W. Jordan.
In Union Spring, 1st, Mrs. M.M. Butterfield.

## THE SOUTHERN ARGUS - DEATHS - JUNE 1869 THROUGH JUNE 1874

In Pickens County, 24th ult., W. Calley.
In Elmore County, recently, Andrew I. Scott.
In Jacksonville, 27th ult., Anna ? Earns, child.
In Tuskaloosa County, 30th ult., Mrs. Martha Hickman.
In Mississippi, 19th ult., J.S. Smith, formerly of Sumter.
Near North Port, 20th ult., Mrs. Nannie Hassell.
In Elmore County, recently, John T. Zimmerman.
In St. Clair County, 19th ult., Mrs. Amanda Rowan.
Near Gadsden, 22nd ult., Mrs. L.A. McGlathery.
In Mobile, 27th ult., John Wolf was shot and slightly wounded by his son-in-law, P.J. Boulo.

The 19th ult. in Attalla, William Humphreys was dangerously cut by Stephen A. Dobb.

William Craft of Etowah County has been pronounced insane.

A negro made a desperate attempt recently to rob and murder Mr. Wayman Herring of Talladega County.

### Issue 12-19-1873

### TEXAS NEWS

At Sempronius, recently, Peter Seales was badly wounded by Jabe Collins.

P. J ?. Willis, Sr. of Galveston died recently in Kansas City, Missouri.

Dedrick Miller, an old citizen of Fayette County, was beaten to death by negroes.

John Patterson was recently killed in Fort Bend County by the falling of a limb from a tree.

Joseph Kuykendall of Fort Bend County is dead.

Died in Paris, recently, Barney Richey.

W.H. Carter, an old citizen of Smith County, died recently.

### ALABAMA NEWS

At Linwood, 9th, William Fryer killed Jacob Kelly.

At Coffeetown, 6th, a Mr. Pruitt was shot and killed by a Mr. Hastins.

## THE SOUTHERN ARGUS - DEATHS - JUNE 1869 THROUGH JUNE 1874

Charles Metcalf, charged with killing Moses Ables in Etowah County in September last, has been admitted bail in $3,000.

Thomas Elder, charged with killing A.M. Carroll in Cherokee County, has fled and a reward is offered for his arrest.

Dr. Carr of Calhoun, Lowndes County, is recovering from a serious illness.

Milas Moorhead of Pickens County recently had one of his hips fractured.

Thomas Horn of Dale County has recently had a leg broke.

George Guice of Barbour County was killed recently by Dan Marshall.

Geo. W. Stearns, Constable of Mobile, has been sentenced to the penitentiary for three years for directing his assistant to shoot a prisoner in his charge, the shot proving fatal.

Judge Brickell has recovered from a serious illness.

### DIED IN ALABAMA

Near Huntsville, 8th, Miss Mollie L. Barham.
In Russell County, recently, Reuben Cooper.
In Livingston, 7th, Dr. Joseph A. Smith.
Near Georgiana, recently, Rev. T.J. Gardner.
In Boligee, 4th, Ida Lavina Hall, infant.
In Montgomery, 11th, Leon Levy.
In Oxford, 4th, Mrs. Anna Hines.
Near Marion, 4th, Mrs. Selvina C. Whitman.
In Gadsden, 7th, infant of T.J. Lamar.
In Jefferson County, 2nd, Lucy Sadler, child.
Near Braggs, 6th, C.D. Snow.
At Braggs, 6th, Minnie Lee, child.
Near Snow Hill, J.J. Burson.
Near Pine Apple, recently, Mrs. Bloxam.
In West Point, Mississippi, 27th ult., Colonel J.S. Garvin, formerly of Tuskaloosa.
In Mississippi, 19th ult., James R. Smith, formerly of Sumter.
In Mississippi, 12th ult., Willis J. Davis, formerly of Pickens.
In Texas, 24th ult., W.W. Harley, formerly of Greene.
In Cherokee County, 8th, Lulah Edwards, child.
In Dale County, 29th ult., Mrs. William Herring.
In Colbert County, 3rd, Mrs. Henrietta Ann Fossick.

## THE SOUTHERN ARGUS - DEATHS - JUNE 1869 THROUGH JUNE 1874

Issue 12-26-1873

TEXAS NEWS

Ex-Congressman J.C. Connor is dead.

W.G. Huddleson killed J.A. Maxwell in Fayette County.

Lovick P. Webb of Fayette County committed suicide.

Thomas Harrison of Parker County is dead.

Died in Llano County, 23rd ult., Mrs. Mary M. Leverett.

Died in Richmond, 10th, W.J. Slack.

A.A. Foster died near Waxahachie, recently.

Monroe Fykes was recently thrown from his horse in Milam County and killed.

Dr. Robert Broadnax of Gonzales is dead.

Miss Lizzie Carrington died in Dallas, recently.

Charles B. Clark, one of the proprietors of the Iron Age at Marshall, is dead.

Luke Howard and Soloman Howard, negroes, were recently killed in Baldwin County while resisting arrest.

Little Bobby Milligan of Newton had his foot amputated the 13th.

In Mobile the 10th, Morris Duclous was shot and killed by John M. Rogers, and John Mandich was wounded.
    John M. Rogers is in the Mobile Jail without bail for killing Morris Duclous.

Died in this city, Saturday, Mary Minter, infant daughter of George L. and Lottie N. Watson.

Dr. E.L. Antony of Huntsville has had a paralytic attack.

An attempt was made in Marion, recently, by a negro to assassinate R.R. Kilfoil.

DIED IN ALABAMA

In Clarke County, 5th, John R. Cox.

## THE SOUTHERN ARGUS - DEATHS - JUNE 1869 THROUGH JUNE 1874

Near Oxford, 14th, I.N. Allen.
In Calhoun County, 3rd, Mrs. Mary Harris.
In Eufaula, 16th, James Martin, infant.
Near Union Springs, 11th, G.W. Germany.
In Tuskaloosa, 12th, Charles Donaho, infant.
At Forkland, 8th, J.R. Brassfield.
In Cherokee, 10th, Jessie B. Wilson.
In Cherokee County, 11th, Melvina Bishop, infant.
In Monroe County, 4th ult., Miss Barbara Jane Talbot.
In Marion, 16th, Alice Speed, infant.
In Wilcox County, 22nd ult., Mrs. Sarah Nugent.
In Texas, recently, Alexander McArthur, formerly of Camden.
Near Livingston, 9th, Austin Prestwood.
In Mobile, 22nd, John E. Herpin.
In Henry County, 17th, James Summerford.

Issue 1-2-1874

DIED IN ALABAMA

In Florence, 21st ult., Robt. C. Foster.
Near Tuskaloosa, 7th ult., John M. Sexton.
In Mobile, 24th ult., Frank Beaumont.
In Montgomery, 25th ult., Reuben Thom.
In Mobile, 25th ult., infant of Ben Lane Posey.
In Pickens County, 19th ult., Mrs. J.B. Newell.

Died at Rehoboth on the 2nd inst., Miss Fannie Kimbrough...being in her eighteenth year.

Died in this city, Saturday, December 27th, the excellent and beloved wife of Samuel P. Steele.

The 15th ult. in Cherokee County a man named Metcalf was killed by one Kennedy.

John Miller of Henry County recently fell into an open cellar in Eufaula and hurt himself badly.

Near Gaylesville, 23rd ult., Dock Metcalfe was fatally stabbed by his brother George.

A little son of Porter Shine of Oakey Streak recently shot himself in the arm.

J.W. Spears, formerly a life insurance agent in Huntsville, was killed recently in Byhalla, Mississippi.

## THE SOUTHERN ARGUS - DEATHS - JUNE 1869 THROUGH JUNE 1874

In Mobile, 25th ult., E.J. Ribert was shot and badly wounded by R. Chatcaux?.

### TEXAS NEWS

John Y. Matthews died in Navasota the 9th ult.

C.W Crane committed suicide in Austin, recently.

Colonel Oscar P. Bowles of Bryan is dead.

In Hempstead, 17th ult., H.T. Ross was killed by J.T. Griffin.

Samuel Hancock died in Paris the 13th ult.

George A. Carter has committed suicide in Hill County.

Captain W.P. Matthews died in Gonzales County, 9th ult.

Thomas Reys of Leon County has committed suicide.

J.C. Rogers of Jefferson accidentally shot and mortally wounded himself.

Mr. Kirk and Willie Holt have been ambuscaded and shot in Jasper.

Issue 1-9-1874

### TEXAS NEWS

Hon. B.C. Franklin, Senator-elect, died in Galveston the 25th ult.

Samuel Hancock recently died in Lamar County.

Mr. J.M. Stammire, who lived near Palestine, was run into by a hack the 15th ult. and fatally injured.

Dr. W.H. Cain of Calvert shot and killed a negro the 24th ult.

In Marlin, 23rd ult., John Easley was killed by J.H. Ewing.

Died in Fort Worth, 12th ult., Mrs. Ella Turner.

Judge W.N. Magrant of Grayson County is dead.

Died in Gatesville, recently, T.J. Fore.

# THE SOUTHERN ARGUS - DEATHS - JUNE 1869 THROUGH JUNE 1874

Died in Gatesville, 12th ult., Rev. B.A. Kemp.

Colbert Shifley/Shitley/Shilley? of Travis County was murdered the 20th ult., by Wiley [sic] Stout, his brother-in-law.

"Mill" Davis of Austin was recently fatally injured by a runaway team.

## ALABAMA NEWS

Near Waterloo, Lauderdale County, the 29th ult., J. Edward Smith of Florence, aged seventeen, was killed by Dr. G.W. Payne of Tennessee.

William L. Ernest of Benton has been very sick.

Mr. George Gulce, who was recently killed near Mt. Andrew, Barbour County, was a Patron of Husbandry, and was buried by Mt. Andrew Grange, of which he was a member, probably the first burial services conducted by the order in the state.

A child of Mr. Comer of Shelby County was recently choked to death by swallowing a bean.

Mrs. Yeatman, wife of the Editor of the *Bladon Springs Herald*, whose death occurred the 19th ult., was a sister of Frank Monroe of the *Evergreen Star*.

On the 31st ult., Curtis Steen and Frank Hall killed each other in a difficulty near Snow Hill.

In Autauga County the 28th ult., William H. Tatum was killed by his brother-in-law, Austin Basil.

Donley Fryer, who had a grocery store at McGhee's switch on the Montgomery and Mobile Road, was murdered the night of the 29th ult. and his store was burned over his body.

In Etowah County, 28th ult., L.B. Archey killed Wesley Sturkey.

Cris Munn recently fell into an old well in Marion, fifty feet deep, without serious injury to himself.

A man named Roberts was shot and wounded in Oxford, Christmas, while assisting the Marshal in arresting some revellers.

## THE SOUTHERN ARGUS - DEATHS - JUNE 1869 THROUGH JUNE 1874

Robert Keeling has been committed to jail without bond for the recent killing of John G. Graham in Tuskegee.

Major A.G. Shackelford, an old citizen of Dallas County, as fine a specimen of the old-time gentleman as we had among us, died at his residence three miles from the city on Tuesday last. He had been in bad health for some time but his sudden death was unexpected. He was in Selma on Monday looking not worse than usual.

Died in this city the 5th inst., Mrs. Frances, wife of Joseph Hampshire.

### DIED IN ALABAMA

In Bladon Springs, 19th ult., Mrs. Mary Yeatman.
In Shelby County, recently, James M. Spearman.
In Shelby County, recently, Charles Bragg.
In Florence, 15th ult., Mrs. Margaret Faulk.
In Nashville, recently, D.R. Whitman, formerly of Madison County.
Near Trianna, 17th ult., James R. Collier.
In Clarke County, recently, J.A. Megginson.
In Tuskegee, 30th ult., Mrs. M.A. Lamar.
Near Farmersville, 12th ult., W. Lankford.
In Decatur, 13th ult., Miss Mollie K. Drake.
In Mobile, 23rd ult., Mrs. Wilson of Grove Hill.
Near Eutaw, 28th ult., Miss Annie Brown.
Near Boligee, 28th ult., James Watson.
In Mobile, 2nd, C.O. Healey.
In Hale County, 26th ult., Mrs. M.G. Pickens.
In Choctaw County, recently, A.R. Doggett.

### Issue 1-16-1874

### TEXAS NEWS

James Neal was killed by a kick from a horse in Palo Pinto County.

U.H. Ustick died in Walker County the 21st ult.

In Parker County a man named Quinn was recently killed while resisting arrest by the Sheriff.

Frank P. Ford died in Austin the 25th ult.

George Howard of Sherman was accidentally killed the 3rd.

Ex-Governor Runnells died in Bowie County the 23rd ult.

## THE SOUTHERN ARGUS - DEATHS - JUNE 1869 THROUGH JUNE 1874

### ALABAMA NEWS

Andrew Glasswell, formerly of Sumter County, died in California, November 26th.

Thomas M.J. Hughes, formerly of Montgomery, was recently accidentally killed on the cars between Louisville and Nashville.

Bill Odom, wife, and two children (negroes) were burned up in their house in Conecuh County the 6th.

Lizzie Carroll committed suicide in Montgomery the 4th.

Near Gadsden, 30th ult., Mat Hendrix was killed by the falling of a tree.

A little daughter of Hon. J.M. Carmicheal of Ozark was badly burned a few days ago by her dress catching fire.

A little son of Cornelius Atkinson of Dale County recently had his right hand terribly crushed in a cotton gin.

Near Gadsden, 30th ult., Mat Hendrix was killed by the falling of a tree.

Gov. Lewis has offered $100 reward for the arrest of G.W. Payne, who recently killed Eddie Smith in Lauderdale County.

### DIED IN ALABAMA

In Eufaula, 2nd, John B. Clark.
In Montgomery, 5th, Mrs. Somerville.
In Mobile, 5th, David Martin Cahill.
In Mobile, 7th, Henry Thomas.
In Shelby County, 4th, Thomas H. Brasher.
In Walker County, 27th ult., Henry Holmes, child.
In Talladega County, Miss Ellen Stockdale.
In Chambers County, 31st ult., Mrs. J.M. Greer.
In Chambers County, 3rd, Mrs. Margaret Carlisle.
In North Port, 5th, Henry P. Green.
In Perry County, 9th ult., Mrs. Rebeca Holmes Dansby.
In Limestone County, 5th, Mrs. B.M. Townsend.
In Eutaw, 5th, Mrs. Sarah Roberts.
In Mobile, 9th, W. Leigh Hopkins.
In Ozark, 2nd, Emanuel Tomlin.
In Huntsville, 6th, Jacob W. David.
Near Cluttsville, 22nd ult., T.J. Douglass.
In Talladega County, 31st ult., Jackson Hammock.

## THE SOUTHERN ARGUS - DEATHS - JUNE 1869 THROUGH JUNE 1874

In San Francisco, 27th ult., W.F. Williams, formerly of Pickens County.

Obituary: Died at her residence in Selma, Alabama, January 5th, 1874, Mrs. Frances Hampshire, beloved wife of Joseph Hampshire, in the forty-second year of her age. In removing from this world the subject of this notice, it was the will of God that she should pass through much suffering...

Issue 1-23-1874

TEXAS NEWS

Died in Sherman, recently, W.E. Tarr.
Died near Navasota, 5th, Mrs. Eliza Johnson.
Died in Navasota, recently, Joseph Lancaster.

Mr. W.S. Trout of Wood County has died from a gunshot wound accidentally received.

A.F. Kelman of Gonzales County died the 1st.

G. Erichson, forty years a citizen of Houston, is dead.

Mrs. Mary Evans died at Waco the 8th.

ALABAMA NEWS

Mr. S.P. Jackson, an old engineer, died the 15th on the steamer *Victoria*, near Bladon.

Joseph Byers, who recently died in St. Clair County, was a lieutenant in the War of 1812.

J.A. Milner of Birmingham, who has been dangerously sick, is getting well.

William Capuion at Fackler's Station, Jackson County, was recently fatally crushed between two cars.

The 3rd, Rev. W. M. Wilson of Cherokee County was thrown from his buggy and badly hurt.

In Lowndes County the other day, John Harris was shot and dangerously wounded by Andrew Pou.

Died in this county, Tuesday morning, January 20th, 1874, Mr. S.L. Coleman.

## THE SOUTHERN ARGUS - DEATHS - JUNE 1869 THROUGH JUNE 1874

General C.M. Shelley has been seriously ill for some days at his residence in this city.

Died in this city the 10th inst., Emma, daughter of Charles Rosenburg, aged five years.

### DIED IN ALABAMA
In Newbern, 10th, J.A. Hendon.
In Marion, 11th, Mrs. Woodson Cocke.
Marion, 8th, George Martin True, infant.
Near Huntsville, 1st, Mrs. Mary Giles.
In Tuskegee, 1st, R.L. Abercrombie, child.
In Talladega, 10th, Mrs. M.V. Plowman.
In Tallasseehatchee, 10th, Lee Coleman.
In Mobile, 14th, W. Laureedine.
In Mobile, 14th, Thomas Little.
Near Jacksonville, 12th, Dr. James Vernon.
Near Cedar Bluff, 30th ult., Mrs. H.J. Wilson.
Near Jasper, 9th, R.J. Richardson.
In Etowah County, 10th, R.W. Wright.
In St. Clair County, 19th ult., J.A. Byers.
In Gordon, 31st ult., S.S. Cawthon.
In Mobile, 8th, Thomas Hogg.
Near Abbeville, recently, Anderson Watson.
In Limestone County, 11th, Mrs. Sallie Bridgeforth.
In Montgomery, 16th, Mrs. George Gammel.
Near Bollgee, 3rd, D.W. Elliott.
Near Clinton, 10th, L.A. Pippen.
In Grove Hill, 6th, Mrs. C.M. Dickinson.
In Clarke County, 7th, Mrs. Sarah Whatley.
In Hayneville, recently, Patrick Leonard.

Dr. W.L. DeBerry died in Rankin County, Mississippi, the other day.

Judge J.E. McNair died in Brookhaven, Mississippi, the 4th.

Issue 1-30-1874

### TEXAS NEWS
At Footout the 4th, Abe Kennedy was killed and Tom Kennedy was wounded in an affray.

Gail Borden, the inventor of condensed milk, died at Columbus the 11th.

## THE SOUTHERN ARGUS - DEATHS - JUNE 1869 THROUGH JUNE 1874

Judge Steiner of Colorado County is dead.

Hugh, Governor Throckmorton's eldest son, died a few days ago.

A Mrs. Swope was run over by a horse in the streets of Austin recently and fatally injured.

Hiram M. Thompson, Jr. died in Richmond the 12th.

Charles Railey, aged seventy-five, died in Hempstead the 18th.

### DIED IN ALABAMA
In Marengo County, 8th, Elijah Rawls.
In Greensboro, 19th, Mrs. S.A. Stokes.
In Montgomery, 20th, Stephen B. Pleasants.
In Toulminville, 22nd, Dan'l Young.
In Mobile, 22nd, James D. Hynes.
In Colbert County, 18th, Mrs. F.M. Sledge.
In Demopolis, 26th, Mrs. D.J. English.
In Etowah County, 16th, Mrs. Letitia White.
In Etowah County, 7th, Edmund Jourdan.
In Talladega County, 10th, Isaac Lawler.
Near Talladega, 14th, Miss Enfield Sinon.
In Birmingham, 18th, child of Dr. Parker.
In Tuskalosa, 21st, R.N. Norris.
In Tuskaloosa, 18th, Mrs. Thomas.
In Evergreen, 15th, Mrs. Eliza Darby.
In Butler County, 26th, Mrs. Ross Callan.
In Mobile, 21st, Miss Kate L. Taber.
In Abbeville, 20th, Mrs. Robert Barr.
Near Madison, 18th, Mrs. Crowley.
In Mobile, 25th, G.M. Parker.
In Marion, 23th, Dennie, daughter of Dr. L.A. Ball.
In Lauderdale, Mississippi, 18th, John Kennedy, formerly of Sumter County.

Rev. Wm. Sparrow, thirty-three years dean of the Episcopal Seminary near Alexandria, Virginia, died recently, aged seventy-three.

The widow of the late Chancellor J.B. Clark of Eutaw has removed to New Orleans to reside with a daughter.

A man named Martin was shot and killed at Ashville Depot the 14th by a Mr. Gibbs.

## THE SOUTHERN ARGUS - DEATHS - JUNE 1869 THROUGH JUNE 1874

Ike Roper, negro, was shot and killed in Huntsville the 19th.

James H. Clark, living near Vienna, Madison County, hung himself the 22nd.

Died in this city, Sunday night, D.E. Schultz.
Died in this county, Tuesday night the ?0th, Mr. Isaac May.
Died at Logan's Station the night of the 20th, James Edwards.

Joe Clarke (negro) was drowned on Saturday last from the sail-boat *Susie Stephens*, near King's Bend.

Died in this city the night of the 27th, Eugenia Gayle, only child of Mr. E.C. and Mrs. Alice Hagood, aged about fourteen months.

Mrs. Louisa Coleman, wife of Captain H.F. Coleman, and daughter of our venerable fellow-townsman, Mr. James D. Craig, died at her residence in Cahaba on Friday last.

Wednesday night of last week, Mr. James Coleman of Orrville died from the effects of a fall received from a horse the previous day.

Tom Sankey, negro, is to be hung in Montgomery today.

John Harris of Lowndes is recovering from the gun shot wound recently received at the hand of Mr. Pou.

Dr. H.V. Smith of Lowndesboro has been very sick.

Edmond Jourdan, who recently died in Etowah County, was one hundred and five years old.

Mr. Fulcher, near Gadsden, has recently lost three children with diphtheria.

*Issue* 2-6-1874

### TEXAS NEWS

J.C. Wilson of Comanche County was killed recently in Kansas.

John H. Sauters of Galveston died recently in Europe.

A brakeman named Jo Swain was crushed to death at Hearne on the 19th ult. while coupling cars.

Died in Waco the 8th ult., Mrs. Mary E. Evans.

## THE SOUTHERN ARGUS - DEATHS - JUNE 1869 THROUGH JUNE 1874

Died in Smith County the 21st ult., Rev. Robert Clay.
Died in Tyler, 19th ult., Mrs. J.L. Stribling, wife of Rev. J.H. Stribling.

Mr. Runnion, an old citizen of Tyler, died the 18th.

Died in Waco the 21st ult., Frank E. Stephens.
Died in Marlin, recently, Mrs. Emma, wife of Dr. J.H. Tripp.
Died in Hempstead the 17th ult., F.F. Hooper.
Died in Austin, 20th ult., Thomas Moore, formerly of Florida.
Died in Burleson County, 18th ult., Mrs. B.A.G. Sorelle.

Dr. F. Hasenburg of San Antonio died in Austin the 19th ult.

Died in Gatesville the 15th ult., Mrs. W.W. Hammack.

### ALABAMA NEWS

On the 24th ult. at Pine Level, Montgomery County, Dr. McLeod was killed by a Mr. Mordecai.

Cas. Battles of St. Clair County was recently badly hurt by being thrown from a mule.

In self-defence, Henry Spratling of Chambers County recently killed a negro man.

Major and Mrs. McWhorter of Birmingham were badly burned a few days ago in saving from injury their little daughter whose clothes had caught fire.

William Tabler, who recently died in Marshall County, was a volunteer of 1812.

Mrs. Rebecca Smith, who recently died in North Port, had lived in Tuskaloosa County fifty-five years.

In Mobile the other day, Willie Curtin, child, was accidently shot and seriously wounded by Jimmy Dugan, a boy of fourteen.

Tom Sankey, the negro hung at Montgomery last Friday, died happy.

Died Sunday night last, in East Selma, Mrs. Elizabeth Schultz.

In Crawford, Russell County, 24th ult., Mr. J.J. Davis was stabbed and killed by A.B. Eiland.

## THE SOUTHERN ARGUS - DEATHS - JUNE 1869 THROUGH JUNE 1874

The funeral of ex-Mayor Parker of Mobile was largely attended.

### DIED IN ALABAMA

Near Montevallo, 20th ult., P.H. West.
In Liverpool, England, 22nd ult., James A. Macauley, formerly of Florence.
In Lauderdale County, 27th ult., Clinton Heslep, Jr.
In Florence, recently, Philip Fables.
In Lauderdale County, 11th ult., Howell Sledge.
In North Port, 25th ult., Mrs. Rebecca Smith.
In Eufaula, 28th ult., Gordie Smith, child.
In Marengo County, 14th ult., H.T. Bennett.
Near Macon Station, 25th, K.C. DuBose.
In Birmingham, 29th ult., Mr. Enslen of Arkansas.
Near Ashville, 21st ult., Mrs. Sallie Montgomery.
In Talladega County, recently, Simon Morris.
In Baldwin County, 23rd ult., Anna Vasser Wheadon, child.
In Elmore County, 24th, Uriah Williams.
In Geneva County, 20th ult., H.T. Wilkinson.
In Dale County, recently, Henry Beverett.
In Jackson County, 16th ult., Mrs. Sarah Hughes.
In Jackson County, recently, Mrs. C.W. Allen.
In Texas, 11th ult., Joshua Stephens, formerly of Jackson County.
In Henry County, recently, James Butler.
In Florida, recently, A.J. Tarver of Russell County.
In Madison County, recently, Jonathan Mayhew.
In Marshall County, 11th ult., William Tabler.
In South Carolina, December 25th, Miss Nancy M. Smarr of Greene County.
Near Boligee, 14th ult., Miss Lucy Bouchelle.

Isaac Hooper (negro) is to be hanged in Augusta, Georgia, March 30th.

Rev. Duncan H. Selph of the Baptist Church died in Missouri the 8th ult.

Rev. Daniel Howard Bittle of Savannah is dead.

General C.M. Shelley has happily recovered from his recent illness.

Died near Selma on the 27th of January, 1874, Mr. James Kenan, son of Colonel Thomas and M.R. Kenan. The subject of this notice was born in Duplin County, North Carolina, June 24th, 1808, being in his sixty-sixth year when he died. He removed with his father to Dallas County, Alabama in 1833. Forty years residence in this county...Ruling elder in Valley Creek Church......

Died Sunday night last in East Selma, Mrs. Elizabeth Schultz.

# THE SOUTHERN ARGUS - DEATHS - JUNE 1869 THROUGH JUNE 1874

Issue 2-13-1874

Dr. A.S. Newton of Louisville is dead.

## TEXAS NEWS

In Marshall, 19th ult., Bob Angel was stabbed and killed by Wm. Russel.

The 24th ult., James B. Helm was shot in the court in Galveston and killed by John Ferguson, whose father he had killed in April last and for which killing he was then on trial.

Died in Gatesville, 18th ult., William Woodburn.

J. Henry Bell was killed at McDade by young John Lawrence.

Judge Leslie A. Thompson died in Galveston the 23rd ult.

Frank S. Stephens died suddenly in Waco a short time ago.

Died near Hempstead, 10th ult., Mrs. Dorcas Matchet.

Captain Thomas I. Poole died at Indianola the 19th ult.

Colonel J.B. Banks of Galveston committed suicide a few days ago.

Colonel J.B. Johnson, master of the state grange, Patrons of Husbandry, died recently at his residence in Free Stone [sic] County.

## DIED IN ALABAMA

In Eutaw, 3rd, Mrs. Virginia McAlpine.
In Dallas, Texas, 28th ult., W. McKerrell, formerly of Eutaw.
In Eutaw the 1st, Mrs. Mary Cook.
In Hale County, recently, Mrs. Ann Jeffries.
In Philadelphia, 5th ult., Mrs. Maria Hawn Patterson, formerly of Tuskaloosa.
At Bell's Landing, 23rd ult., Mrs. Mary A. Nelson.
In Wilcox County, 29th ult., W.M. Goode.
In Madison County, 29th ult., Henry B. Penny, infant.
In Henry County, 29th ult., John Pearre.
In Galveston, 1st, Thomas R. Balling, formerly of Mobile.
In Benton, October 2nd, Edward D. Lacey.
In Eufaula, 31st ult., Emanuel Lang.
In Mobile, 3rd, Mrs. Mary Ann Murphy.
In Etowah County, 28th ult., Mrs. Elizabeth Busby.
In Geneva County, 30th ult., Henry Wilkerson.

## THE SOUTHERN ARGUS - DEATHS - JUNE 1869 THROUGH JUNE 1874

In Mobile, 1st ult., Kate Taber.
Near Moulton, 29th ult., Miss Virginia Chitwood.
In Tuskegee, 6th, Mrs. Jane Mitchell.
In Athens, 5th, Daniel A. Cannon.
In Athens, 1st, Miss Mittie Mingea.
In Limestone County, 28th ult., Maggie Nash Tisdale, infant.
In Jonesboro, Jefferson County, recently, Mrs. S.E. Owen.
In Montgomery, 7th, Patrick Thomas Robinson, child.
In Auburn, 6th, Robert F. Hall.

The representatives of Carey, the railroad conductor recently killed on the Memphis and Charleston Railroad, have brought suit in the Madison Circuit Court against the Southern Railroad Security Company for twenty thousand dollars damages.

Tribute of respect from the board of directors of the Selma and Meridian Railroad Company on the death of General Wm. J. Hardee, late president of this board...lovable husband and father.

Mrs. Jane Lee, wife of Mr. V.C. Lee, who a few months ago removed from this county to Arkansas, died recently in her new home.

James McMillan of Shelby County was accidentally shot the 2nd by Mr. Luther F. Holt and killed.

In Marengo County, recently, Poellnitz Johnson, son of General G.D. Johnson, accidentally shot and wounded his cousin, Charles DeYampert.

Colonel M.A. King of Tuskaloosa, who has been dangerously ill, is convalescing.

Hampton Wade (negro) will be hung in Tuskaloosa sometime next month.

A Mr. Jamison was shot and wounded in Decatur recently.

The negroes of Montgomery believe Tom Sankey, recently executed there for murder, has been resurrected and is preaching a new gospel.

Issue 2-20-1874

TEXAS NEWS

Died in Longview, 26th ult., Mrs. Maria Park.

## THE SOUTHERN ARGUS - DEATHS - JUNE 1869 THROUGH JUNE 1874

James Armstrong, a lawyer, was assassinated in Gatesville the 29th ult. by unknown parties.

Mr. Wharton, a blacksmith, died near Mooresville recently.

Near Cedar Springs the 26th ult., Patrick Clinton, a peddler, was robbed and murdered by a man named Sheffield.

Colonel J.W. Stell of Gonzales died recently.

Died in Matagorda County, Colonel James D. Blair.

In Grayson County, recently, Charles Martin was shot and killed by O. Bourd.

Died recently near Regan's Station, W.G. Etheridge, Sr., formerly of Alabama.

William Pierce, who lived twenty miles west of Denison, was assassinated the 23rd ult.

### DIED IN ALABAMA
In Huntsville, 9th, Mrs. Ann B. Spragins.
In Montgomery, 9th, Berry Cooley.
In Clark County, 8th, Mrs. F.W. Baker.
In Clarke County, 8th, Geo. Walker.
In Carthage, 7th, H.C. Force.
In Butler County, 28th ult., Milton Lloyd.
In Butler County, 2nd, Whitmill Butler.
In Tuskegee, 6th, John Owsley.
Near Greenwood, 5th, Mrs. Nancy R. Stowers.
In Mobile, 9th, R.B. Owen.
In Jefferson County, recently, Warren Martin.
Near Talladega, 9th, James Llewellyn.
In Talladega, 5th, Mrs. Ellen Bibby.
In Montgomery, 14th, R.H. Maddox.
In Ozark, 5th, child of Senator Carmichael.
In Texas, 5th, Mrs. Sarah J. White of Moulton.
In Courtland, 9th, Morris M. Falk.
In Mobile, 13th, Mrs. M.R. Rafferty.
In Huntsville, 19th, Theo. Lacy, Sr.
In Whistler, 26th ult., Mrs. C. Barrett.
In Hale County, 5th, Amanda Clifton Rogers, child.
Near Centre, 28th ult., Amanda Louisiana Smith, child.
Near Bell's Landing, 23rd ult., Mrs. M.A. Nelson.
In Florida, recently, L.L. Cater, formerly of Conecuh County.

## THE SOUTHERN ARGUS - DEATHS - JUNE 1869 THROUGH JUNE 1874

Mrs. Robert S. Todd of Lexington, Kentucky, mother of Mrs. N.H.R. Dawson of this city, died the 14th.

Near Dixie on Saturday evening last, Jordan Seymour (negro) was shot and killed by his son-in-law, Tom Williams (negro).

We are sorry to hear that our distinguished fellow-citizen, Dr. A.G. Mabry, is seriously ill at his residence in this city.

Colonel Russel P. McCord, formerly of Lowndes County, died at Oakfield, near Pensacola, Florida, on the 12th. Colonel McCord was at one time a leading politician in South Carolina; and after his removal to this state, he continued to take an active part in public affairs, and was elected in 1836 and again in 1837 to the Legislature from Lowndes. He was the father of Mrs. William S. Knox of this city.

John B. Rittenhouse, a naval paymaster who recently died in Pennsylvania, was Editor of the *Alabama Beacon* at Greensboro 35-40 years ago.

The estimable wife of Mr. Jordan White, one of the editors of the *Moulton Advertiser*, died in Paris, Texas, the 5th.

In the death of James Kenan, recently announced, the community in which he lived lost one of its effluent and useful members... mind was generously improved by a superior education... quiet, affable, genial with all...

We regret to learn that our venerable friend, Colonel W.B. Haralson, is quite ill at the residence of his son, Colonel John Haralson, in this city.

In Jonesboro, Jefferson County, recently, a Mr. Curren was cut and dangerously wounded by a Mr. Patrick.

Mr. H.C. Force, whose recent death at Carthage, Hale County, is elsewhere announced, was a brother of our esteemed townsman, Dr. C.F. Force, and a son of the late famous Peter Force of Washington City.

Issue 2-27-1874

TEXAS NEWS

Died in Jefferson, 9th, Mrs. Nannie W. Wheatley.

Colonel E.T. Broughton of Sherman died the 11th.

Died in Austin the 31st ult., Miss Mary Hynes, aged eighty-one years.

# THE SOUTHERN ARGUS - DEATHS - JUNE 1869 THROUGH JUNE 1874

Died in Galveston the 8th, Mrs. Ella M. Sherrard.
Died in Brenham the 6th, Mrs. E.G. Hurley.
Died in Hempstead the 4th, Charles Kraus.

In Calvert, recently, Mrs. Minnie C. Wilson and daughter were killed by an overdose of laudanum.

Died in Smith County, 7th ult., Mrs. Rachel D. Arthur, nee Loftin, formerly of Alabama.

## ALABAMA NEWS

Mr. John M. Lansdon, who died recently in Butler County, was ninety-four years old.

On the 17th, William Smith of Central Institute, Elmore County, and the horse he was riding were killed by lightning near Nixburg.

The announcement of the death of Mrs. Mattie S. Cooper, in Mobile on Sunday last, shocked and grieved a large circle of admiring and loving friends here...

Died suddenly on Sunday last, at the residence of Dr. Tipton on the South side of the river, Mr. John Z. Riggs of this city, son of the late Daniel M. Riggs, and brother of our distinguished townsman, Dr. B.H. Riggs.... Born and reared here, he had many friends in this community...

## DIED IN ALABAMA

In Talladega, 13th, child of R.W. Huston.
In Talladega, 16th, child of J.J. Nix.
In Lowndes County, 12th, Thos. S. Coburn.
In Jefferson County, 15th, Rev. Benj. Tarrant.
In Macon County, 16th, Henry McKenzie.
In Choctaw County, 15th, Willis Knighten.
In Tuskaloosa, 15th, Col. Mike A. King.
At Gosport, 10th, W.J. Taylor.
In Huntsville, 15th, R.J. Keel.
In Eutaw, 14th, Mrs. Mary C. Lyeria.
In Eutaw, 17th, S.W. Cockrell.
In Butler County, 15th, John M. Lansdon.
In Greenville, 14th, Mrs. Sarah LeGraff.
Near Moulton, 7th, H.L. Cowan.
In Henry County, recently, L.M. Mozeley.
In Monreville, recently, W.J. Tucker.
Near Florence, 10th, Abia Parsons.

## THE SOUTHERN ARGUS - DEATHS - JUNE 1869 THROUGH JUNE 1874

On Fowl River, 25th ult., H.D. Powell.
In Mobile, 23rd, John McDonald.
In Montgomery, 24th, James Dinsmore.
In Greene County, 19th ult., Mrs. Williamson A. Glover.

Tribute of respect from the Selma Medical Society, held February 24, 1874, on the death of Albert Gallatin Mabry, M.D.... stricken wife, children, relatives...

Tribute of respect from Hall Protection H. & L. Company, Selma, February 23, 1874 on the sudden death of John Z. Riggs...

Information has been received here that Mr. Robert Gardner, formerly of this vicinity, was, on Sunday last, assassinated on his plantation in Louisiana. No particulars have been received. Mr. Gardner was a son of Col. V.H. Gardner of this county and was well known in this community.

Rev. Benjamin Tarrant, who recently died in Jefferson County, was a veteran of 1812.

In Eufaula the other day, Harry Thomas (negro) shot and killed Ned Ogletree (negro).

On the 14th in Huntsville, Dr. J.L. Ridley knocked Nich Davis, Sr. down with a pistol.

Issue 3-6-1874

### TEXAS NEWS

Died in Hamilton County the 14th ult., Sampson McGowan, formerly of Coryelle.

A reward of $500 is offered for the arrest of W. Baltzell, charged with the murder of Charles Mason in Gonzales County in 1867.

A reward of $250 is offered for the arrest of Andrew Shuffield, charged with murdering Patrick Quin in Falls County in 1867.

Died in Cherokee County, recently, Z. H. Spruill.
Died in Smith County, recently, Jesse P. Bruton.

Judge Simeon Hart died recently at El Paso.

Senator Smith of Houston County died in Austin the 16th ult.

## THE SOUTHERN ARGUS - DEATHS - JUNE 1869 THROUGH JUNE 1874

Died in Tyler, recently, Mrs. James S. Moore.

Garland R. Martin died recently in Collin County.

Anderson Boggs, an old citizen of Kauffman County, is dead.

In Calhoun County, John O'Neil killed a man named Bouborn.

Albert Schurenberg of Washington County was recently killed by a man named Warren.

James Allison, an old citizen of Williamson County, is dead.

A.M. Davis was recently shot and wounded near Waco by Bud Weaver.

### ALABAMA NEWS
On the 2nd, Mrs. Ward was dangerously ill in Birmingham.

Miss Dugary, a well known Montgomery milliner, on Sunday last fell through a trap door from her store into the cellar beneath and killed herself.

Russell St. John Parker of Mobile, aged nine years, fell into a kettle of boiling soap last Saturday and was fatally burned.

Tommie Binion of Georgiana was drowned in Sepulga River the 17th ult.

Rev. Timothy Root, formerly of Wetumpka, died in St. Louis the 19th ult.

At Pollard, recently, a Mr. McClelland was fatally shot by a Mr. Ghent.

Captain Witcher of Hayneville has been very sick in Montgomery.

Mrs. Frank Crocheron, late of Hayneville, was recently lying at the point of death at Abington, Virginia.

Asbury Craig of Limestone County was assassinated the 19th ult. by unknown parties.

Dr. G.W. Payne, the murderer of Eddie Smith in Lauderdale County, was captured in Mississippi and is in jail at Tuscumbia.

Alphonso Kelley, son of Mr. Larkin A. Kelly of Madison County, on the 14th ult. in Mississippi, killed two brothers named Choyle by whom he was assaulted.

## THE SOUTHERN ARGUS - DEATHS - JUNE 1869 THROUGH JUNE 1874

A negro was recently shot on Willis Miree's place near Marion, and killed in the act of stealing.

DIED IN ALABAMA

In Scottsboro, 19th ult., Mrs. S.C. Davidson.
In Conecuh County, 20th ult., Mrs. Susan Ray.
In Livingston, 25th ult., Hon. E.W. Smith.
In Mobile, 26th ult., Mrs. Alice Simpson.
In Greenville, 22nd ult., T.H. Kimball.
In Clarke County, recently, P.G.H. Holder.
Near Eutaw, 17th ult., W.H. Bizzell.
In Bullock County, 16th ult., Col. Hubbard.
In Attalla, 21st ult., Miss Martha Echols.
In Montgomery, 25th ult., son of J.O Patton.
In Montgomery, 20th ult., Mrs. P.D. Stuart.
In Lowndes County, 21st ult., T.H. Booth.
In Montgomery, 1st, W.H. McClure.
In Wetumpka, 2nd, Rev. S.J. McMorris.
In Mobile, 1st, Russell St. John Parker.
In Mobile, 2nd, Captain V.M. Byrnes.
In Butler County, 17th ult., Tommie Binion.
In Henry County, recently, child of J.P. Box.
In Henry County, 25th ult., Mrs. Margaret Ward.
In Talladega County, 25th ult., Mrs. Lula Borden.

W.H. McNamee, Register in Chancery of Lee County, accidently shot and wounded himself the 23rd ult.

Dr. C. Ligon of Lawrence County has been very sick.

Issue 3-13-1874

TEXAS NEWS

Died in Austin, 25th ult., Colonel W.T. Austin.

In Red River County, John Maurer was recently killed by John Walker.

Died in Cass County, 15th ult., John M. Fleming.

Mr. Brooks of Wharton County was killed by a negro recently.

In Columbus, recently, Dan Power was shot and killed by William Willis.

## THE SOUTHERN ARGUS - DEATHS - JUNE 1869 THROUGH JUNE 1874

J.A. Wise, correspondent of the *San Antonio Herald* died in Austin the 22nd ult.

Rev. N.P. Moore, formerly of Tyler, died recently in Tennessee.

### ALABAMA NEWS

Tommy Binion was not drowned, as reported, in Sepulga River the 17th ult.

Major Lawrence B. Bradley has been very ill at his home near Mt. Willing.

Samuel Feagin of Midway accidentally shot and killed himself recently.

Alsebrooks, a photographer, was recently killed near Arbacoochie by a negro.

### DIED IN ALABAMA

In Mobile, 6th, Mrs. Fernetta Everist.
In Mobile, 5th, P. La V. Pease.
In Birmingham, 6th, Mrs. M.E. Ward.
In Birmingham, 6th, M.A. Faver.
Near Athens, 2nd, Mrs. Kate Skinner.
In Marion, 3rd, Charles Clement.
In Tuscumbia, 20th ult., J.A. Stoddard.
In Tuscumbia, 1st, James Throckmorton.
In Opelika, recently, Leroy Moore, child.
In Walker County, 1st, son of John Yoe.
Near Grove Hill, 2nd, Wilburn J. Fleming.
In Monroe County, 24th ult., Isaac S. Williams.
In Montgomery, 9th, Mrs. Eliza A. Williams.
In Opelika, 8th, J.H. Richards.
In Marion, 10th, child of W.H. Redding.
In Greene County, 8th, Charlie Edwards, child.
In Marengo County, recently, James R. Quinney.
In California, recently, E.B. Clapp, formerly of Huntsville.
In Tuskaloosa County, 28th ult., Mrs. Eva Brown.
In North Port, 24th ult., Mrs. Nancy Thompson.
In Pickens County, recently, Mrs. F.J. Goodman.
In Walker County, 27th ult., Henry Ferguson, Sen.
In Henry County, recently, child of I.M. Campbell.
In Texas, 9th ult., Miss Chattie Reed, formerly of Fort Deposit.

Mrs. Pettiebone, whose maiden name was Rosa Cramer, formerly of this city where she married, committed suicide in Atlanta the 6th.

## THE SOUTHERN ARGUS - DEATHS - JUNE 1869 THROUGH JUNE 1874

Old man McMillan of Meridian was choked to death the other day by a piece of beef.

Issue 3-20-1874

### TEXAS NEWS

Died in Waller County, 20th ult., Edwin A. Glover, for many years a citizen of Alabama.

Fort Bend County sends George Washington (negro) to the penitentiary for twenty-five years for child murder.

Died in Richmond, 5th, Mrs. Eliza Alexander, daughter of the late Rev. John Newland Maffit.

John W. Kavanaugh has recently died in Lamar County.

The wife of Hon. T.G. Alison of Panola County is dead.

Died in Austin, 3rd, Mrs. M.A. Goodrich.

### ALABAMA NEWS

Mrs. Addison of Greene County was recently badly burned while setting fire to grass in a field.

Mr. James K. Whitman of Lowndesboro has been very sick.

J.E. Littlepage of Choctaw County accidentally shot and seriously wounded himself some time ago.

Reynolds, son of Captain Hugh Haralson, aged about three years, died at the residence of Mr. Reynolds in Talladega County on Tuesday last.

Judge Thomas A. Walker was on Monday last dangerously ill on his plantation near Bellevue; but his friends throughout the state will be glad to know that he is now in this city, and convalescing.

Colonel J.R. Powell of Birmingham has been seriously unwell.

### DIED IN ALABAMA

In Eutaw, recently, A.B. Hanson.
In Talladega, 8th, F.A. McClelan.
In Birmingham, 7th, Maude Bagley, child.
In Marion, 10th, E.W. Redding, child.

# THE SOUTHERN ARGUS - DEATHS - JUNE 1869 THROUGH JUNE 1874

In Sumter County, 8th, Thomas A. Kennard.
In Mobile, 2nd, Mrs. Ann Pearson.
In Lee County, 8th, Addison Frazer, Jr.
In Elkmont, 1st, Miss Delia Lewis.
In Jacksonville, 12th, Mrs. Fielding Snow.
In Lowndes County, 7th, Major Bradley.
Near Auburn, 4th, Horace W. Rundell.
In Blountsville, 7th, R.B. Montgomery.
Near Huntsville, 8th, Mrs. Kate M. Barclay.
In Texas, 1st ult., W.M. Cross, formerly of Talladega.
In Shreveport, Louisiana., recently, Wm. Hayley, formerly of Greenville.
In Baltimore, 27th ult., Henry F. Stickney, formerly of Mobile.
In Coffee County, 8th, daughter of Dudley Barron.
In Abington, Virginia, 6th, Mrs. Crocheron, formerly of Lowndes.
In Texas, recently, John F. Baggett, formerly of Loachapoka.
In Auburn, recently, Professor Frank Lipscomb.

Rev. Jefferson Falkner of Montgomery has been ill.

## Issue 3-27- 1874

Henry W. Longfellow, Edward L. Pierce, and Francis V. Baich are executors of Senator Sumner's will.

Hon. Edmund Smith, a member of the Ohio Constitutional Convention, died suddenly the 13th.

Rt. Rev. Charles H. Harris, D.D., Bishop of Gibraltar, is dead.

Judge W.T. Jones, late of the Virginia Court of Appeals, is dead.

Rear Admiral Lanman died the 14th.

## TEXAS NEWS

Died in Galveston, 10th, Captain Aaron C. Burns.

Major E.W. Rogers, the founder of Waxahachie, a prominent and popular citizen, died on the 28th ult.

Mr. F. King committed suicide at Denison the 5th.

At Barton, recently, Patrick Rafferty fatally stabbed Patrick Henslen.

Little Jake Nussbaum was burned up in the Ward building in Jefferson.

## THE SOUTHERN ARGUS - DEATHS - JUNE 1869 THROUGH JUNE 1874

Mrs. Cinthia Dyer died in Coryelle County the 22nd ult.

Mr. Joseph Kellar of Eagle Lake committed suicide the other day.

In Sherman, Billy Keyes fatally cut Charlie Hoffman.

### ALABAMA NEWS

Mrs. Baird of the vicinity of Tuskaloosa is hopelessly ill.

In a recent affray in Jonesboro, Lawrence County, Cal Bettis was fatally stabbed and Jack Williams was badly wounded.

Perry County sends Giles Clay (negro) to the penitentiary for eight years for wife-murder.

Dr. M.H. Daniel of Perry County, charged with killing W.E. Massey, has obtained a change of venue to Dallas.

W.R. Hardaway of Greene County is suffering with cancer of the tongue.

Frank Demouey of Grand Bay was recently killed by a limb falling from a tree.

The Macon Circuit Court sends Charles Stafford (negro) to the penitentiary for burglary, and Julia Thornton (negro) for child murder.

Charles Chambers of Mobile accidently shot and wounded himself the 17th.

Frank Demoney of Grand Bay was recently killed by a limb falling from a tree.

### DIED IN ALABAMA

In Gadsden, 12th, Mrs. Geo. Atway.
In Stevenson, recently, Geo. W. Newcomb.
In Cherokee County, 8th, Mrs. Lorena Matthews.
In Mobile, 18th, Samuel G. Battle.
In Hale County, 16th, Mrs. F.J. Monette.
In Grove Hill, 1?th, Isham Moore.
In Memphis, Tennessee, 17th, Perry Simpson, formerly of Tuscumbia.
In Limestone County, 19th, Mrs. Dorothy Holt.
In Arkansas, 11th, F.W. Bynum, formerly of Colbert County.
In Calhoun County, 4th, Mrs. Harriet Bush.
Near Oxford, 17th, Julian Frank Acton, child.
In Pickens County, 8th, Andrew Lyon.
In Pickens County, 8th, Richard M. Bunn.
In Montgomery, 21st, Jos. Solomon.

## THE SOUTHERN ARGUS - DEATHS - JUNE 1869 THROUGH JUNE 1874

In Linden, 15th, Mary Clifton Clarke, infant.
In Montgomery, 19th, W.H. Daniels.
In Montgomery, 22nd, John Frazier.
Near Mobile on Sunday evening last, Edward Phifer shot and killed Louis Kazalas.

Thomas Velasco of Mobile attempted suicide on Sunday morning last by cutting his throat.

Mr. Richie, a section master on the Mobile and Montgomery Railroad, was shot and killed at Brewton the 14th inst. by a negro whom he had discharged.

Tribute of respect from the Hall of the Mobile Medical Society, Mobile, Alabama, March 14, 1874 on the death of Dr. A.G. Mabry of Selma......

Larkin Allen of Clay County was recently murdered in Lee County as he was returning home from Columbus, Georgia.

Issue 4-3-1874

TEXAS NEWS

Ben. A. Weir died recently in Austin.

Ex Governor Throckmorton has been quite sick.

Died in Marlin the 6th ult., Mrs. Homer G. Houghton.

R.C. Ashbury of Cedar Springs, Falls County, died recently.

Fort Bend County sends George Washington (negro) to the penitentiary for twenty-five years for murder.

Died in Hempstead, 13th ult., Bennie Porter, son of Captain W.H. and Mrs. Emma P. Bedell, aged four years and three months.

Died in Hempstead the 18th ult., child of Mr. T.S. Reese.

In Bell County, recently, the brothers Wilkinson killed a man named Roach.

Mr. M.C. Strickland of Rusk County died recently.

Died in Harrison County the 16th ult., Dolph Powell.

Frank Herbert Park died in Jefferson the 18th ult.

## THE SOUTHERN ARGUS - DEATHS - JUNE 1869 THROUGH JUNE 1874

William A. George of Dallas County got shot the other day while trying to frighten some boys by playing panther.

Livingston Skinner, a citizen of Texas for thirty-five years, died in Titus County, February 27th.

A Bertham Smith died in Waco the 16th ult.

Judge J.W. Fox was shot and killed at Forrest City, Arkansas the 21st ult. by J.R.P. Aldridge.

In Vicksburg the other day, Colonel R.J. Miller was shot and killed by W.R. Spears.

### ALABAMA NEWS

Saturday night last, Levi Muller (negro) broke into the house of Mrs. Susan E. Crapps in Mobile and murderously assaulted her.

E.G. Burke, an employee of the Conception Street Railroad, Mobile, was fatally kicked by a mule Sunday evening last.

Heinrich Frei committed suicide in Mobile the 26th ult.

In Greenville the 25th ult., William Carroll, in an altercation with Mr. Ellwood and Willie Burnett, received two pistol shot wounds.

Mrs. S.W.L. McCloskey of Tuscumbia has been very ill.

Died in this city, Monday last, J.W. Bogle.

Leonard, infant son of Mr. and Mrs. W.L. Corbin, died Thursday of last week.

### DIED IN ALABAMA

Near Alpine, 26th ult., Isaac Stone.
In Athens, 25th ult., Samuel Tanner, Sr.
In Athens, 21st ult., Mrs. Mary McWilliams.
In Athens, 23rd ult., infant son of T.H. Field.
Near Gosport, 16th ult., John E. Spinks.
Near Grove Hill, 20th ult., Rev. W.J. Parker.
In Hale County, 20th ult., T.H. Evans.
In Demopolis, 26th ult., Rev. C.H. Coley.
In Mt. Hope, 4th ult., C.H.M. Sims.
In Mt. Hope, 5th ult., Dr. J.H. Sims.
In Talladega, 24th ult., Tennie Freeman, child.

## THE SOUTHERN ARGUS - DEATHS - JUNE 1869 THROUGH JUNE 1874

In Barbour County, 26th ult., Andrew Sanders.
In Mobile, 24th ult., William Hanlon.
In Lowndesboro, 15th ult., Mrs. James K. Whiteman.
In Limestone County, 24th ult., Frank Blackburn.
In North Port, 20th ult., Mrs. Mahala A. Odom.
At Choctaw Corner, 11th ult., Pher Thomas Dahlberg, child.
In Hale County, January 4th, Miss Carrie Melton.
At Spring Hill College, 26th ult., Rev. F. Larnandie.
In Rome, Georgia, recently, J.B. Landers, formerly of Talladega County.
In Montgomery, 30th ult., Mrs. Patrick Kenney.
In Lawrence County, 19th ult., Miss Lucy Jamison.

Tribute of respect from Widow's Son Lodge #72, Snow Hill, March 20th, 1874 on the death of I Capers Jones of Richmond Lodge #282. [mentions wife and children]

Issue 4-10-1874

### TEXAS NEWS

George Rabb was shot and killed by J. Thompson near Groesbeck the 24th ult.

Samuel Warrenton recently committed suicide in Hillsboro.

Died near Waco, 20th ult., F.J. Patterson.

George Bishop killed Thomas Rice near Spring Hill, McLennan County, the other day.

Jesse Andrews died recently in Austin.

Died in Marshall the 19th ult., E.P. Wornick.

The wife of Judge Simeon English of Red River County died the 4th ult.

Colonel Isaac T. Tinsley died in Brazoria County the 17th ult. He went to Texas from Alabama in 1830.

### ALABAMA NEWS

Mrs. B.I. Harrison of Tuskaloosa has been quite sick.

Elias A. Leake, formerly of Alabama, was assassinated by negroes on the 30th ult. near Bryan, Texas.

## THE SOUTHERN ARGUS - DEATHS - JUNE 1869 THROUGH JUNE 1874

On the 2nd in Barbour County, Nathan Newton (negro) was brutally murdered by Daniel Brooks and two other negroes.

Dr. James D. Osborn, who recently removed from Greensboro to Yazoo County, Mississippi, recently, in self defense, shot and wounded a man there.

Carter Harrison was recently shot and killed in Escambia County by a man named Owens.

Tribute of respect from Cold Springs, Texas, March 7, 1874: On the fourth instant John S. Cleveland of this place died at his residence and was buried on the fifth instant... Captain Cleveland was born in Selma, Alabama in 1822; served with distinction as Captain of Company H. Fifth Texas Regiment, and was a member of the Representatives of Texas before the war...

### DIED IN ALABAMA
In Demopolis, 2nd, Mrs. Adele S. Inge.
In Mobile, 30th ult., Mary Gunn.
In Brooklyn, New York, 30th ult., Mrs. Susan T. Hester, formerly of Montgomery.
In Montgomery, 13th ult., Miss Rosalie Patton.
In Mobile, 31st ult., H. Barkuloo.
In Montgomery, 1st, Mrs. N. Lelievre.
In Lauderdale County, 27th ult., W.C. Reeder.
In Clarke County, 26th ult., Marion S. York.
In Lowndes County, 22nd ult., Mrs. J.N. Cowen.
In North Carolina, 15th ult., Cecil White, late of Lowndes County.
In Greene County, 26th ult., Moses L. White.
In Tuskaloosa County, 15th ult., Elizabeth Sanders.
In Mobile, 2nd, Herman Lawitzky.
In Pensacoola, 4th, Mrs. E.D. Leak, formerly of Montgomery.
In Mobile, 2nd, Mary C. Jordan, infant.
In Jefferson County, 25th ult., E.D. Kennedy.

Issue 4-17-1874

### ALABAMA NEWS
Dr. C.J. Pope of Eufaula has been dangerously ill.

On the 1st, Green Bush of Calhoun County accidentally shot John Miller, of the same neighborhood, through the left arm, necessitating its amputation.

In the Etowah Circuit Court, Wm. Hall of Cherokee County was sentenced to the penitentiary for life for the murder of his wife in 1865.

## THE SOUTHERN ARGUS - DEATHS - JUNE 1869 THROUGH JUNE 1874

At the late term of the Etowah Circuit Court, Metcalfe was sentenced to the penitentiary for thirty-five years for killing a man named Ables some time ago.

Frank Moon, arrested in Tallapoosa County for the murder three years ago of his uncle, Thad Pennington, was recently rescued by unknown parties from the jail in Opelika, whither he had been taken for safety.

T.J. Pullen and James M.P. Coker of Cherokee County are dangerously ill.

Died at Bastrop, Louisiana, March 5th, Pinkie, only child of William C. and Mary Madden, aged fifteen years.

### DIED IN ALABAMA
In Eufaula, 8th, Kate Wellborn, infant.
In Pickens County, 5th, A.M. Windle.
In Cherokee County, 20th ult., Thos. Combs.
In Marion, 2nd, Mrs. Eliza West.
In Decatur, recently, J.H. King.
Near Snow Hill, 18th ult., Elder J.C. Jones.
In Sumter County, 30th ult., E.C. Gibbs.
In Gadsden, 31st ult., infant of Mr. Atway.
In Eufaula, 12th, Dr. C.J. Pope.
In Montgomery, 6th, Mrs. E.H. Harris.
In Fayette County, recently, Henry Logan.
In Meridian, 3rd, C.N. Wilcox of Choctaw County.

Issue 4-24-1874

### TEXAS NEWS
Died near Austin, recently, James N. Gresham.

In an affray near Granbury recently three brothers named Prewit were killed by a man named Mitchell and four of his friends.

Died in Sherman, recently, from an overdose of morphine, Dr. Craig.

Captain George Teneyek died in Austin the 10th.

In a rencontre in Austin the 10th between Dr. C. Thomas and Dr. Throckmorton, the throat of the latter was probably fatally cut.

Died in Coryelle County, 26th ult., Mrs. Emily W. Hearne.

## THE SOUTHERN ARGUS - DEATHS - JUNE 1869 THROUGH JUNE 1874

Near Orange the 8th, Mrs. Jett and two children were brutally murdered by a straggling Italian sailor.
    The murderer of the Jett family was taken from the Orange Jail and hung the night of the 8th.

S.A. Houston died recently in San Saba County.

Andrew Wilson, who lives near Jewett, was murdered the night of the 5th for his money.

### ALABAMA NEWS

The Hale Circuit Court sent Charles Jemison (negro) to the penitentiary for life, for murder.

Bowen, the murderer of Carter Harrison, has escaped from the Escambia Jail.
Joshua P. Coman of Athens has been quite sick.

Died in Orrville 19th, Imogene Russell Berry, infant daughter of L.S. and F.M. Berry.

### DIED IN ALABAMA

Near Hayneville, 14th, Mrs. Ellen Meadows.
In Courtland, 10th, B.B. Hawkins.
In Etowah County, 12th, Mrs. Wiley Nelms.
In Etowah County, 9th, Anderson Brannan.
In Courtland, 12th, Mrs. M.J. Cravens.
In Bibb County, 5th, Blassingame Nabors.
Near North Port, 12th, Thomas Hughes.
Near Mantua, 9th, John S. Lavender.
In Eutaw, 12th, W.W. Hawkins.
In Eutaw, 12th, W.R. Hardaway.
Near Opelika, 17th, Mrs. Yarbrough.
In Pickens County, recently, Mrs. R.R. Bogle.
In Pickens County, recently, Mrs. C.B. Cook.
In California, recently, General D.P. Baldwin, formerly of Wilcox.
In Tennessee, 29th ult., E.C. Nicholson of Montgomery County.
In Pickens County, recently, Mrs. W.B. Peebles.
In Pickens County, recently, Mrs. A.B. Hughes.
In Aberdeen, Mississippi, 7th ult., Mrs. Jane A. Gladney, formerly of Pickens County.

## THE SOUTHERN ARGUS - DEATHS - JUNE 1869 THROUGH JUNE 1874

Issue 5-1-1874

### TEXAS NEWS
Died in Galveston, 10th ult., Colonel W.H. Sellers.
Died in Galveston, 13th ult., Mrs. Martha E. Andrews.

The elder of the Pruitt's recently reported killed near Granbury is not dead. [see issue April 24, 1874]

D.J. White was assassinated in Sherman the 23rd ult.

In Kimball, recently, a man named Abell was killed by one named Shoat, and the latter was hung by mob.

### ALABAMA NEWS
J.H. Woodward of Sumter has been convicted of manslaughter and sentenced to the penitentiary for one year for killing a Mr. Lindsay in 1865.

Sam Slaton and Moses Mann were recently drowned in Mobile Bay.

Mrs. Sam Turner, Jr. of Athens has been very ill.

In the Coosa Circuit Court, the case of Wilson for killing Nabors, from Shelby, was continued by the state.

### DIED IN ALABAMA
In Pike County, 9th ult., Mrs. Sarah Sanders.
In Montgomery, 19th ult., Wright Groome.
At Triana, recently, W.B. Edwards.
In Eufaula, 22nd ult., Miss Eliza Courtney.
Near North Port, 21st ult., Fletcher Jones.
Near Gaylesville, 14th ult., John Little.
In Montgomery, 31st ult., James R. Lewis.
In Greenville, 19th ult., Fannie Ashford, child.
In Choctaw County, 4th ult., Mrs. Leah Burns.
In Mobile, 22nd ult., Mrs. Mary F. Crippen.
In Monroe County, 15th ult., John Peebles.
In Barbour County, 20th ult., Larkin Baker.
In Tuskegee, 24th ult., Rev. Isaac Spangler.
In Greenville, 15th ult., Miss Amanda Murphree.
In Talladega County, 23rd ult., Rev. Oliver Welch.
In Lawrence County, 12th ult., Mrs. Samuel Wallace.
In Brooklyn, New York, 16th ult., Rush Fuller, late of Mobile.
In California, 25th ult., Adam Schuessler, formerly of Montgomery.

# THE SOUTHERN ARGUS - DEATHS - JUNE 1869 THROUGH JUNE 1874

Issue 5-8-1874

## TEXAS NEWS

Died in Waco, recently, G.W. Prather.
Died in Waco, recently, Thomas J. Owen.
Died recently, in San Antonio, Mrs. David Y. Portis.
Died in Smith County, recently, Warren Williams.
Died in Smith County, March 10th, Mrs. Josephine Amanda Jones, formerly of Sumter County, Alabama.

Mem. Murphy, a desperado of Hill County, was recently taken from jail in Hillsboro by a mob and shot to death.

Mayor White was recently struck by lightning, near Galveston, and killed.

Died in Austin, 15th ult., James S. Hunt.

## ALABAMA NEWS

Near Marion, recently, Jordon DeYampert, negro, was shot and killed by W.E. Warford.

Frank Duran of Columbiana has been seriously ill.

Mr. James Edward Morrison, one of the oldest and best citizens of the county, died Friday the 1st inst.

Dr. J. Martin Lee, a well known and long honored citizen of Dallas, died in Carlowville, Thursday, April 30th, in the 64th year of his age.

Mrs. Nancy Ellis, wife of Nathan Ellis, died the 1st at her residence in this county, aged eighty-one years, two months, and three days. She had been in Dallas County since 1819; had been married sixty years; and had been a member of the Methodist Protestant Church forty-five years. Her husband, Nathan Ellis, still lives at the age of eighty-one years, full of years, and endowed with the confidence and respect of all who know him.

## DIED IN ALABAMA

Died in Mobile, 29th ult., Daniel Kelly.
Died in Greene County, recently, Z.M. McGehee.
In Eufaula, 27th ult., Dr. E. Sheppard.
In Jasper, 23rd ult., Joseph Richardson.
In Eutaw, 28th ult., Mrs. Virginia Palmer.
In Elyton, 24th ult., Mrs. Mary E. Place.
Near Moulton, 10th ult., Mrs. Margaret Kelly.

# THE SOUTHERN ARGUS - DEATHS - JUNE 1869 THROUGH JUNE 1874

In Lawrence County, 9th ult., Wm. Wasson.
In Tuscumbia, 28th ult., Wm. Farley, infant.
In Athens, 24th ult., Nina E. Tanner, infant.
In Huntsville, 29th ult., Mrs. Martha E. Dill.
In Opelika, 25th ult., Mrs. S.C. Tally.
In Marion, 2nd, Mrs. Gray Huckabee.
In Texas, recently, Mrs. Julia A. Woodward, formerly of Talladega.
In Talladega County, 23rd ult., Sue Ida Harrison.
In Gadsden, 24th ult., Mrs. Emma A. Johnson.
In Sandy Hill, New York, March 15th, Henry Lewis, formerly of Mobile.
In Lee County, Mississippi, 14th ult., Miss Laura V. Shawver, late of Eutaw.
In Blount Springs, 25th ult., Dr. R.S. Williams of Mobile.
In Coosa County, 28th ult., Mrs. Mary Garland Marks Moore.
In Texas, 15th March, Bennet Easterling, formerly of Pickens County.
In Montgomery County, 15th ult., Mrs. R.H. Cross, Sr.

Issue 5-15-1874

## TEXAS NEWS

T.M. Leach, G.W. Goforth, and W.W. Thompson, have recently died in or near Killgore, Rusk County.

Died in Grayson County, 4th ult., J.T. Lackey.

Louis Logan died in Coryelle County recently.

Rev. G.W. Prather died in Waco, 18th ult.

## ALABAMA NEWS

R.W.H. Armstrong of Colbert County has been seriously ill.

Died in East Selma, 12th inst., Mrs. J.J. McMahon.

Died in this city, Monday last the 11th inst., in the 65th year of his age, Joel Early Matthews.

On the 15th, J.W. Carter of Limestone County was attacked at his house by J.D. Stevenson, an insane man, whom, in self defence, he killed.

General J.M. Lane of Athens was, on the 8th, reported dying.

In Pine Level a few months ago, Dr. Morrisey killed Dr. McLeod.
   In Pine Level a few days ago, Dr. James D. Townsend shot and wounded Dr. Morrisey.

## THE SOUTHERN ARGUS - DEATHS - JUNE 1869 THROUGH JUNE 1874

In Montevallo, recently, W.B. Brown was shot and wounded by R.D. Harris.

Dr. Kendall of Benton has been very sick.

Mrs. General Robinson of Loundes County has been very sick.

General H.H. Higgins of Athens has been quite sick.

### DIED IN ALABAMA

In Perry, 3rd, Mrs. Martha Hogue.
In Linden, 3rd, Mrs. R.H. Clarke.
In Mobile, 8th, A.M. Sprague.
In Pickens County, 3rd, James Kerr.
In Tuscumbia, 6th, Mrs. Ann Farrar.
In Colbert County, 29th ult., Dr. J. Douglass.
In Florence, 3rd, Charles McAllister.
In Birmingham, 4th, G.W. Clift.
In Tuskaloosa, 4th, Rev. A.S. Hamilton.
In Dale County, 30th ult., Mrs. Gideon Massey.
Near Oxford, 5th, Mrs. William Johnson, Sr.
In Hale County, 5th, Mrs. J. Howard.
In Lowndes County, 3rd, Jos. Rudolph, child.
In Sanford County, 27th ult., Mr. Lokey.
In Mobile, 19th, David Cumming.
In Montgomery, 12th, W.F. Witcher.
In Bradford, Coosa County, recently, Mrs. Mary Moore.
Near Grove Hill, 30th ult., Mrs. Henrietta Pogue.
In Petersburg, Virginia, 28th ult., Mrs. Julia Perkins Watson, formerly of Eutaw.
In Shreveport, Louisiana, 21st ult., Mrs. Nettie Leonard Ashmore, formerly of Tuskaloosa.
In Columbus, Mississippi, recently, Dr. C.W. Westmoreland, formerly of Greene County.

James Edward Morrison sweetly, calmly fell asleep in Jesus at his residence near Selma, Alabama, on the first day of May, 1874, being in the sixty-third year of his age. He was born in Cabarras County, North Carolina, June 3rd, 1811, and came to Alabama when quite young... For nearly twenty years he filled the office of ruling Elder in Valley Creek Church.

Issue 5-22-1874

Redden Hodges of St. Clair County has been very ill.

## THE SOUTHERN ARGUS - DEATHS - JUNE 1869 THROUGH JUNE 1874

Mr. E. James has been made a member of the Lowndes County democratic executive committee, vice W.F. Witcher, dead.

W.F. Witcher, who recently died in Hayneville, had his life insured for $10,000.

The Bar of Lowndes and the Democrat Executive Committee have passed resolutions in memory of the late W.F. Witcher.

Mr. M.A. Sheehan, Editor of the *Henry Co. Register*, has been quite sick.

Rev. T.R. Parker of Lineville has been missing some time and his friends fear foul play.

In the case of Hooper, charged with killing Phillips in Opelika in May last, tried last week in the Russell Circuit Court, the jury returned a verdict of not guilty.

Captain W.F. Karsner of Tuskaloosa has been quite ill.

The dead body of a man named Lunceford was recently found near Union Church in Tuskaloosa County.

Dr. W.P. Cabe, formerly of Dallas County, died near Durand, Mississippi, April 11th.

Died in this city, Monday last the 18th, Miss Camilla Mims, daughter of the late George W. and Joanna S. Mims of Holmes County, Mississippi.

### DIED IN ALABAMA

In Clinton, 2nd, Jesse Hill
In Florence, 12th, David H. Hudson.
In Pickens County, 6th, E.P. Hill.
In Mobile, 15th, Geo. Murphy, child.
Near Centre, 7th, Jas. A. Long.
In Lowndes, 10th, Mrs. Roderick Morrison.
In Opelika, 15th, Henry Bird.
In Limestone County, 12th, H.P. Elliott.
In Athens, 8th, James M. Lane.
In Athens, 10th, Mrs. Samuel Tanner, Jr.
In Athens, 12th, Gen. H.H. Higgins.
In Wilcox County, recently, Dr. T.C. Strother.
In Montgomery, 14th, Bruce Joiner.
In Mobile, 8th, A.M. Sprague.
In Cherokee County, 26th ult., J.M.P. Coker.
In Gadsden, 8th, Miss Rosa Ross.
In Montgomery, 12th, Isaac Cohen.

## THE SOUTHERN ARGUS - DEATHS - JUNE 1869 THROUGH JUNE 1874

In Clayton, 13th, Mrs. John Rees.
In Mobile, 1st, Miss C.A.E. McCune.
In Mobile, 30th ult., A.M. Phillips.
In Mobile, 16th, Geo. W. Tarleton.
At Castleberry, 7th, Mrs. Amanda Howard.
Near Springville, 8th, Miss Sarah A. Greene.
Near Ashville, 7th, John W. Hodges.
In Mobile, 21st ult., Mrs. Mary Florence Morrow of Greene County.
In Mayhew, Mississippi, 18th ult., Mrs. M.C. Thompson, formerly of Florence.
In Lauderdale County, recently, Mrs. Milly Tate.
In Milan, Tennessee, recently, Mrs. J.F. Parker, nee Hart, formerly of Tuskaloosa.
In Tennessee, 8th, Mrs. Mollie A. Mitchell, formerly of Athens.
In Montgomery, 18th, infant child of C.P. Storrs.

Issue 5-29-1874

### TEXAS NEWS

Died in Marlin, 13th, W.I. Adair.

Col. P.T. Tannehill of Henderson County died recently in Bryan.

The night of the 20th, J.H. McEachern, Editor of the *Jefferson Democrat*, was shot twice, and perhaps fatally wounded, by Wm. Richardson, a bar-keeper.

A man named Coleman in Coryelle County recently shot and killed his wife.

John Fullerton, Michael Morton, P.F. Coakley and H. Filgner, were murdered at Penescal, near Corpus Christi the 9th.

F.R. Turner, an old citizen of Hopkins County, died recently.

### ALABAMA NEWS

Adrian Robinson of Forkland recently had his arm so mutilated in the machinery of a steam mill as to necessitate amputation near the shoulder.

Dan Shelby of Lowndes County is very ill.

In Monroe County the other day, John Cross was killed by the falling of a piece of timber, which he was raising into a ginhouse.

B.P. Worthington, near Birmingham, has been very sick.

Died in Selma, Friday last, James Tomlinson.

## THE SOUTHERN ARGUS - DEATHS - JUNE 1869 THROUGH JUNE 1874

Miss Mary Ann Daley died in this city Thursday of last week.

Died in this city, Friday last, of diphtheria, little Willie, son of Mr. and Mrs. C.W. Hooper, aged eighteen months.

### DIED IN ALABAMA

In Fayette County, 10th, James Jenkins.
In Baldwin County, 10th, H.H. Coster.
In Montgomery, 22nd, infant of W.H. Hill.
In Mobile, 18th, Henry Stauter.
In DeKalb County, 14th, R. Estes.
In Etowah County, 5th, son of Edward Cox.
In Birmingham, 17th, Hattie Wheeler, infant.
In Birmingham, 18th, Thomas O'Brien, boy.
In Lowndes County, 11th, Mrs. S.C. Bell.
In Demopolis, 17th, Charles K. Breitling.
In Athens, 15th, Mrs. Rebecca J. Hendricks.
In Eufaula, 22nd, W.H. McNamee.
In Tuskegee, 15th, Mrs. Pauline Felts.
In Talladega County, 19th, Mrs. W.P. Shelley.
In Elmore County, 5th, John Holley, aged eighty-two.
In Cusseta, 20th, Thomas L. Penn, Sr.
In Opelika, 23rd, Mrs. Margaret Perry.
In Etowah County, 26th, P.M. Turner.
In Birmingham, 25th, infant of John Glovannl.
In Randloph County, 20th, W.A. Grant.
In Randolph County, 14th, Mrs. T.E. Stone.
In Louisa, 15th, child of Z.T. Phillips.
Near Paris, Tennessee, 7th, Miss Bettie Polk McKay, formerly of Lawrence County.
Near Mt. Hope, March 22nd, Miss Lucy Jemison.
In Etowah County, 10th, Mrs. Elizabeth Alford, aged one hundred three years.
In Eufaula, 22nd, Allie Warren Dickinson, child.
In Shelby County, 17th, Embery Spence Horton.
In Pike County, March 18th, Mrs. Mary McBryde.
In Jonesboro, Jefferson County, 25th, Mrs. Ellen, wife of Capt. S.A. Tarrant.

Issue 6- 5-1874

### TEXAS NEWS

Rev. Henry Renick of Travis County died the 24th ult.

J.M. McMullen, late of Troupe County, died in Tyler recently.

# THE SOUTHERN ARGUS - DEATHS - JUNE 1869 THROUGH JUNE 1874

A little son of Capt. Ayers of Paris accidentally shot and badly wounded himself a few days ago.

J.H. McEachern, Editor of the *Jefferson Democrat*, recently shot in a difficulty in which he was not a participant, is dead.

In Hill County, recently, a man named Willis was killed by Stephen Wright, who was subsequently killed while resisting arrest.

## ALABAMA NEWS

T.J. Pierce, late of Russell County, is very ill in Columbus, Georgia.

Near Pine Apple, recently, James Owens shot and killed a negro.

William Snyder of Tuskaloosa County was recently shot and killed by a young man named Beavers.

In Courtland, a man named Horne was recently hung by a mob for an outrage upon the person of a little girl.

Little Willie, son of Mr. and Mrs. Charles Kuhne, died Tuesday last.

We regret to learn that Miss Hattie Works, a very charming young lady, is quite ill at the residence of her mother in this city.

W.L. Kerley, recently of Clay County, was the other day reported dying at Collinsville.

## DIED IN ALABAMA

In Henry County, recently, F.M. Weems.
In Abbeville, recently, child of W. Skinner.
In Montgomery, 1st, W.M. Finley.
In Mobile, recently, Capt. Peter Aunspaugh.
Near Clayton, 26th ult., Peter Cunningham.
In Wilcox County, 17th ult., M.W. Cook.
In Russell County, recently, Caswell Black.
In Montevallo, 24th ult., John T. Davis.
In Hale County, 21st ult., Richard Avery.
In Hale County, 24th ult., James Junkins.
In Hale County, 24th ult., J.H. Syring.
In Mobile, 28th ult., Thos. Macartney, infant.
In Monroe County, 15th ult., J. Leslie Johnson.
Near Alpine, 16th ult., Mrs. Dr. J.C. Heacock.
In Troy, recently, Mrs. Samuel Trotter.
In Pike County, recently, William Mills.

## THE SOUTHERN ARGUS - DEATHS - JUNE 1869 THROUGH JUNE 1874

Near Enon, 16th ult., Martin Howard.
In Troy, 25th ult., R.H. Park.
In Opelika, 22nd ult., W.H. McNamee.
In Montgomery, 27th ult., Dr. Frank Lynch.
In Clarke County, 3rd ult., W.J. Cole of Mobile.
In Bibb County, 2nd, Judge J.W. Suttle, aged sixty-nine.
In Elmore County, 9th ult., Miss Gussie Meadors.
Near Mt. Andrew, 17th ult., Mrs. Rebecca Upton.
In Calhoun County, John W. Ledbetter.
Near Reform, 24th ult., infant of Dr. S.L. Bonner.
In Waynesboro, Mississippi, 24th ult., Mrs. Agnes Webster, formerly of Mobile.

Died April 11th, 1874, near Durand, Mississippi, in the twenty-sixth year of his age, Dr. William Paul Cabe, formerly of Dallas County, Alabama... a member of the Presbyterian Church.

Issue 6-12-1874

### TEXAS NEWS

Thomas J. League died in Galveston 28th ult.

Mrs. Dr. W.T. Moore, eldest daughter of ex-Governor Throckmorton, died in McKinney, 20th ult.

### ALABAMA NEWS

Mrs. B.B. Lewis of Tuskaloosa has been quite ill.

Allen Wambold of Pike County was recently accidentally killed.

Near Hilliardsville, Isaac T. Calver recently, in self defence, shot and killed a negro named Buford Whitehurst.

A young man named Pennington, or Pendleton, recently stole a horse in Geneva County and was pursued, overtaken, and shot to death.

S. Dennis, Sr. of Dadeville has been very sick.

The Barbour Circuit Court sentences Jack Horn (negro) to death for robbery.
    Abe Cotton and Jack Horn (negroes) will be hung at Clayton, July 17th.

Rev. A. Jay of Conecuh County was recently badly hurt by a kick from a horse.

## THE SOUTHERN ARGUS - DEATHS - JUNE 1869 THROUGH JUNE 1874

In the neighborhood of Hilliardsville, Mr. Peacock recently shot and killed a negro named Crawford Skipper.

J.C. Montgomery has been appointed solicitor of St. Clair County, vice Finley dead.

Nicholas, son of N.D. Talley of Jefferson County, was killed the 1st by a horse kick.
The 2nd inst., a child of N.D. Talley of Jefferson County died of meningitis.

Judge John B. Jones, many years ago a lawyer in Selma, died recently in Galveston.

Died in this city the 7th at the residence of her son-in-law, Mr. E. Stanton, Mrs. O. Sutherland.

Father O'Leary, the beloved pastor of the Catholic Church here, is again at his post after an absence and dangerous illness of months.

John Anderson, the negro manager on Dr. D.C. Anderson's place in Greene County, was recently shot and killed by a negro named Louis Connegan.

### DIED IN ALABAMA
In Elyton, 3rd, Lizzie Kelly Wildsmith, infant.
In Colbert County, 28th ult., J.J. Russell.
In Cross Plains, 1st, C.W. Sharp.
In Collinsville, 22nd ult., W.L. Kerley.
In Greensboro, 4th, F.P. Ravesies.
Near Greensboro, 16th ult., Mrs. Orry Williams.
In Greene County, 20th ult., W.M. Taylor.
On Sand Mountain, recently, Baxter Gilbreth.
In Camden, 30th ult., Mrs. Augusta Gaillard.
In Limestone County, 28th ult., T.M.L. Reid.
In Tuskaloosa, 29th ult., infant of T.B. Waller.
In Gadsden, 26th ult., Joseph White.
In Ashville, 25th ult., W.M. Finley.
In Mobile, 31st ult., Mrs. Jane Ann Stuart.
In Opelika, 6th, Dr. T.W. Newsome.
Near Tuskegee, 29th ult., Miss Amelia Abercrombie.
In Escambia County, 4th ult., daughter of Reuben Hart.
In Carrolton, 27th ult., Mrs. Rebecca A. Gresham.
In Etowah County, 29th ult., Mrs. W.B. Gilliland.
In Randolph County, 27th ult., Mrs. Lizzie Weaver.

## THE SOUTHERN ARGUS - DEATHS - JUNE 1869 THROUGH JUNE 1874

Issue 6-19-1874

TEXAS NEWS

Died in Hempstead, 1st, Jesse R. Ward.
Died in Marlin, 30th ult., Dr. G.W. Outler.

James L. Haswell recently died in Fayette County.

ALABAMA NEWS

The 11th, Mr. F.S. Hermitage of Mobile was thrown from the truck of a hook and ladder company and fatally injured.

Richard Lindsay of Russell County was dangerously ill last week.

Col. N.W. Long, many years a citizen of Russell County, is in very bad health in Columbus, Georgia.

Hannah Trice, widow of Captain W.R. Trice, late of Summit, was declared a lunatic by a jury on the 13th.

Mr. and Mrs. John Sampey of Belleville have been seriously ill.

Col. C.C. Langdon was quite sick at Bladon Springs last week.

Joseph Betancourt was drowned in Mobile River the other day.

In Jasper, recently, J.C. Lollar was killed by Isaac Brown.

The venerable John Smith of Jones' Valley, has been quite sick. He is over eighty years old. In sight of him now, is Rev. Reuben Phillips, seventy-nine years old.

Mrs. E.H. King of Tuskaloosa has been very ill but is convalescent.

O. Ereckson of Mobile was accidentally drowned the other day.

Mrs. Jones, who died in Clay County a few days ago, was one hundred seven years old.

Mrs. Hart, sister of Mr. Neal of the *Daily Echo*, died in Wetumpka the 10th inst.

"Little Shepherd", only child of Mr. Hecker(?) of the *Daily Echo*, died in Linden on Friday last the 12th.

## THE SOUTHERN ARGUS - DEATHS - JUNE 1869 THROUGH JUNE 1874

Col. N.W. Long, many years a citizen of Russell County, is in very bad health in Columbus, Georgia.

### DIED IN ALABAMA

Near Wedowee, 27th ult., W.A. Grant.
In Mobile, 11th, F.S. Hermitage.
In Mobile the 11th, Mrs. Willie V. Figures.
In Pickens County, 4th, Mrs. Ann Hodge.
In Russellville, 14th ult., Mrs. Eva Clarke.
Near Moulton, 7th, Mrs. James Woodruff.
In Mobile, 12th, infant of W.B. Holt.
In Clay County, recently, Mrs. Jones.
In Mobile, 12th, O. Ereckson.
In Newbern, 9th, Mrs. C.C. Huckabee.
In Perry County, 13th, Mrs. Robert Craig.
Near Bladon Springs, 3rd, Mrs. R. Harwell.
Near Bladon Springs, 2nd, Mr. McBatley.
In Conecuh County, 3rd, Charles Beddingfield.
Near Gravilla, 25th ult., Mrs. Philyow.
In Mobile, 14th, Mrs. Elizabeth Hepburn.
In Tuskaloosa, 8th, Miss Virginia Donoho.
In Tuskaloosa, 4th, Miss Mary Kerr.
In Tuskaloosa, 10th, infant of Prof. Peck.
In North Port, 8th, Mrs. E. Norris.
In Jefferson County, 7th, T.F. Waldrop.
In Birmingham, 10th, Mrs. R.A. Hughes.
In Eufaula, 12th, Lafayette Stow.
In Opelika, 15th, Mrs. Fletcher.
In Mobile, 14th, infant of Charles Stuart.
In Paris, France, 9th, Joseph Godard of Mobile.
In Columbus, Georgia, 9th, Walker, son of Col. Walker Richardson of Glennville.
In Glennville, 9th, Sanford, son of Col. Walker Richardson.
At Macon Station, 30th ult., Mrs. Narcissa Tayloe.
In Marion, 10th, C.C. Pegues, infant son of John Walthall.
In Morgan County, 31st ult., Mrs. Sarah F/E. Chunn.
In Tuskaloosa County, 29th ult. Julia A. Robinson.

Issue 6-26-1874

### TEXAS NEWS

Died in Navasota, 9th, Philo B. Perry.

Hon. James Love of Galveston is dead.

## THE SOUTHERN ARGUS - DEATHS - JUNE 1869 THROUGH JUNE 1874

Died near San Felipe, 9th, Joseph Greer.
Died in Austin, 15th, Augustus Gebhard.
Died in Jefferson, recently, Major James A. Crump.

Marmaduke Box, a veteran of 1812, died at Rockport the 18th.

### ALABAMA NEWS

Mike Fitzgerald, the accomplished engineer of the Little Mechanic fire engine, left with his family, on Wednesday, to spend the summer with his relatives in Hamilton County, Ohio. We regret that Mr. Fitzgerald's health makes a rest of some months necessary. We hope he may return with the frost, with health and strength completely restored.

Seaborn Walker (negro) has been arrested near Sparta for killing Mr. Halliday in Russel County about two years ago.

Col. Long of Huntsville is in hopelessly feeble health.

The wife of Dr. N. D. Richardson of Athens has been dangerously ill.

At Garland, Butler County, 19th, James Bradley was shot and mortally wounded by a Mr. Hays.

On the 11th, three little children of William Cook, who lives near Hanceville, fell into an old well and were drowned.

Mrs. B. B. Lewis of Tuskaloosa is still very ill.

L. B. Howard, son of Mrs. W. W. Howard of Lowndes County, was killed the 18th by the accidental discharge of his gun.

### DIED IN ALABAMA
In Decatur, 14th, W. H. Horne.
In Baldwin County, 18th, Theodore Graham.
In Dale County, 14th, Sam'l. Grice.
In Pike County, 10th, Mrs. John J. Blair.
In Pike County, 16th, Mrs. Douglass.
In Tallapoosa County, recently, Mrs. Young.
In Columbiana, 16th, infant of Dr. Hubbard.
In North Port, 16th, W. Seth Bolton.
Near Opelika, 15th, Mrs. John Fletcher.
Near Warsaw, 3rd, Mrs. Tabitha Rogers.
In Courtland, recently, J. D. Rebman.

## THE SOUTHERN ARGUS - DEATHS - JUNE 1869 THROUGH JUNE 1874

In St. Clair County, 5th, Mrs. Joice Newton.
In St. Clair County, 7th, John Collins.
Near Ashville, 15th, Oscar F. Neely.
Near Oxford, 14th, John Floyd Smith, Jr.
In Uehee, 16th, Rev. J. C. Carter.
In Chambers County, recently, Howard Finney.
In California, 26th ult., Theo Revault, formerly of Mobile.
In Gadsden, 18th, W. L. Cain.

Mrs. Mary J. White, the estimable wife of Captain John White, died in this city on Tuesday last.

Sunday last, Mrs. M. A. Nicol was seriously injured by a fall from a second story window of her residence.

William Lothrop, infant son of Mr. W. V/N. R. and Mrs. Minnie L. Watson, died in Galveston the 16th, aged two months and nine days.

Mrs. Elizabeth Prestridge, a venerable lady well-known in this county, where until recently she had resided for many years, died a few days ago near Alvarado, Johnson County, Texas.

After a long and painful illness, Dr. George H. Lenoir died in this city on Thursday last. He was a native of Tennessee, but came to this county in 1867 and married Miss Fannie Barker of Cahaba. He had been a resident of Selma about three years.

Died at Logan's Station the 19th, Mrs. Mary Elliott.

At Garland, Butler County, 19th, James Bradley was shot and mortally wounded by a Mr. Hays.

**THE SOUTHERN ARGUS - DEATHS - JUNE 1869 THROUGH JUNE 1874**

NAME INDEX

Abbott 181, 233
Abell 346
Abercrombie 39, 119, 167, 189, 323, 355
Abernathy 8, 192, 248, 272
Aberson 144
Ables 64, 108, 293, 315, 344
Abney 12
Abram 190
Abston 88
Achille 67
Acker 261
Ackerman 20, 71
Acklen 79, 216
Acre 313
Acton 313, 339
Adair 351
Adam 208
Adams 7, 45, 47, 63, 65, 66, 67, 75, 81, 82, 85, 95, 96, 104, 105, 107, 125, 190, 193, 194, 195, 198, 208, 254, 259, 265, 269, 300
Addison 337
Aderhold 48
Adkins 78
Adkinson 15
Adolphe 125
Adrain 98, 244
Affron 47, 197
Agee 68
Agner 290, 293
Aiken 86, 143
Aikenhead 50
Ainchbacker 204
Ainsworth 1
Airey 174
Aite 118
Akin 117
Albertine 117
Albright 221, 303
Albritton 189

Alcorn 289
Alderburg 79
Aldridge 56, 81, 181, 276, 341
Alexander 15, 111, 154, 195, 197, 198, 209, 235, 240, 245, 294, 295, 306, 310, 337
Alford 112, 132, 239, 303, 352
Alfred 46
Alisando 259
Alison 337
Allard 304, 310
Allbrook 35
Allen 16, 54, 55, 100, 140, 145, 163, 182, 187, 199, 217, 221, 231, 235, 236, 239, 241, 250, 256, 273, 290, 294, 299, 312, 317, 327, 340
Alley 216, 231
Allicin 145
Allington 240
Allison 86, 87, 183, 283, 334
Allread 299, 302
Alnchbacker 204
Alrey 174
Alsebrook 246
Alsebrooks 336
Alston 89, 100
Alte 118
Alvarez 139
Amand 48
Ambrose 219
Amonett 91, 271
Amos 111
Amsden 177
Anchors 168
Anderson 20, 34, 36, 38, 49, 56, 73, 76, 85, 106, 108, 113, 132, 133, 136, 140, 179, 229, 246, 247, 248, 274, 311, 355
Andre 210
Andrew 92, 144, 212

## THE SOUTHERN ARGUS - DEATHS - JUNE 1869 THROUGH JUNE 1874

Andrews  119, 149, 259, 276, 342, 346
Angel  328
Angell  295
Angle  22
Anthony  85, 137, 267
Antony  316
Anyan  141
Applewhite  259, 269
Appling  241, 242
Apsey  50, 67
Arbucle  259
Archer  92, 245
Archey  319
Archibald  195
Arendale  254, 268
Armer  52
Armstead  66
Armstrong  77, 101, 141, 179, 180, 214, 243, 244, 249, 286, 330, 348
Arnold  5, 109, 163, 194
Arrington  136, 236
Arter  86
Arthur  72, 133, 332
Aschenbaum  220
Ash  158, 178
Ashbury  340
Ashe  104, 310
Ashford  14, 81, 97, 236, 346
Ashland  249
Ashley  36, 125, 142, 162, 302
Ashmore  138, 349
Ashurst  49, 278, 279
Atkins  75, 79, 116, 249
Atkinson  42, 131, 157, 321
Attaway  20, 301
Atway  339, 344
Atwood  57, 177
Auderson  239
Aunspaugh  353
Aurieres  185
Austin  21, 74, 266, 335
Autery  33

Autunez  70
Avcrytt  243
Avent  215, 216
Averett  104
Avery  182, 247, 270, 353
Averytt  239, 243
Axem  139
Aycock  179
Ayers  85, 89, 353
Baas  170
Back  191
Bacon  140
Bagby  136, 292
Baggett  8, 118, 338
Bagley  162, 337
Baich  338
Bailey  72, 150, 173, 177, 179, 194, 246, 281, 282, 304, 310
Bails  55
Baird  339
Baker  20, 44, 51, 53, 55, 61, 79, 89, 100, 162, 165, 168, 174, 177, 211, 231, 232, 233, 248, 263, 265, 299, 301, 305, 310, 330, 346
Baldwin  109, 129, 226, 294, 300, 345
Balkum  300
Ball  16, 47, 188, 278, 283, 324
Ballard  57, 60, 79, 81
Ballew  290
Balley  179
Balling  328
Baltzell  333
Balzegar  83
Bancroft  31, 49, 54
Banks  113, 115, 255, 328
Bannister  308
Banta  74
Banting  197
Barber  67, 164
Barbour  42, 175
Barclay  12, 43, 112, 277, 338
Barefield  111

## THE SOUTHERN ARGUS - DEATHS - JUNE 1869 THROUGH JUNE 1874

Barelli  306
Barfield  311
Barger  131
Bargliss  250
Barham  262, 315
Barker  77, 81, 174, 297, 359
Barkuloo  343
Barley  109
Barlow  83, 110, 146
Barman  150
Barner  79
Barnes  1, 84, 102, 120, 172, 204, 263, 273, 301, 310, 312
Barnet  274
Barnett  102, 133, 231, 236, 272
Barnewell  170
Barnum  251, 310
Barnwell  101
Barr  117, 164, 219, 225, 324
Barrackman  250
Barrett  87, 192, 330
Barrier  175
Barron  1, 40, 60, 94, 150, 166, 203, 230, 269, 338
Barson  230
Bart  176
Bartee  291
Barthelot  302
Barton  12, 89, 113, 136, 191
Basham  108
Basil  319
Basinger  244
Basken  81, 224
Baskin  38, 46, 83
Bass  214, 231
Bassel  14
Bassett  108, 168
Bassford  213
Batcheller  194
Batchelor  110
Bates  11, 36, 80, 93, 135, 161, 219
Batre  105
Battey  61

Battle  59, 63, 84, 155, 172, 289, 339
Battles  326
Baudion  43
Bauerlien  214
Baugh  100, 195, 233
Baxter  79, 108, 198, 279
Bayard  33
Bayne  221
Bayol  206, 304
Bazemore  95
Beach  43
Beaird  180
Beale  291
Beall  85, 156
Beallo  43
Beaman  117
Bean  262
Beard  123, 192, 240, 310
Beasley  214, 309
Beasly  36
Beason  236
Beatty  135
Beauchamp  85
Beaumont  212, 317
Beavers  353
Becham  217
Beck  84, 312
Becker  290
Beddingfield  357
Bedee  188
Bedell  6, 81, 151, 270, 340
Beeker  290
Beers  59
Beggs  134, 300
Belcher  24
Belden  101
Belgart  160, 171
Bell  9, 19, 35, 65, 97, 111, 120, 124, 149, 159, 161, 181, 241, 242, 254, 272, 281, 282, 284, 285, 328, 330, 352
Belser  33-35
Belthoo  74

## THE SOUTHERN ARGUS - DEATHS - JUNE 1869 THROUGH JUNE 1874

Beltzhoover  107
Bemuth  310
Benbow  313
Bender  181, 303, 304
Benge  77
Benjamin  279, 280
Bennet  206
Bennett  44, 82, 104, 213, 260, 268, 291, 327
Benson  38, 83, 95, 204, 234, 290
Bentley  44, 70, 174
Bently  155
Benton  5, 92, 116
Beresford  301
Bergman  301, 310
Berney  75, 153, 200, 205
Beroujon  227
Berrier  11
Berrs  300
Berry  90, 144, 156, 188, 226, 284, 295, 345
Berthelot  303
Best  59, 96
Betancourt  356
Betrie  73
Bettis  339
Beuford  77
Beutly  155
Bevans  87, 124
Beverett  327
Bevington  170
Beyseigel  52
Bibb  14, 16, 43, 98, 108, 118, 141, 151, 300
Bibby  330
Bice  138
Bickenstaff  2
Bickly  244
Bidgood  296
Bierly  259
Bilberry  76
Bilbro  299
Bill  203

Billberry  77
Billen  257
Billings  23, 152
Billingslea  197
Bingham  105, 278
Binion  297, 334-336
Bird  148, 150, 237, 266, 350
Bishop  143, 147, 176, 317, 342
Bittle  327
Bizzell  335
Blacand  215
Black  13, 63, 143, 160, 161, 164, 311, 353
Blackburn  227, 276, 282, 292, 342
Blackman  85, 126
Blackmon  24, 207
Blacksbeer  109
Blackwell  21, 257, 295
Blair  68, 70, 79, 98, 134, 137, 282, 330, 358
Blake  31, 310
Blakely  95
Blakewood  205
Blakey  307
Blanton  234
Bledsoe  131, 143, 181, 240, 286
Blevins  190
Bliss  150, 156, 158, 204
Bloodworth  272
Blount  68, 97
Blow  244, 305
Bloxam  315
Blue  95
Blunt  63, 64, 66
Boan  183
Boardman  98, 253
Boby  197
Bogan  251
Boggan  179
Boggs  104, 108, 113, 242, 334
Bogle  341, 345
Bohlea  91
Boinkman  290

## THE SOUTHERN ARGUS - DEATHS - JUNE 1869 THROUGH JUNE 1874

Boland 152
Boldan 22
Bolinger 126
Bolles 294
Bolling 60, 240
Bolman 147
Bolton 23, 142, 167, 233, 242, 358
Boltz 201
Bonaparte 216
Bond 184, 311, 312
Bone 302
Bonham 9
Bonnell 170
Bonner 7, 249, 269, 290, 354
Bookout 178
Boon 46, 92
Boone 98, 204
Booth 10, 92, 192, 256, 298, 300, 302, 335
Boozer 311
Borden 108, 146, 179, 323, 335
Borders 297
Boring 63
Boseman 272
Boshell 290
Bostock 218
Bostwick 97, 98
Boswell 206, 259, 297
Bosworth 274
Bouborn 334
Bouchelle 17, 227, 327
Bouillemet 307
Boullement 111
Boullemet 128
Boulo 314
Boune 78
Bourd 330
Bowden 247
Bowen 51, 305, 345
Bowers 123
Bowhannon 83
Bowie 266
Bowlen 115

Bowles 147, 318
Bowlin 130
Bowls 146
Bowman 58
Box 290, 335, 358
Boyce 280, 313
Boyd 1, 24, 31, 33, 56, 60, 69, 175, 179, 205, 215, 246, 292
Boykin 16, 62, 150, 190
Boyle 78, 109, 185
Bozeman 188, 271, 282, 291
Bradfield 193
Bradford 3, 20, 55, 65, 96, 108, 274, 292, 313
Bradley 107, 125, 158, 159, 184, 221, 235, 336, 338, 358, 359
Bradly 255
Bradshaw 43, 157
Brady 52, 81, 111, 124
Bragaw 98
Bragg 24, 28, 75, 81, 96, 109, 118, 177, 180, 244, 320
Brame 194, 216
Bramlette 2, 151
Branch 206, 260
Brand 35
Brannan 345
Brannon 67, 219, 234, 262
Bransford 133
Brantley 127, 128, 147
Brantly 80, 164
Brashear 76
Brasher 115, 321
Brassfield 317
Braton 194
Braune 311
Brawner 54
Bray 17, 79, 112, 296
Brazelton 176
Breathwaite 135
Breedlove 248, 256
Breitling 352
Brennan 249

**THE SOUTHERN ARGUS - DEATHS - JUNE 1869 THROUGH JUNE 1874**

Brewer  24, 34, 37, 117, 155, 226, 267, 272, 281
Brewster  313
Brewton  68
Brey  185
Brickell  309, 315
Bridgeforth  218, 323
Bridges  180, 200, 232, 283
Bridgman  1
Briggs  1
Brightman  208
Brindley  126
Brinlee  107
Bristow  238
Britt  312
Brittan  303
Britten  4
Brittle  85
Britton  170, 191, 223
Brizziolari  55
Broadfoot  118
Broadmax  123
Broadnax  316
Brock  119, 183
Brockett  224
Bromberg  176
Brooke  199
Brooks  57-59, 68, 89, 112, 127, 136, 183, 194, 220, 221, 239, 241, 250, 296, 297, 299, 301, 310, 335, 343
Broughton  147, 331
Browder  20, 85
Brown  8, 19, 21, 41, 45, 58, 64, 72, 81, 90, 91, 94, 96, 100, 105, 115, 120, 122, 125, 132, 134, 140, 161, 162, 167, 179, 183, 190, 195, 204, 217, 225, 227, 234, 241, 252, 257, 258, 260, 262, 267, 275, 283, 291, 306, 310, 320, 336, 349, 356
Browne  82
Browning  289
Brownlow  161

Bruce  143, 175, 219
Brunscomb  103
Bruster  230
Bruton  333
Bryan  81, 110, 115, 152, 162, 223, 241, 251, 267
Bryant  29, 72, 111, 139, 179
Bryce  76
Buchanan  238
Buck  164, 166
Buckalew  164
Buckhalter  284
Buckley  149, 210
Buell  279
Buford  139, 209
Bugg  102, 103, 140
Buhler  255, 293
Bulger  24
Bullard  35, 301
Bullock  102
Bumpers  226
Bunckley  183
Bunn  292, 339
Bunting  74, 197
Burchfield  271
Burfield  182
Burfield/Barfield  182
Burfoot  75
Burford  186
Burgamy  313
Burge  66
Burgess  85, 95, 170
Burgin  12
Burgwin  198
Burke  72, 73, 261, 273, 341
Burket  307
Burkett  17
Burks  136
Burn  284, 308
Burnett  18, 137, 139, 256, 300, 341
Burnley  307
Burns  72, 137, 145, 180, 190, 229, 265, 270, 309, 338, 346

**THE SOUTHERN ARGUS - DEATHS - JUNE 1869 THROUGH JUNE 1874**

Burrell  16
Burrows  236
Burrus  114
Burson  42, 230, 315
Burt  55, 98, 173, 176
Burton  85, 126, 141, 202, 225, 298
Burtwell  135
Burtz  228
Burwell  132
Busby  328
Bush  84, 294, 310, 339, 343
Busteed  313
Buster  130
Butherick  206
Butler  53, 78, 100, 140, 177, 287, 327, 330
Butt  43, 150, 208, 225, 267
Butterfield  160, 313
Butts  189
Byars  103
Byers  227, 279, 322, 323
Bynum  339
Byrd  66, 144, 163, 188
Byrne  59, 231
Byrnes  335
Bythewood  150
Cabaniss  15
Cabe  350, 354
Cabell  117
Cabot  296
Cade  46
Cadliff  79
Cady  42
Caffey  218
Cahall  285
Cahill  71, 321
Cain  2, 40, 56, 301, 310, 318, 359
Caldwell  28, 43, 64, 70, 71, 73, 96, 106, 120, 146, 153, 197, 211, 233, 289
Caleff  52
Calhoun  5, 82, 108, 160, 258

Callahan  8, 99, 126, 128
Callan  324
Callen  189
Callenge  128
Calley  314
Callighan  76, 272
Callin  8
Calloway  157, 221
Calver  354
Calvin  99
Camak  253
Cameron  124, 148, 177, 189, 234
Caminade  296, 303
Camp  128, 131
Campbell  8, 29, 33, 40, 46, 166, 172, 185, 198, 239, 244, 272, 279, 336
Canby  101
Candy  26
Canning  252
Cannon  215, 239, 329
Cantwell  16
Caperton  28
Capuion  322
Card  23
Carden  265
Carew  150
Carey  329
Cargile  136, 237
Cargle  110
Carlen  152
Carlisle  215, 216, 218, 321
Carlos  176
Carlton  274
Carmelich  177
Carmichael  89, 113, 330
Carmicheal  321
Carnes  166, 292
Caro  41
Carothers  108, 132
Carpenter  16, 19, 71
Carr  125, 150, 178, 189, 315
Carraway  244, 247

## THE SOUTHERN ARGUS - DEATHS - JUNE 1869 THROUGH JUNE 1874

Carrel  45
Carrender  120
Carrington  124, 128, 316
Carroll  168, 306, 315, 321, 341
Carson  124, 276, 277, 311
Carte  88
Carter  14, 38, 94, 96, 110, 119, 132, 134, 140, 171, 176, 187, 208, 212, 262, 263, 267, 270, 275, 282, 314, 318, 348, 359
Cartledge  297
Cartwright  101, 195
Carver  89
Cary  152, 160, 282, 309
Casal  212
Case  155
Casey  49, 139
Cash  256
Cason  9
Cassaday  303
Cassdes  301
Cassin  168
Castles  310
Cater  330
Cates  285, 309
Cather  228
Cato  13
Caver  204
Cavett  266
Cawthon  323
Cayce  97
Certain  226
Chadwick  244
Chamberlain  63, 233
Chambers  74, 120, 129, 172, 262, 268, 339
Chamblee  114
Chambliss  72, 175
Champion  14, 236
Chancellor  100
Chancy  220
Chandler  117, 120
Chapin  232

Chapman  36, 56, 74, 77, 92, 126, 129, 139, 148, 150, 159, 193, 196, 249, 266, 279
Chappel  23
Chappell  103, 307
Chappelle  269
Charborinet  204
Charles  33
Chassart  289
Chastain  204
Chatcaux  318
Chaudron  171, 307
Cheatham  5, 54
Cheney  37, 117
Cherry  56, 210, 258
Chesnut  207
Chestnut  182, 253
Chevalier  301
Chevelier  310
Chighizola  166
Child  144
Childers  27, 310
Childress  272
Childs  262
Chiles  29, 88, 141, 144
Chilton  86, 88, 134
Chisenhall  279
Chisholm  166, 247
Chisolm  102, 156
Chitwood  35, 329
Chotteau  13
Choutteau  11
Choyle  334
Christian  25, 68, 75, 92, 125, 128, 258, 274, 290
Christopher  51, 268
Chrystal  192
Chunn  357
Cirruth  47
Claiborn  124, 247
Clanton  42, 125, 136, 215, 225, 309
Clapp  336
Clarance  112

**THE SOUTHERN ARGUS - DEATHS - JUNE 1869 THROUGH JUNE 1874**

Clare  82
Clarissa  27
Clarity  249
Clark  47, 50, 68, 70, 80, 81, 104, 113, 128, 131, 162, 165, 178, 236, 255, 273, 275, 276, 290, 291, 316, 321, 324, 325
Clarke  92, 165, 277, 290, 300, 325, 340, 349, 357
Clarkson  161
Claughton  184, 188
Clausen  35
Clausson  43
Clay  37, 169, 326, 339
Clayton  85, 308
Cleary  173
Clem  284
Clemens  204
Clement  336
Clements  47, 120, 126, 192, 254, 288, 294, 295
Cleveland  35, 343
Clifford  308
Clift  349
Clifton  73
Clint  52
Clinton  33, 49, 261, 330
Clitherall  198
Cload  230
Clopton  43
Clouch  52
Cloud  123
Cloudes  164
Clough  261
Clyde  254
Cnsack  177
Coakley  351
Coalman  40
Coates  224
Cobb  24, 26, 44, 46, 78, 85, 97, 149, 154, 307
Cobbs  133, 134, 184
Coblentz  11
Coblentza  11
Coburn  176, 332
Cochran  3, 105, 169, 192, 197, 220, 225, 252, 255, 257, 313
Cochrane  309
Cockburn  256
Cocke  19, 128, 323
Cockrell  64, 98, 112, 225, 332
Cockrill  44
Cody  111
Coffee  140, 217
Cohen  350
Cohill  70
Coker  54, 111, 126, 150, 305, 307, 344, 350
Colby  19, 80, 177
Cole  2, 38, 116, 156, 158, 185, 245, 249, 290, 305, 354
Coleman  57, 66, 111, 117, 137, 143, 150, 193, 238, 239, 260, 285, 290, 310, 322, 323, 325, 351
Coler  274
Coley  341
Collier  13, 111, 165, 172, 222, 232, 238, 283, 320
Collins  9, 11, 31, 46, 67, 107, 126, 129, 153, 166, 168, 185, 189, 192, 194, 200, 201, 208, 237, 274, 285, 314, 359
Colsey  151
Colson  166
Colsson  144
Colt  167
Coltart  75, 107, 254
Colton  302
Colvin  30, 32, 91
Coman  345
Combs  344
Comegys  271, 274
Comer  262, 319
Commlus  212
Condon  284
Cone  80
Coney  242

**THE SOUTHERN ARGUS - DEATHS - JUNE 1869 THROUGH JUNE 1874**

Conley  226
Connally  10
Conne  214
Connegan  355
Connelly  253
Conner  57, 277
Connerly  76, 126, 174, 252
Conners  122, 140
Connine  91
Conning  88
Connolly  178
Connor  316
Connoway  89
Constantine  126, 216
Conter  310
Conuerley  156
Conway  6, 221
Cook  11, 20, 24, 35, 45, 58, 59, 73, 79, 127, 142, 157, 158, 163, 169, 195, 245, 247, 274, 328, 345, 353, 358
Cooke  297
Cooley  41, 191, 330
Cooper  4, 16, 120, 148, 232, 302, 315, 332
Copeland  71, 102, 210
Corbett  28
Corbin  341
Corbitt  278
Corcoran  84
Corege  48
Cornavilla  290
Cornette  154, 155
Corniff  50
Corry  182
Corvin  283
Corzelius  111
Cosgrove  295
Coster  352
Costly  208, 210
Cotehett  93
Cothran  75, 76, 139, 222
Cotten  138, 220
Cottingham  76
Cotton  354
Couch  114, 115, 152
Coulson  101
Counts  99
Coupee  300
Courie  312
Courson  32, 121
Courtney  346
Couter  310
Covington  153, 287
Cowan  157, 306, 332
Cowen  69, 343
Cowin  84, 247
Cowles  51, 67, 105, 123
Cowley  131
Cowling  166
Cox  4, 16, 24, 42, 43, 48, 77, 93, 110, 113, 133, 136, 162, 171, 177, 187, 204, 209, 210, 230, 281, 288, 316, 352
Coyle  82, 151
Crabbe  173
Craft  314
Craig  27, 48, 66, 70, 172, 185, 189, 243, 289, 325, 334, 344, 357
Cramer  26, 336
Crane  218, 318
Crapps  341
Crassette  173
Cravens  345
Cravy  72, 73
Crawford  134, 143, 152, 174, 189, 198, 211, 253, 310
Creach  131
Creagh  166
Crease  209
Creed  220
Creighton  281
Crenshaw  33, 36, 82, 110, 149, 233, 239, 285
Crews  147, 153
Cribbs  247
Crippen  346

## THE SOUTHERN ARGUS - DEATHS - JUNE 1869 THROUGH JUNE 1874

Crisp  250
Crittenden  163
Crocheron  334, 338
Crockett  100
Croft  155
Crone  102
Crook  265
Croom  36
Crosby  182
Croshever  286
Cross  16, 98, 120, 212, 338, 348, 351
Crosswell  228
Crouch  229
Crow  107, 109, 166, 221
Crowder  231, 299
Crowe  49, 52, 307
Crowell  222
Crowley  324
Croxten  262
Croxton  168, 232
Crozier  244
Cruchfield  309
Crum  16, 82, 126
Crump  300, 358
Crusius  127
Crutchfield  313
Crymer  152
Culbert  34
Culpepper  6, 98
Culver  46
Cumming  70, 188, 349
Cummings  50, 105, 262, 263, 268
Cummius  212
Cunningham  2, 50, 62, 63, 68, 88, 115, 146, 166, 179, 193, 196, 218, 255, 263, 296, 309, 353
Curb  64, 282
Curren  331
Currence  127
Currier  249
Curry  40, 90, 169, 231, 308
Curtin  326

Curtis  36, 263
Cusack  177
Cushing  236
Cushman  222
Cusick  197
Cuthbert  73
D'Aubigne  201
Dabney  237
Dacus  230, 261
Dahlberg  342
Daily  153, 226, 260
Dale  274
Daley  124, 352
Daly  269
Daman  117
Dane  72, 74, 206
Danforth  38
Daniel  58, 85, 112, 164, 228, 276, 283, 284, 288, 293, 296, 299, 339
Daniels  145, 340
Danklin  197
Danly  280
Dannelly  282
Danner  212
Dansby  321
Darby  324
Darden  119
Dare  138
Darman  137
Darrell  204
Darwin  162
Daughdrill  31, 54
Davenport  71, 238, 264
David  244, 251, 321
Davidson  45, 82, 119, 142, 184, 206, 227, 265, 282, 313, 335
Davis  2, 8, 12, 14, 50, 58, 61, 70, 71, 79, 83, 95, 100, 113, 132, 153, 162, 166, 168, 175, 176, 177, 182, 200, 206, 215, 216, 221, 223, 229, 236, 237, 244, 246, 247, 250, 251, 259, 262, 264, 267, 268, 278, 281,

**THE SOUTHERN ARGUS - DEATHS - JUNE 1869 THROUGH JUNE 1874**

Davis (continued) 284, 292, 315, 319, 326, 333, 334, 353
Daw 94
Dawkins 176
Dawns 156
Dawson 104, 128, 137, 157, 208, 254, 331
Day 41, 101, 184, 201, 208, 305, 313
De Beaulieu 59
Deale 90
Dean 66, 98, 220, 270, 272, 292
Deane 234
Dear 98
Dearing 30, 100, 197
DeArmar 135
Dearne 123
Deas 71
Deason 192, 229, 232
Deaton 187, 259
Debardelaban 238
DeBardelaben 60, 185
DeBendetti 270
DeBerry 323
Dedlake 311
Dedman 207
Deer 136
Deering 226
Dees 196
Deford 278
DeFreese 212
Delbridge 64
Delecamps 58
Delevan 87
Demasters 206
Dement 226
Deming 6, 198
Demoney 54, 339
Demouey 339
Denman 206
Dennis 128, 129, 158, 159, 354
Denny 204
Densler 175
Denson 92, 219, 231, 271

Dent 12, 13
Denton 245
Deoille 67
Derby 125
Desharo 182
Deshier 140
Desporte 49
Detz 249
DeVotie 201
Dewitt 61, 128, 177, 208, 210
DeYampert 41, 141, 236, 329, 347
Diamond 301
Diaz 101
Dick 171
Dickens 199
Dickenson 114
Dickerson 60, 105, 283
Dickey 46
Dickinson 20, 123, 131, 194, 323, 352
Dickson 204
Dignon 248
Dill 109, 185, 233, 348
Dillahunfy 224
Dillard 2, 113, 179, 180
Dillon 21, 144, 199
Dinsmore 333
Disque 185
Dixon 44, 119, 121, 286
Dobb 314
Dobbins 54
Dobbs 102
Dodson 52, 201
Doggett 103, 320
Doherty 115
Dolbear 285
Donaho 219, 317
Donahoo 158
Donaldson 248
Donavan 150
Donegan 50, 143
Donelson 251
Donoho 357

# THE SOUTHERN ARGUS - DEATHS - JUNE 1869 THROUGH JUNE 1874

Donohoo  54
Donovan  141
Dorman  5, 102, 112, 131, 147
Dorrance  225
Dorroh  311
Dorset  261
Dorsey  176, 270, 273
Doss  20
Dotton  173
Dotty  308
Dougall  304
Dougherty  113
Douglas  32, 34, 43, 63, 71, 141, 164, 262, 268, 278, 295
Douglass  165, 321, 349, 358
Douson  168
Douthit  60
Dowdell  124
Dowdy  187
Dowell  163
Dowling  297
Downing  116, 125
Downs  223
Dox  124
Doyle  24, 61, 161
Dozier  127, 252
Drake  12, 15, 39, 48, 91, 151, 164, 212, 276, 291, 320
Drakeford  105
Drane  154
Driggers  176
Drinkard  175
Driver  137
Drummond  126, 176, 192
Dryer  171
DuBois  14, 18
Dubose  48, 254, 294, 296, 327
Dubroca  247
Duclous  316
Dudley  96, 102, 197, 224, 266, 293, 303
Duerson  51
Duff  226
Duffie  174

Dugan  326
Dugary  334
Duggan  261
Duke  101, 288
Dukes  141, 207
Dulaney  4, 276
Dumas  80, 223
Dunbar  2, 63, 246
Duncan  81, 176, 178, 190, 195, 263, 300
Dunkin  29, 198
Dunklin  173
Dunlap  20, 22, 228, 308, 310
Dunn  18, 140, 146, 194, 308
Dupree  87, 223
Dupuy  7
Duran  347
Durand  77
Durham  210
Durr  313
Duryee  49
DuTour  275
Duvall  149, 281
Dwinelle  109
Dyer  21, 81, 339
Dykous  146, 152
Eady  57
Eagon  131
Earle  83, 278
Early  17, 22, 248, 348
Earns  314
Earp  307
Earrand  304
Easley  276, 318
Eason  135
East  284
Eastburn  291
Easter  16, 17
Easterling  348
Eastin  90
Eaths  237
Eatman  16
Eaton  301
Eaves  216, 267

**THE SOUTHERN ARGUS - DEATHS - JUNE 1869 THROUGH JUNE 1874**

Eberhart  152
Echerberger  311
Echols  8, 22, 88, 94, 335
Eckels  171
Eckles  229
Eddings  132
Eddins  155, 287
Edds  287
Edgar  159
Edmenson  272
Edmonds  162, 221
Edmondson  74, 196
Edmunds  134, 220
Edward  196
Edwards  2, 40, 54, 56, 64, 75, 97, 158, 169, 175, 206, 221, 225, 264, 286, 315, 325, 336, 346
Efurd  79
Eggleston  111, 218
Eich  262
Eigleberger  41
Eiland  326
Einstein  310
Elam  201, 273
Elder  315
Eldridge  54
Elgin  48
Eliasberg  1
Elkins  310
Ellard  187
Ellet  68
Ellington  75, 307
Elliott  65, 85, 94, 130, 133, 193, 196, 212, 223, 323, 350, 359
Ellis  104, 117, 238, 266, 303, 347
Ellison  127, 256
Ellwood  341
Ellyson  106
Elmore  168, 311
Elsberry  10
Ely  42
Elzy  91
Embrey  27

Emerson  213
Emmerson  127
Emmons  104
Emsell  75
England  38, 237
English  59, 107, 135, 169, 213, 244, 248, 279, 324, 342
Enslen  327
Enzor  17
Epperson  309
Epping  278
Ereckson  356, 357
Erichson  322
Ernest  226, 319
Ernst  141
Ervin  74
Erwin  72, 89, 121, 240
Eshelby  141
Eskridge  80, 127
Eslinger  110
Espy  300
Esslinger  21
Estep  103
Estes  287, 310, 352
Estis  234
Etchison  292
Etheridge  53, 55, 330
Ethridge  36
Evans  13, 36, 40, 45, 47, 55, 74, 80, 82, 94, 179, 181, 198, 210, 221, 238, 272, 289, 299, 302, 322, 325, 341
Evarts  234
Eve  108
Everett  164
Everist  336
Evins  97
Ewing  211, 318
Extima  55
Fables  327
Fabush  51
Fackler  5, 6, 140, 322
Fahs  193, 309
Fail  103, 107

**THE SOUTHERN ARGUS - DEATHS - JUNE 1869 THROUGH JUNE 1874**

Fain  171, 237, 258
Fair  83, 109, 163
Faith  212
Falconer  7, 209, 298
Falk  68, 330
Falkner  288, 338
Fallon  193
Falres  152
Falson  183
Fancher  176
Fannen  85
Fannin  204
Fariss  26
Farley  15, 20, 279, 284, 298, 348
Farmer  133, 247, 287
Farnham  176, 178
Farrand  232, 304
Farrar  349
Farris  15, 292
Farrow  284
Fars  305, 309
Fason  185, 196, 278
Faulk  320
Faulkner  308
Faver  336
Fawcett  303
Fay  49
Feagin  336
Fearn  13, 49, 232
Fedder  176
Fee  115
Feeney  88
Felder  71
Felton  188
Felts  352
Fenderson  6
Fennel  12
Fennet  307
Fenton  4
Fergarson  305
Ferguson  27, 37, 118, 132, 177, 258, 328, 336
Ferrell  37, 136, 200

Ferrent  43
Ferris  72, 249
Fetchner  157
Fettyplace  88
Ficklin  95
Field  80, 106, 299, 310, 341
Fielder  249
Fields  257, 301
Fife  256
Figh  46, 74
Fight  298
Figures  203, 233, 357
Fike  238
Files  146, 158
Filgner  351
Fillebrowne  121
Finch  104, 269
Findley  60, 165
Fink  299
Finlayson  74
Finley  183, 215, 353, 355
Finney  359
Fiquet  36
Fisher  107, 115, 130, 224, 227
Fisk  142, 175, 227
Fitch  70, 218
Fitts  213
Fitzgerald  83, 151, 187, 358
Fitzgibbon  181, 184
Fitzhugh  293
Fitzpatrick  192, 311
Flanagan  123, 167, 241
Flanegan  122
Fleming  67, 335, 336
Flemming  30
Fletcher  11, 60, 109, 144, 194, 265, 357, 358
Fletchner  158
Flint  267
Flora  87
Flournoy  29, 171, 279
Flowers  90
Floyd  73, 265
Fluker  82

## THE SOUTHERN ARGUS - DEATHS - JUNE 1869 THROUGH JUNE 1874

Flynn  190
Foggy  226
Follansbee  257
Fondreu  39
Fonville  12, 45
Foote  30
Forbes  198, 287
Force  128, 330, 331
Forcheimer  188
Ford  92, 152, 164, 203, 217, 226, 247, 264, 266, 320
Fore  49, 283, 318
Foreheimer  52
Foreman  224
Forney  37
Forniss  79
Forrest  22, 137
Forsander  310
Forss  93
Forstelle  212
Forsyth  27, 78, 153
Forsythe  195
Fort  177, 181
Fortes  66
Foscue  97
Fosdick  236
Fossick  315
Foster  12, 23, 45, 69, 77, 105, 132, 141, 147, 160, 186, 188, 244, 260, 264, 298, 309, 316, 317
Fountain  31, 66, 237
Fountaine  171
Foust  295, 303
Fowler  25, 33, 191, 206, 210, 249, 276, 285, 313
Fox  162, 233, 341
Foy  297
Francis  70, 103, 293
Frank  36, 75, 135
Franklin  94, 296, 299, 318
Frazer  151, 197, 240, 263, 287, 338
Frazier  95, 107, 242, 251, 340

Free  114
Freeland  71
Freeman  58, 206, 235, 246, 341
Frei  341
French  15, 307
Frenkel  185
Friel  262
Frierson  66
Fries  308
Froman  43
Frotman  296
Fry  162
Frye  176
Fryer  85, 107, 314, 319
Fulcher  325
Full  211
Fuller  52, 102, 140, 219, 252, 253, 346
Fullerton  281, 351
Fulmer  145
Fulmore  234
Fulson  123
Fulton  46, 211, 267
Futrell  123
Fykes  316
Gab  55
Gabe  100
Gadder  58
Gaddis  52
Gafford  57
Gage  96, 195, 219
Gager  168
Gaillard  355
Gaines  68, 225
Gains  249
Galbraith  118
Gallagher  61
Galland  253
Galley  228
Galliard  26
Gallier  118
Galloway  274
Galvin  4, 113
Gambel  1

## THE SOUTHERN ARGUS - DEATHS - JUNE 1869 THROUGH JUNE 1874

Gamble  56, 152, 237, 240
Gammel  323
Gandy  69, 116
Garber  116
Gardner  55, 70, 108, 146, 194, 245, 247, 284, 315, 333
Garick  269
Garland  192, 303, 348
Garley  100
Garner  6, 32, 36, 59, 93, 170, 209, 234, 242, 284
Garnett  141, 284
Garrett  18, 59, 117, 131, 145, 158, 183, 205, 250, 295, 296
Garrigas  263
Garrison  274
Garrott  136
Garside  48
Gartrell  87
Garvin  315
Garvis  5
Gary  42, 235
Gaskin  307
Gaston  238
Gates  14, 87, 281, 305, 312
Gavin  238
Gay  125, 162, 308
Gayle  137, 147, 180, 237, 293
Gebhard  358
Gentry  141, 155
George  28, 310, 341
Gerald  311
German  128
Germany  38, 317
Geron  128
Gerson  239
Ghent  334
Gibbons  58, 65, 173
Gibbs  157, 208, 324, 344
Gibson  33, 39, 129, 132, 183, 184, 190, 201, 219, 276, 282, 301
Gidley  233
Gifford  131

Gilbert  83, 92, 118, 170, 222, 233, 279, 282
Gilbreth  355
Gilchrist  11, 135, 136
Giles  82, 150, 169, 286, 323
Gilhland  31
Gilkey  277
Gill  85, 166, 171, 184, 197
Gillam  271
Gillaspie  280
Gillespie  7, 124
Gilley  210
Gilliespie  126
Gilliland  355
Gillman  248
Gilman  151
Gilmer  23, 57, 69, 114, 118, 129, 266, 279
Gilmore  19, 47, 97, 113, 120, 125, 205, 217, 218, 220, 223
Gilon  310
Gilson  299, 310
Gilston  115
Giovanna  255
Girard  74, 206, 260, 263, 301, 310
Girrard  21
Givens  147
Gladden  158
Gladney  345
Glass  16, 17, 19, 95, 204, 301, 310
Glasscock  267
Glasswell  321
Gleason  114
Glen  132, 279, 313
Glenn  1, 94, 144, 197
Gliddon  149
Glovannl  352
Glover  47, 143, 177, 256, 296, 333, 337
Godard  357
Godbee  70
Godden  248

## THE SOUTHERN ARGUS - DEATHS - JUNE 1869 THROUGH JUNE 1874

Godfrey  19
Goforth  348
Goldsby  175
Goldsmith  95, 138, 278
Goldsten  293
Golighly  135
Golightly  135
Golson  79
Gomez  171
Gonzalez  256
Goodbrad  46
Goode  10, 49, 200, 239, 328
Goodin  113
Goodman  124, 198, 336
Goodrich  337
Goodwin  25, 73, 148, 151, 217, 227, 257, 277
Goodwyn  14
Gordon  54, 133, 152, 153, 158, 197, 206, 254, 274, 306, 307
Goree  284
Gorman  154, 284
Gornlay  140
Goss  90, 200
Gossett  230
Goubil  117
Gould  64
Grace  200, 247, 248
Grady  136
Graham  45, 75, 77, 82, 98, 123, 142, 156, 168, 185, 187, 193, 195, 251, 271, 313, 320, 358
Grant  12, 57, 70, 74, 170, 250, 311, 352, 357
Grantham  212, 284
Grantlan  125
Grass  221
Grattan  262
Graves  9, 95, 124
Gray  31, 53, 89, 107, 153, 157, 183, 192
Grayson  259
Greeley  167, 199

Green  21, 52, 65, 77, 93, 97, 149, 187, 226, 227, 251, 260, 272, 274, 321
Greene  16, 124, 204, 205, 210, 220, 231, 274, 281, 284, 312, 351
Greenwood  230, 247
Greer  106, 111, 321, 358
Gregg  114, 118
Gregory  28, 50, 86, 298
Gresham  95, 137, 150, 344, 355
Gresser  134
Gretofull  197
Grey  175, 313
Grice  358
Grider  70, 148
Griffin  20, 57, 137, 155, 194, 196, 203, 265, 281, 318
Griffith  48, 145
Griflin  277, 293
Grigg  114, 118
Griggs  130, 300
Grillo  304
Grimes  129, 292
Grimsley  198
Grissit  164
Griswold  162, 303
Groce  45, 188, 282
Groome  346
Grote  180
Groves  4, 122
Grubbs  44, 176, 177
Gruber  3
Grumbles  303
Gruzelier  41
Gue  115
Guerry  92
Guesnard  223
Guess  84
Guice  315
Guild  58, 59, 160, 222
Gulce  319
Gullatt  265
Gulley  134

## THE SOUTHERN ARGUS - DEATHS - JUNE 1869 THROUGH JUNE 1874

Gully  143, 248
Gunn  26, 64, 76, 136, 238, 240, 343
Gunnison  246
Gunter  6, 12, 15, 72, 290, 313
Gunthorpe  75
Gurley  91
Guthery  234
Guthrie  173, 183
Guttery  272
Guy  162
Guyler  99, 102
Guynes  75
Gwin  121, 284
Gwinn  130, 192
Gwynn  226
Haas  59
Hackett  142
Hacklander  168
Haddox  47, 215
Hadley  285
Hadson  250
Haessell  179
Hagins  206
Hagler  126
Hagood  220, 262, 268, 301, 325
Hahn  96
Haig  126
Haigier  41, 71
Haigle  200
Haigler  224
Hail  52, 251
Haily  283
Halbrook  279
Halbrooks  116
Haldeman  310
Hale  46, 260, 262, 267, 301, 305, 310
Haley  112, 232, 239, 306
Hall  2, 4, 23, 25, 48, 59, 83, 114, 117, 154, 182, 187, 195, 198, 209, 230, 237, 245, 246, 247, 261, 292, 295, 305, 315, 319, 329, 343

Hallett  133
Halliday  228, 358
Hallinguist  233
Hallins  110
Hallowell  149
Halls  100
Halpin  82
Halsey  88, 156, 188, 244
Haly  160
Ham  40, 119
Hamblett  197
Hambrick  88, 276
Hamer  125
Hamiel  32
Hamilton  27, 77, 125, 178, 228, 240, 246, 255, 291, 312, 349
Hamiter  61
Hamlet  55, 198
Hamlin  60
Hammack  326
Hamman  51
Hammand  74
Hammen  301
Hammett  200
Hammock  321
Hammon  310
Hammond  73, 114, 283
Hammonds  16, 296
Hamner  251
Hamp  34, 190
Hampshire  320, 322
Hampton  110
Hancock  149, 318
Handley  245
Hanghey  228
Hanghy  228
Hanks  45, 180
Hanlein  143
Hanlon  342
Hanna  7, 244
Hannah  233
Hannon  54, 103, 193
Hannum  157
Hansell  95

## THE SOUTHERN ARGUS - DEATHS - JUNE 1869 THROUGH JUNE 1874

Hanson  69, 302, 306, 337
Hanuum  157
Haralson  51, 331, 337
Harcourt  302
Hard  300
Hardaway  218, 291, 339, 345
Hardee  275, 305, 306, 329
Hardie  148, 192
Hardin  194, 272
Hardman  82, 103, 105, 145, 212, 214
Hardwick  14, 26, 27, 227, 230
Hardwicke  141
Hardy  58, 59, 113
Hare  33, 35, 38, 172
Hargove  163
Hargraves  286
Hargrove  89, 115
Hargue  187
Harkins  307
Harkness  99, 102
Harless  206
Harley  315
Harmen  93
Harold  210
Harper  124, 131, 164, 233, 297
Harraway  115
Harred  310
Harrel  300, 310
Harrell  49, 76, 77, 156, 157, 168, 181, 182, 257, 259, 274, 277, 301
Harrington  300
Harris  16, 18, 19, 33, 50, 51, 54, 64, 80, 83, 84, 87, 104, 114, 116, 118, 122, 131, 134, 140, 151, 170, 180, 206, 219, 236, 237, 240, 252, 253, 269, 273, 277, 279, 283, 290, 298, 317, 322, 325, 338, 344, 349
Harrison  4, 15, 69, 92, 108, 111, 158, 176, 177, 211, 215, 216, 248, 270, 275, 279, 283, 296, 316, 342, 343, 345, 348

Harriss  24, 153
Harrow  196
Hart  17, 31, 143, 169, 333, 351, 355, 356
Hartel  155
Hartley  282, 295
Hartnett  294
Harton  236
Hartung  159, 209
Hartwell  17, 162, 300, 303
Harvell  227, 300
Harvey  107, 195, 268
Harvy  57
Harwell  34, 97, 168, 178, 180, 215, 217, 228, 357
Harwood  72, 73, 132
Hase  264
Haseltine  132
Hasenburg  326
Haskett  147
Hassell  314
Hastings  50
Hastins  314
Haswell  356
Hatch  110, 302
Hatcher  106, 122, 154, 163, 198, 239
Hatchmeyer  59
Hatfield  106
Hatte  172
Hatten  170
Hatter  35, 180
Hatton  61
Haughey  8, 9, 11, 228
Haupt  42
Hauser  92
Hawk  157
Hawkins  69, 121, 144, 164, 168, 216, 254, 257, 267, 345
Hawley  290
Hawn  328
Hawthore  193
Hawthorn  284
Hawthorne  193, 194

**THE SOUTHERN ARGUS - DEATHS - JUNE 1869 THROUGH JUNE 1874**

Hayes 45, 209, 210, 221, 223, 276
Haygood 150, 212
Hayley 338
Haynes 75, 110, 226, 301, 310
Haynie 232
Hays 43, 101, 121, 191, 207, 220, 233, 267, 290, 358, 359
Hazard 27, 64
Hazel 107
Hazzard 51
Heacock 353
Head 3, 177, 277
Healey 320
Heard 106, 150, 167, 271
Hearn 312
Hearne 344
Hearon 250
Hearren 185
Heath 156
Heawood 218
Hecker 356
Heddin 248
Hedges 34
Heenan 58, 304
Heflin 157, 218
Heidelberger 118
Heidt 213
Heilen 83
Heinz 90, 199
Heitman 220
Hellen 83
Helm 282, 328
Helmer 193
Henderlaing 124
Henderson 34, 43, 45, 52, 54, 70, 122, 124, 125, 133, 140, 197, 226, 236, 253, 288, 290, 294
Hendley 289
Hendon 42, 46, 155, 323
Hendree 175
Hendrick 16, 36, 248
Hendricks 18, 132, 170, 352
Hendrix 237, 321

Henley 133, 240
Henly 268
Henry 37, 42, 48, 110, 159, 232, 294, 295, 297, 308
Henshaw 91
Henslen 338
Henson 228, 308
Henstis 130
Hepburn 357
Herbert 42, 98, 113, 152, 189, 277
Herd 93, 245
Hereford 145, 300, 302
Herman 64, 191, 310
Hermann 301
Hermitage 356, 357
Herndon 1, 73, 75, 146, 147
Heron 248
Herpin 317
Herren 171
Herring 32, 90, 231, 281, 284, 314, 315
Herrington 164
Herron 15, 188, 198
Herschfelder 252
Herts 10
Heslep 154, 327
Hester 71, 308, 343
Hesterly 288
Hestle 77
Hetterstein 4
Heustis 130, 210
Heutsch 69
Hewett 125
Hewitt 114, 131, 200
Hewlett 179
Hickerson 217
Hickey 102
Hickman 86, 91, 179, 229, 314
Hicks 73, 106, 186. 274
Hickson 250, 279
Higdon 50, 125
Higgins 68, 75, 97, 155, 303, 304, 349, 350

## THE SOUTHERN ARGUS - DEATHS - JUNE 1869 THROUGH JUNE 1874

High  26, 81, 142, 200
Hill  10-12, 17, 25, 34, 45, 52, 54, 58, 90, 111, 113, 135, 136, 143, 145, 155, 162, 176, 179, 201, 209, 220, 221, 250, 253, 258, 268, 271, 284, 289, 299, 350, 352
Hille  303
Hilliard  268
Hinderer  230
Hindes  29
Hinds  28, 57, 197
Hines  42, 251, 315
Hinson  49, 276
Hinton  104, 192, 248
Hirsch  273
Hitzheim  313
Hobbie  129, 130
Hobbs  161, 185, 234, 262
Hobby  76
Hobdy  81
Hobgood  64
Hobson  300
Hodge  94, 128, 291, 310, 357
Hodges  349, 351
Hodgson  188
Hoffman  50, 74, 95, 133, 243, 339
Hogan  33, 34, 217, 223
Hogg  146, 323
Hogue  13, 189, 349
Hoke  235
Holcomb  156
Holcombe  279
Holder  83, 335
Holifield  245
Holland  101, 107, 224, 230, 244, 266, 267, 269, 290, 307
Hollenbach  66
Holley  190, 256, 308, 352
Hollingsworth  230
Hollingworth  180
Holloway  53
Holly  27, 123, 168

Hollyman  40
Holman  106, 226
Holmes  91, 223, 234, 247, 254, 321
Holsey  245
Holt  41, 66, 83, 133, 145, 160, 188, 214, 272, 287, 318, 329, 339, 357
Holzer  300
Hood  96, 244, 247, 297, 300
Hook  198, 242
Hooker  153
Hooks  89, 180
Hoope  219
Hooper  9, 208, 247, 255, 306, 326, 327, 350, 352
Hooten  185
Hope  160
Hopgood  18
Hopkins  101, 186, 200, 252, 270, 272, 321
Hopper  31, 33, 269
Horan  287
Horlock  284, 285
Horn  72, 74, 75, 274, 295, 315, 354
Hornady  131
Hornbeak  189
Horne  353, 358
Horton  44, 63, 95, 115, 166, 226, 240, 292, 352
Hosfeldt  215
Hosmer  112
Hosner  140
Hough  166
Houghan  268
Houghton  188, 340
Houston  39, 50, 61, 73, 94, 111, 112, 128, 150, 232, 345
Howard  3, 23, 35, 71, 79, 88, 130, 165, 199, 208, 216, 240, 295, 303, 304, 307, 316, 320, 349, 351, 354, 358
Howell  29, 31, 145, 152

## THE SOUTHERN ARGUS - DEATHS - JUNE 1869 THROUGH JUNE 1874

Howland  40
Howle  228
Howling  308
Howze  49
Hoxter  224
Hoyt  74
Hrabonski  131
Hrabouski  131, 171
Hubbard  287, 290, 335, 358
Hubert  77
Huckabee  60, 197, 348, 357
Huddleson  316
Hudgins  110
Hudson  10, 56, 117, 156, 158, 243, 246, 269, 270, 276, 350
Huff  196
Huffman  155
Hufford  250
Hugenard  270
Huggins  37
Hughes  34, 40, 68, 71, 152, 165, 185, 188, 198, 215, 226, 227, 234, 235, 238, 262, 268, 271, 310, 321, 327, 345, 357
Hughey  95
Hughs  74
Hughston  55
Hugo  20
Hull  194
Humes  190
Humphrey  6, 29, 186, 188, 190, 243, 272
Humphreys  145, 314
Humphries  47, 81
Hundley  288
Hunnicut  114
Hunnicutt  160
Hunt  75, 79, 167, 195, 230, 278, 280, 347
Hunter  48, 77, 119, 240, 269, 272
Huntingdon  82
Huntington  222
Hurd  300

Hurley  332
Hurry  204
Hurst  268
Hurt  146, 244
Hurtel  307
Huske  16
Hussey  27
Hust  310
Huston  74, 77, 91, 217, 231, 263, 332
Hutchins  160, 171
Huth  129
Hutton  14, 67, 112, 144
Hyde  285
Hyden  192
Hydrick  207
Hyland  210
Hymas  310
Hynes  3, 324, 331
Idom  54
Idorn  70
Igou  223
Ihringer  310
Inge  169, 214, 231, 257, 343
Ingersoll  78
Ingram  189
Inman  204
Irby  7, 218
Irvin  16, 19, 162
Irvine  292
Irwin  57, 106, 243, 288
Isbell  93, 130, 139, 272
Ives  105
Ivey  52, 103, 125, 157, 278
Ivie  137
Ivy  26, 289
Jack  17, 294
Jackson  12, 37, 47, 48, 58, 70, 78, 106, 107, 114, 139, 164, 185, 229, 244, 292, 322
Jacob  285
Jacobs  64, 185
Jainer  171

**THE SOUTHERN ARGUS - DEATHS - JUNE 1869 THROUGH JUNE 1874**

Jaines 155
James 72, 93, 102, 103, 125, 155, 156, 160, 173, 223, 225, 292, 350
Jamison 100, 329, 342
Jarett 53, 55
Jarman 29, 255, 291
Jarrett 206, 218
Jarvis 7, 127, 188, 247
Jasper 147
Jay 186, 354
Jefferies 310
Jefferson 252
Jeffries 328
Jemison 45, 64, 77, 131, 136, 249, 345, 352
Jenkens 182
Jenkins 35, 77, 88, 118, 155, 286, 352
Jennings 197, 207, 271, 272, 275, 277, 292
Jennison 152
Jernigan 312
Jesper 266
Jeter 70
Jett 345
Jetton 123
Jewell 216, 217, 300
Jewett 345
Jinkens 130
Jinkins 52
John 178
Johnson 10, 23, 30, 51, 53, 68, 77, 78, 87, 89, 91, 92, 101, 108, 115, 130, 131, 132, 134, 135, 143, 145, 148, 153, 169, 178, 179, 182, 185, 192, 195, 200, 208, 214, 215, 223, 225, 229, 233, 237, 240, 244, 248, 249, 272, 279, 282, 289, 290, 295, 307, 311, 313, 322, 328, 329, 348, 349, 353
Johnston 12, 153, 215, 226, 268, 304

Joiner 82, 182, 245, 350
Jolley 253
Jolly 37, 91, 128, 150
Jonas 150
Jones 9, 10, 12, 14, 20, 21, 33, 34, 36, 41, 42, 44, 51, 52, 53, 59, 61, 63, 77, 86, 91, 96, 98, 100, 101, 103, 104, 108, 109, 112, 126, 131, 134, 144, 146, 157, 158, 164, 170, 176, 180, 183, 186, 195, 201, 202, 204, 207, 209, 210, 215, 216, 217, 218, 222, 228, 234, 236, 240, 244, 245, 248, 252, 254, 257, 260, 262, 264, 270, 272, 273, 274, 276, 278, 280, 281, 283, 286, 289, 290, 291, 293, 294, 295, 296, 303, 305, 306, 338, 342, 344, 346, 347, 355, 356, 357
Jordan 33, 77, 111, 115, 141, 143, 171, 178, 219, 224, 227, 232, 235, 238, 244, 260, 261, 291, 313, 343
Joseph 242
Jourdan 324, 325
Jowers 266
Joy 95
Joyce 1
Jude 176
Judkins 30, 92, 130
Junkins 353
Jupiter 66
Justice 126
Kaelin 7
Kahn 221
Kaiser 310
Kamp 310
Kapahn 93
Karny 248
Karsner 7, 152, 212, 350
Kavanaugh 337
Kay 287
Kazalas 340

## THE SOUTHERN ARGUS - DEATHS - JUNE 1869 THROUGH JUNE 1874

Kean  121
Keane  206
Kearney  100, 272
Kearns  98
Keb  2
Keeble  280, 285, 286
Keel  332
Keeling  313, 320
Keen  64
Keeze  301
Kehoe  123
Keith  88, 94, 106
Kellar  339
Keller  126, 194
Kelley  30, 153, 268, 334
Kellum  254
Kelly  44, 70, 71, 89, 120, 187, 267, 314, 347
Kelman  322
Kelso  87
Kelsoe  106
Kelton  201
Kemp  319
Kenan  271, 327, 331
Kendall  256, 297, 304, 349
Kendrick  18, 231
Kennaird  13
Kennard  237, 247, 338
Kennedy  10, 27, 68, 87, 137, 146, 169, 261, 262, 268, 275, 280, 287, 298, 299, 312, 317, 323, 324, 343
Kennemore  215
Kenney  342
Kennon  39, 301, 313
Kerley  353, 355
Kerr  25, 259, 349, 357
Kessee  310
Ketchum  85
Key  72, 122, 123
Keyes  339
Keys  89, 256, 257
Kibbie  300
Kidd  207, 299

Kilfoil  206, 316
Kilfoll  206
Kilgore  145
Killiard  213
Killough  67
Kilpatrick  92
Kimbal  260
Kimball  63, 98, 335
Kimbrough  29, 187, 188, 231, 317
Kincey  278
Kindell  221
Kineey  278
King  34, 37, 41, 68, 78, 81, 82, 121, 126, 137, 144, 149, 167, 168, 206, 207, 216, 231, 252, 255, 262, 267, 272, 277, 278, 292, 294, 325, 329, 332, 338, 344, 356
Kinghorne  230, 231
Kinkle  20, 36, 155
Kinnaird  82
Kirby  48, 216
Kirk  221, 318
Kirkbride  206
Kirkland  68, 105
Kirkman  98
Kirkpatrick  24, 140, 187, 193
Kirksey  120
Kiser  128
Kitchens  256
Kittrell  63
Klein  105, 125
Knapp  7, 301, 310
Knight  53, 91, 97, 194, 253, 301
Knighten  332
Knott  208, 311
Knowles  117
Knox  9, 15, 25, 47, 67, 136, 138, 142, 212, 224, 225, 284, 331
Kohlen  37
Kohn  109
Kornegay  207

## THE SOUTHERN ARGUS - DEATHS - JUNE 1869 THROUGH JUNE 1874

Kosciusko 149
Kraus 332
Krebs 166
Krout 255
Kuhne 353
Kulper 237
Kuykendall 314
Kyle 21, 192, 296, 305
Kynard 172
Kynerd 239
La?clle 104
Lacey 328
Lackey 226, 348
Lacy 330
Lafan 173
Lafaulette 308
Laffre 127
LaForce 49
Lahue 310
Laird 279, 289
Lake 83
Lamar 69, 315, 320
Lamb 217
Lampkin 80
Lampson 63
Lancaster 322
Land 90, 276
Landers 17, 342
Landford 85
Landingham 40, 171
Landlingham 121
Landman 123
Lane 140, 210, 296, 317, 348, 350
Laney 40
Lanford 182
Lang 75, 162, 183, 328
Langdon 81, 166, 236, 356
Langston 145, 296
Lanier 35, 284
Lankford 320
Lanman 338
Lansdon 332
Lapsey 4

Lapsley 148
Larkin 67
Larkins 296
Larnandie 342
Laser 77
Laslie 12
Lassiter 94, 151
Latham 117, 232
Latimer 201
Lauderdale 128
Lauer 161
Laureedine 323
Laurence 282
Lavallette 32
Lavender 257, 345
Lavretta 282
Law 114, 304
Lawitzky 343
Lawler 74, 124, 188, 262, 283, 324
Lawless 44
Lawrence 28, 103, 111, 136, 240, 257, 328
Laws 264
Lawson 14, 96, 172, 250
Lawton 9
Layne 157
Layton 266
Lazard 310
Lea 243, 299
Leach 348
Leagan 234
League 354
Leak 208, 343
Leake 17, 183, 342
Lealie 147
Leatherwood 124, 176
LeBaron 251
LeBarron 247
Ledbetter 282, 287, 354
Ledyard 14, 192, 272, 274
Lee 2, 4, 6, 7, 23, 32, 47, 48, 58, 60, 66, 83, 89, 102, 131,

## THE SOUTHERN ARGUS - DEATHS - JUNE 1869 THROUGH JUNE 1874

Lee (continued) 183, 192, 214, 283, 297, 301, 315, 329, 347
Leek 311
Leeky 291
Leeper 117, 139
Lefevre 213
Leftwich 33, 186
Legg 277, 281
Leggett 158, 183, 185
LeGraff 332
LeGrand 67
Lehing 276
Leigh 271, 274
Leiser 120
Lelievre 343
Leman 269
Lemley 154, 165
Lenoir 89, 186, 203, 264, 285, 359
Lentz 253
Leonard 99, 138, 299, 310, 323, 349
Leonhart 282
Lesesne 26
Leslie 127, 147, 225, 311
Lespes 206
Lester 24, 44
Letson 292
Leverett 316
Leverson 187
Levert 27, 101, 112, 206
Levie 92
Levins 129
Levison 182
Levy 126, 168, 315
Lewers 48
Lewis 3, 9, 37, 43, 44, 53, 66, 67, 80, 96, 132, 139, 147, 163, 165, 186, 214, 219, 226, 248, 270, 298, 303, 307, 321, 338, 346, 348, 354, 358
Lewy 113
Libby 122
Lide 74

Liebman 46
Lightfoot 36, 82, 218
Lightner 251
Ligon 123, 151, 335
Lillienstein 194
Lilly 74
Lincoln 113
Linddeman 162
Lindman 110
Lindsay 44, 48, 59, 86, 105, 147, 197, 215, 346, 356
Lindsey 80, 244
Linebaugh 200, 207
Lingo 136
Links 303
Linn 174, 177, 191, 262, 268
Lipke 299, 301, 310
Lippincott 84
Lipscomb 9, 135, 235, 275, 293, 338
Litesey 190
Little 14, 117, 149, 169, 181, 191, 201, 236, 283, 289, 297, 311, 323, 346
Littlejohn 22
Littlepage 61, 337
Litton 46
Livingston 126, 133
Llewellyn 330
Lloyd 56, 159, 218, 232, 297, 330
Lobman 281
Lock 29
Lockard 166
Locke 60, 101, 148, 185, 267
Locket 229
Lockett 175
Lockhart 162, 202, 205, 239
Loftin 61, 65, 332
Logan 10, 111, 190, 258, 325, 344, 348, 359
Lokey 349
Lollar 356

## THE SOUTHERN ARGUS - DEATHS - JUNE 1869 THROUGH JUNE 1874

Long  146, 197, 283, 289, 300, 350, 356, 357, 358
Longacre  223
Longfellow  338
Longmire  294
Longstreet  57
Lony  196
Loomis  111, 188
Loper  257
Lopez  282
Lord  287
Loring  40
Lothrop  359
Lotspeich  98
Lott  136, 228, 229
Love  61, 108, 124, 250, 257, 260, 276, 295, 310, 357
Lovel  102
Lovelace  234
Loveman  104
Lovett  310
Low  40
Lowe  34, 155, 183, 302
Lowery  202
Lowrey  190
Lowry  44, 94, 178, 202, 208, 254
Lowther  95
Lucas  164, 206
Luckett  180
Lucy  56
Ludeman  77
Ludwig  48
Luke  89
Lumery  70
Lumsden  1, 234
Lunceford  350
Lundy  85, 125, 274, 279, 310
Lung  2
Lunsford  1, 109
Lupton  213
Luter  118
Luther  232, 307
Lyeria  332

Lyle  135, 161
Lyles  51, 111, 242
Lynch  37, 167, 169, 274, 289, 311, 312, 354
Lyne  204
Lynn  53, 300
Lyon  8, 71, 112, 138, 149, 172, 339
Lyons  141, 144
Lyster  261
Lytle  249
Mabarry  214
Mabrey  92
Mabry  207, 209, 210, 256, 331, 333, 340
Mabson  60
Macartney  353
Macauley  327
Machen  170
Machin  247
Mack  73, 84, 151
Mackey  298
Maclin  194
Macon  104, 157, 194, 197, 199, 203, 287, 306, 308, 309
Madden  4, 344
Maddox  205, 304, 310, 330
Mader  274
Maderia  295
Madigan  204
Madison  1
Maffit  337
Magrant  318
Magruder  71
Mahaffey  88
Mahew  73
Mahone  221, 223
Malakoff  212
Mallett  98
Mallory  64, 70
Malone  91, 106, 113, 180, 194, 201, 238, 239, 241, 242, 251, 288, 294
Maloney  242, 262

## THE SOUTHERN ARGUS - DEATHS - JUNE 1869 THROUGH JUNE 1874

Manack 9
Mandich 316
Mandley 180
Mangham 283
Mangold 258
Mangum 19
Manley 104
Manly 99, 235
Mann 13, 118, 150, 166, 232, 255, 346
Manning 40, 67, 68, 155
Manuccy 22
Maples 110
Marburg 60
March 203
Mardis 45
Marivitz 71
Markham 49, 119
Markle 23
Marks 252, 290, 301, 303, 310, 348
Marlowe 237
Marona 159
Maroney 126
Marrast 226, 265
Marriott 253, 260
Marschalk 72, 109, 110, 119
Marsh 41, 179, 242
Marshall 54, 163, 213, 273, 315
Marshman 117
Marston 131
Martin 15, 22, 29, 55, 59, 60, 64, 67, 70, 82, 120, 132, 134, 137, 145, 156, 158, 164, 168, 171, 173, 177, 180, 183, 186, 187, 220, 232, 234, 236, 245, 248, 261, 266, 272, 278, 288, 293, 300, 306, 317, 324, 330, 334
Martinez 96
Marvin 100, 115, 150
Marx 85, 102

Mason 4, 18, 99, 103, 106, 130, 162, 193, 235, 271, 275, 306, 333
Mass 303
Massey 39, 131, 138, 182, 212, 214, 247, 285, 288, 296, 339, 349
Massingale 297
Massingill 85
Mastin 17, 133, 134, 260, 284, 306
Matchet 328
Matheson 150
Mathews 74, 227, 263, 271, 287
Matkin 194
Mattchett 16
Matthews 52, 56, 79, 110, 133, 189, 194, 290, 300, 302, 318, 339, 348
Mattison 170
Mauldin 79
Maumme 183
Maupin 152
Maurer 335
Maxman 1
Maxwell 37, 95, 231, 266, 316
May 53, 55, 64, 130, 161, 205, 238, 255, 325
Mayberry 231
Mayer 124
Mayes 140
Mayfield 185
Mayhew 327
Maynes 205
McAdams 50, 105
McAdory 139, 222
McAfee 12, 75
McAlilly 195
McAlister 118, 158, 285
McAllister 94, 126, 220, 245, 349
McAlpin 134
McAlpine 147, 192, 328
McArthur 103, 150, 317

## THE SOUTHERN ARGUS - DEATHS - JUNE 1869 THROUGH JUNE 1874

McAuley  201, 221
McAuliffe  219
McBatley  357
McBroom  164
McBryde  235, 352
McCain  251, 287
McCaleb  199
McCall  113, 135, 202, 207, 212
McCalley  11, 55
McCally  13
McCann  58, 295
McCargo  63
McCarkle  299, 301
McCarra  276
McCarthy  65, 176, 310
McCartney  286
McCarty  280, 290
McCarver  288, 290
McCasky  164
McCaslan  313
McClanahan  62
McClelan  337
McClellan  123, 180, 197
McClelland  43, 72, 101, 334
McClenahany  48
McClister  221
McCloskey  110, 341
McClung  269
McClure  36, 60, 81, 335
McCluskey  105, 193
McClusky  197
McCoin  202
McCollough  156
McCollum  39, 237
McConnell  128, 298
McConnico  215
McCord  120, 177, 331
McCoritin  180
McCorkle  310
McCorley  120
McCormack  117, 256
McCormick  32, 217, 230
McCorvey  31
McCourt  112

McCoy  76, 176, 211
McCracken  48, 183
McCrary  46, 94
McCraw  50, 51, 305
McCreary  113, 125
McCreless  230
McCullom  157
McCullough  36, 209
McCune  351
McCurdy  103
McCutchen  305
McDaniel  9, 40, 63, 100, 145, 243, 301, 304
McDaniels  299
McDanniel  310
McDiarmid  265
McDonald  4, 10, 18, 47, 109, 141, 143, 150, 224, 246, 251, 292, 305, 333
McDougal  164
McDougall  308
McDowell  214, 268
McDuff  301
McDuffie  190, 212
McEachan  162
McEachern  351, 353
McEachin  121
McEackin  294
McElderry  157, 247
McElrath  241, 292
McElzia  183
McFalls  209
McFarland  57, 290, 294
McFerrin  160
McGaha  74, 239
McGaughy  75
McGee  57, 233, 246, 256
McGehee  134, 136, 167, 219, 267, 347
McGhee  118, 131, 180, 218, 281, 302, 312, 319
McGibbin  270
McGlathery  214, 314
McGlynn  54

## THE SOUTHERN ARGUS - DEATHS - JUNE 1869 THROUGH JUNE 1874

McGonegal  75
McGonigal  130
McGovern  79, 136, 182, 214
McGowan  333
McGrath  14, 131, 150
McGraw  101
McGree  71
McGriff  287
McGuire  52, 120, 187, 250, 251, 265, 286
McHugh  310
McIlwain  28, 39
McIntosh  99, 212, 222
McIntyre  151
McIver  26
McKay  88, 120, 131, 184, 352
McKee  13, 122, 153, 172
McKellar  223
McKelvey  11
McKelvy  68
McKenzie  332
McKerall  179
McKerrall  92, 183, 256
McKerrell  155, 328
McKevy  311
McKibbon  57, 169
McKinney  96, 296
McKinnon  143
McKinstry  156
McKissack  252
McKittrick  254, 298
McLain  290
McLane  171
McLarin  282
McLaughlin  48, 107, 194, 268
McLean  70, 93, 264, 278, 279, 312
McLemore  196, 276
McLendon  254, 266, 298
McLeod  23, 52, 59, 198, 221, 326, 348
McLeon  228
McLeroy  295
McMahan  162, 240, 242

McMahon  91, 205, 348
McMain  192
McManus  311
McMath  15
McMichen  259
McMillan  9, 18, 73, 248, 259, 266, 269, 329, 337
McMillian  306
McMinn  9
McMinnis  53
McMorris  335
McMullan  201
McMullen  11, 15, 352
McMurry  246
McNair  323
McNairy  227
McNally  221
McNamarry  140
McNamce  168
McNamee  335, 352, 354
McNeely  27
McNeill  40
McNermee  185
McNully  221
McNutty  66
McPherson  87
McQueen  23, 47, 55, 104, 113, 224, 274, 292, 306
McRae  37, 243
McRee  192
McSquirt  94
McVay  121
McVoy  14
McWharton  264
McWhorter  326
McWilliams  139, 140, 234, 341
Mead  148
Meadors  354
Meadows  143, 200, 279, 345
Mealing  18
Means  218, 293
Mears  280
Medcalf  293
Medley  96

## THE SOUTHERN ARGUS - DEATHS - JUNE 1869 THROUGH JUNE 1874

Meeker  35
Meeks  134, 260, 267
Meenan  193
Megginson  169, 320
Meharg  140
Melford  84
Mellown  34, 67, 269
Melner  182
Melson  275
Melton  119, 207, 231, 256, 260, 342
Mendenhall  279
Mendez  304
Menifee  242
Menke  169
Menses  310
Menzer  279
Mercer  73
Meredith  42
Merritt  131
Merriweather  26, 224
Merriwether  298
Mervin  197
Metcalf  70, 219, 239, 315, 317
Metcalfe  317, 344
Metevier  110
Meyer  156, 244, 250
Meyers  192
Michael  183
Michaella  228
Michell  254
Mickelboro  225
Mickleboro  12
Middlebrooks  198, 306
Miers  144
Milan  30
Miles  55, 111, 174, 268, 287
Milhous  268
Miller  5, 20, 32, 45, 58, 65, 67, 68, 74, 78, 91, 93, 101, 103, 114, 121, 123, 136, 153, 205, 234, 254, 259, 280, 282, 293, 302, 303, 311, 314, 317, 341, 343

Millican  58
Milligan  316
Millingham  225
Mills  83, 93, 166, 236, 353
Millsap  258
Milner  165, 322
Milwee  49
Mims  350
Mince  67
Mingea  225, 329
Minter  243, 316
Miree  335
Mitchell  18, 43, 90, 105, 107, 134, 140, 162, 176, 186, 195, 198, 199, 228, 234, 242, 260, 291, 293, 301, 307, 329, 344, 351
Mixson  172, 174
Mizel  300
Mizell  297
Moat  229
Moates  89
Mobley  45, 56, 77, 192, 238
Mock  54
Modawell  81
Molette  211
Molton  230
Moncrief  128, 298
Monerief  128
Monette  24, 70, 212, 339
Monier  28
Monk  131
Mononl  147
Monroe  49, 211, 239, 319
Montague  109, 161
Monteaboro  201
Montgomery  72, 144, 153, 180, 191, 202, 228, 296, 299, 301, 310, 327, 338, 355
Moody  4, 11, 64, 112, 208, 248, 290
Moon  27, 344
Mooney  55, 119, 182

## THE SOUTHERN ARGUS - DEATHS - JUNE 1869 THROUGH JUNE 1874

Moore  13, 22, 29, 34, 45, 50, 52, 65, 70, 74, 97, 112, 115, 133, 147, 148, 149, 156, 162, 164, 168, 183, 194, 196, 197, 209, 217, 231, 235, 240, 242, 244, 246, 266, 269, 282, 301, 310, 326, 334, 336, 339, 348, 349, 354
Moorer  76, 100, 174, 224, 306
Moorhead  315
Moragne  213, 245
Morague  116
Moran  144
Mordecai  54, 73, 326
Morehead  155, 192
Morel  310
Moreland  230
Morgan  31, 32, 48, 72, 81, 101, 116, 118, 130, 133, 147, 152, 156, 179, 242, 290, 291, 292
Morningstar  141, 142
Morrill  31
Morring  65
Morris  36, 38, 104, 140, 170, 193, 204, 224, 245, 252, 261, 327
Morrisette  60, 126
Morrisey  348
Morrison  78, 224, 282, 347, 349, 350
Morrow  5, 63, 124, 136, 209, 222, 238, 242, 257, 289, 351
Morse  2, 47, 208
Morton  92, 140, 253, 351
Mosely  101, 122, 149, 192, 258, 262, 281, 290
Moses  194
Moss  73, 163, 180, 183
Motes  85
Motley  247, 248
Moton  288, 294, 297
Moulton  182
Moyler  75, 217
Mozeley  332

Muldon  128
Muller  131, 341
Mullins  259
Mumford  22
Munchus  303
Munerlyn  161
Munford  284
Munn  319
Munnerlyn  37
Murdock  126, 158, 279
Murphee  181
Murphey  180
Murphree  274, 346
Murphy  1, 14, 18, 81, 101, 136, 175, 179, 236, 257, 261, 298, 328, 347, 350
Murray  2, 44, 139, 210, 228
Murrell  98, 100
Murrills  296
Murry  278
Muse  197
Mushat  127, 140
Musten  76
Mustin  84, 240
Myers  58, 161, 283, 298
Myerseay  106
Nabors  92, 106, 130, 168, 262, 268, 345, 346
Nagle  2, 53
Nall  140
Nance  219
Napier  311
Nash  14, 67, 106, 111, 123, 329
Nason  130, 140, 164
Nathan  61, 87
Nations  308
Nauce  118
Naughan  247
Nave  79, 115
Neal  20, 101, 173, 320, 356
Neaves  303
Neeley  307
Neely  39, 57, 359
Neighbors  68, 94

## THE SOUTHERN ARGUS - DEATHS - JUNE 1869 THROUGH JUNE 1874

Neilson  45
Nelms  129, 345
Nelson  125, 134, 138, 140, 148, 158, 253, 274, 299, 301, 311, 328, 330
Nesbitt  227
Nesmith  208
Nettles  76
Nevins  73
Newberry  191
Newbold  221
Newby  51, 53
Newcomb  339
Newell  234, 317
Newland  337
Newman  107, 135, 212, 272
Newsome  355
Newson  293
Newton  61, 67, 168, 292, 328, 343, 359
Nichol  6, 245
Nicholls  289, 290, 311
Nichols  5, 45, 125, 143, 179, 203, 210, 245, 253, 286
Nicholson  18, 128, 345
Nickel  188
Nickerson  276
Nickols  212
Nicol  359
Nicoll  213
Niel  56
Niles  149
Nix  38, 130, 332
Nixon  15, 119, 287
Nobles  152, 305
Noel  112
Nolan  6, 142, 228
Noland  292
Norand  77
Norman  22, 61
Norred  307
Norrell  71
Norris  69, 211, 219, 307, 324, 357

Northrop  269
Norton  23, 72, 74, 162, 165, 201, 223, 225, 227, 257
Norvil  123
Norwood  194, 207, 229
Nott  21, 234, 235
Nuckolls  94
Nugent  296, 317
Nunnemacher  105
Nusom  20
Nussbaum  338
Nutting  21, 46, 70, 234, 244, 276
O'Brien  174, 176, 262, 268, 274, 352
O'Connell  42
O'Conner  97
O'Connor  200, 240
O'Day  253
O'Donnell  95
O'Dwyer  307
O'Farrell  100
O'Gwynn  95
O'Hare  120
O'Keefe  201
O'Leary  355
O'Meara  132
O'Neal  27, 52, 155, 260
O'Neil  334
Oakley  132
Oakman  47
Oates  2, 40, 114, 131
Oats  288
Oberry  71
Odam  57
Odele  131
Oden  8
Odermatt  132
Odom  176, 321, 342
Odum  94, 195
Ogborn  3
Ogbourne  176
Ogburn  70
Oglesbie  75

## THE SOUTHERN ARGUS - DEATHS - JUNE 1869 THROUGH JUNE 1874

Oglesby  214, 260, 274
Ogletree  232, 333
Ohlman  132, 169
Oldham  52
Olds  129
Olive  242
Oliver  21, 40, 99, 155, 197, 202, 205
Ollis  240
Olson  99
Oppenheimer  51, 162, 208
Ormand  297
Orme  281
Ormesby  227
Ormond  147
Orr  206
Orth  98
Osborn  153, 273, 343
Osburn  146
Osgood  92
Oswalt  277
Otero  129
Ott  14, 142
Otts  106
Outler  356
Owen  24, 44, 45, 55, 92, 163, 300, 311, 329, 330, 347
Owens  57, 100, 162, 194, 218, 240, 311, 312, 343, 353
Owsley  330
Oxford  262-264, 268
Ozanne  158
Pace  249
Packer  65
Padgett  119, 120, 303
Padleford  268
Page  59, 111
Pagles  291
Paiton  113
Palmer  9, 121, 133, 213, 235, 256, 269, 347
Palmore  136
Parham  24, 123, 175
Parish  258

Park  85, 88, 160, 241, 329, 340, 354
Parker  38, 50, 77, 79, 127, 183, 196, 197, 223, 224, 256, 265, 298, 308, 310, 324, 327, 334, 335, 341, 350, 351
Parkes  152
Parks  137, 139, 176, 259, 277
Parmer  250, 254, 287
Parmlee  231
Parrot  62, 289
Parrott  44
Parshall  2, 288, 291
Parsons  103, 139, 209, 332
Parton  236, 248, 295, 306
Pascal  287
Passmore  60
Paterson  4
Patey  208
Paton  223
Patrick  69, 266, 331
Patridge  242
Pats  167
Patten  93
Patterson  4, 9, 29, 33, 38, 73, 169, 216, 223, 225, 228, 257, 269, 283, 314, 328, 342
Patton  154, 162, 335, 343
Paty  57, 205
Paul  66
Paullin  104, 219
Payne  67, 87, 125, 195, 319, 321, 334
Peacock  355
Peagler  18, 153, 168
Peake  7
Peaks  84
Pearce  74, 75, 105, 276
Pearre  21, 328
Pearsall  143, 180
Pearson  38, 48, 103, 294, 338
Pease  147, 336
Peck  357

## THE SOUTHERN ARGUS - DEATHS - JUNE 1869 THROUGH JUNE 1874

Peebles  117, 124, 208, 210, 306, 307, 345, 346
Peende  123
Peeples  124
Peete  83
Peevey  259, 310
Pegues  70, 218, 357
Pelham  37, 106, 191
Pendleton  64, 354
Penick  234
Penn  58, 352
Pennick  123
Pennington  81, 143, 211, 272, 303, 344, 354
Penniss  271
Penny  328
Percy  114
Perdne  305
Perdue  69, 121
Perey  36
Perkins  11, 108, 200, 270, 311, 349
Perrick  204
Perrin  105, 276
Perry  2, 4, 75, 159, 183, 204, 208, 259, 306, 352, 357
Perryman  18, 39, 127, 222
Persell  4
Pesknell  38
Peteet  276
Peters  31
Peterson  96, 97, 159, 235
Pettiebone  336
Pettigrew  67, 81, 104, 108, 113, 239, 281
Pettus  17, 63, 65, 135
Petty  68, 69, 87, 114, 162, 232, 278
Petway  236
Pevey  117
Pharr  27
Phelan  50, 55
Phelps  12, 47, 195
Phifer  340

Phillippe  155
Phillips  5, 20, 34, 39, 50, 53, 88, 96, 98, 101, 141, 171, 173, 180, 185, 189, 191, 198, 225, 230, 231, 233, 247, 255, 272, 278, 296, 306, 350, 351, 352, 356
Philpot  53
Philyow  357
Picard  264
Pickens  160, 232, 244, 269, 320
Pickett  10, 66, 72, 286
Pickford  28
Pidal  116
Pierce  29, 37, 129, 135, 204, 275, 330, 338, 353
Pierson  117
Piggott  150
Piily  312
Pillow  32, 34, 229
Pills  264
Pinckston  128
Pinkney  139
Pinson  83
Pipin  67
Pipkin  233
Pippen  20, 21, 231, 323
Pipper  20
Pippin  142
Pittman  163
Pitts  132, 191, 205, 206, 263, 276, 278
Pizzala  22, 23
Place  347
Pleas  184
Pleasant  64
Pleasants  7, 266, 324
Plowman  323
Plummer  106
Pogue  349
Pointe  190
Pointer  46
Points  190
Polk  352

## THE SOUTHERN ARGUS - DEATHS - JUNE 1869 THROUGH JUNE 1874

Pollard  2, 42, 52, 93, 104, 202, 254, 297
Pollock  172
Polly  133, 186, 189
Polnitz  196
Pond  111
Pool  116, 155
Poole  13, 65, 136, 328
Pooser  182
Pope  8, 48, 54, 56, 60, 95, 96, 194, 269, 278, 343, 344
Porter  29, 76, 211, 224, 292, 340
Portis  56, 347
Posey  88, 317
Post  73, 124, 297
Postell  125
Posteur  116
Poston  101
Potter  29, 41, 171
Potts  35, 149, 185, 212, 223, 236
Pou  322, 325
Pouncey  149, 235
Powe  107
Powell  43, 67, 114, 115, 117, 155, 163, 170, 171, 256, 295, 296, 306, 311, 333, 337, 340
Power  335
Powers  11, 68, 238, 253, 262, 272, 312
Poyner  216
Prather  94, 347, 348
Pratt  15, 55, 110, 113, 120, 203, 238, 241
Preiss  216
Prentice  95
Prescott  217
Pressly  197
Presswood  167
Prestridge  359
Prestwood  317
Prevost  120
Prewit  344

Prewitt  233
Price  8, 23, 46, 48, 122, 170, 180, 182, 225, 227, 290
Prichard  139, 204
Prichett  141
Pride  111, 149
Prince  19, 131, 157, 185, 237
Pringle  187
Pritchard  56
Pritchett  107, 146, 147, 226, 257
Proby  37
Proctor  82, 223
Profit  5
Progay  275
Province  272
Prudden  141
Pruden  41
Pruett  92, 215
Pruit  40
Pruitt  124, 187, 278, 314, 346
Pryor  59, 118, 194, 268
Puett  294
Pugh  55, 138, 147, 148, 225
Pullam  113
Pullen  100, 344
Pulliam  15, 44
Pullum  201
Purdon  113
Purifory  43
Purifoy  149
Purnell  200, 278
Pursley  83
Purvis  104
Puryear  272
Putnam  154, 165
Pynes  226
Qualls  152
Quarles  185
Queen  185
Quigley  72
Quillar  245
Quin  333
Quinlan  279

**THE SOUTHERN ARGUS - DEATHS - JUNE 1869 THROUGH JUNE 1874**

Quinn  320
Quinney  336
Rabb  162, 176, 179, 204, 206, 342
Rachels  85
Rafferty  330, 338
Ragan  22
Ragden  269
Raglan  301
Ragland  157, 206, 298, 304
Railey  324
Rain  93
Raines  294
Rainey  77, 235, 265
Rains  199, 312
Raisler  156
Ralls  284
Rally  244
Ralph  85, 287
Rambo  176
Ramer  287, 288
Ramie  194
Ramond  74
Ramsey  33, 86, 97, 112, 128, 228, 235, 291
Randall  125, 129, 302
Randle  73
Randolph  30, 110, 162, 310
Rankin  171
Rann  135
Raoul  43
Raphael  32, 300
Rapier  291
Rash  143
Rasher  203
Raspberry  151
Rast  60, 71, 91, 173, 274
Rather  85, 239, 284
Ravesies  355
Rawlins  120
Rawls  88, 324
Ray  18, 66, 97, 152, 208, 335
Rayburn  7
Rayford  94

Raymond  274
Raymur  242
Rea  254
Read  182, 183, 286, 310
Real  215
Reale  101
Reams  151
Reardon  149
Reaves  206
Reavis  45, 82, 171
Rebman  12, 358
Rector  301, 310
Reddick  44
Redding  184, 221, 229, 336, 337
Reddish  101, 110
Redmon  123, 228
Redus  14
Redwood  153
Reed  22, 80, 122, 129, 167, 179, 191, 193, 204, 212, 237, 272, 336
Reeder  29, 343
Reedy  33
Rees  351
Reese  19, 62, 65, 68, 69, 85, 98, 102, 141, 230, 233, 272, 286, 340
Reesgraff  283
Reeve  111
Reeves  223, 237, 287
Regan  330
Regensberger  301
Regensburger  310
Regina  291
Register  176, 226
Reid  99, 114, 171, 205, 208, 253, 355
Reins  296
Reitts  291
Relf  10
Rembert  152
Remhard  75
Remy  101

# THE SOUTHERN ARGUS - DEATHS - JUNE 1869 THROUGH JUNE 1874

Renalde  83
Renaldi  89
Rencan  210
Renean  210
Reneau  210
Renfroe  108, 112, 278
Renick  352
Revault  242, 359
Reynolds  101, 107, 150, 171, 198, 231, 236, 240, 241, 257, 337
Reys  318
Rhea  141, 173
Rhett  168, 199
Rhodes  12, 27, 52, 110, 155, 238, 262
Rian  284
Ribert  318
Rice  27, 41, 112, 147, 160, 201, 242, 256, 264, 304, 342
Richards  51, 210, 224, 301, 336
Richardson  13, 54, 94, 98, 119, 227, 245, 305, 323, 347, 351, 357, 358
Richey  314
Richie  340
Ricker  300
Ridgeway  70, 151
Ridgill  54
Ridgway  69
Ridley  333
Ried  75
Rigg  197
Riggs  266, 304, 332, 333
Rikard  76
Riley  56, 64, 67, 68, 87, 97, 120, 138, 196, 214, 286
Ringo  15, 282
Ripley  142
Risen  122
Ritchey  305
Rittenhouse  331
Ritter  187, 204
Ritters  309

Rivers  233, 278, 307
Rives  153, 201
Roach  25, 157, 340
Roads  221
Robbins  56, 147, 156, 181
Robert  137, 310
Roberts  18, 20, 21, 31, 54, 69, 81, 82, 105, 136, 152, 166, 171, 177, 193, 200, 205, 221, 223, 225, 227, 231, 263, 281, 290, 292, 295, 319, 321
Robertson  57, 63, 77, 109, 131, 155, 188, 204, 210, 239, 254, 276
Robins  260
Robinson  7, 55, 64, 94, 100, 103, 132, 133, 157, 193, 204, 206, 230, 269, 279, 287, 307, 329, 349, 351, 357
Roby  197
Rodding  221
Roden  45
Rodgers  46
Rodon  45
Roebuck  144, 265
Roesenan  154
Rogers  37, 42, 46, 95, 108, 162, 172, 195, 213, 218, 223, 227, 232, 316, 318, 330, 338, 358
Roland  74
Rolfe  132, 235
Rolie  235
Roller  288
Romine  311
Rone  155
Roop  255
Root  107, 334
Roper  33, 88, 325
Rose  11, 157, 274
Rosenau  301
Rosenberger  204
Rosenburg  323
Rosenquest  280
Rosenstiel  225

**THE SOUTHERN ARGUS - DEATHS - JUNE 1869 THROUGH JUNE 1874**

Ross  68, 98, 110, 113, 126, 229, 237, 318, 350
Rossen  279
Rosser  6, 120, 135, 272
Rosson  158
Rothrock  218
Roughton  301
Roulston  42, 88
Roundtree  105
Rountree  105
Rouse  129, 208
Routon  201
Rowan  138, 314
Rowden  247
Rowe  48, 161
Rowell  255, 295, 310
Rowland  28
Roy  175, 305
Royster  200
Royston  202
Rucker  84
Rudd  266
Rudolph  349
Rudulph  16
Ruff  273
Ruffin  265
Rugely  188, 190
Rumly  233
Rumph  127
Rundell  338
Runnells  320
Runnion  326
Rupel  224
Rupert  89, 100
Ruppenthal  218
Rush  152, 300
Rushing  23, 212
Rusk  233
Russel  247, 328
Russell  52, 79, 81, 87, 98, 123, 133, 155, 157, 162, 186, 214, 270, 283, 284, 304, 345, 355
Rutland  35
Rutledge  130, 287

Ryalls  218
Ryals  68
Ryan  44, 51, 74, 212, 218, 283, 298, 301
Ryder  55
Ryland  140
Sabin  310
Saddler  291
Sadler  315
Saffold  211, 241, 306
Safford  207, 273
Sails  252
Salle  223
Sally  266
Salomon  132
Salter  151, 157
Sampey  297, 356
Sample  311
Sampley  131
Sampson  60, 84, 215
Samuel  100, 158
Samuels  164
Sandefur  212
Sanders  19, 67, 96, 113, 127, 137, 157, 165, 239, 240, 342, 343, 346
Sanderson  224
Sandford  187
Sandidge  93
Sandlin  291, 292
Sands  37
Sandusky  12
Sanford  78, 222, 224
Sankey  313, 325, 326, 329
Sanky  186
Sanson  242, 243
Sargent  48, 162
Sartain  71
Sasman  284
Satterwhite  5, 217
Saunders  50, 147, 150, 243, 302
Sauters  325
Savage  116, 117, 156, 280, 281

## THE SOUTHERN ARGUS - DEATHS - JUNE 1869 THROUGH JUNE 1874

Savary  78
Savory  116
Sawtelle  150
Sawyer  127, 287
Sawyers  96
Sayre  164
Saywood  63
Scade  287
Scale  287
Scales  29
Scarborough  8, 149
Scarbrough  99
Scarey  168
Scears  223
Schafer  192
Schaffer  12
Schau  292
Schemerhorn  165
Schimerhorn  163
Schmeidler  301, 310
Schmidt  93
Schnebley  310
Schneider  165
Schoenfeld  124
Schoolar  76
Schoppert  85
Schott  171
Schrigner  304
Schrimsher  187
Schuessler  346
Schular  70
Schultz  325-327
Schurenberg  334
Schuster  278
Schwabacher  200
Schwarz  257
Scofield  237
Scott  35, 50, 88, 101, 141, 151, 159, 179, 193, 209, 211, 223, 231, 242, 245, 283, 298, 299, 313, 314
Scroggins  165
Scruggs  120, 236, 240
Scullins  303

Scully  295
Scurry  141
Seagroves  141
Seale  43, 78, 147, 209
Seales  314
Seals  95
Seaman  145
Searcy  168, 208
Seatal  284
Seawell  183, 208
Seawright  192
Seay  144
Seaymer  264, 269
Secor  93, 297
Sedberry  262
Sedbury  205
Seed  194
Seeforth  85
Seemuller  218
Selfrank  3
Sellars  116
Sellers  25, 82, 100, 157, 346
Selliman  21
Selman  308
Selph  327
Semple  185
Senter  289
Servatius  75
Sewad  313
Seward  114, 199
Sewell  32
Sexton  317
Seymour  35, 166, 331
Shackelford  76, 297, 320
Shackleford  226
Shanahan  172
Shancer  1
Shannon  21
Sharp  54, 75, 88, 107, 118, 289, 355
Shaver  19
Shaw  177, 210, 251
Shawver  348
Shearer  15, 124, 203, 211, 309

## THE SOUTHERN ARGUS - DEATHS - JUNE 1869 THROUGH JUNE 1874

Sheatly  52
Shedden  303
Shedecor  283
Sheehan  134, 194, 268, 350
Sheehane  311
Sheffield  231, 297, 330
Shehan  118
Shelby  72, 98, 210, 266, 351
Sheldon  116, 187, 256
Shell  185, 313
Shelley  25, 323, 327, 352
Shelly  28
Shelton  30, 82, 105, 153, 193, 250
Shenfessle  243
Shephard  183
Shepherd  124, 262, 305
Sheppard  112, 215, 347
Sherlock  63
Sherman  160, 204
Sherrard  332
Sherrill  57
Sherrod  32, 162, 224
Sherry  311
Sherwood  239, 245
Shields  82, 117, 124, 149, 303
Shifley  319
Shilley  319
Shinault  182
Shine  146, 317
Shinkley  230
Shirley  301, 310
Shitley  319
Shives  312
Shoat  346
Shoenberger  63
Sholl  187
Short  73, 168
Shorter  166, 167
Shortridge  58, 60, 62, 266
Shouse  169
Shreve  226
Shrewsbury  226
Shropshire  117

Shuffield  333
Shumake  49
Shumaker  41
Sibert  262
Sibley  204
Siddons  117
Sides  256
Siemens  286
Siler  47
Silliman  42
Silver  9
Simison  129
Simmons  33, 61, 164, 168, 214, 227, 279
Simms  67, 228
Simons  220, 243, 244
Simonton  7
Simpson  5, 13, 43, 70, 154, 197, 198, 200, 225, 255, 335, 339
Sims  86, 102, 183, 234, 341
Sinclair  25, 26
Singleton  18, 148, 223
Singley  129
Sinon  324
Sise  147
Sisk  64
Sister Agatha  127
Skaggs  257
Skegog  78
Skelton  146, 194
Skidmore  123
Skillman  198
Skinner  10, 112, 120, 234, 336, 341, 353
Skipper  246, 355
Slack  290, 316
Slade  68, 73, 271
Slater  212
Slaton  144, 155, 346
Slaughter  124, 150, 201, 235, 277, 282
Sledge  13, 28, 192, 244, 324, 327

## THE SOUTHERN ARGUS - DEATHS - JUNE 1869 THROUGH JUNE 1874

Sloan  281
Slocum  132
Slorah  306
Sloss  74, 79, 108
Slough  152
Small  211
Smarr  327
Smart  49, 182, 239
Smaw  277
Smiley  278
Smilie  98
Smith  1, 15, 16, 21, 22, 26, 33, 34, 35, 37, 40, 46, 47, 52, 53, 75, 76, 79, 87-89, 91, 92, 101, 107, 108, 113, 115, 117, 118, 120, 124, 131, 132, 133, 138, 141, 142, 143, 146, 150, 152, 163, 171, 172, 173, 174, 176, 178, 183, 195, 196, 206, 207, 219, 221, 222, 223, 224, 226, 228, 234, 237, 238, 239, 240, 246, 251, 255, 258, 261, 262, 266, 267, 268, 269, 272, 273, 281, 284, 285, 289, 297, 302, 306, 307, 312, 314, 315, 319, 321, 325, 326, 327, 330, 332, 333, 334, 335, 338, 341, 356, 359
Smoke  170
Smoot  71, 79, 180
Smyly  241, 281
Sneed  237, 286
Snell  43
Snidow  307
Snoddy  30, 32
Snodgrass  8, 9, 23, 179
Snow  104, 231, 315, 338
Snyder  310, 353
Soles  64, 88, 283
Solomon  304, 310, 339
Solomons  217
Somerville  321
Sommerkamp  183
Sorelle  326
Sorsby  25, 171, 211, 259, 267
Southard  37
Southerland  113
Spalding  180
Spangler  311, 346
Spanland  175
Spanlard  175
Spann  20, 253
Sparrenberger  218, 233, 298
Sparrenger  302
Sparrow  324
Spaulding  199
Speak  30
Speake  74, 243
Spear  132, 226
Spearman  320
Spears  317, 341
Speed  39, 233, 317
Speight  162, 261
Spence  352
Spencer  81, 82, 96, 204, 216, 219, 221
Spicker  210
Spigner  196
Spiller  52
Spindle  130
Spinks  341
Spinner  73
Sporman  217, 254
Spottswood  9
Spracklin  137
Spragins  118, 330
Sprague  349, 350
Sprangler  236
Spratling  326
Spratt  98
Springer  200
Springfellow  291
Sprott  29, 44, 311
Sprout  46
Spruill  284, 333
Spurlock  174, 176, 232, 243
St. John  98
St. Lanier  35

**THE SOUTHERN ARGUS - DEATHS - JUNE 1869 THROUGH JUNE 1874**

St. Leger  58
Stabler  72
Stacey  64
Stafford  48, 213, 227, 271, 339
Staggers  10, 88
Stainton  283
Stakeley  169
Stallings  78
Stallsworth  32
Stallworth  65, 132
Stallwoth  59
Stammire  318
Stamp  299, 301
Stamps  14
Stanley  117, 125, 169, 239, 258
Stanton  222, 301, 355
Stanwood  216
Staples  101
Stapp  234
Stark  37, 50, 51
Starke  16
Starkey  225
Starr  38, 40
Starrett  254
Staton  260
Stauter  352
Steadman  57, 93
Stearnes  165
Stearns  77, 315
Stedham  95
Steedman  256
Steel  162
Steele  22, 45, 47, 54, 75, 78, 176, 179, 241, 266, 269, 276, 297, 317
Steely  57
Steen  319
Steidel  307
Steiner  217, 222, 258, 324
Stell  330
Stellars  268
Stellers  251
Stephens  110, 157, 175, 230, 291, 326, 327, 328

Stephenson  146, 208, 210
Sterling  310
Sterne  199, 202
Sterns  27
Stevens  39, 90, 124, 140, 262, 311
Stevenson  182, 348
Stewart  6, 29, 30, 34, 35, 43, 53, 55, 125, 141, 158, 160, 177, 184, 242, 267, 283, 295, 300, 305
Stickle  75
Stickney  8, 52, 338
Stiefiel  212
Stiff  115
Stigler  313
Stiker  248
Stillings  93, 162
Stillman  79
Stinnett  129, 280
Stinson  37, 63
Stites  171
Stith  54
Stockdale  321
Stocker  117
Stocks  199
Stoddard  66, 93, 336
Stokes  115, 142, 175, 232, 298, 324
Stollenwerck  291
Stonaker  177
Stone  19, 21, 97, 104, 170, 171, 227, 276, 287, 295, 297, 308, 341, 352
Storer  64, 221
Storrs  351
Stott  206
Stoudenmire  81, 230
Stout  319
Stovall  8, 9, 23
Stow  357
Stowers  97, 330
Strain  52
Strait  138

## THE SOUTHERN ARGUS - DEATHS - JUNE 1869 THROUGH JUNE 1874

Stramler 78
Strang 168
Strange 114, 302
Strans 251
Strater 156
Stratton 66
Straub 257
Straus 251
Strawbridge 207
Streater 171, 209, 291
Street 216, 310
Stribling 250, 326
Stricker 310
Strickland 1, 240, 302, 340
Strillitz 3
Stringfellow 7, 50, 112, 201, 237
Strock 140
Strode 33, 127
Strong 92, 147, 229
Strother 135, 272, 350
Stroub 268
Stroud 245
Strudwick 60, 208
Strupper 310
Stuart 47, 272, 304, 335, 355, 357
Stubblefield 261
Stubbs 284
Stuckey 227
Stump 310
Sturges 263
Sturkey 319
Stutts 166
Sublett 179
Suggert 4
Sullivan 134, 158, 183, 208, 229, 260, 283
Summerford 120, 317
Summers 153, 297
Summersault 44
Summerville 307
Sumner 115, 338
Sunnerer 126
Suther 112

Sutherland 355
Sutherlin 210
Suttle 129, 245, 354
Sutton 37, 103, 221, 300
Swain 325
Swan 96
Swank 307
Swann 177
Swasy 185
Sweeney 109
Swift 129, 261
Swigert 143
Swint 247
Swoope 110, 147
Swope 324
Swords 134
Sylvester 43
Syring 353
Tabb 276, 287
Taber 324, 329
Tabler 326, 327
Taff 297
Tait 120, 233, 312
Talbot 317
Talbott 160, 273
Taliaferro 108
Tallaferro 291
Talley 355
Tallman 45
Tally 348
Tankersley 100, 157
Tankersly 298
Tannehill 351
Tanner 35, 86, 188, 253, 265, 276, 341, 348, 350
Tannock 266
Tardy 34
Tarleton 351
Tarr 322
Tarrant 27, 69, 88, 266, 332, 333, 352
Tarry 25, 26
Tart 170
Tartt 169, 201

## THE SOUTHERN ARGUS - DEATHS - JUNE 1869 THROUGH JUNE 1874

Tarver  59, 327
Tate  79, 179, 351
Tatnall  106
Tatum  194, 319
Taul  227
Tayloe  357
Taylor  23, 28, 40, 41, 47, 57, 63, 65, 71, 83, 137, 140, 171, 186, 196, 198, 218, 230, 252, 257, 274, 276, 282, 289, 296, 301, 307, 310, 332, 355
Teague  120, 154, 212
Teal  62, 182, 227
Teer  84
Telfair  48
Tell  254
Templeton  291
Templin  6
Teneyek  344
Tennant  169
Tepper  160
Terrel  175
Terrell  3, 5, 150
Terry  124, 170, 186, 188, 198, 262, 268, 270, 298, 301
Tew  113
Thacher  48
Thacker  159
Thames  115, 117
Thaxon  5
Theis  249
Thielyard  136
Thigpen  302
Thom  317
Thomas  2, 24, 40, 47, 85, 88, 91, 93, 97, 103, 110, 125, 126, 128, 170, 181, 187, 191, 203, 208, 223, 226, 235, 252, 281, 284, 321, 324, 333, 344
Thomason  217, 256
Thomaston  136
Thomlin  114
Thompkins  254

Thompson  9, 20, 25, 29, 51, 73, 77, 79, 80, 81, 86, 91, 94, 96, 97, 101, 107, 111, 114, 129, 132, 138, 143, 160, 171, 176, 193, 204, 223, 253, 275, 281, 284, 287, 289, 295, 311, 324, 328, 336, 342, 348, 351
Thorington  91, 115
Thorn  167, 205
Thornston  260
Thornton  62, 107, 120, 159, 166, 174, 260, 268, 290, 339
Thorp  97
Thrash  109, 183
Threadgill  143
Throckmorton  324, 336, 340, 344, 354
Thurber  79, 232
Thweatt  50
Tidwell  179, 311
Tier  137
Tieree  290
Tilford  186
Tillery  118
Tillman  236, 301, 310
Tilman  183
Timmons  13
Timms  186
Tims  273
Tinch  244
Tindale  45
Tinker  17
Tinsley  342
Tippett  52
Tipton  2, 46, 82, 191, 332
Tisdale  63, 77, 231, 237, 252, 298, 329
Titcomb  125
Tobey  93
Todd  25, 36, 99, 113, 146, 184, 187, 201, 309, 331
Tolbett  212
Tolson  137
Tom  56

## THE SOUTHERN ARGUS - DEATHS - JUNE 1869 THROUGH JUNE 1874

Tomlin  158, 321
Tomlinson  117, 308, 351
Tones  177
Tony  90
Tood  104
Toomer  154, 155
Torbett  149
Torrence  75
Touart  98
Toulmin  279
Towles  254
Townly  296
Townsen  71
Townsend  119, 128, 274, 321, 348
Toxey  73
Trague  72
Trammell  232
Trant  302
Trask  208
Travis  75, 301
Trawick  100, 174
Treadway  231
Treadwell  230
Tress  283
Trice  200, 356
Trimble  41, 88
Tripp  74, 326
Trotman  70, 276
Trott  18, 30
Trotter  353
Troup  74
Trout  322
Troutman  101
Troy  124, 184
True  50, 323
Truss  96
Trussell  130
Tubb  155, 219
Tucker  24, 26, 68, 84, 101, 107, 113, 150, 230, 300, 332
Tuggle  136
Tulles  128
Tuomey  182

Turk  261, 278
Turner  17, 35, 40, 52, 63, 68, 93, 94, 102, 109, 115, 117, 126, 129, 138, 144, 150, 171, 194, 197, 206, 208, 217, 224, 240, 241, 248, 251, 300, 318, 346, 351, 352
Turnipseed  241
Turnley  102
Turrentine  274
Tutill  75
Tutt  17, 56, 189
Twithey  56
Tyler  142, 283, 293
Ulmer  26, 65, 112, 277, 281
Ulrick  179
Underwood  13, 38, 76, 86, 153, 225, 291, 302, 307
Upchurch  110, 266
Upton  18, 354
Ussery  281
Ustick  180, 188, 320
Vail  64
Valentine  277
Vallandingham  227
Vanderhook  170
Vandiver  179
Vanghan  283
VanHoose  277
Vann  260, 284
VanWinkle  159
Vanzant  305
Varner  35, 44, 107, 112, 298
Varnum  215
Vasser  26, 327
Vaughan  44, 83, 89, 113, 161
Vaughn  90, 222
Vaur  228
Veal  141
Velasco  340
Venable  152, 256
Verdot  185
Vermilya  145
Vernon  323

## THE SOUTHERN ARGUS - DEATHS - JUNE 1869 THROUGH JUNE 1874

Vesey 117
Vessels 143
Vick 35
Vickers 121, 280
Vincent 127, 171, 235, 238
Volle 310
Voss 251
Wachtee 134
Waddell 209, 291
Waddle 46
Wade 128, 245, 254, 257, 259, 261, 297, 309, 329
Wagenbrener 183
Wagner 21, 117, 132, 194, 290
Wailes 145
Wainwright 176
Walden 111, 172, 234, 265
Waldrom 272
Waldrop 357
Walker 3, 7, 15, 16, 20, 34, 41, 52, 53, 54, 60, 68, 72, 75, 76, 79, 82, 105, 112, 114, 117, 118, 124, 149, 162, 194, 200, 204, 207, 216, 228, 233, 256, 259, 271, 275, 276, 292, 293, 294, 295, 307, 330, 335, 337, 358
Walkins 203
Walkley 46
Wall 40, 82, 132
Wallace 11, 18, 46, 48, 57, 106, 114, 136, 218, 224, 261, 274, 288, 291, 310, 346
Waller 146, 150, 184, 299, 307, 355
Walls 126, 203
Walsh 159
Walshe 158
Waltall 42
Walter 171
Walters 24, 223
Walthalf 42
Walthall 192, 200, 357
Walton 80, 91, 130, 203, 205, 260, 265, 279

Wambold 354
War 266
Ward 65, 82, 103, 132, 183, 191, 215, 221, 225, 278, 284, 334, 335, 336, 356
Ware 8, 101, 126, 257, 296, 304, 305
Warford 347
Waring 77, 82, 178, 187
Warner 83
Warren 45, 57, 82, 95, 287, 334, 352
Warrenton 342
Warwick 228
Washburn 192
Washington 118, 337, 340
Wasson 148, 348
Waters 52, 215, 307, 309
Watkins 66, 192, 195, 196, 197, 234, 286, 291
Watson 27, 62, 63, 65, 78, 89, 114, 142, 143, 170, 178, 208, 214, 216, 269, 272, 291, 301, 310, 316, 320, 323, 349, 359
Watt 96, 126, 193, 196
Watters 63
Watts 126, 240, 265, 276, 283, 284, 303, 304
Waugh 20, 50
Wave 89
Wayne 238
Wear 79
Weatherford 88, 300
Weatherly 164
Weaver 45, 47, 60, 112, 128, 137, 143, 164, 173, 193, 202, 285, 295, 334, 355
Webb 33, 60, 66, 88, 103, 230, 258, 278, 316
Webing 65
Webster 64, 67, 78, 177, 239, 259, 287, 290, 354
Wedgeworth 152
Weekes 296

**THE SOUTHERN ARGUS - DEATHS - JUNE 1869 THROUGH JUNE 1874**

Weems  184, 353
Weidman  268
Weir  123, 340
Welborn  155
Welch  133, 187, 191, 272, 346
Weldon  37, 51, 56, 75
Wellborn  344
Wellhorn  156
Wellington  304
Wells  69, 142, 196, 198
Welsh  74, 75, 210
Werdle  260
Werner  251
Werneth  48
Wert  255
Wesley  10
Wesson  200, 271
West  40, 164, 166, 168, 209, 238, 327, 344
Westbrook  9, 26, 139
Westbrooks  228
Westcott  111
Wester  113, 115, 234, 300
Westerfield  176
Western  95
Westmoland  299, 302
Westmoreland  172, 349
Westmorland  101
Weyer  230
Whaley  56
Wharton  256, 330
Whatley  113, 154, 161, 182, 240, 323
Whatson  244
Wheadon  75, 327
Wheatley  331
Wheeler  41, 46, 121, 242, 270, 303, 352
Wheelock  9
Whelan  1, 5, 19, 32, 33, 125, 214
Whetstone  37, 197, 232, 312
Whipple  215, 277
Whisenant  83

Whit  86
Whitby  75
White  4, 32, 39, 49, 75, 89, 90, 91, 101, 107, 108, 127, 132, 148, 174, 184, 190, 192, 203, 220, 221, 242, 270, 293, 300, 310, 312, 324, 330, 331, 343, 346, 347, 355, 359
Whitecotton  91
Whitehead  282, 313
Whitehurst  354
Whiteman  342
Whitesides  152
Whitfield  17, 95, 192, 215, 219
Whiting  42
Whitley  222
Whitlock  113, 142
Whitman  43, 82, 221, 242, 315, 320, 337
Whitney  132
Whitsett  183
Whitson  244
Whitt  172
Whittaker  296
Whittemore  126
Whitten  200, 227, 268
Whittle  96
Whorton  66, 67, 150
Wicke  301, 310
Wickel  304
Wickham  114
Wicks  301
Widmer  300
Wiggins  140, 292
Wigginton  253
Wilcox  30, 238, 344
Wilder  83, 146
Wildman  145
Wildsmith  355
Wiles  225
Wiley  7, 21, 202, 295, 298
Wilhelm  46
Wilkerson  133, 183, 328
Wilkins  41, 87, 214

## THE SOUTHERN ARGUS - DEATHS - JUNE 1869 THROUGH JUNE 1874

Wilkinson  39, 268, 327, 340
Wilks  107
Willard  67, 291
Willett  128, 183, 283
Williams  7, 14, 15, 48, 49, 54, 58, 63, 64, 65, 73, 74, 78, 90, 93, 98, 106, 123, 138, 140, 144, 167, 171, 172, 176, 178, 179, 182, 185, 187, 190, 197, 198, 205, 207, 212, 217, 219, 225, 230, 232, 233, 239, 244, 246, 252, 253, 255, 270, 275, 276, 294, 298, 301, 308, 310, 312, 313, 322, 327, 331, 336, 339, 347, 348, 355
Williamson  50, 66, 72, 182, 247
Williford  41, 195, 253, 255, 256
Willingham  17, 92, 135
Willis  55, 146, 177, 179, 208, 216, 314, 335, 353
Wills  178
Wilson  23, 32, 36, 42, 51, 57, 60, 64, 69, 97, 103, 106, 109, 118, 120, 130, 132, 133, 135, 139, 146, 164, 181, 182, 187, 192, 194, 203, 216, 228, 245, 246, 249, 250, 256, 261, 262, 274, 281, 285, 291, 300, 301, 303, 305, 310, 317, 320, 322, 323, 325, 332, 345, 346
Wimberly  50, 155, 280
Winbourne  33, 105, 123
Windham  90, 139, 218, 240
Windle  344
Wingate  130
Wingo  245
Winkler  199, 200
Winslett  164
Winston  13, 44, 49, 89, 103, 128, 141, 282
Winter  112, 143, 302, 306
Winters  4, 81
Wisdom  177
Wise  94, 306, 336

Wistenhunt  250
Witcher  79, 200, 334, 349, 350
Withers  104, 301
Witherspoon  104, 105
Wittman  69
Wolf  44, 248, 314
Wolff  284
Womack  15, 48
Womble  76, 176
Wood  22, 52, 64, 84, 103, 108, 109, 112, 114, 119, 127, 156, 178, 186, 233, 291, 302, 311
Woodall  300
Woodard  117
Woodburn  328
Woodbury  57
Woodfin  95
Woodford  162
Woodham  139
Woodliff  177, 302
Woodruff  62, 112, 116, 357
Woods  90, 241, 250, 253, 259
Woodson  175, 238
Woodward  124, 139, 346, 348
Woodyard  141, 142
Woolf  155
Woolley  39
Woolsey  144, 178, 295
Woosley  27
Wootan  307
Wooten  115, 263
Word  143
Works  174, 177, 353
World  97
Wornick  342
Worrell  303
Wortham  158, 160
Worthen  159
Worthington  99, 179, 262, 268, 351
Worthy  210
Wren  240, 247

## THE SOUTHERN ARGUS - DEATHS - JUNE 1869 THROUGH JUNE 1874

Wright  24, 42, 50, 84, 88, 147, 214, 269, 274, 286, 301, 310, 323, 353
Wyatt  32, 44, 50, 110, 119, 133, 163, 165, 174
Wylie  32
Wynn  61, 252
Wynne  8, 59, 81, 117
Yarborough  271
Yarbrough  65, 231, 345
Yarbrow  270
Yarrington  49
Yates  117
Yeatman  319, 320
Yeend  223
Yeldell  239
Yerby  284
Yoe  336
Yonge  255, 258
York  343
Yost  275
Young  16, 28, 38, 46, 76, 93, 94, 117, 124, 174, 177, 203, 216, 223, 228, 230, 256, 257, 262, 291, 324, 358
Yuille  37, 126
Yung  300
Zepernick  51
Zimmerman  7, 49, 314
Zorkowski  110
Zorn  147

www.ingramcontent.com/pod-product-compliance
Lightning Source LLC
Chambersburg PA
CBHW050832230426
43667CB00012B/1965